Assessing China's Impact on Poverty in the Greater Mekong Subregion

The **Institute of Southeast Asian Studies (ISEAS)** was established as an autonomous organization in 1968. It is a regional centre dedicated to the study of socio-political, security and economic trends and developments in Southeast Asia and its wider geostrategic and economic environment.

The Institute's research programmes are the Regional Economic Studies (RES, including ASEAN and APEC), Regional Strategic and Political Studies (RSPS), and Regional Social and Cultural Studies (RSCS).

ISEAS Publishing, an established academic press, has issued more than 2,000 books and journals. It is the largest scholarly publisher of research about Southeast Asia from within the region. ISEAS Publishing works with many other academic and trade publishers and distributors to disseminate important research and analyses from and about Southeast Asia to the rest of the world.

Cambodia Development Resource Institute (CDRI)

The GMS Development Series is an initiative of CDRI. Established in 1990, CDRI is Cambodia's leading independent development policy research institute. Its mission is to contribute to Cambodia's sustainable development, and the well-being of its people, through the generation of high quality policy-relevant development research, knowledge dissemination and capacity development.

CDRI works to achieve this mission in partnership with Cambodian public institutions and civil society, and their regional and international development partners, with respect for the capacity of the Cambodian people and their institutions, for the value of local knowledge and experience, and for Cambodia's history and culture.

CDRI produces policy-relevant development research on:

- Economy, trade and regional cooperation
- Agriculture and rural development
- Democratic governance and public sector reform
- Natural resources and the environment
- Social development

with cross-cutting themes of inclusive growth, poverty reduction, sustainability, governance and institutional arrangements, gender equity, and conflict prevention and resolution.

Located in the Phnom Penh suburb of Tuol Kork, CDRI has ninety-five staff, including management, professional and technical staff, operations and support staff, of whom ninety-two are Cambodian. It also houses Cambodia's most extensive development research library and resource centre. Its publications, in both English and Khmer, are available as free PDF downloads from its website at <www.cdri.org.kh>.

The Greater Mekong Subregion Development Analysis Network (GMS-DAN)

The Greater Mekong Subregion Development Analysis Network (GMS-DAN) is a collaborative research network of leading development policy research institutes in Cambodia, Laos, Thailand, Vietnam and Yunnan province of China. GMS-DAN's current core members are:

- Cambodia Development Resource Institute (CDRI), Cambodia
- National Economic Research Institute (NERI), Laos
- General Department of Statistics, National Committee for Planning and Investment, (formerly National Centre of Statistics), Laos
- Thailand Development Research Institute (TDRI), Thailand
- Central Institute for Economic Management (CIEM), Vietnam
- Institute of Economics, Vietnam Academy of Social Sciences, Vietnam
- ASEAN Regional and Industrial Development Research Centre, Faculty of Management and Economics, Kunming University of Science and Technology, Yunnan, China.

GMS-DAN has, with the support of the Rockefeller Foundation, undertaken collaborative research and published research reports and associated publications, on the following topics:

- The Impact of the Asian Financial Crisis on the Southeast Asian Transitional Economies
- Labour Markets in Transitional Economies in Southeast Asia and Thailand
- Off-farm and Non-farm Employment in Southeast Asian Transitional Economies and Thailand
- The Cross-Border Economies of Cambodia, Laos, Thailand and Vietnam
- Pro-poor Tourism in the Greater Mekong Subregion
- Labour Migration in the Greater Mekong Subregion
- Agricultural Trade in the Greater Mekong Subregion
- Assessing China's Impact on Poverty Reduction in the Greater Mekong Subregion.

LIST OF AUTHORS BY GMS-DAN COUNTRY RESEARCH TEAM

Hossein Jalilian	Reader, University of Bradford; former Director of Research, CDRI
Cambodia	
Ouch Chandarany	Researcher, CDRI
Saing Chanhang	Researcher, CDRI
Phann Dalia	Researcher, CDRI
Benjamin C.R. Flower	Researcher, CDRI
Laos	
Leeber Leebuapao	Acting Director General, NERI
Saykham Voladet	Director of the Policy Research Division, NERI
Thailand	
Dr Wisarn Pupphavesa	Researcher, TDRI
Dr Srawooth Paitoonpong	Researcher, TDRI
Montinee Chaksirimont	Researcher, TDRI
Siam Sakaeo	Researcher, TDRI
Vietnam	
Nguyen Thi Kim Dung	Researcher, CIEM
Nguyen Manh Hai	Researcher, CIEM
Tran Trung Hieu	Researcher, CIEM

Yunnan Province, China

Lei Qin	Faculty of Management and Economics, Kunming University of Science and Technology
Shuhui Wen	Faculty of Management and Economics, Kunming University of Science and Technology
Tu Xinquan	China National Institute of WTO, University of International Business and Economics, Beijing
Xiong Bin	Faculty of Management and Economics, Kunming University of Science and Technology
Xuan Juneng	Faculty of Management and Economics, Kunming University of Science and Technology

GMS Development Series 3
A CDRI Publication

Assessing China's Impact on Poverty in the Greater Mekong Subregion

EDITED BY **Hossein Jalilian**

ISEAS
INSTITUTE OF SOUTHEAST ASIAN STUDIES
Singapore

and

GMS - DAN

THE ROCKEFELLER FOUNDATION

First published in Singapore in 2013 by
ISEAS Publishing
Institute of Southeast Asian Studies
30 Heng Mui Keng Terrace
Pasir Panjang
Singapore 119614

E-mail: publish@iseas.edu.sg
Website: http://bookshop.iseas.edu.sg

ISEAS Library Cataloguing-in-Publication Data

Assessing China's impact on poverty in the Greater Mekong Subregion / edited by Hossein Jalilian.

1. Poverty—Mekong River Region.
2. Poverty—China—Yunnan Sheng.
3. Investments, Chinese—Mekong River Region.
4. Mekong River Region—Economic conditions.
5. Yunnan Sheng (China)—Economic conditions.

I. Jalilian, Hossein.

HC441 Z9P6A84 2013

ISBN 978-981-4311-87-8 (soft cover)
ISBN 978-981-4414-19-7 (hard cover)
ISBN 978-981-4311-88-5 (e-book, PDF)

Typeset by Superskill Graphics Pte Ltd
Printed in Singapore by Oxford Graphic Printers Pte Ltd

CONTENTS

LIST OF FIGURES, TABLES AND BOXES

Chapter 1

Chapter 3

Chapter 4

Chapter 5

Chapter 7

Chapter 8

FOREWORD

This volume presents the findings of the Greater Mekong Subregion Development Analysis Network (GMS-DAN) research on "Assessing China's Impact on Poverty Reduction in the Greater Mekong Subregion", which was undertaken through the generous support of the Rockefeller Foundation. GMS-DAN comprises leading development policy research institutes in Cambodia, Lao PDR, Thailand, Vietnam and Yunnan Province of China.[1] Since its inception in 1997, GMS-DAN has undertaken collaborative research, and published research reports and associated publications, on a range of significant cross-border socio-economic issues for the GMS — the impact of the Asian financial crisis on the Southeast Asian transitional economies; labour markets in transitional economies in Southeast Asia and Thailand; off-farm and non-farm employment in Southeast Asian transitional economies and Thailand; the cross-border economies of Cambodia, Laos, Thailand and Vietnam; pro-poor tourism in the GMS; labour migration in the GMS; agricultural trade in the GMS; and, most recently, assessing China's impact on poverty reduction in the GMS.

GMS-DAN's vision is for a peaceful, prosperous and integrated Greater Mekong Subregion that has achieved inclusive growth and sustainable development for its peoples. GMS-DAN's mission is to

1. The GMS-DAN currently comprises the Cambodia Development Resource Institute (CDRI); National Economic Research Institute (NERI) and Bureau of Statistics, Lao PDR; Thailand Development Research Institute (TDRI); Central Institute for Economic Management (CIEM) and Institute of Economics, Vietnam; Faculty of Management and Economics, Kunming University of Science and Technology (KUST), Yunnan, China.

collaborate effectively as a network of leading GMS development research institutions; to generate high-quality collaborative development policy research on issues of importance to the GMS; to disseminate it effectively to policy-makers and influencers; and to strengthen the capacity of its member institutes and researchers. GMS-DAN's researchers include both senior experienced researchers with decades of experience working on development issues in ASEAN and the GMS, and a younger generation of emerging researchers who are building their knowledge and skills at a time of rapid change and development in their own countries and in the broader region — economically, socially and geopolitically. Of all these changes, none has more significant implications for these countries, for the GMS, and for ASEAN and the broader East Asian region, than the re-emergence of China as a major regional and global economic and geopolitical power, and the deepening of its relations, both economically and strategically, with the countries of the GMS, particularly the least developed countries (LDCs), Cambodia, Lao PDR and Myanmar.

In 2009, when this project was conceived, the global and regional economies, including the GMS countries in this study, were still feeling the impact of the global financial crisis and associated economic downturn. As a result of the crisis, China, with sustained robust growth, and already deeply engaged economically and geopolitically in ASEAN and its subset of GMS countries, further strengthened its global and regional influence through mechanisms such as the G20, ASEAN+3 cooperation, and increased contributions to the Asia Development Bank (ADB), and led a remarkable recovery in East Asia from the crisis. In the case of Cambodia, for example, by 2010 China had become the largest source of both foreign direct investment and development assistance, with a significant deepening of bilateral relations, also the case with the other two GMS LDCs, Lao PDR and Myanmar.

With much writing, both popular and academic, already available on the so-called "rise of China" globally and regionally, some of it balanced, analytical and constructive, some ideological and alarmist, the GMS-DAN project "Assessing China's Impact on Poverty Reduction in the Greater Mekong Subregion" was conceived to objectively explore the broad question of what is the overall impact of China on economic growth within the GMS countries, how does this differ between these countries given their different economies, stages of development and political systems, and what policy issues might this surface for the GMS as a subregion. The study explored these questions through an analysis of Chinese trade, investment and development assistance, and their impacts, with empirical case studies of specific GMS economies undertaken by researchers from leading policy influencing research institutions within the GMS itself.

As part of the project's research process, in August 2010, GMS-DAN co-hosted a consultation and dissemination workshop with the Institute of World Economics and Politics and the Institute of Asia-Pacific Studies of the Chinese Academy of Social Sciences at CASS headquarters in Beijing. The workshop involved the GMS-DAN researchers, officials from each of the GMS-DAN member countries including Yunnan province of China, and CASS scholars. For many of the younger GMS-DAN researchers, this was both their first opportunity to visit Beijing but more importantly, also their first opportunity to engage in dialogue with Chinese scholars and officials on such a significant and potentially controversial subject. The discussion was frank, robust and constructive, with acknowledgement of both the benefits and opportunities for the GMS countries of a deeper engagement with China, and the issues, real and perceived, that require careful management. Such dialogue, and over time the building of an "epistemic community" of policy researchers, policy-makers and officials in the GMS countries and China, working together to resolve policy challenges, will only serve to enhance the quality and relevance of regional policy research, and build trust and cooperation, particularly for a younger generation of researchers and officials.

The GMS-DAN project and the Beijing workshop identified some important opportunities and challenges, and issues of policy and practice in China's economic engagement with the GMS. These include: the substantial benefits to the GMS of Chinese development assistance, both bilateral and through its increased contributions to the ADB's GMS programme, along with Chinese tourism and trade, investment in infrastructure, agriculture and agribusiness, and mineral resource exploitation, and their contribution to economic growth and diversification, poverty reduction and the narrowing of the development gap between the GMS and ASEAN countries and more broadly in East Asia; the need to better manage the reality and perception of Chinese companies' corporate practices in the GMS in relation to the use of Chinese labour on significant investment and development assistance projects, and to engage more effectively in local community consultation and participation to better share the benefits of such projects; the provision of high levels of development assistance by China that, while responsive to government-defined needs and free of much of the conditionality attached to more traditional development assistance, is criticized for a lack of transparency; the need to better balance economically productive investment, particularly in agriculture and agribusiness, with more responsible environmental management practices to reduce deforestation and environmental degradation; and the need for effective regional and subregional cooperation to ensure that the exploitation of the resources of the Mekong River system are better managed to enable both much-needed hydro-power development and protection of the eco-systems on which local communities rely for their livelihoods.

The strategic location of the GMS countries included in this study, situated as they are in an increasingly integrated Greater Mekong Subregion, and ASEAN, and in close proximity to China, is a major asset, but it also creates policy challenges. The increasingly likely prospect of an integrated production network and market, extending from China, through the GMS countries to the rest of Southeast Asia and beyond, provides the GMS countries with great opportunities for growth and socio-economic development, prosperity, private sector development and poverty reduction. The role of China, both economically and geopolitically, and the way the GMS countries individually and jointly manage their relations with China, will be central to this. We hope this volume will make a useful contribution to the research literature and stimulate questions for further research on major development trends and issues in the Greater Mekong Subregion, and on China's global and regional role and impact.

Larry Strange
Executive Director CDRI

LIST OF CONTRIBUTORS

Benjamin C.R. Flower is Researcher at Cambodia Development Resource Institute (CDRI), Phnom Penh, Cambodia.

Hossein Jalilian, Reader, University of Bradford, U.K. was Director of Research at Cambodia Development Resource Institute (CDRI), Phnom Penh, Cambodia (2007–2010).

Leeber Leebuapao is Acting Director General of the National Economic Research Institute (NERI), Vientiane, Laos.

Lei Qin is with the Faculty of Management and Economics, Kunming University of Science and Technology, Yunnan, China.

Montinee Chaksirinont is Researcher at Thailand Development Research Institute (TDRI), Bangkok, Thailand.

Nguyen Manh Hai is Researcher at the Central Institute for Economic Management (CIEM), Hanoi, Vietnam.

Nguyen Thi Kim Dung is Researcher at the Central Institute for Economic Management (CIEM), Hanoi, Vietnam.

Ouch Chandarany is Researcher at Cambodia Development Resource Institute (CDRI), Phnom Penh, Cambodia.

Phann Dalia is Researcher at Cambodia Development Resource Institute (CDRI), Phnom Penh, Cambodia.

Saing Chanhang is Researcher at Cambodia Development Resource Institute (CDRI), Phnom Penh, Cambodia.

Saykham Voladet is Director of the Policy Research Division, National Economic Research Institute (NERI), Vientiane, Laos.

Siam Sakaeo is Researcher at Thailand Development Research Institute (TDRI), Bangkok, Thailand.

Srawooth Paitoonpong is Researcher at Thailand Development Research Institute (TDRI), Bangkok, Thailand.

Tran Trung Hieu is Researcher at the Central Institute for Economic Management (CIEM), Hanoi, Vietnam.

Tu Xinquan is with the China Institute for WTO Studies, University of International Business and Economics, Beijing, China.

Wen Shuhui is with the Faculty of Management and Economics, Kunming University of Science and Technology, Yunnan, China.

Wisarn Pupphavesa is Researcher at Thailand Development Research Institute (TDRI), Bangkok, Thailand.

Xiong Bin is with the Faculty of Management and Economics, Kunming University of Science and Technology, Yunnan, China.

Xuan Juneng is with the Faculty of Management and Economics, Kunming University of Science and Technology, Yunnan, China.

PART I

The Context

1

ASSESSING CHINA'S IMPACT ON POVERTY IN THE GREATER MEKONG SUBREGION
An Introduction

Hossein Jalilian and Benjamin C.R. Flower

Since the dawn of the industrial revolution, and the ushering in of an era of global economic relations, the United States and Europe have been the core poles of economic power. However, China along with India and a select group of other rapidly developing (and mostly East Asian) countries are increasingly challenging the traditional economic hegemony. Such is the level and significance of this challenge that Gu, Humphrey and Messner (2008, p. 275) are moved to assert that this generation is "witnessing a fundamental shift in power centres in the global economy". Indeed, in 2010, in a moment laden with symbolism, China eclipsed Japan to become the world's second largest economy, cementing its position as one of the globe's foremost economic powerhouses.

An issue of great importance is how this shift in the global economic balance of power will affect developing economies, and in particular the poor residing within them. Developing countries will be offered opportunities by China's growth, but also face challenges. It is important to identify the likely routes of impact so policy can be designed to optimize opportunities and lessen the potential for negative impacts. Nowhere are these issues more relevant than in the transition economies of the Greater Mekong Subregion (GMS),[1] which are located in China's backyard and deeply integrated into its economy through regional supply chains. This volume examines the relationship between transition economies and the rise of China through presenting empirical case studies from the GMS. In doing so, it offers insights into the effect of China on developing countries in general, and offers practical policy directions for the place-specific economies of the GMS.

This chapter starts by giving an overview of the Chinese economy and the key routes through which its rise may affect developing countries. It then focuses on the relationship between China and the GMS, and highlights the key issues that may arise from economic interaction. A method to analyse China's impacts on poverty in the GMS is then forwarded; which informs the empirical studies that follow. The results of the case studies presented in this volume are then surmised, and the organization of the following chapters is detailed.

1. KEY ISSUES

1.1 China and Developing Countries

From an economic perspective, the speed and strength of China's growth trajectory is as sobering as it is well documented. With the ascension of Deng Xiaoping in 1978, China embarked on a state-led transition to capitalism. Since then the country has progressed inexorably up the global economic hierarchy, its strong and consistent GDP growth resultant of high levels of investment and ever-growing participation in world trade.

Since the late 1970s China has consistently averaged around 9–10 per cent GDP growth (Figure 1.1). Political factors have greatly influenced China's growth trajectory: between 1960 and 1980, China's GDP grew from US$63 billion to US$189 billion, and then, following the economic reforms that began in the late 1970s, it exploded to US$4.9 trillion in 2009. Stiglitz (2001, p. 18) does not overstate the significance of these figures when he says that "China's recent experience is one of the greatest economic success stories in history". In the 2000s China's economy has continued to exceed

FIGURE 1.1
China's GDP Growth

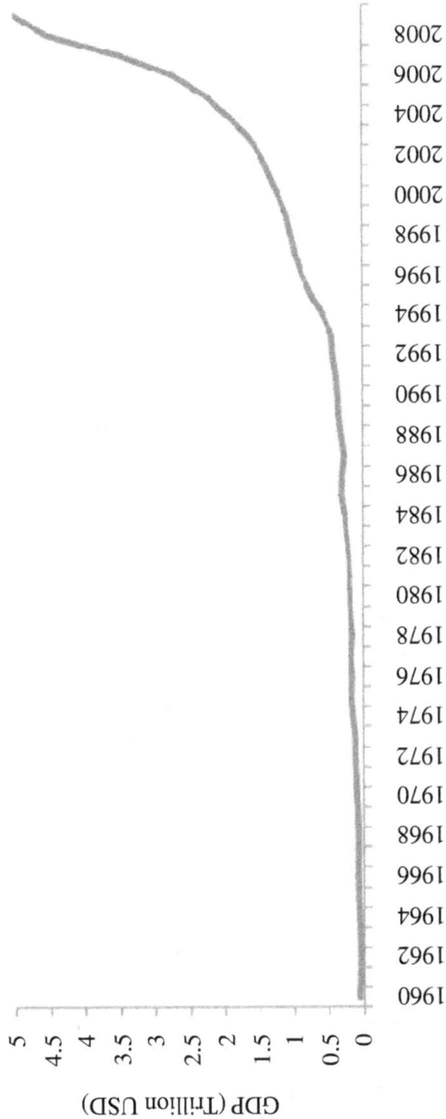

Source: World Bank (2010).

expectations, growing phenomenally to become the second largest in the world; if current trends persist it will be the largest in the world before the middle of this century.

Although there is no such thing as a "sure thing" in economic history, the structure of the Chinese economy seems to indicate it is built to last. A recent United Nations Development Programme (UNDP 2010) report praises the solid foundations underlying the shining statistics. While exports and foreign direct investment (FDI) have contributed to China's GDP, growth has been underpinned by domestic investment funded by domestic savings, suggesting a stable long-term economic outlook (Prasad 2009). Building on these foundations, the government hopes to rely less on exports for generating future growth, and instead tap huge potential domestic demand. Diversifying its growth in this way will mean the economy will be less vulnerable to shocks resulting from falling external demand for manufactured products.[2]

The aspect of China's growth that makes it unparalleled in history is the size of the population experiencing it in tandem with its high rate. Stigliz (1998, p. 2) notes:

> If China's 30 provinces were treated as separate economies — and many of them have populations exceeding those of most other low-income countries — the 20 fastest-growing economies between 1978 and 1995 would all have been Chinese provinces.

China's East Asian neighbours Taiwan, South Korea and Japan have shown equal or more impressive rates of growth, but on a global scale China's growth is more significant. Illustrative of this fact is the impact of China's domestic growth on the structure of the global economy, its contribution to global GDP increasing from 1.8 per cent in 1978 to 6.42 per cent in 2008 (World Bank 2010 cited in UNDP 2010, p. 8). This growing prominence has increasingly meant that domestic economic conditions have large effects globally. This has been especially noticeable in the current global economic recovery: while the advanced economies of Europe, the United States and Japan are stagnating, China's consistently strong growth figures are buoying the global economy.

Because of its huge population, it is China's growth in per capita GDP that could have the largest effect on the future structure of the global economy. Wage rises across China and increased consumerism could benefit both advanced and developing countries by opening a huge and potentially highly lucrative market for them. Per capita GDP increased from around US$330 in 1990 to around US$950 in 2000 — an almost threefold increase in just ten years. Since 2000 this growth has been even stronger, and in 2009 per capita GDP stood at US$3,744 — an elevenfold increase in less than twenty years (Figure 1.2). These per capita increases have been spread across a population of over 1.3 billion people.

As China's consumption patterns change, demand for products — both manufactured and those used in manufacturing processes — will soar. To take a striking example of this potential for growth in domestic consumption, the prominent neo-Malthusian scholar Lester Brown (2005, p. 45) notes that "if automobile ownership in China were to reach the USA level of 0.77 cars per person, China would have a fleet of 1.1 billion cars in 2031 — well beyond the current world fleet of 795 million". The knock-on effects of these changes would manifest globally, potentially affecting economies and government policies around the world, which would adapt both to take advantage of emergent opportunities, but also to try and mitigate threats arising from issues such as global warming. Increases in per capita GDP will stimulate other processes, such as increased rates of saving, financial sector development and FDI that will also have significant impacts far from China's own shores.

The place-specific impacts of China's ascension will depend on the individual and regional structure of economies as well as geopolitical considerations. In general it is thought China's rise may have both positive (complementary) and negative (competitive) effects on the economies of developing countries (for example, Jenkins and Edwards 2004). It is in this context that the ADB-GMS initiatives aim to increase interaction between the GMS and China and also to develop policies that enable these interactions to have beneficial outcomes. However, the potential for negative outcomes must also be acknowledged. In assessing and identifying complementary and competitive impacts in developing economies resulting from China's economic growth, it is necessary to examine the main spheres of economic interaction between China and developing counties in general, and the GMS in particular. These spheres of economic interaction are trade, FDI and overseas development assistance (ODA), and increasingly, impacts arising from China's growing participation in global economic governance.

FIGURE 1.2
GDP per capita in China

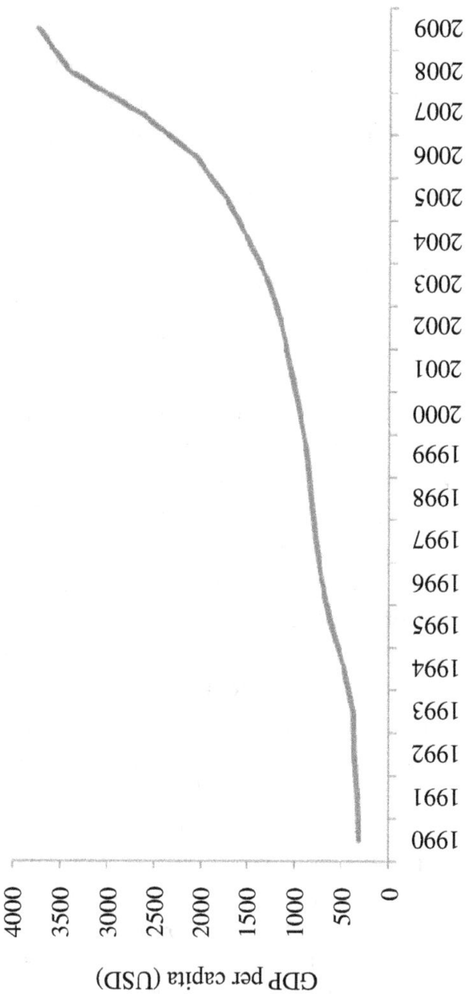

Source: World Bank (2010).

1.2 Trade

China's growing participation in world trade has been a defining trait of its transition. During the period 1985–2005, exports rose from US$50 billion to US$798 billion (Kaplinsky and Messner 2008, p. 199): China is now the third largest exporter of goods in the global market place, behind the United States and Germany. In addition, China has seen huge increases in imports, which have mirrored exports and been largely driven by demand for materials used for production in the manufactured products export sector. This trend has been particularly apparent in the past decade (Figure 1.3), and is primarily seen as a result of a surge of manufactured output driven by the huge growth of small- and medium-sized enterprises and careful management of state-owned enterprise.

The growth of China's manufacturing sector has provided a huge potential market for the goods of developing countries, particularly those that rely heavily on export revenues derived from primary products. Davies (2009, p. 23) observes that China's "imports have grown rapidly, increasing from 6 per cent of GDP in 1980 to 29 per cent of GDP in 2006 and increasing by 90 per cent in real (US) dollar terms between 2003 and 2006". A large proportion of this import demand has been in primary products such as raw materials or minerals for use in manufacturing and industrial activities, resulting in a surge in demand, which has had the effect of pushing commodity prices up.

Many least developed countries have gained in the short term as a result of this facet of China's economic structure. In particular the sub-Saharan African (SSA) countries, being reliant on primary product export revenues, have seen their export volumes grow quickly in response to China's growth (Figure 1.4). SSA export profile mirrors China's surge in imports and exports starting in the early 2000s, helping satiate its demand for materials used in the production of manufactured products. In the long term, this increase in demand for primary products may encourage primary product dependency in some least developed nations and hence, heighten vulnerability to shocks and stifle industrial development.

For countries trying to get a foothold on the industrial ladder, competition from Chinese goods in domestic and third markets could be a potential cause for concern. In particular, China's global dominance in the textile industry, which is traditionally seen as the first rung of the industrial ladder, is often considered a core challenge to many countries

FIGURE 1.3
China's Imports and Exports

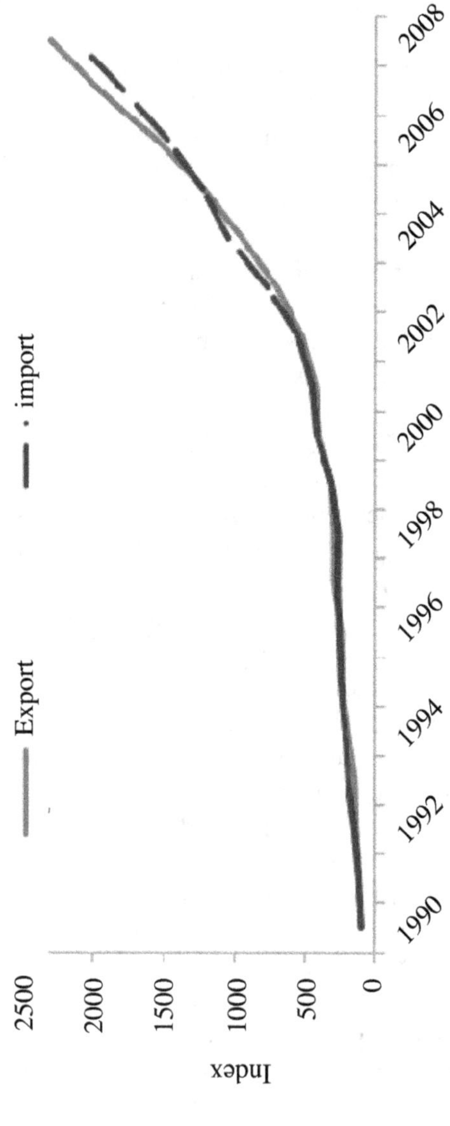

Source: World Bank (2010), adapted.

FIGURE 1.4
Growth (%) of Total Exports to China from SSA against Primary Commodities

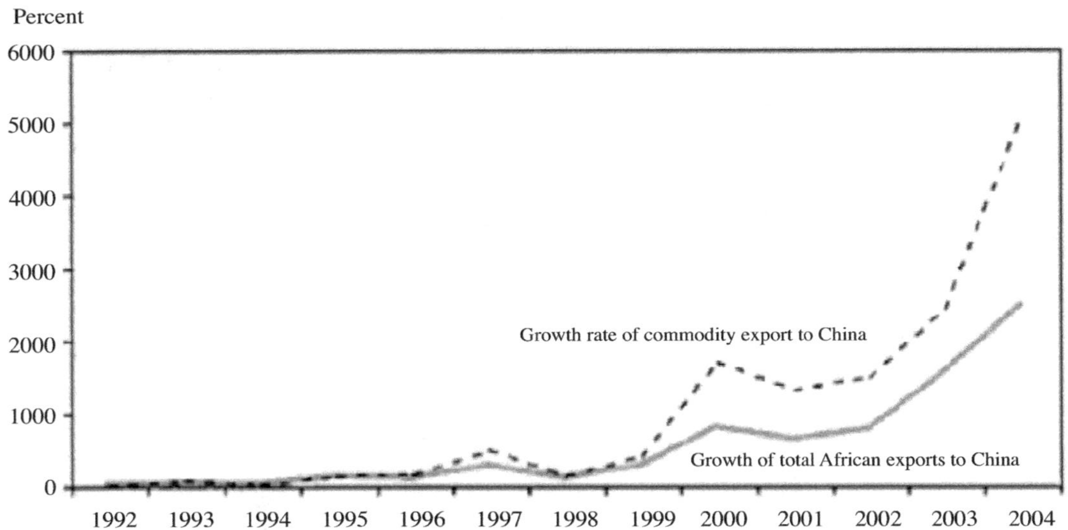

Source: Goldstein et al. (2006, p. 24).

seeking to industrialize. Collier (2008), for example, sees the rise of China as a constraint to many SSA countries developing garment industries; China is established, well connected to supply chains and has access to a large pool of cheap labour. As Kaplinsky and Morris (2008, p. 269) assert "the blunt reality is that SSA clothing and textile exporters cannot compete with Asian producers in general and Chinese exporters in particular".

It does not seem likely in the short to medium term that as China develops, and the structure of the Chinese labour market changes, its labour-intensive industrial exports (particularly garments) will become uncompetitive and shift to less developed countries. Akamatsu's (1962) flying geese model predicts that as a country moves up the industrial ladder from labour- to capital-intensive industrial processes, less developed countries fill the void and start utilizing their labour advantage to produce labour-intensive industrial products. But Shenkar (2005, p. 134 cited in Kaplinksy and Messner 2008, p. 200) contends that

> China's enormous labour reserves, with pay scales radically lower in the hinterland than the coast and urban areas (the average income on the farm, where more than half the Chinese population lives, is less than US$25 per month), create the equivalent of a country within a country; so instead of Vietnam or Bangladesh replacing China as a labour-intensive haven, Yunnan province will replace Guangdong.

Thus China is able to support and remain competitive in both capital- and labour-intensive industries. This is a major barrier to many countries nascent attempts to industrialize.

1.3 Capital Inflows: FDI and ODA

A second potential route of impact of China's rise on developing countries is through changes in the structure of their capital inflows. In regards to the "competitive" outcomes of China's growth there is the possibility that its correspondingly increased attractiveness to investors may have diverted FDI destined for other developing markets, and thus reduced their FDI inflow. Indeed, it is true that China has become an increasingly attractive proposition for foreign investors — the explosion in township village enterprises (TVEs) in particular has attracted a lot of FDI to China, rendering it a significant driver of these industries (for example, Fu and Balasubramanyam 2003). But as Figure 1.5 shows, though the

FIGURE 1.5
Inflow of FDI and Developing Countries (1990=100)

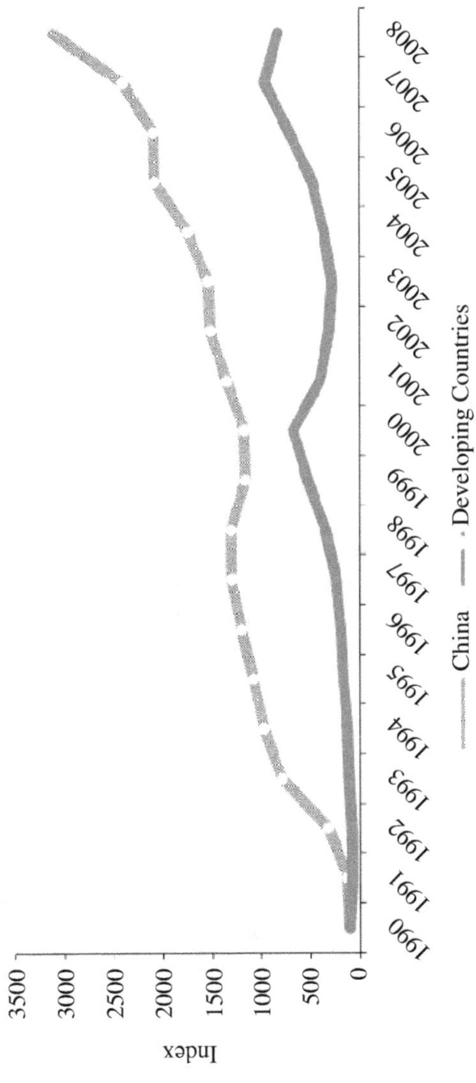

Source: World Bank (2010), adapted.

rate of increase of FDI to China has risen rapidly over the last two decades, FDI has also increased to other developing countries in the same period, albeit at a slower rate. Given the inherent complexity of factors underlying FDI inflows, it is very hard to say whether FDI to other developing countries would increase if China's economy was not growing at such a fast rate.

China's rise has meant that an increasing volume of FDI coming from it is destined for developing countries. In general a defining trait of China's FDI has been its strategic and coordinated nature. A case in point is the garment industry: in light of the quotas put on Chinese exports to Western markets, Chinese FDI destined for garment factories has been seen from SSA (Lall 2005 on Lesotho) to Southeast Asia (Jalilian and Reyes 2010 on Cambodia). Other FDI has been used to secure natural resource supplies, such as minerals, rubber plantations, and land for crops, etc., from developing nations in SSA, Latin America and Asia, for China's future needs (WB 2010).

Like FDI, official development assistance (ODA) from China has been forthcoming, but has often been tied to conditionality and has been seen as strategically serving China's interests rather than that of the host country. For example, referring to Chinese aid in SSA, Zafar (2007, p. 120) notes its strategic nature in combining "financial assistance and funding of construction projects to build influence in exchange for oil and create a network of reliable allies and suppliers". The planning element, and the ever-present role of the state, that has proved so successful in China's transition from communist to capitalist state, is also the hand guiding outflows of capital in the form of FDI and ODA.

1.4 Global Governance

A final route of impact is the Chinese government's role in constructing the agendas of global governance institutions. Figure 1.6 indicates just how much China has increased its participation in global forums. A good example of this can be found in China's participation in the Dispute Settlement System of the World Trade Organisation (WTO) as a third party mediator. Through this system it has gained knowledge of the institutional and regulatory apparatus of the WTO and has become active "in the making and application of WTO rules" without becoming directly involved in trade disputes with member countries (Gu, Humphrey and

FIGURE 1.6
China's Membership of International Organizations

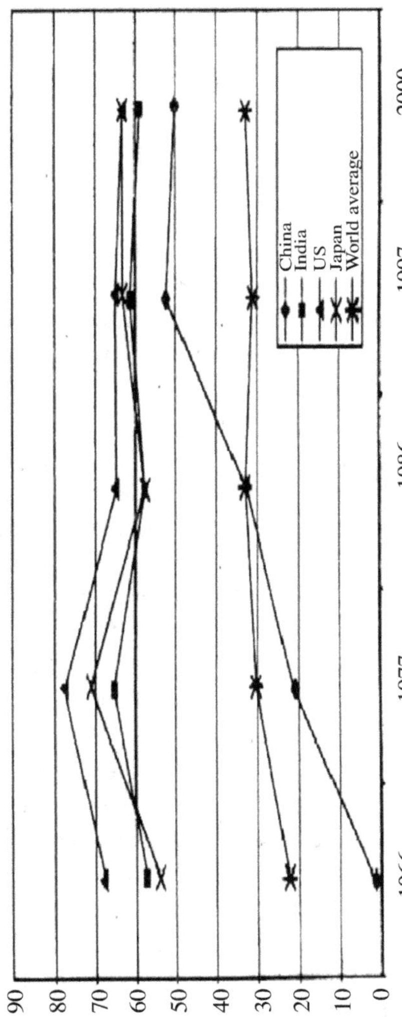

Source: Johnston (2003 cited in Kaplinsky & Messner 2008).

Messner 2008, p. 284). Thus, strategically and relatively silently, China has been able to strengthen its position in the WTO and use its knowledge to get the decisions that serve its interests.

China's increasing prominence in the mechanisms of global — particularly economic — governance has the potential to greatly affect developing countries. On a global scale, if one uses the binary distinction of "developed" and "developing" world, then China's participation in global governance bodies, particularly the WTO, is of great significance in altering the global balance of power potentially in favour of developing regions. However, the specific impacts will again vary between countries and regions. As China's actions are motivated by self-interest, regions that compete in markets such as textiles could lose out, for example, those in SSA. There is the potential for those integrated into China's regional supply chains to benefit; having an economic superpower representing the interests of the region could be particularly beneficial to low- and middle-income Asian countries.

1.5 China and the GMS

The countries of the Greater Mekong Subregion[3] (GMS) in many ways face the same opportunities and challenges resultant of China's ascension as other transition economies. A key difference, however, is that China is closely integrated with the region and shares some common interests. The GMS-4[4] share a key attribute that set them apart from most developing countries in that they are China's backyard: their political and socioeconomic stability, and indeed development and prosperity, can have direct impacts on China. As Krongkaew (2004, p. 980) notes, the "GMS economic zone should provide an excellent 'southern gateway' that could bring greater economic prosperity to the south and southwestern provinces of China". The relative poverty of western China is a major issue for the government. While the east coast of China is prosperous, areas such as Yunnan province are land locked and far from markets and the coast. A prosperous GMS would be beneficial to China, and in particular the inland provinces bordering the GMS countries.[5]

To take advantage of the opportunities afforded by close geographical proximity and geopolitical circumstance, a number of ADB projects aimed at fostering increased regional integration between the GMS and China have been initiated since the early 1990s. The main focus of these programmes has been the development of Economic Corridors that link the GMS and China. Economic corridors consist of many facets, including hard infrastructure such as roads and railway — including a project that seeks to connect Kunming in China to Singapore via the GMS — electricity and water supply and communications. In addition to upgrading hardware, programmes have focused on institutional and policy reform to better facilitate increased trade and investment. For example, there have been reforms of customs procedures to encourage cross-border trade and the development of regional institutional mechanisms to enhance private sector participation in policy making (Krongkaew 2004).

A key facet of the relationship between China and the GMS is trade. China relies on and is well integrated into regional production networks. To promote these interests, economic regionalism has become a strong trait of a modern China; as McDonald, Robinson and Thierfelder (2008, p. 210) assert, China is "an integral part of the regional trading bloc in East and South East Asia ... with regional production characterised by cross country value chains". Agreements to foster increased economic interaction between China and GMS countries are already in place. Indeed, the GMS countries included in this volume (Cambodia, Laos, Thailand, Vietnam) are part of the ASEAN Free Trade Area (AFTA) and in the near future are to be part of the ASEAN-China Free Trade Area (ACTFA). The province of Yunnan is now a part of this agreement. Resultant of this, trade between China and the GMS has steadily increased over the past decade, though China's exports to the GMS have risen at a faster rate (Figure 1.7).

While the GMS countries share common traits, it should be noted that the GMS is not a homogeneous group, and thus outcomes of a growing China and increased interaction with it are likely to vary from country to country. In particular, the GMS-4 (i.e., excluding Yunnan and Myanmar), vary greatly in their level of economic development. For example, in 2009 Thailand had a GDP of over US$263 billion, Vietnam of around US$97 billion, Cambodia at US$10.4 billion, and Laos at US$9.7 billion (Figure 1.8). Thailand, the most developed of the four countries, has sophisticated infrastructure, electricity provision, public services, financial and banking sectors, and exports a wide range of products including high value-added electronics — it is the only one of the four that the World Bank classifies as middle income. Also within this group is Laos — a country with a GDP more than twenty-five times smaller than Thailand, with an economy based mainly around the export of primarily commodities, and with limited

FIGURE 1.7
China's Trade with GMS-4

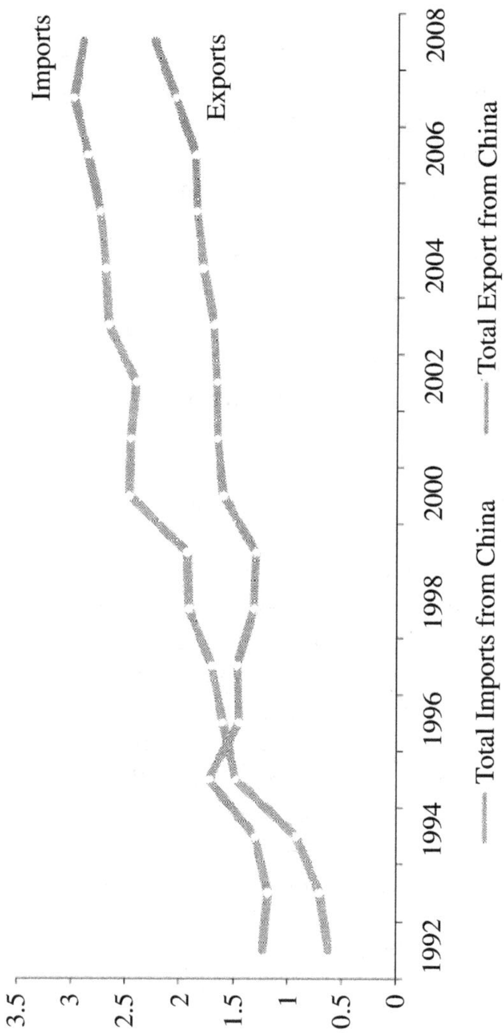

Source: Ministry of Commerce, PRC (2010).

FIGURE 1.8
GDP of the GMS-4

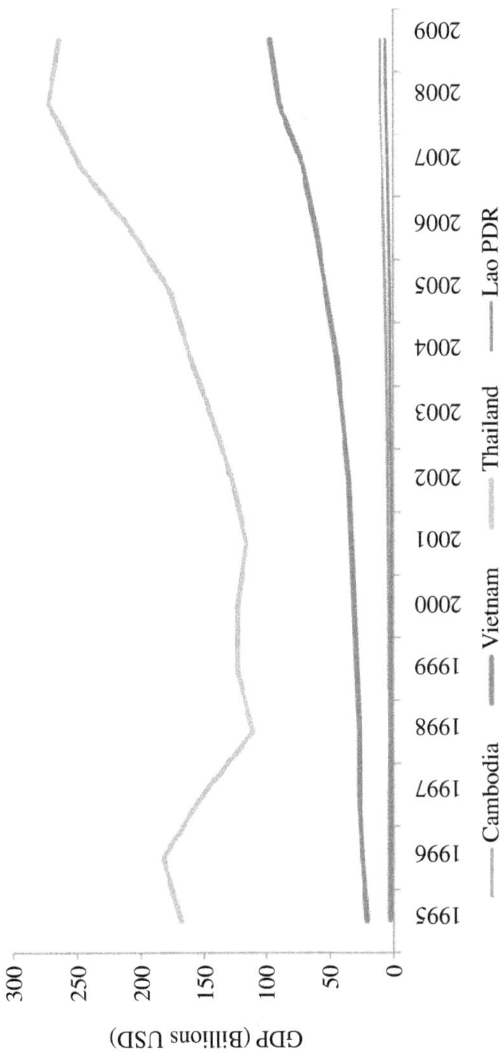

Source: World Bank (2010).

infrastructure. With such diversity within the GMS, there is potential for a variety of economic interactions with China.

Eichengreen, Rhee and Tong (2007) note that while China's imports have a great diversity, they are mainly made up of either primary products or capital goods. Exports to China are likely to increase among the more advanced ASEAN countries that export capital goods, or the lesser developed countries that export primary products. Those that rely on export revenues from consumer goods are unlikely to see such returns and may face significant challenges from China in third markets. There could also be negative long-term effects for primary product exporting countries, which could see resources diverted from industrial pursuits and suffer overvalued currencies as a result of primary product exports making manufactured products uncompetitive in export markets. As Devadason (2010, p. 660) asserts, ACTFA could prove challenging to the smaller ASEAN countries (i.e., GMS-4 excluding Thailand) "given their weak industrial structures ... ACTFA will render domestic markets swamped by better quality, cheaper Chinese goods".

Flows of Chinese FDI and ODA into the GMS have been increasing as a result of ever-closer economic relations (Figure 1.9). The total amount of Chinese FDI to the GMS increased from US$92.9 million to US$456.9 million in 2008. This, however, still accounts for a tiny fraction of China's total FDI (less than 1 per cent). The distribution of China's FDI in the GMS reflects the diversified nature of the economies of the GMS, and also the profile of Chinese FDI, which is generally geared towards garment manufacturing or natural resource extraction in developing economies. Indeed, it is for this reason that most of China's FDI is going to lesser developed GMS countries where these industries operate.

2. ASSESSING CHINA'S IMPACT: METHODOLOGIES

The country studies following this introduction provide a poverty-centred analysis of the effects of China on the GMS-4, and the effects of the GMS-4 on Yunnan province of China. Principally they look at how China's rise has affected the economies of the GMS-4 in general and the poor located within the GMS-4 in particular. The volume utilizes the overarching analytical framework for assessing the impacts on developing countries posited by Jenkins and Edwards (2004).

FIGURE 1.9
FDI Outflow to GMS-4

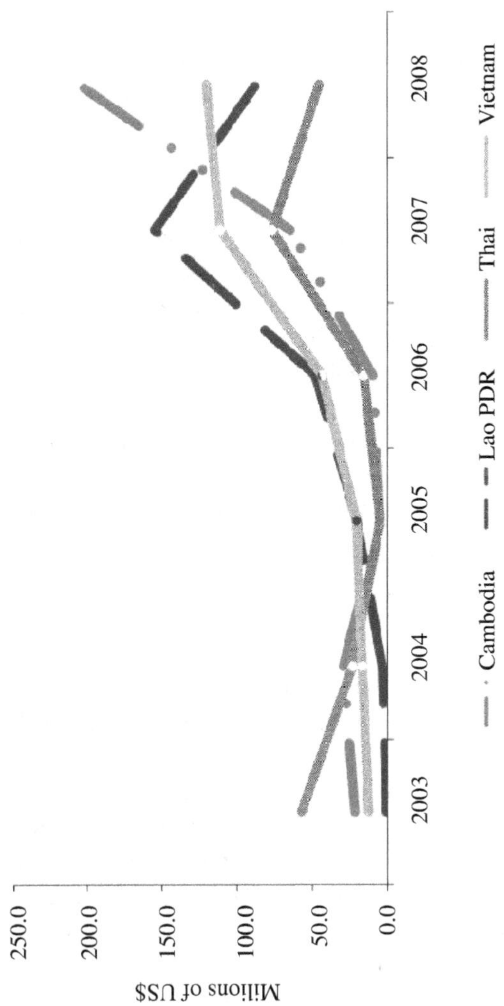

Source: Ministry of Commerce, PRC (2010).

The Jenkins and Edwards (2004) model is useful for analysis of the GMS because it provides a universally applicable framework for analysing China's impact on developing countries that is both country specific and poverty focused, allowing comparisons to be made between and within regions. The framework represents "a disaggregated approach to analysing the impact of China on national economies and … to tracing through the effects on poverty, with some recognition of broader issues of vulnerability" (ibid., p. 10). It is able to capture the effects of potential factors such as integration into regional supply networks that are present in the economies of GMS nations, but less apparent in other developing regions, such as Latin America or SSA. Following the Jenkins and Edwards tradition, this volume contributes to the emerging literature analysing the impact of the rise of China on developing economies by focusing on the GMS-4 and Yunnan province in China as distinct, but interlinked, entities.

The conceptual basis of the Jenkins and Edwards model rests on analysis of key attributes of developing economies where China will have the biggest impact. Because it focuses on individual countries, it sidesteps more indirect issues such as China's role in global governance and issues regarding environmental, trade and other global policies instigated through global institutional frameworks. For example, there is no analysis of China's participation in the WTO which has better terms of trade for trade blocs of developing nations, or its role in securing better carbon emissions quotas for developing nations; instead the framework focuses on China's impact on specific countries.

According to the Jenkins and Edwards' model, areas where China's impact is most direct, quantifiable and observable in developing countries are in the realms of trade, FDI and ODA. With regards to trade, China can affect developing economies through providing new export markets and/or through competing in domestic and third markets. Regarding investment, there is the threat of FDI destined for GMS countries being diverted to China; alternatively there is the potential for increased FDI flow from China to developing economies, including the GMS. Increases in Chinese ODA can have both positive and negative short- and long-term impacts on developing economies. In their study, Jenkins and Edwards (2004) apply this framework to a host of countries to analyse the potential impacts of China. In order to capture the impact of China on a particular country, Jenkins and Edwards distinguish between four different stages, which are summarized in Table 1.1.

While the Jenkins and Edwards model provides the overarching conceptual and structural framework for this volume, it should be remembered that a key facet of their model is the recognition of variation between developing economies. With this in mind the various country chapters place emphasis on different sectors and use methodological approaches that best serve their case study research. For instance, in the case of Thailand an ODA section is absent because there is negligible effect on the economy through this mechanism. The research focuses mainly on trade, which has a massive impact on the Thai economy. The authors of this report use gravity models to predict the impact that future changes in the Chinese economy would have on Thailand's trade profile.

TABLE 1.1
Jenkins and Edwards' Analytical Framework

STAGE 1	Identify direct channels of impacts through: – Export to China – Competition with China in third markets – Competition with China in domestic markets – FDI – ODA
STAGE 2	Identify sub-channels through which poverty effects are likely to be transmitted: • Export to China: – Agriculture, Extractive, Manufacturing • Competition with China in third markets: – Labour intensity in products exported • Competition in domestic market: – Competition with domestic or foreign producers • FDI, ODA – Diversion to China or inflow from China
STAGE 3	Consider effects on: – Production – Prices, and – Government revenue
STAGE 4	Consider effects on the Poor through changes in: – Production by the poor – Consumption by the poor – Support received from government – Spillovers effects affecting the poor.

The other key attribute of the Jenkins and Edwards model is its poverty focus. It assesses how China's rise has influenced sectors, such as agriculture, where the percentage of households that live in poverty is highest. Improving the market for agricultural goods, for instance, may have a greater pro-poor impact than increasing markets for capital goods. Utilizing this poverty focus, the country chapters presented in this volume examine case studies of particular sectors where China has had greatest impact on rates of poverty. For instance, the Vietnam country study pays close attention to fruit and vegetable and fishery exports to China, which are sectors where workers involved in the production processes suffer high instances of poverty. Using a gravity model it is predicted that China's future growth could significantly reduce poverty among workers and their dependent households in these sectors.

3. KEY FINDINGS

3.1 Trade

Because of the variance in the economies and tradable commodity profiles of the GMS-4, there has been a large amount of variance in how China has manifested in terms of bilateral trade. It is argued that China has a great elasticity of imports, but they are mainly either primary products or capital goods. Thus, those low-income countries that export neither will have limited opportunity in Chinese markets. This has been found to be the case with Cambodia, where the majority of exports are labour-intensive garments and the increasing potential of China as a new export market has not as yet had a highly significant impact on the economy. During the period 2000–08, the value of Cambodia's exports to China has on average been a mere US$36.34 million a year, accounting for just 1 per cent of the country's total exports.

Laos, though economically underdeveloped, has seen increases in exports to China from US$7 million to US$41 million in the period 2004–08, representing a rise in share of total exports from 1.8 per cent to 3.2 per cent. These have been mostly in the form of primary products: minerals such as coal and copper account for 75 per cent of exports to China. In Vietnam, which shares a border with China, exports provided significant revenues of US$4,010 million in 2009, again mostly derived from exports of primary products such as oil, coal and, particularly, rubber. Thailand, the most developed of the GMS-4, has a profile that dwarfs the rest: total exports in 2009 stood at US$16,183 million. Indeed, this year (2010) China is expected to replace the United States as Thailand's main export destination. For these countries, a growing Chinese market will mean real GDP growth in the future.

All of the GMS-4 countries have a trade deficit with China. The question is: do these imports hurt domestic production? In Laos the extraction of primary products is seen as environmentally damaging. Further, while Laos currently has no industries that directly compete with Chinese manufactured imports, the focus on primary product dependency could be negative for the country's long-term industrial development. In Thailand, domestic producers have suffered as a result of cheap Chinese imports, particularly in the agricultural sector. In Vietnam and Cambodia, the country studies found no significant effect. In third markets, Cambodia is the only country to register any real competition from Chinese exports. This is mainly because its primary export is labour-intensive garments, which are similar to those exported from China.

The pro-poor effects of China's growth have also varied across the region. From a pro-poor perspective, the changing profile of Cambodian goods exported to China is a positive development: labour-intensive textiles and garments rose from 3.2 per cent of all exports in 1992 to 28.2 per cent in 2008. This has contributed to poverty reduction through creating employment for unskilled workers from poor households. However, given the small value of exports, the contribution is small. Greater pro-poor benefits have been found in Vietnam where increased trading activity has benefited remote border regions, exports to China have boosted sectors which have high incidences of poverty, and imports from China have provided poor households with cheap consumer goods. Thailand's export of rubber to China, it was found, has had the effect of creating employment for a staggering 465,836 unskilled workers, thus significantly reducing poverty. However, the competition from Chinese imports has put more unskilled people out of work, so the net result for poor households has been negative. Laos found that on a microscopic level, trade in sugar cane decreased poverty in the short term, but questions the environmental sustainability of the intensive farming methods used on sugar cane plantations.

3.2 Foreign Direct Investment and Overseas Development Assistance

From a Chinese perspective, the Yunnan study team found that FDI to the GMS-4 was relatively small in scale, accounting for just 0.032512 per cent of China's outgoing FDI. Although small at the moment, the figure underscores the potential for growth in this sector in the future. Across the GMS-4, the Yunnan study found that, in general, Chinese FDI was limited to sectors that produced primary products, and was not concerned with environmental sustainability. In the long run this could damage the future stock of local primary products and energy that are needed to fuel the Chinese economy.

While FDI to the GMS-4 from a Chinese point of view is small, from the perspective of certain GMS-4 countries, it is a vital source of investment. In Laos for example, China is the third largest source of FDI after Thailand and Vietnam, accounting for 17.8 per cent of the country's total FDI in the period 2004–08. The Thai study found, that while less significant than trade, FDI contributed to the creation of 43,363 jobs. In Cambodia, there has been significant development of the garment industry that has benefited from inflows of Chinese FDI.

There is some concern as to the structure of Chinese FDI. While FDI is always going to be profit orientated, and though it is clear that from a macroeconomic perspective there have been short-term benefits from Chinese FDI in many respects, the studies show a tendency to extract more on capital and resources with maximum haste rather than to invest in longer term, sustainable ventures. The Vietnamese study found that the majority of Chinese FDI in the country was destined for natural resource extraction, which did little to reduce poverty and degraded the natural environment.

Even in areas where Chinese FDI has contributed to poverty reduction, there has been a lack of skills transference. For example, the Cambodia study found that very little FDI went to research and human resource development. Thus, while Chinese FDI contributed to short-term declines in poverty, there was barely any evidence that it contributed to the long-term development and sustainability of the Cambodian garment industry. The Lao team found a similar effect in the mining sector: only low-skilled workers were employed from the local populace.

Perhaps because of the limited data on Chinese ODA, the findings of the country chapters regarding ODA and poverty reduction are mixed. Certain projects have yielded positive pro-poor outcomes. The Cambodia study found that from 2000 to 2009, ODA from China totalled US$465 million, furthermore, that this aid had pro-poor benefits: a Chinese-sponsored infrastructure project increased the poor's access to markets, education and healthcare, and thus improved their standard of living. Similarly, the Lao study notes the importance of Chinese ODA to the country's development and also found that infrastructure projects funded by Chinese ODA had pro-poor impacts.

The Vietnam chapter, however, finds a striking feature of China's ODA is that it is not designed with social development first in mind: "very little linkage can be found from China's implemented ODA projects to the poverty alleviation priority areas such as education, health, and employment creation. This is because the ultimate goal of the projects is either political or economic, not the purpose of social improvement i.e. enhancing people's living standards." Indeed, from this perspective, the poverty alleviation facets of Chinese infrastructure in Laos and Cambodia are more a by-product of Chinese political and economic interests than benevolent interventions. The end product, however, has been the same.

Finally, it should be noted that none of the country studies found any evidence of China diverting FDI flows from their economy.

4. ORGANIZATION OF THIS COLLECTION

This volume is split into three parts. The first part provides the context underlying the country studies. Following this introduction, a literature review by Lei Qin expands on and augments the themes highlighted here. She draws salient issues from the literature on five key points. First, she reviews literature on the possible effects of economic growth on poverty reduction: are policies that pursue aggregate growth inherently pro-poor or do interventions focusing on issues such as inequality need to be targeted? She explores the roles that sectoral composition and trade have on poverty reduction initiatives, focusing on agriculture as the key driver of sustainable development in developing economies. In the second and third sections, she assesses how China's growth has affected Asian economies, expanding on its "competitive" and "complementary" manifestations in the area of trade, and reviews methodological approaches to quantify this impact. Fourth, she gives a conceptual critique of FDI with special reference to the GMS and China, before finally noting the characteristics of Chinese ODA, and highlighting its often strategic nature.

The second part presents a study of China's impact on the GMS-4 from the perspective of the Chinese study team and is divided into two chapters. First, how the GMS-4 has affected the Chinese province of Yunnan is overviewed, focusing on the effect regional cooperation has had on trade, economic growth and poverty reduction. Using a gravity model, it is shown that GMS cooperation and the implementation of related GMS initiatives have significantly promoted trade between Yunnan and most of the GMS countries. Further, the field survey and case studies on selected main export products show that Yunnan's exports to the GMS countries have a direct and indirect impact on income growth in rural areas. However, there is little evidence to show that the income growth of poor people in the poverty-stricken areas is significantly related to trade expansion. The second chapter assesses China's FDI and ODA to the GMS-4. The first section of this chapter deals with FDI from China, highlighting their changing distribution and function; namely diversifying from primary commodity extraction in Thailand and Vietnam to manufacturing in Cambodia. China's key investment motives — to seek out natural resources, new markets, improve capital efficiency and promote regional economic networks — are identified. It is asserted that the outcomes have been mutually beneficial for both China and host countries. The results reveal that China's investment in this region holds great potential. The second section of the chapter then analyses the motivations and goals of China's ODA to the GMS countries, concluding that China's aid is mostly politically oriented with the purpose of consolidating its good relations with neighbouring countries in the region and that it is used as a tool to help Chinese companies take part in the economic growth of emerging economies.

The third part examines China's impact on poverty reduction from the perspective of each of the GMS-4 countries. First the Vietnamese study, uses a gravity model to predict that future rises in China's GDP will decrease poverty through increasing exports from sectors with high instances of poverty. Using a computer general equilibrium (CGE) model, the effect of Chinese imports on poverty is estimated. It is also predicted that falling costs of imports from China will reduce poverty and may even offset a scenario where exports to China decrease in value. Next the Thai study, similar to the Vietname report utilizes gravity models to predict the future impact that China's growth will have on Thailand's trade and FDI profiles. Bilateral trade is found to be the most significant "Chinese" factor affecting the Thai economy. Significantly, it is predicted that Thailand's exports to China will rise as China's GDP grows. Further, it is anticipated that this trend will be enhanced by China-ASEAN Free Trade in the longer term. From a pro-poor perspective, a net positive effect from trade with China was found as more unskilled jobs are created from exports to China than are lost from exports. The Cambodia chapter that follows next provides a macro and microscopic analysis of China's impact on the economy, with particular reference to poverty. It provides a detailed analysis of bilateral trade, Chinese competition in third markets and how Chinese FDI and ODA have affected Cambodia in this respect. The study identifies a key line of effect through the garment industry. Garments have become Cambodia's main export product to China, and Chinese FDI has underpinned the development of the industry. It is argued that there have been significant pro-poor benefits from this intervention, but that these would be more effective if policies were put in place to ensure knowledge and skill transference to the Cambodian workers. Finally following the qualitative approach of the Cambodian chapter the Lao chapter pays particular attention to the microscopic aspects of China's rise and poverty reduction in that country. Using detailed case studies of sugar cane production (for trade), mining (for FDI) and infrastructure development (for ODA), not only positive pro-poor short term impacts, but also issues of sustainability are highlighted.

Notes

1. The Greater Mekong Subregion (GMS) is a term coined by the ADB to refer to Cambodia, Laos, Myanmar, Thailand, Vietnam and Yunnan Province of China. Myanmar, however, is not included in this study.
2. This has been evident in recent years following the global financial and economic crisis of 2008. By relying on domestic demand, China, unlike the Western world, has so far avoided the negative impacts.
3. In this volume GMS refers to all of the states that constitute the ADB's definition with the exception of Myanmar for which no study has been carried out.
4. In this volume, country studies analysing the impact of China on GMS countries include Cambodia, Laos, Thailand and Vietnam, or the GMS-4.

5. A separate case study in this volume deals with these and other similar issues.

References

Akamatsu K. "A Historical Pattern of Economic Growth in Developing Countries". *Journal of Developing Economies* 1, no. 1 (1962): 3–25.

Brown, L.R. "China is Replacing US as World's Leading Consumer". *New Perspectives Quarterly* 22, no. 5 (2005): 41–45.

Collier, P. *The Bottom Billion*, New York: Oxford University Press, 2008.

Davies, M. "The Rise of China: Implications for the Mekong Countries". In *Globalization and Development in the Mekong Economies*, edited by Leung, S., B.F.W. Bingham and M. Davies. Massachusetts: Edward Elgar Publishing, 2010.

Devadason, E.S. "ASEAN-China Trade Flows: Moving Forward with ACFTA". *Journal of Contemporary China* 19, no. 66 (2010): 653–74.

Eichengreen, B., Y. Rhee and H. Tong. "China and the Exports of Other Asian Countries". *Review of World Economics* 143, no. 2 (2007): 201–26.

Fu, X. and V.N. Balasubramanyam. "Township and Village Enterprises in China". *Journal of Development Studies* 39, no. 4 (2003): 27–46.

Goldstein, A., D. Pinaud, H. Reisen and X. Chen. "The Rise of China and India, What's in it for Africa". Paris: OECD, 2006.

Gu, J., J. Humphrey and D. Messner. "Global Governance and Developing Countries: The Implications of the Rise of China". *World Development* 36, no. 2 (2008): 274–92.

Jalilian, H. and G. Reyes. *Global Financial Crisis Discussion Series Paper 14: Cambodia*. London: ODI, 2010.

Jenkins, R. and C. Edwards. *How Does China's Growth Affect Poverty Reduction in Asia, Africa and Latin America?* Expanded Report to DFID, 2004. http://www.sarpn.org.za/documents/d0001045/P1159-China_Impact_Report_Dec2004.pdf. Accessed 9 December 2010.

Kaplinsky, R. and D. Messner. "Introduction: The Impact of Asian Drivers on the Developing World". *World Development* 36, no. 2 (2008): 197–209.

Kaplinsky, R. and M. Morris. "Do the Asian Drivers Undermine Export-orientated Industrialization in SSA". *World Development* 36, no. 2 (2008): 254–73.

Krongkaew, M. "The Development of the Greater Mekong Sub-region (GMS): Real Promise or False Hope?". *Journal of Asian Economics* 15 (2004): 977–98.

Lall, S. "FDI, AGOA and Manufactured Exports by a Land Locked, Least Developed, African Country: Lesotho". *Journal of Development Studies* 41, no. 6 (2005): 998–1022.

McDonald, S., S. Robinson and K. Thierfelder. "Asia Growth and Trade Poles: India, China and East and Southeast Asia". *World Development* 36, no. 2 (2008): pp. 210–34.

Ministry of Commerce, PRC: Ministry of Commerce, People's Republic of China, 2010.

Prasad, E.S. "Is the Chinese Growth Miracle Built to Last?". *China Economic Review* 20 (2009): 103–23.

Stiglitz, J. "More Instruments and Broader Controls: Moving towards the Post-Washington Consensus". In *Joseph Stiglitz and the World Bank: The Rebel Within*, edited by H.J. Chang, pp. 17–49. London: Anthem Press, 2001.

UNDP. *China Human Development Report 2009/2010; China and a Sustainable Future, Towards a Low Carbon Economy and Society*. Beijing: China Translation and Publishing Corporation, 2010.

World Bank. *World Development Indicators*. Washington, D.C.: World Bank, 2010.

Zafar, A. "The Growing Relationship between China and Sub-Saharan Africa: Macroeconomic, Trade, Investment, and Aid Links". *The World Bank Research Observer* 22, no. 1 (2007): 103–30.

2

ASSESSING CHINA'S IMPACT ON POVERTY REDUCTION IN THE GREATER MEKONG SUBREGION
Literature Review

Lei Qin

This literature review, comprising four main sections, discusses the key conceptual and empirical debates around poverty, the rise of China, and the Greater Mekong Subregion (GMS). Principally, the literature on economic growth and poverty reduction in general — and in the GMS region in particular — is reviewed. These key issues are then linked to trade, investment and official development assistance (ODA) as they are the three most important factors that drive national and regional growth. All GMS member countries (except Yunnan province and the Guangxi region of China) are member countries of the Association of Southeast Asian Nations (ASEAN). Therefore the literature review looks at China's growth, its overall impact on ASEAN and its specific impact in terms of trade, investment and ODA in the region on individual GMS countries. This overview gives an academic background to the key issues addressed in the following country studies that follow.

1. ECONOMIC GROWTH AND POVERTY REDUCTION

While there is a consensus that pro-poor growth strategies play a crucial role in poverty reduction, there is wide debate about what exactly constitutes pro-poor growth and how it can be measured (Ravallion and Chen 2003; Kakwani and Pernia 2000; Klasen 2004). The traditional orthodox economics view (for example, Dollar and Kraay 2001; Ravallion and Chen 2003) suggests that any growth that reduces poverty is pro-poor — unless the incomes of poor people stagnate or decline — irrespective of inequality.

Another view holds that, as poor people are the least likely to share the benefits of growth, pursuing policies that actively focus on reducing poverty through "inclusive growth" should be made a priority. They argue that pro-poor growth should focus not just on reducing poverty, but also inequality. White and Anderson (2000), for example, define pro-poor growth as growth where poor households enjoy higher income growth than other segments of society. Kakwani and Pernia (2000) suggest that pro-poor growth not only reduces poverty, but also results in a more equitable distribution of income. H. Son (2007) adopts the equitable distribution of income definition proposed by Kakwani and Pernia (2000) and examines this issue by using a cross-country analysis of seventeen Asian countries during the period 1981 to 2001. He assesses how much growth is required to offset the adverse effect of an increase in inequality on poverty and notes the importance of specifically pro-poor growth strategies in augmenting GDP growth.

Broadly speaking, it can be said that pro-poor growth is "inclusive growth"; inclusive in the sense that it entails formulating policy that includes and empowers the most vulnerable in society, ensuring that they share the benefits of GDP growth in formulating policies to promote inclusive growth, many (for example, Ali and Zhuang 2007) have stressed the need to promote growth with equal access to opportunity. Here, inclusive growth has two key aspects: (i) it creates employment and other opportunities for development, and (ii) it promotes equalization of opportunities for development. At a policy level, inclusive growth requires rapid and sustained economic growth; it also calls for increased social equity and inclusiveness by reducing or eliminating inequality of opportunity. These two dimensions complement each other. High economic growth provides opportunities, including opportunities for improved equity and greater inclusiveness. If opportunities are not equal and social inclusiveness is lacking, economic expansion is not sustainable.

Inclusive growth strategies reduce inequality by pursuing employment policies that focus on low income groups (Felipe 2007). In Felipe's (2007) opinion, the key to harmonious development is ensuring that the incomes of low-income group increase faster than those of the rich so as to bridge the gap between rich and poor. The poor mainly obtain their income through labour while the rich earn primarily through capital. Therefore, if the poor's income is to grow faster than those of the rich, the poor must have access to full employment and enjoy wages that rise faster than growth on the rate of return on capital.

Concerning the relation between growth and poverty reduction, it has often been argued that the sectoral composition of growth determines whether it is pro-poor. Growth that is driven by primary sectors, especially agriculture, has been more inclusive than growth relying on secondary and tertiary sectors. According to Oshima (1993), agriculture spearheads the way in inequality reduction. In countries where poverty is predominately a rural phenomenon, the raising of rural productivity levels has been an important element in poverty reduction. Chatterjee (1995) addresses this point in a cross-country study, finding that agriculture sector growth (mainly studying cereal production) plays a large role in explaining lower poverty levels; the growth of industries and services appear to have little relevance in explaining lower poverty levels. Similarly, Lipton and Ravallion (1995) conclude that at a global level generally, and in Asian contexts specifically, relatively high (growing) farm outputs have also featured relatively low (falling) rural poverty. That primary sector growth has played an important role in poverty reduction has also been stressed in a more rigorous study by Ravallion and Datt (1996) using Indian household survey data.

In other contexts, growth of secondary industry is important in reducing poverty in developing countries. While Hasan and Quibria (2004) confirm Ravallion and Datt's finding of the role of primary sector growth for South Asia, they also find that secondary (and not primary) sector growth plays an important role for poverty reduction in East Asia. Their explanation for the difference is that East Asia has a more flexible labour policy regime, and a higher degree of openness, which enabled a more rapid structural transformation and consequently faster poverty reduction through the rapid growth of the secondary sector.

Following from this, many studies (for example, Fields 1991; Winters, McCulloch and McKay 2002, 2004; Niimi and Winters 2003) examine the relationship between trade reform and poverty reduction. Fields (1991) estimates that, on average, for every percentage point decline in growth, poverty rises by 2 per cent. International trade liberalization has a potentially important role to play in poverty alleviation in the GMS. Niimi and Winters (2002) assess the evidence on the widely debated issue of the impact of trade policy reform on poverty in developing countries. Their study uses an analytical framework which addresses four key areas: economic growth and stability; households and markets; wages and employment and government revenue. They argue that there can be no simple generalizable conclusion about the relationship between trade liberalization and poverty. However, in the long run and on average, trade liberalization is highly likely to be poverty alleviating. Trade reform also involves important adjustments, and there is evidence that the poor may be less well placed in the short run to protect themselves against adverse effects and take advantage of favourable opportunities. In a follow-up study they present evidence which suggests that carefully implemented trade liberalization can contribute significantly to pro-poor development (Winters, McCulloch and McKay 2004).

The issue of trade liberalization and poverty has received much attention in the literature and its effects on poverty reduction have been explored in an array of studies. Niimi and Winters (2003) study the poverty impacts of Vietnam's trade liberalization over the 1990s and assess how well they could have been predicted from earlier data. They identify policy changes and their major effects on trade and prices and then seek the effects of these changes in a panel comprising 4,302 households observed in 1993 and 1998. By using a multinomial logit model, they find evidence that trade liberalization influenced household poverty status and reduced poverty substantially over the period 1993–98. Winters (2002) points out that though a liberal trade regime almost certainly helps to reduce poverty in the long run, the direct and indirect effects of trade reform on poverty could also be negative depending on patterns of consumption and production and on the exact nature of the reform. Some prices will rise while others may fall; some sectors will expand while others will contract. Whether these changes help or harm the poor depends on many factors including what the poor produce and consume and the extent to which they adjust to the changing economic environment.

Several studies note that facilitating increased access to global markets is a possible alternative to providing development aid as a means to reducing poverty. Binswanger and Lutz (2000) argue that harmful trade policies substantially negate the aid provided by rich countries. They suggest that the welfare losses from industrialized countries' protection amount to more than three times the value of grant aid which flows to developing countries. Francois (2001) models the reduction of global import protection by up to 50 per cent finding that gains to developing countries could well outweigh recent annual flows of official development aid from industrialized countries. Watkins and Fowler (2002) also argue that trade has an enormous potential to lift people out of poverty, noting that when countries lock poor people out of their markets, they close the door to an escape route from poverty.

2. THE RISE OF CHINA AND ASIAN ECONOMIES

China has experienced rapid economic development: GDP growth rate has averaged 9 per cent per annum in the past two decades. Its GDP was estimated at US$500 billion in 1992 and reached US$3,282 billion in 2007 (UNCTAD 2008). Per capita income has grown tremendously, surpassing US$2,000 in a population of 1.3 billion. Zhang (2004) estimated that within a few years China's economy would be the third largest in the world after the United States and Japan, and may be the second largest after the United States within two or three decades — this is now a reality, a mere six years later. Dwyer (2006) asserts that China and India will regain their mantle as the world's largest and most powerful economies after three centuries of lagging behind.

With its strong and enduring growth rate, China's contribution to the world economy and especially to the regional economy has become increasingly visible. For some years, China's economic growth has been one of the key factors behind global economic growth. (Zhang 2004): China is now a key force behind regional and world growth. Its relatively rapid expansion over the past two decades has boosted growth figures for South and East Asia and, from a global perspective, compensated subdued economic performances in the United States, Europe and Japan (Dwyer 2006). As a vast and diverse economic entity, China's participation in regional growth and development will not only boost the region's overall growth potential, but also profoundly affect the region's patterns of production, trade and investment, and resource flows (Wong 2004). Its deepening economic integration with economies in Southeast Asia has led to substantial structural changes in regional production and trade (Tong and Lim 2009).

With total foreign trade valued at US$2,561.6 billion, China is the third largest trader in the world after the United States and Germany (WTO 2009). Along with China's development strategy, China's exports expanded rapidly and it was the second largest exporter in the world in 2008. In addition, China's domestic market of 1.3 billion people is becoming the largest consumer market in the world. With economic development and improvements in living standards, demands for more agricultural products, consumer goods and services are driven higher. Hence, China — as now the third biggest importer in the world — has a huge demand for primary commodities such as crude oil and copper, intermediate inputs and capital goods. China's rapidly rising imports have supported the strong performances of neighbouring economies and contributed to the recent strength in world commodity prices (Spatafora, Yang and Feyziog 2004).

2.1 China, Trade and the Developing World: Competing or Complementary?

For Eichengreen, Rhee and Tong (2004) China's export profile has implications for national development trajectories in Asia and elsewhere. It will heighten the incentive for other countries to move up the technological ladder into the production of more technologically intensive, less labour-intensive exports in order to better insulate themselves from Chinese competition. At regional level, China's emergence suggests that any regional free trade arrangement or effort to more closely coordinate monetary and financial policies will not be attractive if it does not involve the economy which will eventually be the largest in the region.

Indeed, China's economic growth has generated significant impacts, both challenges and opportunities, to the outside world. With regards to trade, different perceptions of China's growth across Asia fall into two opposing views. From one perspective, China and other Asian economies can grow in harmony. Okita (1985) notes that the great diversity among Asian nations in their stages of development and resource endowments works to facilitate the flying geese pattern (Akamatsu 1961, 1962) of shared development. That is to say that each is able to benefit because their respective comparative advantages facilitate the migration of production processes from one to another. Kwan (2002) also takes the view that economies in Asia share mutual benefits resultant of the potential of greater integration of product lines across the region and the increased incomes of Chinese consumers, both of which are reflected in expanding intra-regional trade in Asia (Zebregs 2004).

The other view sees China and other Asian economies as competitors: they specialize in the production of export goods that are relatively close substitutes and compete for market share in major export markets. A 2001 White Paper on International Trade by Japan's Ministry of Economy, Trade and Industry represents this view. It argues that, through receiving direct foreign investment, China has been gaining the competitive edge not only in labour-intensive products, but also IT and other technology-intensive products. As a result, the complementary international division of labour according to level of economic development has been disrupted by China, giving way to stiffer competition, including in high-tech industries. In the long-term, such increased competition could bring overall benefits to the regional economy by improving productivity. However, in the short-term, increasing competition between China and ASEAN members could have negative repercussions on the latter, as illustrated by the 1997–98 Asian financial crisis (quoted in Kwan 2002). Thus as Tong and Lim (2009) suggest, there are challenges for ASEAN countries hoping to maintain their competitiveness with China. ASEAN's relatively more developed economies face the task of industrial upgrading to maintain a technological lead over China. ASEAN's newer members must develop labour-intensive industries that are competitive in domestic and third markets.

2.2 China, Trade and ASEAN

Existing studies on China's impact on ASEAN export include two opposing viewpoints. The first holds that the consumption power of Chinese citizens and demand for industrial investment will grow at the same pace as China's economy. This will lead to an expansion of demand for foreign products, therefore promoting within the region and benefiting the ASEAN economies. The other view holds that with the consecutive upgrading of China's industrial structure, the gradual progress of technical capability, a large inflow of foreign direct investment (FDI) and the deepening of localization, the comparative advantage China enjoys in low labour costs will bring remarkable competitive pressure on other Asian economies. Using this framework China could be described as "comrades" and/or "competitors" (Loungani 2000; Ahearne et al. 2003; Fernald and Loungani 2004).

Rumbaugh and Blancher (2004), supporting the "comrades" conceptualization of China's rise, estimate that approximately half of China's imports from around the region are for domestic consumption. This indicates that though China is emerging as a new economic power in the Asia region, it also benefits Asian countries in that it provides a huge market for Asian countries' export. Hart (2005) also holds that ASEAN countries have generally been beneficiaries in terms of supplying China's growing resource demands, but are facing competition over labour-intensive goods in third markets. Abeysinghe and Lu (2003) believe that the rise of China's economy significantly benefits the East Asia region. This is due to the shift of China's economy from an export-oriented to a more domestic demand-driven one. Such a shift, against the background of China's accession into the WTO, is opening up the country's huge domestic market for imports.

To analyse the effect of China on trade, some empirical studies have used aggregate trade data and the standard or revised gravity model. Such research uses the correlated coefficient between total trade volume and market share to illustrate the relations between China and other Asian economies. The conclusions of some studies suggest that they are complimentary (Ahearne et al. 2003; Laila 2006), whereas other studies conclude that they are competing (Eichengreen, Rhee and Tong 2004). Ahearne et al. (2003) use a panel of annual data spanning the period 1981 to 2001 for four newly industrialized economies (NIEs) (Korea, Singapore, Taiwan and Hong Kong) and four additional ASEAN members (Indonesia, Malaysia, the Philippines and Thailand). They consider the impact of China's exports on the exports of these neighbouring countries, and suggest complementarities between its exports and those of its Asian neighbours. The authors conclude there is little evidence that increases in China's exports reduce the exports of other emerging Asian economies. Eichengreen, Rhee and Tong (2004) also analyse the impact of China's growth on the exports of its Asian neighbours using the gravity model. They try to distinguish the increase in China's own demand for imports from the effects of its increased penetration of export markets, and the tendency for the latter to crowd out the exports of its Asian neighbours.

The impacts are differentiated by the different classification of the products by using Standard International Trade Classification (SITC) 2-digit data: capital goods, consumer goods and intermediates. They conclude that an increase in China's output, and thus in both China's demand for imports and capacity to export, positively affects the exports of its high-income neighbours but negatively affects the exports of less developed countries in the region.

Other disaggregate studies focus on countries' sectoral composition or types of products it manufactures as well as considering the Chinese labour market and trade conditions (for example, Shafaeddin 2002; Ravenhill 2006). Ravenhill (2006) chooses three representative capital-intensive and two labour-intensive products for study. By comparing changes in absolute volume and market share of imports from China and ASEAN by the United States and Japan before and after China's WTO accession, he illustrates that in the competition between ASEAN and China's manufactured products, ASEAN loses in the high-income market. However, along with China's economic growth, China's imports from ASEAN countries are growing, which could partially offset such losses. At the same time, as a result of China's growing demand for raw materials and spare parts (Abeysinghe and Lu 2003; Shan and Sun 1998), China also provides increasing export opportunities for ASEAN countries (Loungani 2000; Ahearne et al. 2003; Fernald and Loungani 2004). Ianchovichina and Walmsley (2003) calibrate and simulate a multi-country, multi-sector model of international trade, and find that China's WTO accession, while increasing the country's own exports, reduces the exports of Vietnam, the Philippines, Thailand, Indonesia and Malaysia (due mainly to the negative impact on their textile and garment sales). They find that WTO accession has a positive impact on the exports of Japan and the NIEs. Their simulations suggest a decline in exports (mainly of textiles and garments) and a reduction in GDP relative to baseline levels in East Asia's developing countries.

Yang and Vines (2000) simulate a multi-sector, multi-country model with differentiated products as a way of analysing the impact of China's growth on exports from other Asian countries, finding that the exports of ASEAN countries drop slightly, while those of Japan and the NIEs rise. These general effects are the combination of positive effects on exports to China and negative effects on exports to third markets, which differ in size depending on the Asian exporter concerned. The International Monetary Fund (IMF) (2004) uses a computable general equilibrium model designed to analyse the geographical and sectoral structure of trade flows. This analysis shows a small negative impact on the exports and output of all regions. In terms of output, this negative effect is largest for the Middle East and North Africa and smallest for the advanced economies. The ASEAN economies experience a slightly above-average impact, while the NIEs and South Asian economies show a slightly below-average impact. The precise effects vary by sector and country. Countries that rely heavily on exports of textiles and clothing— labour-intensive manufactures in which China also has a comparative advantage — tend to suffer particularly large negative effects.

While the above studies provide useful insights into how China affects developing economies through trade, they do not focus *per se* on the poor located in developing countries. Jenkins and Edwards (2004) evaluate the impact of China's growth on poverty reduction in Asia, Africa and Latin America by applying the Winters Approach. Exports to China, competition in the third market and imports from China are analysed and SITC 3-digit data of the products related to the poor are collected based on the classification of labour-intensive agricultural products, other agricultural products, forestry, minerals and petroleum, labour-intensive manufacture, labour-intensive textiles and garments, and other manufacturing. The research reveals that exports to China have little effect on Cambodia and Vietnam. Both Cambodia and Vietnam benefit from cheaper consumer goods imported from China. However, the competitive threat from China means Cambodia faces significant harm and Vietnam faces moderate harm in third markets.

Many researchers have focused on the bilateral trade relationship between China and specific GMS countries, notably Thailand and Vietnam. Analysing the impact on individual GMS members, Stone and Strutt (2009) illustrate the variation across the region in terms of intra-regional trade dependence and the degree to which China plays a role in that dependence. The highest dependency rate is found in Myanmar, China appears to play a small but significant role in Cambodia and Laos, though they do not appear to be overly dependent on China as trading partners. In fact, their intra-GMS trade shares change little whether China is included or not. The two economies most dependent on trade with China appear to be Thailand and Vietnam. However, it is of note that China's trade with lesser developed ASEAN countries seems to be growing. According to Kagami (2010) China's trade with Cambodia, Laos, Myanmar and Vietnam (CLMV) increased by 449 per cent from US$3,352 million in 2000 to US$18,393 million in 2007, significant rate of growth. Noting the variance in impacts in developing countries as a result of trade with a growing China, Kaosa-ard (2006) concludes effects could be complimentary and/or competing depending on the products produced by the given country. The food sector is one in which the impact of China will be significant. He concludes that the prevailing assumption about food trade with China is that the GMS will benefit greatly from "feeding the dragon", China. This assumption seems to be plausible, but at an individual level, not every commodity or group of farmers will benefit nor will they benefit equally.

3. CHINA'S IMPACT ON TRADE IN ASIAN ECONOMIES

3.1 FDI and Developing Countries

A key aspect of the studies in this volume is the issue of FDI from China, a developing country, to the countries of the GMS, a subregion composed of developing economies. Broadly speaking, economists hold two different views about FDI flows between developing countries. One view is that it shares the same characteristics as FDI flows between developed and underdeveloped countries. Therefore, the reasons and decisive factors influencing FDI between developing countries are similar to those of developed countries investing in underdeveloped economies. The other view believes that FDI among developing countries has its own characteristics.

The earliest theories on FDI stem from research on the foreign investment of developed countries from a microeconomic perspective. Mundell (1957), for example, assesses the relationship between investment and trade, but from a relatively static perspective. According to Mundell, FDI could act as an alternative to trade in cases where trade barriers impeded market penetration: the flow of production processes would replace commodities as a kind of market entry alternative for international trade. Vernon (1966) puts forward the theory of Product Life Cycle (PLC). In his opinion, the life cycle of products is similar to the life cycle of people, going through the process of formation, growth, maturity and then decline. However, there is a big distance and time lag in such a cycle, manifesting in a technology gap between countries. The stage of a country in this cycle indicates their competitiveness in producing a given product, which consequently determines changes in international trade and international investment. He holds the view that it is the international transfer of developed countries' production to areas that have a comparative advantage that drives FDI.

Another explanation of FDI distribution rests on the concept of monopoly advantage, which was first proposed by American scholar Hymer (1960) and developed by Kindleberger (1969, 1975), Caves (1971), and Buckley and Casson (1976). J.H. Dunning (1977) uses this concept in his eclectic theory of international production and FDI. He concludes that three conditions are required for FDI in his "OIL" analysis paradigm: (1) ownership (advantages produced by the monopoly of intangible assets and the scale effect of enterprises); (2) internalization (the capability of saving or eliminating transaction costs through adopting ownership); and (3) location (the resources and political advantages of the host country). He maintains that only with all of these three advantages can enterprises invest abroad directly.

There is wide literature that examines FDI flows specifically among developing countries. Lecraw (1977), for example, investigates twenty Thai enterprises partly funded with FDI from a variety of Asian countries, and notes that the bulk of these enterprises are labour-intensive and target both domestic and export markets. The characteristics of such investments are compatible with small-scale, labour-intensive production of common goods. Frequently investors prefer to hold shares in a joint venture; their investment, and often family connections in the enterprises of the host country, plays an important role in business operations. As a result of these arrangements FDI of this kind has a higher degree of autonomy in terms of management compared to FDI from developed countries.

Transnational companies located in developing countries are also a source of FDI to developing economies. Wells (1983) argues that the transnational corporations of developing countries share many of the same characteristics as those of developed ones. The difference, however, is that the transnational companies of developing countries may be better suited to the socioeconomic and cultural contexts of developing countries. Unlike corporations of developed countries which have ownership advantages (for example, mature and advanced technology and managerial experience), corporations of developing countries have the technical and managerial strengths which are more applicable to the economic environment of other developing countries. Following from this, FDI from developing countries has the following distinctive advantages: (1) less specialized low-technology local equipment is used as alternatives; (2) mature and compatible products are more suitable to lower standard machinery and equipment of the local down-stream enterprises; (3) a lower degree of specialization can reduce the scale, so as to adapt to local small markets; (4) in case of a change in market environment, these enterprises can change their products more flexibly.

In his theoretical framework "Investment Development Path" (IDP), Dunning (1988) regards a country's FDI outflow as corresponding to its economic development. For a developing country, FDI outflow depends on whether its enterprises have ownership and management advantages necessary to overcome the challenges posed by investing in other countries. The expansion of FDI depends on further accumulation of ownership over time. In most cases, he argues, a country first accepts FDI inflow, and then gradually FDI will flow out as a result of economic development, and for a developing country, it would become an FDI outflow country only when its per capita GDP approaches US$3,000.

Another theory holds that FDI flows between developing countries are often from a comparatively disadvantaged investor country to a comparatively advantaged host country (Kojima 1978). The host countries either do not realize the potential of their advantages or do not have the capacity to exploit them. It is assumed that the investing country is able to exploit these advantages through FDI. Adopting a macro approach to study firms' motives in foreign investment, he argues that there are three main factors influencing FDI flows:

(1) Natural resources: The investing country either moves its production to the area which possesses the desired resource or chooses to import them depending on comparative costs.
(2) Labour: The host countries' labour costs (predominantly wages) are lower so the investing country can reduce its costs by moving some or all of its production to that location.
(3) Market: Trade barriers facilitate FDI because they create a substitution of finished goods exports for the export of components and intermediate products such as machinery and technology. Such barriers mean that the location advantages can only be partially exploited and can create a waste of resources despite still holding a net cost advantage.

Kojima (1978) uses the concept of profits to show how host countries' economies benefit from receiving FDI in order to fully utilize their comparative advantage without massive capital expenditure and thus promotes his model as a basis for economic development especially for developing countries.

Focusing on the relationship between FDI inflow and economic development in Asia, Ozawa (1992, p. 33) proposes a "dynamic paradigm of FDI facilitated development". He argues that industrialization has essentially been based on copying ever since the industrial revolution. In Ozawa's model, FDI patterns change with the structural transformation of the economy. Through the development of new technologies, FDI pushes nations to develop new comparative advantages and eventually to move to the next stage of economic development. He gives the example of the Asian "tigers" that have progressed from the factor-driven stage to the investment-driven stage. The author concludes that more conceptual work is needed to investigate the effects of FDI on innovation-driven economies.

Hiratsuka (2006) holds that the decisive factor for ASEAN cross-regional FDI is the cost of transportation: if the cost of transportation is too high, the enterprise would locate its production base somewhere close to the market. According to Hiratsuka, there are four driving forces behind ASEAN transnational enterprises' foreign investment: (1) efficiency-oriented FDI which pursues the lower wage margin of the host countries; (2) market-oriented FDI that aims to enter the host countries' enormous market; (3) FDI characterized by the model of "supplier following production line", which means that the suppliers of the host countries follow the production line in foreign countries to make direct investment; (4) function-oriented FDI. The subject of this research is ASEAN, especially developed ASEAN member countries like Singapore, Malaysia and Thailand, and ASEAN's partners such as Hong Kong, Japan and Korea.

3.2 The Role of Chinese FDI in the GMS

Chinese researchers have focused on China's FDI outflow to ASEAN members, especially the less developed members. For instance, Li (2003) evaluates the distribution of China's FDI outflow to ASEAN countries by industry. Of particular note is the increased analysis of China's FDI outflow to Vietnam. Xu and Chen (2008) analyse the Vietnamese investment environment and Chinese Enterprises' investment situation in Vietnam and conclude that current Chinese FDI in Vietnam is still at a small value and the level of the projects remains low-end. Ha Thi Hong Van and Do Tien Sam (2008) reveal that the impact of China's FDI on Vietnam's progress is not obvious because the volume is still small.

Despite significant increases in the volume of Chinese FDI, Jenkins and Edwards (2004) hold that China has played a much smaller role in exporting FDI than in importing it, and that the effect of outward FDI from China on developing countries in Latin America, Africa and Asia has (so far) been slight, especially relative to the effects of trade. A 2006 ADB report analysing FDI in GMS countries, and focusing on the emerging role that China's outward investment played, found mixed outcomes. In Laos, ASEAN investors still accounted for over 40 per cent of total investment by 2005. The relative importance of China and South Korea as FDI source countries has increased sharply in recent years, but their combined share is still small. In contrast, in Cambodia Northeast Asia and China accounted for 44 per cent of total approved investment, OECD countries 36 per cent and ASEAN 20 per cent, from 2000 to 2005. Vietnamese investment from China has increased rapidly, but from a low base, reaching 4 per cent of total investment during 2000–05.

According to the International Institute for Sustainable Development (IISD 2008), China's economic growth and consequent demand for a reliable and steady supply of inexpensive natural resources have led to a rapid increase in Chinese FDI expansion to Africa and Latin America. In the GMS, however, Chinese FDI has produced different, more positive results. For example, it has improved the infrastructure for transporting commodities, in part through the ADB's GMS Economic Corridors, extended the regional power grid and has invested in planned railway links from Kunming to Singapore.

3.3 China: FDI Diversion?

ASEAN is often taken as an example of a loser in the face of China's competition in receiving FDI. Zhang (2004), however, questions this finding. He argues that the slowdown of FDI flow to ASEAN after the 1997 financial crisis is not because of China's competition, but because of the worsened economic and political situation there.

While China enjoys some advantages in attracting FDI (for example, abundant labour supply, low costs and a huge potential market based on its uniquely large population), the resources that can be used for FDI are rich, diverse and abundant. Thus, it is unclear whether increased FDI flow to China would divert FDI flows from other economies. Several studies have attempted to bring some clarity to this issue. Yang (2003), for example, finds that it is difficult to judge the extent to which the redistribution of FDI among Asian developing countries has been the result of China's increased attractiveness to FDI, while Panitchpakdi and Clifford (2002) have argued that FDI flows to China and other Asian economies have been complementary rather than competitive. Chantasasawat et al. (2004) confirm this in their study of eight East and Southeast Asian economies, arguing that this complementary effect reflects the development of production networks in the region.

Other studies have found a more ambiguous relationship between China and FDI diversion. Jenkins and Edwards (2004), for example, conclude that in the short run China's FDI inflows may have led to a slight diversion from some developing countries. Further, because FDI in China has been linked so closely to exports the effect on poverty may have been accentuated as labour-intensive industrial exports from other countries suffer the biggest competitive threat from China. However, they find that even in the short run, the poverty effect is almost certainly minimal. Moreover, in the long run there is probably no diversionary effect because China has been more successful than most countries in underpinning and augmenting FDI inflows with domestic investment.

There are also cultural factors to consider, such as the role of overseas Chinese or the so-called "bamboo network". An Asian Development Bank (ADB) 2006 report examines actual Chinese FDI sources and points out that FDI flows from Hong Kong and Taipei to China accounted for approximately 66 per cent of the total FDI inflows to China between 1983 and 2004. These flows are presumably driven largely by Chinese ethnic links in addition to the general economic considerations determining overseas investment decisions. But even so it is not realistic to assume that these flows are completely at the expense of other investment locations. Further, the ADB report argues that data on global investment patterns indicate that the decline in ASEAN's share in FDI compared with other developing countries is not a result of increased FDI inflows to China.

4. CHINA'S IMPACT ON CAPITAL INFLOWS TO ASIAN ECONOMIES

Since the mid-1950s, China has provided aid to other countries. However, China only began to attract more attention as a donor of development assistance in recent years. Few studies touch on China's development assistance with regard to GMS countries.

One of the few papers to address this is issue is by Lum et al. (2009). They state that China's foreign assistance during the past several years has been driven primarily by Beijing's desire to secure and transport natural resources, and secondarily for diplomatic reasons. Concerning Chinese aid to Southeast Asia, the report argues that though access to natural resources plays a prominent role in China's engagement in the region, strategic interests are likely to influence China's activities in Southeast Asia to a greater extent than they do in Africa and Latin America. Many of China's aid activities in the region appear to provide long-term diplomatic benefits and comparatively few short-term economic ones.

Based on investigations into China's foreign aid to Africa, Davies (2008) concludes that the main driver of China's interest in Africa is to secure energy and resource assets. In order to hedge against immediate rising commodity prices and possibly long-run supply shortages, the Chinese government has encouraged its companies to secure a wide range of commodity assets. The Chinese government's aid policy plays an important role in supporting these companies (mostly state-owned enterprises [SOEs]) in outbidding foreign companies to secure these resource assets. Political factors continue to play an important part in the relationship.

In the GMS the case of Laos provides a useful example as to the nature of Chinese ODA. There, the China Development Brief (2006) argues that China's aims have shifted from securing political to economic gains, namely tapping Laos' rich supply of natural resources. Along with its aid, China has also paid more attention to technical and human resource assistance to Laos. Hubbard (2007) suggests that the purpose of Chinese concessional lending has more to do with the promotion of Chinese export products than the economic development of recipient countries.

When considering Chinese ODA, it should be kept in mind that the Chinese government publishes hardly any information on foreign aid. This makes it very difficult to analyse the pattern of ODA. A few studies (for example, Lum et al. 2009), however, have tried to quantify it. The 2009 report by Lum et al., largely based on news reports of Chinese foreign economic activity, finds Chinese foreign assistance and government-supported economic projects in Africa, Latin America and Southeast Asia. They assert that Chinese ODA grew from less than US$1 billion in 2002 to US$27.5 billion in 2006 and US$25 billion in 2007. These figures are far larger than foreign aid statistics announced by the Chinese government possibly because there are significant discrepancies on what should be included in foreign aid. Chin and Frolic (2007) also attempt an analysis of Chinese aid, but they can only deliver sporadic, rather than systematic, information because citing the Chinese government's inability, or unwillingness, to provide basic data.

An article in the *Economist* (2009) represents the typical Western concern over China's foreign aid to developing countries. They contend that the growing importance of Chinese ODA represents "the spread of authoritarian aid [and] is a challenge to more than just Western ideas of the right sort of giving". Lancaster (2007) raises questions about China's aid in Africa; principally, will it discourage much-needed economic and political reforms in Africa? They explore the key issues around Chinese aid — how much it is currently and how fast it is growing? How are decisions made on how much aid is provided each year? Which countries receive it and how much do they get? How is the aid managed within the Chinese government and how it is evaluated? But most of these questions remain unanswered, mainly because the Chinese government has not yet tried to address them. But as Maskishima and Mitsunori (2009) point out, China is not an OECD country; it is hard to compare or apply the same standards to its ODA as, for example, that of Japan's.

Despite this ambiguity over the international distribution of Chinese aid, it is clear that the influence of Chinese ODA has been rising among CLMV countries. The IISD (2008) states that the Chinese government provides considerable foreign aid to Cambodia, Laos and Vietnam, often without any major conditions attached and frequently integrated with cultural exchange and support. Although it is significant in comparison with other donors, China's ODA is often not in sectors such as agribusiness, hydropower and mining but mostly includes support for transport, communications, health, education and human resources development, and construction (including sports, culture and government buildings) sectors. Cambodia is the only country among the three where the Chinese government has provided aid for hydropower development projects.

References

Abeysinghe, T. and D. Lu. "China as an Economic Powerhouse: Implications on its Neighbours?". *China Economic Review* 14, no. 2 (2003): 164–85.

ADB. *The Mekong Region Foreign Direct Investment*. Manila: Asian Development Bank Institute, 2006.

Ahearne, Alan G., John G. Fernald, Prakash Loungani and John W. Schindler. "China and Emerging Asia: Comrades or Competitors?". International Finance Discussion Paper, No. 789, 2003.

Ahearne, Alan G., John G. Fernald, Prakash Loungani and John W. Schindler.

"Flying Geese or Sitting Ducks: China's Impact on the Trading Fortunes of other Asian Economies". International Finance Discussion Paper, No. 887. Board of Governors of the Federal Reserve System, Washington, D.C., 2006.

Akamatsu, Kaname. "A Theory of Unbalanced Growth in the World Economy". *Weltwirtschaftliches Archive* 86 (1961): 196–217.

———. "A Historical Pattern of Economic Growth in Developing Countries". *The Developing Economies* No. 1 (1962): 3–25.

Ali, I. and J. Zhuang. *Inclusive Growth toward a Prosperous Asia: Policy Implications*. ERD Working Paper No. 97. Manila: ADB, Economics and Research Department, 2007.

Binswanger, H. and E. Lutz. "Agricultural Trade Barriers, Trade Negotiations and the Interests of Developing Countries". Paper presented at the Round Table for the United Nations on Trade and Development, Bangkok, February 2000.

Buckley, P.J. and M. Casson. *Multinational Enterprises in the World Economy: Essays in Honour of John Dunning*. Aldershot: Edward Elgar, 1976.

Caves, Richard E. *Multinational Enterprises and Economic Analysis*. 2nd ed. Cambridge: Cambridge University Press, 1971.

Chantasasawat B., K.C. Fung, H. Iizaka and A. Siu. "Foreign Direct Investment in East Asia and Latin America: Is There a People's Republic of China Effect?". ADB Institute Discussion Paper No. 17, 2004.

Chatterjee, S. *Growth, Structural Change and Optimal Poverty Interventions*. Occasional Paper No. 13. Manila: Economics and Development Resource Centre, Asian Development Bank, 1995.

Chatterjee Shiladitya. "Poverty Reduction Strategies-Lessons from the Asian and Pacific Region on Inclusive Development". *Asian Development Review* 22, no. 1 (2005): 12–44.

Chen, S. and M. Ravallion. "What Can New Survey Data Tell Us about Recent Changes in Distribution and Poverty". *World Bank Economic Review* 11, no. 2 (1997): 357–82.

Chin, Gregory T. and B. Michael Frolic. *Emerging Donors in International Development Assistance: The China Case*. Canada: International Development Research Centre, 2007.

China Development Brief. "Communist Capital Flows Downstream: China's Aid to Laos", 2006. <http://www.chinadevelopmentbrief.com/node/454>. Accessed 3 November 2009.

Daisuke Hiratsuka. "Outward FDI from and Intra-regional FDI in ASEAN: Trends and Drivers". ASEAN-UNCTAD Annual Seminar 2006.

Davies, Martyn. *How China Delivers Development Assistance to Africa*. Stellenbosch, SA: Centre for Chinese Studies, University of Stellenbosch, 2008.

Dollar, David and Aart Kraay. *Growth is Good for the Poor*. World Bank Policy Research Working Paper No. 2587, Washington, D.C.: World Bank, 2001.

Du Qunyang and Song Yuhua. "FDI Effect of China-ASEAN Free Trade Economic Area". *International Business Issues*, No. 3 (2004): 51–54.

Dunning, J.H. "Trade, Location and Economic Activity and the Multinational Enterprise: A Search for an Eclectic Approach". In *International Allocation of Economic Activity*, edited by B. Ohlin, P. Hesselborn and P. Wijkman. London: Macmillan, 1977.

———. *Explaining International Production*. London: Unwin Hyman, 1988.

Dwyer, Wayne. "China and India: Their Impact on Regional and World Economies". *Eco Date* 20, no. 4 (2006).

Economist. "Development Aid from Authoritarian Regimes: An (Iron) Fistful of Help". 4 June 2009. <http://www.economist.com/node/13799239>.

Eichengreen, Barry and Douglas Irwin. "Trade Blocs, Currency Blocs, and Reorientation of Trade in the 1930s". *Journal of International Economics* 38 (1995): 1–24.

———, Rhee Yeongseop and Hui Tong. "The Impact of China on the Exports of Other Asian Countries". 2004. <www.econ.berkeley.edu/.../kiep-claremont8sep7sep28-04.pdf>. Accessed 5 November 2009.

Felipe, J. *Macroeconomic Implication of Inclusive Growth: What Are the Questions?* Manila: ADB, 2007.

Fernald, John and Prakash Loungani. "Comrades or Competitors? On Trade Relationships between China and Emerging Asia". *Chicago Fed Letter*, Issue 200, March 2004, pp. 1–4.

Fields, Gary S. *Growth and Income Distribution, Essays on Poverty, Equity and Growth*, edited by George Psacharopoulos. Oxford, UK: Pergamon Press, 1991.

Francois, Joseph F. "Trade Policy Transparency and Investor Confidence: The Implications of an Effective Trade Policy Review Mechanism", edited by Bernard Hoekman and Will Martin. *Review of International Economics* 9, Issue 2 (2001). <http://www3.interscience.wiley.com/journal/118998866/issue>. Accessed 30 November 2001.

Ha Thi Hong Van and Do Tien Sam. *Vietnam and China Trade, FDI and ODA Relations (1998–2008) and Impacts upon Vietnam*. 2008. <http://www.ide.go.jp/English/Publish/Download/Brc/pdf/01_vietnamandchina.pdf>. Accessed November 2009.

Hart, Robin. "China's Economic Growth and its Global Impact". Report on Wilton Park Conference, WP800, 2005.

Hasan, R., and M.G. Quibria. "Industry matters for poverty: A critique of agricultural fundamentalism". *Kyklos* 57, no. 2 (2004): 253–64.

Hiratsuka, Daisuke. "Outward FDI from ASEAN and Intra-regional FDI in ASEAN: Trends and Drivers". Discussion Paper No. 77. Institute of Developing Economies, Japan, 2006.

Huang, Yanghua. "An Interpretation on the Exports of China and East Asia from

Evolutionary Development Economics". CAEA Discussion Paper No. 163. Kyoto University, 2007.

Hubbard, Paul. "Aiding Transparency: What We Can Learn about China ExIm Bank's Concessional Loans". Centre for Global Development, Washington, D.C., 2007. <http://www.cgdev.org>. Accessed 25 November 2009.

Hymer, S.H. *The International Operations of National Firms: A Study of Direct Foreign Investment*. (Ph.D. Dissertation (1960) published posthumously.) Cambridge, MA: MIT Press, 1976.

Ianchovichina, Elena and Terrie Walmsley. Impact of China's WTO Accession on East Asia? Washington, D.C.: World Bank, 2003.

IISD (Institute for Sustainable Development). "Rethinking Investments in Natural Resources: China's Emerging Role in the Mekong Region". Policy Brief, Heinrich Boll Stiftung Institute, WWF & IISD, Phnom Penh, 2008.

International Monetary Fund. "China's Emergence and its Impact on the Global Economy". *World Economic Outlook*, April 2004, Chapter 2, pp. 63–102.

Jenkins, Rhys and Chris Edwards. "How Does China's Growth Affect Poverty Reduction in Asia, Africa and Latin America?". Expanded Report to DFID. University of East Anglia, Norwich, 2004.

Kagami Mitsuhiro, ed. "Economic Relations of China, Japan and Korea with the Mekong River Basin Countries". Research report No. 3, Bangkok Research Centre, IDE-JETRO, 2010. <http://www.ide.go.jp/English/Publish/Download/Brc/03.html>. Accessed 15 May 2010.

Kakwani, N. and E. Pernia. "What is Pro-poor Growth?". *Asian Development Review* 16, no. 1 (2000): 1–22.

——— and H.H. Son. "Poverty Equivalent Growth Rate Review of Income and Wealth". IMF Working Paper 04/36, 2008.

———, S. Khandker, and H. H. Son. "Pro-poor Growth: Concepts and Measurement with Country Case Studies". Working Paper No. 1. UNDP International Poverty Centre, Brasilia, 2004.

Kaosa-ard, Mingsarn. "Flying with the Dragon? Opportunities and Challenges for the GMS Countries" 2006. <http://www.sri.cmu.ac.th/~gms/joomla/publish/MK_Paper.pdf>. Accessed 13 November 2009.

Kindleberger, C.P. *American Business Abroad*. New York: Yale University Press, 1969.

———. "The Monopolistic Theory of Direct Foreign Investment". In *Transnational Corporations and World Order*, edited by G. Modelski, pp. 91–107. San Francisco: W.H. Freeman, 1975.

Klasen, S. "In Search of the Holy Grail: How to Achieve Pro-poor Growth". In *Towards Pro-Poor Policies: Aid, Institutions and Globalisation*, edited by B. Tungodden, N. Stern and I. Kolstad. New York: Oxford University Press, 2004.

Kojima K. *Direct Foreign Investment: A Japanese Model of Multinational Business Operations*. London: Croom Helm, 1978.

Kwan, C. "The Rise of China and Asia's Flying-Geese Pattern of Economic Development: An Empirical Analysis Based on US Import Statistics". NRI Paper No. 52, 2002.

Laila, N. "The Impact of China's Growth on the Exports of Asian Countries". 2006. <http://wwwdocs.fce.unsw.edu.au/fce/Research/NHCPapers2006/econlaila.pdf>. Accessed 20 November 2009.

Lancaster, C. *The Chinese Aid System*. Washington, D.C.: Centre for Global Development, 2007. <http://www.cgdev.or>. Accessed 20 December 2009.

Lecraw, D.J. "Direct Investment by Firms from Less Developed Countries". *Oxford Economic Papers* 29, no. 3 (1977): 442–57.

Li Jianwei. "The Study on the Industrial Choice of China's FDI to ASEAN". *Around Southeast Asia*, 2003, pp. 49–53.

Lipton, M. and M. Ravallion. "Poverty and Policy". In *Handbook of Development Economics, Vol. 3B*, edited by J. Herman and T.N. Srinivasan. Amsterdam: North Holland, 1995.

Loungani P. "Comrades or Competitors? Trade Links between China and Other East Asian Economies". *Finance and Development* 37, no. 2 (2000). <http://www.imf.org/external/pubs/ft/fandd/2000/06/loungani.htm>.

Lum, Thomas, Hannah Fisher, Julissa Gomez-Granger and Anne Leland. "China's Foreign Aid Activities in Africa, South America, and Southeast Asia". Washington, D.C.: Congressional Research Service, 2009.

Maskishima Minoru and Yokoyama Mitsunori. "Japan's ODA to Mekong River Basin Countries". 2009. <http://www.ide.go.jp/English/Publish/Download/Brc/pdf/01_japansoda.pdf>. Accessed 30 December 2009.

Mundell, Robert A. "International Trade and Factor Mobility". *American Economic Review* 47, no. 3 (1957): 321–35.

Niimi, Dutta and Winters. "Trade Liberalisation and Poverty Dynamics in Vietnam". (Published posthumously, 2003.) *Journal of Economic Integration* 22, no. 4 (December 2007).

Okita. "Special Presentation: Prospect of Pacific Economies, Korea Development Institute, Pacific Cooperation: Issues and Opportunities, Report of the Fourth Pacific Economic Cooperation Conference", Seoul, Korea, 29 April–1 May 1985, pp. 18–29.

Oshima, H.T. *Strategic Processes in Monsoon Asia's Economic Development*. Maryland: John Hopkins University Press, 1993.

Ozawa, T. "Foreign Direct Investment and Economic Development". *Transnational Corporations* 1, no. 1 (1992): 27–54.

Panitchpakdi, S., and M. Clifford. *China and the WTO; Changing China, Changing World Trade*. Singapore: John Wiley and Sons (Asia), 2002.

Quibria, M.G. "Growth and Poverty: Lessons from the East Asian Miracle Revisited". Research Paper Series No. 33. Asian Development Bank Institute, Tokyo, 2002.

Ravallion, M. and G. Datt. "How Important to India's Poor is the Sectoral Composition of Economic Growth?". *World Bank Economic Review* 10, no. 1 (1996): 1–25.

——— and G. Datt. "Why has Economic Growth been More Pro-poor in Some States of India than Others?". *Journal of Development Economics* 68 (2002): 381–400.

——— and S. Chen. "Measuring Pro-poor Growth". *Economics Letters* 78 (2003); 93–99.

———, G. Datt and S. Chaudhuri. "Does Maharashtra's Employment Guarantee Scheme Guarantee Employment? Effects of the 1988 Wage Increase". *Economic Development and Cultural Change* 41, no. 2 (1993): 251–75.

Ravenhill, J. "Is China an Economic Threat to Southeast Asia?". *Asian Survey* 46, no. 50 (2006): 653–74.

Rumbaugh T. and N. Blancher. "China; International Trade and WTO Accession". IMF Working Paper No. 04/36. International Monetary Fund, Washington, D.C., 2004.

Shafaeddin S.M. "Is China's Accession to WTO Threatening Exports of Developing Countries?". *China Economic Review* 15 (2004): 109–44.

Shan, J. and F. Sun. "On the Export-led Growth Hypothesis: The Econometric Evidence from China". *Applied Economics* 30, no. 8 (1998): 1055–65.

Son, H. "Interrelationship between Growth, Inequality, and Poverty: The Asian Experience". *Asian Development Review* 24, no. 2 (2007): 37–63.

Spatafora, Nicola, Yang, Yongzheng and Tarhan Feyziog. "China's Emergence and Its Impact on the Global Economy". World Economic Outlook, April 2004, Chapter 2, pp. 82–102.

Stone, Susan and Anna Strutt. "Transport Infrastructure and Trade Facilitation in the Greater Mekong Sub-region". ADBI Working Paper 130, 2009.

Tang, Min. "Inclusive Growth and the New Phase of Poverty Reduction in the People's Republic of China". *Asian Development Review* 25, nos. 1 and 2 (2009): 81–99.

Tong, Sarah Y. and Tin Seng Lim. *Sino-ASEAN Economic Integration and Its Impact on Intra-ASEAN Trade*. EAI Working Paper No. 144, 2009.

UNCTAD. *Handbook of Statistics 2008*. UNCTAD, 2008.

Vernon, R. "International Investment and International Trade in the Product Cycle". *Quarterly Journal of Economics* 80, no. 3 (1966).

Watkins, Kevin and Penny Fowler. *Rigged Rules and Double Standards: Trade, Globalisation and the Fight against Poverty*. United Kingdom: Oxfam, 2002.

Wells, L.T. *Third World Multinationals: The Rise of Foreign Investment from Developing Countries*. Cambridge, MA: MIT Press, 1983.

White, H. and E. Anderson. "Growth versus Distribution: Does the Pattern of Growth Matter?". *Development Policy Review* 19, no. 3 (2000): 267–89.

Winters, L. Alan. "Trade Liberalisation and Poverty: What are the Links?". *The World Economy* 25 (2002): 1339–67.

———, Neil McCulloch and Andrew McKay. "Trade Liberalisation and Poverty: The Empirical Evidence". CREDIT Research Paper No. 02/22, 2002.

———, Neil McCulloch and Andrew McKay. "Trade Liberalisation and Poverty: The Evidence So Far". *Journal of Economic Literature* XLII (March 2004): 72–115.

Wong, John. "China's Economic Rise: Implication for East Asian Growth and Integration". *Bulletin on Asia-Pacific Perspectives 2004/05*, 2004.

World Trade Organisation (WTO). *International Trade Report 2009*. World Trade Organisation, 2009.

Xu Mei and Chen Wei. "The Analysis of Vietnamese Investment Environment and Chinese Enterprises' Investment Situation in Vietnam". *Southeast Asian Studies* 5 (2008).

Yang, Tongzheng and David Vines. "The Fallacy of Composition and the Terms of Trade of Newly Industrialising Economies". Unpublished manuscript. Oxford University, 2000.

Yang, Y. "China's Integration into the World Economy; Implications for Developing Countries". IMF Working Paper 03/245, 2003.

Zebregs, Harm. "Intraregional Trade in Emerging Asia". IMF Policy Discussion Paper, 04/1, 2004.

Zhang, Yunlin. "China's Economic Emergence and Its Impact". 2004. <http://iaps.cass.cn/English/articles/showcontent.asp?id=397>. Accessed 11 November 2009.

PART II

China and the GMS-4

3

ASSESSING THE IMPACT OF GMS TRADE ON POVERTY REDUCTION IN YUNNAN PROVINCE, CHINA

Xiong Bin and Xuan Juneng

1. INTRODUCTION

1.1 Overview

Located in the southwest border area of China, Yunnan province is one of the key economies that constitute the GMS area of regional cooperation, bordering Myanmar to the west, and Laos and Vietnam to the south, with a boundary of 4,060 kilometres. The total size of Yunnan is about 394,000 square kilometres. Its population amounts to 47.5 million, one-third of which is composed of ethnic minorities. As a landlocked province, it is listed in the category of underdeveloped areas. The gross domestic product (GDP) of Yunnan province was RMB570.0 billion in 2008, ranking it twenty-fifth of China's thirty-four provinces and regions. The poor population in Yunnan accounted for 13.9 per cent of China's total poor in 2008.

As early as the 1990s, the Yunnan government highlighted an export-oriented economic strategy as a priority for economic development and poverty reduction. In addition, the province has participated in regional and subregional cooperation such as Yunnan-North Laos (nine provinces northern Laos), Yunnan-North Vietnam (four provincial cities in northern Vietnam), and Yunnan-North Thailand (eight provinces in northern Thailand). Apart from this bilateral cooperation, Yunnan's participation in the GMS Programme assisted by the Asian Development Bank (ADB) aims to establish it as the gateway to Southeast Asia by developing its infrastructure and promoting the free flow of goods and people in the subregion.

However, little research has been done on assessing the poverty reduction effect of Yunnan's participation in the GMS. By applying the gravity model, Poncet (2006) finds that GMS integration contributed to the trade relationship between Yunnan and other GMS countries to some degree over the period 1988 to 1999, but the effects varied between different countries. This chapter assesses the impact of the GMS on Yunnan's international trade and poverty reduction at both macro and micro levels. At the macro level, Poncet's (ibid.) methodology is used to evaluate the impact of subregional cooperation on trade between Yunnan and other GMS countries. At the micro level, the province's major export products are selected to identify the quantitative and qualitative poverty reduction effect of trade on those specific industries.

1.2 Local Literature Review

Numerous studies by Chinese researchers analysing China's (and in particular Yunnan's) changing trade profile and its relationship with GDP growth have been published in recent years. For example, Shen Chengxiang (1999) employed the Granger causality test and the cointegration test method to assess if exports will be generated from China's economic growth. The results show a reciprocal causation between China's exports and output, and a high degree of export-orientation in China's economic growth. Focusing on Yunnan, Xiao Zhou, Zhou Gu and Li Bin (2006) explored the province's annual economic data by adding the border market trade variable, and examine the relationship between trade and economic growth in Yunnan by employing the cointegration test and the Granger causality test. Their study shows that there is a strong correlation between imports and exports, border market trade and economic growth; further, they attach great importance to the contributions of border trade in the economic growth of Yunnan. On the basis of the Vector Autoregressive (VAR) Model, Chai Zhengmeng (2009) applies the cointegration test, the

Granger causality test and a variance decomposition method to study the dynamic relationship between economic growth and import-export trade in Guangdong and Yunnan, which indicate that exports are the driving force for the economic growth of Yunnan province.

The impact of regional cooperation on trade in particular has attracted much attention from Chinese researchers in the past few years. Some scholars have used actual trade data for their analyses on the effect of regional cooperation. Mao Hui (2006), for instance, holds that regional economic cooperation has strengthened and drawn strength from the complementary nature of the economies within the region. This has brought about new changes in the movement of production factors and industrial transfer among regions, optimized industrial structure and resource allocation, avoided obstacles hindering the movement of products and production processes among different districts, strengthened regional economic ties and improved the integrity and coordination of regional economic operation, thus boosting local economies. Similarly, Zhou Xiaoli (2008) reviews the process of China-GMS economic cooperation and emphasizes that regional economic cooperation has expanded the export of traditional products, labour-intensive manufactured goods and high value-added commodities, and has developed a lively border trade. Moreover, regional economic cooperation has established a production and processing base within the five GMS countries (Cambodia, Vietnam, Laos, Thailand and Myanmar), put low-cost labour to better use and optimized resource structure.

Some scholars focus their attention on trade facilitation to identify its significance in stimulating trade in regional cooperation. Wilson, Mann and Otsuki (2003) use the gravity model to analyse the relationship between trade facilitation, trade flows and GDP per capita in the Asia-Pacific region and find that intra-APEC trade could increase by US$254 billion, which would represent approximately a 21 per cent increase in intra-APEC trade flows. Four dimensions of trade facilitation — improvements in port efficiency, customs environment, regulatory environment and e-business — have been focused on. The results indicate that port efficiency has the greatest impact, and improvements in the customs environment have a positive, but modest impact. Edmonds and Fujimura (2007) focus on the impact of cross-border roads on trade in the GMS region by using the gravity model to analyse bilateral trade and FDI flows by each pair of GMS members. The results indicate that the cross-border economic corridor initiative has boosted intra-GMS trade above what would otherwise have been expected given member countries' income and the distances between them.

While many studies highlight the fact that regional cooperation has increased trade, the precise stimulating effect of the GMS's institutional and policy apparatus in this process is not greatly explored in the literature. However, studies by Poncet (2006) and Zhang (2009), who apply the gravity model approach to the GMS itself, are more directly relevant in this regard. Poncet (2006) estimates how far Yunnan's trade growth with other GMS members can be attributed to GMS initiatives. His analysis covers the period 1988–99 and reveals that GMS cooperation has boosted trade between Yunnan and the GMS countries, though the level of significance is low. However the picture varies substantially between GMS members. Yunnan's trade with Myanmar and Laos is significantly greater than the predicted level, while its trade with Thailand is significantly less than predicted. Trade with Vietnam is in line with the predicted level. In addition, the decrease in trade between Yunnan and its closest neighbours and increase in relations with the original members of ASEAN suggest a progressive reorientation of its trade towards more developed partners. One of the problems of Poncet's research is that most of the GMS initiatives had not been implemented during the period 1988–99. Hence the results need to be updated. In his empirical analysis and assessment of the factors influencing trade between China and the GMS, Zhang Tianjia (2009) introduced two dummy variables to further elaborate on the trade effect of the GMS. His research indicates that GDP and distance are two variables which have a significant influence on the bilateral trade between China and the GMS. From the perspective of trade effects, China's participation in regional economic cooperation has generated a significant trade creation effect, but bilateral trade has a limited impact on the trade between China and non-member countries; consequently, the trade diversion effect is not significant.

There is little direct evidence to show that regional cooperation contributes to poverty reduction. However, previous studies suggest that poverty reduction is indirectly correlated with regional cooperation as the economic growth that has contributed to poverty reduction is one of the results of the expansion of international trade that has been boosted by regional cooperation. Since many studies prove the positive effect of regional cooperation on trade promotion, studies indicating that foreign trade is significantly correlated with economic growth are easily accessed. Indeed, to date, the bulk of research has been related to the impact of economic growth and foreign trade on poverty reduction. Roemer and Gugerty (1997) divide the poorest people into quintiles and regress the income growth for the poorest two groups against the growth of GDP per capita for the entire population. This shows that GDP growth of 10 per cent per year is associated with income growth of 10 per cent for the poorest 40 per cent of the population. For the poorest 20 per cent, the elasticity of response is 0.921, indicating that GDP growth of 10 per cent is associated with income growth of 9.21 per cent. Dollar and Kraay (2004) use a regression model to analyse the trade effect both for individual cases and cross-country, and use a simple elasticity model to estimate the effect of trade on per capita GDP. This shows that trade liberalization leads to faster growth in average incomes. By analysing the responsiveness of the poverty reduction on 1 per cent per capita income growth and the growth –distribution–poverty nexus, Chatterjee (2005) concludes that the greater impact of growth on poverty reduction in Asia is attributed to several factors including, importantly, lower initial inequality in distribution of income, and that economic growth has undoubtedly become a dominant factor.

Concerning poverty reduction and trade in China, Li Shixin, Zou Xinyue and Guo Xinhua (2005) maintain that trade facilitation has expanded foreign trade in agricultural products and increased farmers' income, which is conducive to the rapid reduction of rural poverty. Xue Baoshe (2009) reviews China's achievements in poverty reduction after three decades of reform and opening up and reveals that sustained and stable economic growth is a solid foundation for reducing poverty. Chen Lizhong (2009), employing the dynamic characteristics of poverty elasticity, discusses the influence of income increase and income distribution on reducing poverty from both theoretical and empirical perspectives. He concludes that economic growth has both positive and negative impacts on poverty reduction in China; the improvement of income distribution takes first priority in contemporary poverty reduction.

2. MACROECONOMIC IMPLICATIONS

Given its landlocked location, Yunnan is considerably less open to foreign trade and has a relatively limited volume of international trade compared to the rest of China. In 2008, the province's total trade value contributed less than 1 per cent to China's total trade. As Table 3.1 shows, exports counted for just 7.54 per cent of Yunnan's GDP in 1992 (about half the national average), and 8.75 per cent in 2008 (about one-quarter of the

TABLE 3.1
GDP Shares of Exports and Imports (%)

Year	Yunnan		National average	
	Exports	Imports	Exports	Imports
1992	7.54	3.30	17.37	16.50
1996	7.35	5.54	17.67	16.24
2000	6.01	3.26	20.80	18.79
2004	7.27	4.90	30.71	29.04
2008	8.75	8.09	22.30	26.45

Source: National Bureau of Statistics (various years); Yunnan Province Bureau of Statistics (various years); Yunnan Provincial Department of Commerce <http://www.bofcom.gov.cn/bofcom/432345564227567616/>.

national average). Indeed, combined imports-exports accounted for 16.84 per cent of the province's GDP in 2008, while in China in the same year the figure was 59.84 per cent — about 3.5 times higher.

Despite its remoteness, international trade is an especially important engine for growth in Yunnan and its foreign trade has maintained a fast growth rate compared to the rest of China. Table 3.2 shows the yearly development of trade in Yunnan and the rest of China over the period 1993–2007. The growth rate of Yunnan's exports rose to 27 per cent between 2003 and 2007 following the downturn during the period 1998–2002 which was influenced by the Asian financial crisis. Import evolution in Yunnan converged with that of other provinces after 1992 (with a 39 per cent average annual growth rate between 2003 and 2007).

TABLE 3.2
Annual Trade Growth in Yunnan and China (%)

Year	Yunnan		Rest of China	
	Exports	Imports	Exports	Imports
1993–1997	23.36	32.61	16.77	11.74
1998–2002	4.53	1.37	13.21	17.08
2003–2007	27.37	38.69	30.40	26.45

Note: Average annual growth rates over the sub-periods.

Sources: National Bureau of Statistics (various years) and Yunnan Provincial Bureau of Statistics (various years).

Table 3.3 shows the changes in Yunnan's top ten trading partners from 2000 to 2008. While Myanmar remains Yunnan's largest trading partner, the importance of Vietnam and India in Yunnan's trade relationships keeps increasing.

Yunnan's trade with its GMS neighbours grew rapidly after 1992 and it now represents a very significant share of Yunnan's total international trade. The annual growth rate of trade is much higher than that of the province's average level (Table 3.4). Since 2000, Yunnan's exports to the GMS have accounted for approximately 30 per cent of its total exports, whereas its imports from the GMS have accounted for approximately 15 per cent (Table 3.5). Exports from Yunnan to Myanmar, Laos and Vietnam are significantly greater than exports from other Chinese provinces to those countries in 2008 (ratios reported in the last column of Table 3.6 equal 166.4, 77.4 and 9.6 times, respectively).

2.1 Methodology

A simple gravity model was applied to analyse the development of trade relations between Yunnan and the GMS countries. The original form of a gravity model is:

TABLE 3.3
Top Ten Trading Partners of Yunnan, 2000 and 2008 (%)

Share of Yunnan's trade			
2000		2008	
Myanmar	20.02	Myanmar	12.43
Hong Kong	18.85	Vietnam	6.72
Japan	7.08	India	6.10
Australia	6.60	Japan	4.83
Vietnam	5.53	Australia	4.57
USA	5.14	USA	4.49
Germany	3.07	Brazil	4.14
Indonesia	2.66	Canada	4.07
Canada	2.56	Chile	3.49
India	2.49	Germany	3.48

Source: Yunnan Provincial Bureau of Statistics (various years); Yunnan Provincial Department of Commerce <http://www.bofcom.gov.cn/bofcom/432345564227567616ra/>.

TABLE 3.4
Annual Growth in Trade between Yunnan and GMS (%)

Sub-periods	Exports	Imports
1989–1993	–	112.28
1994–1998	–	525.13
1999–2003	14.25	31.19
2004–2008	20.72	31.85

Note: Average annual growth rates over the sub-periods.
Sources: Yunnan Provincial Bureau of Statistics (various years) and Yunnan Provincial Department of Commerce <http://www.bofcom.gov.cn/bofcom/432345564227567616/>.

TABLE 3.5
Yunnan's Trade with GMS (%)

Year	Exports to GMS/ total exports	Imports from GMS/ total imports
1992	–	2.17
1996	–	12.01
2000	36.01	14.35
2004	36.26	16.08
2008	30.56	15.34

Source: Yunnan Province Bureau of Statistics (various years) and Yunnan Provincial Department of Commerce <http://www.bofcom.gov.cn/bofcom/432345564227567616/>.

TABLE 3.6
Relative Importance of GMS Countries in Yunnan's Exports, 2000 and 2008 (% of total)

Country	Yunnan		Rest of China		Ratio (Yunnan/rest of China)	
	2000	2008	2000	2008	2000	2008
Myanmar	24.93	14.59	0.08	0.09	303.1	166.4
Cambodia	0.06	0.34	0.07	0.08	0.9	4.5
Laos	1.14	1.15	0.01	0.01	133.9	77.4
Thailand	2.00	4.59	0.89	1.08	2.2	4.3
Vietnam	7.88	9.89	0.58	1.03	13.5	9.6
Japan	9.98	7.35	16.75	8.12	0.6	0.9
Australia	0.93	1.74	1.38	1.55	0.7	1.1
USA	5.25	4.58	20.98	17.69	0.3	0.3

Source: National Bureau of Statistics (various years), Yunnan Provincial Bureau of Statistics (various years) Yunnan Provincial Department of Commerce <http://www.bofcom.gov.cn/bofcom/432345564227567616/>.

$$T_{ij} = G\frac{Y_i^{\alpha}Y_j^{\beta}}{D_{ij}^{\beta}} \tag{1}$$

This gravity equation of trade explains aggregate bilateral trade flows. T_{ij} between country *i* and country *j* are explained by including both attraction and repulsion elements. The attraction aspect corresponds to the economic size represented by GDP (Y_i and Y_j) of the exporter and importer. The repulsion element is the geographical distance between them represented by a great circle distance between the capital cities (D_{ij}).

A linear relationship between trade flows, joint economic size and distance can be obtained by taking the natural logarithms of the original gravity equation, so

$$\ln T_{ij} = c + \alpha \ln(Y_iY_j) - \theta \ln D_{ij} + \varepsilon_{ij} \tag{2}$$

where C is a constant term, T_{ij} represents bilateral trade flows between country *i* and country *j*, Y_i and Y_j are the GDP of the importing and exporting country respectively, D_{ij} is the distance between the capital cities of the two trading partners, and ε_{ij} is the disturbance term.

Poncet (2006) also added the variable of joint GDP per capita in the form:

$$\ln T_{ij} = c + \alpha \ln(Y_iY_j) + \beta \ln({}^{Y_i}\!/_{P_i})({}^{Y_j}\!/_{P_j}) - \theta \ln D_{ij} + \varepsilon_{ij} \tag{3}$$

The populations of the two countries are represented by P_i, P_j and the GDP per capita indicates not only the degree of economic development but also the demand preference. The demand for the differentiated products will rise when the net income per person increases. Hence, the expected sign of β is expected to be positive, as countries tend to trade more.

Considering the influence of the exchange rate on bilateral trade, a variable of the U.S. dollar against the renminbi exchange rate is added (Fex_i) in equations (2) and (3). It is expected to be positive in the export model and negative in the import model as the increasing U.S. dollar against the renminbi exchange rate will promote exports and discourage imports. Hence, the new equation form is:

$$\begin{aligned} \ln T_{ij} = c + \alpha \ln(Y_iY_j) + \beta \ln({}^{Y_i}\!/_{P_i})({}^{Y_j}\!/_{P_j}) \\ - \gamma \ln Fex_i - \theta \ln D_{ij} + \varepsilon_{ij} \end{aligned} \tag{4}$$

To measure the impact of the GMS, a dummy variable equal to one when the trading partner is located in the GMS, and zero otherwise, is introduced. A positive and statistically significant coefficient for this dummy variable implies that trade flows exceed the normal level predicted by the countries' economic size and the distance between them, and can be interpreted as a measure of the potential benefits from GMS cooperation. By contrast, a negative and statistically significant coefficient implies that the trade flows are below the normal level.

In order to obtain more detailed results, the aggregate GMS region is divided using individual dummies for member countries, though for Cambodia this is only possible for the export data. Moreover, a dummy is introduced to estimate border effects, which is equal to one if the trading partner borders on Yunnan. The three countries in the GMS that share a border with Yunnan are Laos, Myanmar and Vietnam.

Finally, to compare the effect of Yunnan's integration with the GMS member countries and non-member countries, annual country dummies are introduced for Yunnan's neighbouring countries and its major trading partners to assess the reorientation of Yunnan's trade. The trade partners are: Myanmar, Vietnam, Laos, Thailand, Cambodia (export only), Australia, India, Japan, and the United States. The data covers aggregate bilateral trade flows between Yunnan and approximately fifty-five of its international trading partners between 2000 and 2008. The data set covers 483 observations for the estimation based on exports and 394 observations for that on imports. All data on trade flows and GDP for Yunnan are from the Yunnan Statistical Yearbook (various years). Import data from Cambodia is not available but export data from Yunnan to Cambodia is. All these data are officially recorded by customs and they exclude small-scale free border trade and informal trade. In this case, the regional integration effect on bilateral trade would be underestimated.

Most data on GDP and population statistics come from the World Bank's World Development Indicators (various years). GDP and population data for Hong Kong and Macau are taken from the China Statistical Yearbook (various years), and data for Taiwan is from the Taiwan Statistical Yearbook. Any gaps in the data are filled with data from the Asian Development Bank Key Indicators of Developing Asian and Pacific Countries (various years). The distance between Kunming and the capital city of each country is obtained from the travel distance calculator website (www.mapcrow.info). To eliminate the influence of inflation, all GDP and trade data are transferred from the nominal value to the real value by taking 2000 as the base year.

2.2 Results of the Gravity Model

Equation (4) is used separately for exports and imports on pooled cross-section and time-series panel data. Robust regression is performed to correct the heteroscedasticity by using Stata 10.0. The results are presented in Table 3.7. Columns 1–4 of the table present the impact of GMS cooperation on Yunnan's exports, and columns 5–8 show the impact on its imports. The regression results using an aggregate GMS dummy to measure the impact of GMS membership are shown in columns 2 and 6. In addition, the individual GMS dummy variables are shown in columns 3 and 7. Columns 4 and 8 show the border effect on the trade relationship between Yunnan and its neighbouring countries of Laos, Myanmar and Vietnam.

The results show that the gravity model gives a reasonable explanation on the aggregate bilateral trade between Yunnan and its trade partners, evidenced by the relatively high value of R-squared (approximately 80 per cent for exports and 66 per cent for imports). Results obtained using export data are better than those of the import data. The two basic explanatory variables (GDP and distance) have the expected signs and are statistically significant at the 1 per cent level.

Results obtained using import data show that the coefficient on joint GDP has the expected sign and is statistically significant at the 1 per cent level, suggesting that trade will be promoted with economic development. The coefficient of the distance has the expected sign and is statistically significant at the 1 per cent level for the baseline estimation (column 5) but not statistically significant for the other three sub-models in columns 6–8, which are added with dummies. It is possible that bias in the trade data created by smuggling may be greater on the import side than on the export side. Unofficial trade within the GMS is significant, but precisely how this affects the analysis is unclear.

The sign of the variable of the U.S. dollar against the renminbi exchange rate in the import model is negative and statistically significant as expected, and it is negative but statistically significant at 1 per cent which differs from our expectation in the export model. Since the renminbi exchange regime reform in 2005, the renminbi value has appreciated by 20 per cent and the

TABLE 3.7
Estimation of the Impact of GMS Integration on Yunnan's Exports and Imports

Dependant variable	Exports to GMS partners				Imports from GMS partners			
	1	2	3	4	5	6	7	8
Joint GDP	0.851***	0.845***	0.868***	0.860***	0.453***	0.435***	0.468***	0.466***
Ln (Y_iY_j)	(0.030)	(0.030)	(0.031)	(0.029)	(0.048)	(0.046)	(0.049)	(0.045)
Distance	–2.017***	–1.828***	–1.860***	–1.849***	–0.467***	–0.061	–0.112	–0.121
Ln (D_{ij})	(0.076)	(0.083)	(0.087)	(0.078)	(0.138)	(0.166)	(0.174)	(0.152)
FEX (official exchange rate)	–0.540*	–1.286***	–1.416***	–1.380***	–2.214***	–3.782***	–3.947***	–3.886***
Ln (Fexi)	(0.320)	(0.312)	(0.308)	(0.305)	(0.489)	(0.567)	(0.566)	(0.537)
GMS: (Cambodia, Laos, Myanmar, Thailand, Vietnam)		1.097*** (0.248)				2.208*** (0.341)		
Cambodia			–0.231 (0.212)				— —	
Laos			1.407*** (0.184)				2.155*** (0.299)	
Myanmar			3.635*** (0.211)				3.852*** (0.312)	
Thailand			0.039 (0.152)				0.620** (0.303)	
Vietnam			0.670*** (0.196)				2.184*** (0.384)	
Shared borders with Yunnan (Laos, Myanmar, Vietnam)				1.366*** (0.279)				2.693*** (0.307)
Observations	483	483	483	483	396	396	396	396
R-squared	0.78	0.79	0.81	0.79	0.63	0.66	0.67	0.67

Note: Robust standard errors in parentheses, ***, ** and * indicate significance at the 1 per cent, 5 per cent and 10 per cent level.

U.S. dollar against the renminbi exchange rate has kept dropping in the past few years. However, Yunnan's total export maintains strong growth with an annual growth rate of 20.7 per cent (see Table 3.4). Taking some of the main export products as an example, the total export value of phosphorus chemicals increased by 65.8 per cent, electromechanical products rose by 48.4 per cent and agricultural products by 20.2 per cent in 2008 compared to 2007, accounting for 67 per cent of Yunnan's total exports. Although the export of non-ferrous metals dropped significantly by 49 per cent in 2008 compared to 2007, the factor that most contributed to this was the national export tax refund policy changes which discouraged the export of non-ferrous metals, i.e. natural resource-consuming goods.[1]

The GMS coefficients for both export and imports are positive and statistically significant at the 1 per cent level, underlining the above-standard trade flows between Yunnan and these five countries. Yunnan's exports to its five neighbours are 2.99 times greater than the predicted normal level [exp (1.097) = 2.99] and imports from four of its neighbours (except Cambodia) are 9.10 times greater than the normal level [exp (2.208) = 9.10] predicted by the gravity model.

The country effects within the GMS differ for different members. In the export model, the Laos, Myanmar and Vietnam dummies are positive and statistically significant, indicating that the exports from Yunnan are greater than the normal level (4.08 times for Laos, 37.9 times for Myanmar and 1.95 for Vietnam). The divergence between actual and expected exports to Myanmar is much higher than that to other GMS countries, indicating Myanmar is an important export market for Yunnan. In addition, the significance of Laos and Vietnam suggests the increasing importance of these two countries in Yunnan's export trade. The Cambodia and Thailand dummies are statistically insignificant within 10 per cent level, implying the exports from Yunnan to these two countries have not been significantly influenced by regional cooperation.

In the import model, the Laos, Myanmar and Vietnam dummies are positive and statistically significant at 1 per cent, indicating that the GMS cooperation has significantly improved the imports to Yunnan from these three countries. It is worth noting that trade integration in terms of Yunnan's imports from Laos, Myanmar and Vietnam appears greater than its exports to those countries. The result is consistent with the annual 30 per cent rapid growth rate of total imports to Yunnan from the GMS countries, which is greater than the annual 20 per cent growth rate of Yunnan's total exports to the GMS countries from 2004 to 2008. It also highlights the strong demand of Yunnan for natural resources and crude materials from the GMS countries. The Thailand dummy is positive and statistically significant at 5 per cent level, indicating the modest influence of the GMS cooperation on Yunnan's imports from Thailand. It is 1.86 times greater than the normal level [exp (0.62) = 1.86] predicted by the gravity model. Recent years have witnessed that Thailand is an important import resource of raw materials for Yunnan, such as ferrous metal ores and scrap metal, rubber products, natural rubber etc. In 2008, imported crude materials accounted for 63.5 per cent of Yunnan's total imports from Thailand.

The coefficient of the dummy variable testing the border effects in columns 4 and 8 is positive and significant, indicating that trade with the countries sharing Yunnan's borders is 2.0 times greater than the predicted normal level of export, and 8.3 times greater than the predicted normal level of import. These results are the same as those for the individual GMS country dummies since the coefficients on Laos, Myanmar and Vietnam are also significant. This also suggests that regional cooperation has significantly promoted border trade between Yunnan and its neighbouring countries.

We used variations of equation (4); the basic model excludes joint GDP per capita as a variable. Inclusion of joint GDP per capita does not change the models, except that the coefficients of joint GDP increase slightly. The variable joint GDP per capita is significant with a negative sign, indicating the relatively low income elasticity of demand for the products concerned. However, joint GDP per capita fails to indicate the differences in the degree of GDP per capita between Yunnan and other GMS countries. In 2008, GDP per capita in Yunnan was US$1,638, Thailand US$3,148, Vietnam US$544, Cambodia US$454, Laos US$332 and Myanmar US$60. GDP per capita in all the countries except Thailand was much lower than in Yunnan.

According to the Linder hypothesis (Linder 1961), the more similarity there is in countries' demand structures, the more they will trade with one another. Similar demand preferences can be derived from similar income levels. More specifically, when countries with high income per capita enjoy high income per capita growth rate, they will tend to trade more with non-member countries with high income per capita. On the other hand, when countries with low income per capita enjoy high income per capita growth rate, they will tend to trade more with other member countries. Hence, as Yunnan's GDP per capita has grown, it has tended to trade more with non-GMS countries which have relatively high GDP per capita. This result is evidenced by the fact that trade with the GMS countries only accounted for 23 per cent of Yunnan's total trade in 2008 and the majority of its trade was with non-GMS countries. The insignificant Thailand dummy can also be explained. With the highest GDP per capita of the GMS countries, Thailand tends to trade more with non-GMS countries which have a similar income level since they share a similar demand preference. Hence, Thailand-Yunnan trade only amounts to 2–3 per cent of the total value of Yunnan's trade from 2000 to 2008.

To further assess the country effect, Figures 3.1 and 3.2 show the coefficients on the countries' dummies for exports and imports, to and from the GMS countries and Yunnan's major trading partners during the period 2000–08. To do this, the export and import equations are re-estimated by introducing time-varying country dummies for each of Yunnan's five neighbouring countries and four major trading partners. Owing to missing data, this procedure adds eighty-one variables to the export equation and seventy-two variables to the import equation. For any trade partner, the estimated coefficients on its dummies indicate how its trade with Yunnan has developed over time. They correspond to the deviation from the average norm over the entire time period. Following Poncet (2006), for any one trade partner, the estimated coefficients on its dummies can indicate how its trade with Yunnan has evolved over time.

The findings highlight the diversification of the export market and the import resources of Yunnan province between 2000 and 2008. Preferential trade integration between Yunnan and Myanmar has declined continuously. In 2000, Yunnan exported 40 times more to Myanmar than the expected level. This ratio decreased to just 11 times in 2008. In terms of imports, the relative intensity of Yunnan's imports from Myanmar declined from 27 times to 13 times the norm, over the same period. Another important evolution is the decline in imports from Australia from 18 times higher than the expected level in 2000 to 9 times in 2008.

India and Vietnam have turned out to be important import resources for Yunnan, as evidenced by their above-normal levels since 2000. Imports from India increased from 1.8 times more than the expected level in 2000, to 3.2 times in 2008. Imports from Vietnam increased from 1.2 times more than the expected level in 2000, to 2.8 times in 2008.

Table 3.8 presents the changes of coefficient estimates for the annual country dummies of Yunnan-GMS trade. Cambodia is eliminated from the import model because data on imports from Cambodia could not be

FIGURE 3.1
Coefficients on Dummies for Exports

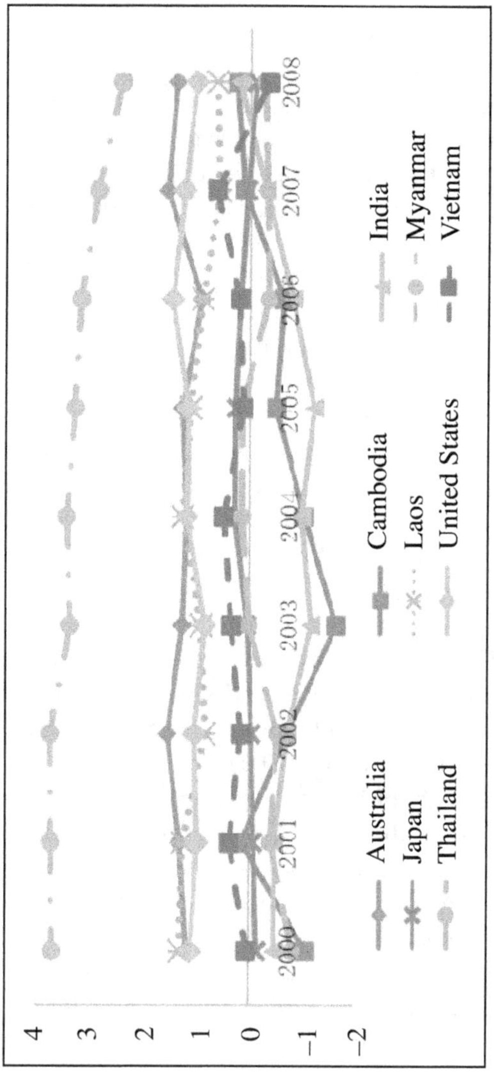

Source: Calculated by the FME research team.

FIGURE 3.2
Coefficients on Dummies for Imports

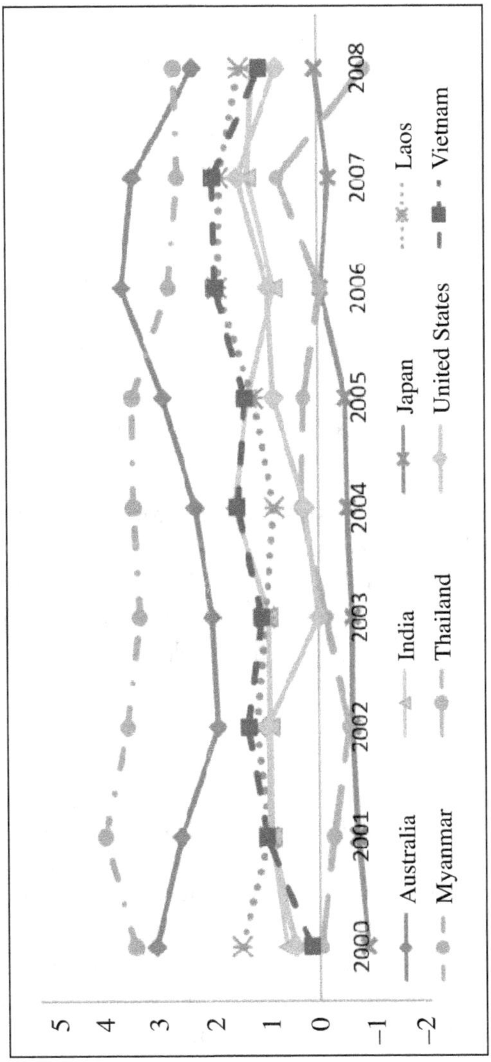

Source: Calculated by the FME research team.

TABLE 3.8
Coefficient Estimates for Annual Country Dummies, Yunnan-GMS Trade

Country	2000	2004	2008
Yunnan's exports to:			
Cambodia	–1.09	–1.04	0.25
Laos	1.56	1.47	0.71
Myanmar	3.69	3.42	2.39
Thailand	–0.82	0.14	–0.28
Vietnam	0.04	0.47	–0.36
Yunnan's imports from:			
Laos	1.39	0.79	1.39
Myanmar	3.28	3.29	2.56
Thailand	–0.04	0.30	–0.84
Vietnam	0.15	1.44	1.03

Source: Calculated by the FME research team.

found for most years. The other three GMS countries (Myanmar, Laos and Vietnam) had above-normal levels from 2000 to 2008, indicating the positive impact of GMS cooperation. Trade with Thailand fluctuated around the normal level and was above normal level in 2004 and 2005, suggesting the positive impact of the implementation of the Early Harvest Programme in 2004.

2.3 Summary

The focus of the study is on the impact of GMS membership in stimulating Yunnan's trade with the subregion between 2000 and 2008. The gravity model of trade is used to assess trade relationships between Yunnan and its trade partners by introducing joint income, distance and exchange rate factors. Export and import equations are estimated separately.

It is shown that Yunnan's trade with most GMS members is now considerably greater than would be predicted from the gravity model and that the implementation of the GMS initiatives positively promotes trade in the subregional countries. Although positive bias towards Myanmar decreases over the 2000–08 period, a large degree of trade integration between Yunnan and Myanmar is observed for both exports and imports. Trade between Yunnan and Laos also significantly exceeds the levels predicted by distance, relative economic size and development. The insignificant coefficient of the Cambodia dummy in the export model indicates that Yunnan's trade with Cambodia is in line with the relative size of, and distance between, the two trade partners. The coefficient of the Thailand dummy in the export model is insignificant because different income levels determine that Thailand trades more with non-GMS countries. However, the complementarities of the import structure explain that imports from Thailand to Yunnan are modestly higher than expected given their distance and other gravity variables. The border effect is positively significant and promoting border trade in the GMS areas is viable.

3. MICROECONOMIC IMPLICATIONS

Due to the nature of poverty, and the breadth of its impacts and connotations, it is a very difficult concept to singularly define. Moreover, the understanding and definition of poverty varies between countries, regions, groups and even from one individual to another. For the purposes of this chapter, poverty is defined as "a state in which basic living needs cannot be satisfied continuously".

Different countries define their poverty in accordance with their respective economic development level and actual consumption capacity. Therefore, the poverty line varies both between different countries and over time. The statistics of poverty calculated in line with one country's "poverty line" cannot be compared with that of another. This is because statistics for formulating poverty-reduction policies and supervising the progress of poverty reduction for a given country are highly context specific. When it comes to measuring poverty in China, there are two frequently used standards: (1) the international poverty standard of "one day, one dollar" defined by the World Bank; and (2) the poverty standard for rural areas issued by the National Bureau of Statistics, which is also known as the government poverty standard.

3.1 International Poverty Standard

In order to get a general picture of poverty in different countries, the World Bank carried out studies on the poverty standards of thirty-four countries in 1990. It took US$370 per capita per year as the recognized international standard to measure each country's poverty, and this standard was simplified to the poverty standard of "one day, one dollar", and is well known and widely accepted internationally (Xiang, Zhu and Yan 2009). The commodity prices and consumption structure of various countries have changed in the past two decades. Although the actual value of the poverty standard is no longer "one day, one dollar", we still regard it as the poverty standard in the research and measurement of poverty.

3.2 China's Poverty Standard

The 1980s saw China formulate the poverty standard for rural residents, but not a unified national poverty standard suitable for both rural and urban areas. In 2002, the World Bank, in collaboration with the Development Research Centre of State Council and Urban Economic and Social Development Survey Corps of the National Bureau of Statistics, found that the poverty standard for urban areas is about 3.7 times that for rural areas. However, since the poverty standards for rural and urban areas do not have a comparison value and most of China's poverty-stricken population live in rural areas, the unified national poverty standard for both rural and urban areas takes second place to the poverty standard for rural areas.

The (rural) poverty standard in China was formulated keeping in mind the distinct conceptions of poverty as both an absolute and a relative phenomenon. In formulating the poverty standard, the Chinese Government took the international poverty standard, the poverty standards of other countries and, in line with China's actual conditions, the actual level of commodity prices, into account. To be specific, China had two standards to eliminate poverty before 2008: one was the absolute poverty standard formulated in 1986, which regarded farmers having a net annual income of less than RMB206 in 1985 (increased to RMB785 in 2007) as the target for poverty reduction. Using this standard as a measure, people living in absolute poverty in China dropped from 125 million in 1986 to 14.79 million in 2007, and the percentage of poor people among the rural population dramatically decreased from 14.8 per cent to 1.6 per cent. The other standard was the low income standard formulated in 2000, i.e. rural people having a net income of less than RMB865 were classed as being in the low income bracket. This standard also identified the low income population which met the requirement of the absolute poverty standard and the low income standard; it was increased to RMB1,067 in

2007. In line with this standard, China's low income population dropped from 62.13 million in 2000 to 28.41 million in 2007.

By the end of 2008, the Chinese government announced an increase in the poverty-reduction standard (mainly due to sharp commodity price increases), and integrated the absolute poverty standard into the low income standard, abolished the differentiated treatment for people in absolute poverty and low income in rural areas, and set the net income of RMB1,196 as the new threshold for poverty elimination. Using this new standard, 40.07 million were classed as poor in 2008. Table 3.9 shows the changes in China's poverty standard from 2000 to 2007.

While it is notable that China upgraded its poverty standard in 2008, this standard still fell short of the "one day, one dollar" standard of the World Bank. There are, however, a variety of factors that could explain this disparity. When the World Bank was formulating the poverty standard, it intended to make comparisons with other countries in terms of poverty level. However, formulation of the poverty standard is related not only to statistical issues, but also to pragmatic decision-making. From this perspective, the formulation of a national poverty standard should be in line with, and take into account, a country's actual condition. Indeed, most of the poverty standards in the seventy plus countries that China's State Council has information on are different from the standard formulated by the World Bank.

TABLE 3.9
Changes in Poverty Standards, 2000–07

Year/unit	Poverty standards for rural areas		Low income standards for rural residents	
	RMB	US$	RMB	US$
2000	625	75.50	865	104.49
2001	630	76.11	872	105.35
2002	627	75.75	869	104.99
2003	637	76.96	882	106.56
2004	668	80.71	924	111.64
2005	683	83.38	944	115.24
2006	693	86.93	958	120.17
2007	785	103.24	1,067	140.32

Source: Collated from *The Yearbook of China's Statistics*.

From the actual practice of poverty reduction in the past, we can see that the poverty standard adopted by the Chinese government in the 1980s is in line and congruous with China's poverty reduction work. The relatively lower poverty standard adopted by China has provided the government with a different reference in assembling resources for poverty reduction, sustainably supporting large numbers of poverty-stricken people in rural areas, implementing socio-economic development policies in underdeveloped regions and its ongoing work related to the relief and disaster assistance of poverty-stricken people. The practice of poverty reduction indicates that the poverty reduction policy under this standard is feasible. As a result of this strategic approach, China's poverty reduction has transformed to a new stage which requires not only providing adequate food and clothes for the poverty-stricken, but also consolidating the achievements made so far. Further, the government is broadening the goals of poverty alleviation programmes, prioritizing not only improvement in living conditions, but also the poor's overall quality of life and increasing their income. The achievements of these policy prescriptions have been recognized and lauded by the international community.

3.3 Poverty Issue in Yunnan Province

Located in southwest China, Yunnan is a multi-ethnic and mountainous province which shares international borders. Due to historical, geographical and socio-economic factors, Yunnan lags behind other provinces or regions in terms of development and, except for the basin areas between mountains, most of its counties are in poverty elimination areas. The province is classed as one of China's main target areas for combating poverty.

There have been many advances in Yunnan's fight with poverty. Its population living below the poverty line dropped from 8.2 million in 2003 to 5.55 million in 2008, a decrease of 32.3 per cent. However, the pace of poverty reduction in Yunnan still lags behind that of the whole of China, and the ratio of people living below the poverty line nationwide has risen from 9.6 per cent in 2000 to 13.9 per cent in 2008. Figures 3.3 and 3.4 present the details.

The distribution of the poor population in Yunnan province is characterized by macro-scattering and micro-concentration and the coexistence of points (villages), areas (particularly poor areas) and lines (the poverty-stricken belt along the border). Yunnan has many cross-border

FIGURE 3.3
Total Poor Population and Poverty Reduction Rate in Yunnan, 2003–08

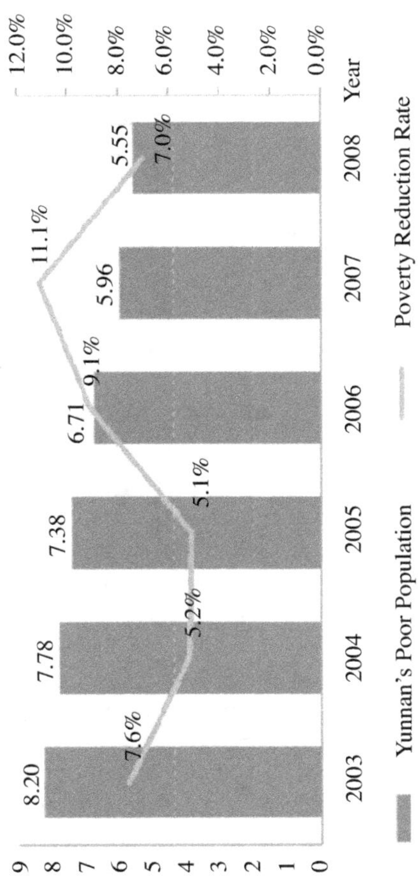

Source: Yunnan Provincial Investigation Corps of the National Bureau of Statistics.

FIGURE 3.4
Yunnan's Poor Population (million) and Share of Poor Population in China (%)

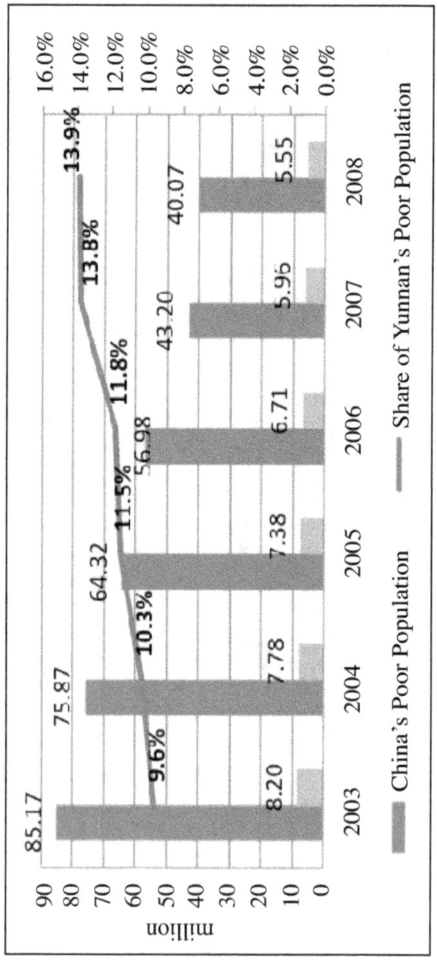

Source: Yunnan Provincial Investigation Corps of the National Bureau of Statistics.

migrants and ethnic groups. Topographically speaking, the key areas of Yunnan are the Jinsha River, the Lancang River (known internationally as the Mekong River), the Nujiang River, the border areas, the rock desertification areas, the areas deprived of basic living conditions, the particularly poor areas of Zhaotong, Diqing and Nujiang, and the twenty-five border counties. These areas have large concentrations of poor people, higher levels of poverty and face particular difficulties in reducing poverty.

According to the latest figures from the National Bureau of Statistics, among the poor rural populations of different cities and prefectures in Yunnan in 2008, Diqing ranked top with a poor population of 919,300, while Xishuangbanna had the smallest with 66,400. From a regional perspective, the northeast ranks first with 28 per cent of the total poor population in Yunnan, central Yunnan has the smallest poor population with only 9 per cent of the total poor population, and the northwest and southwest each have a 21 per cent share. Figures 3.5 and 3.6 give more detail.

3.4 Methodology

The gravity model has explained that Yunnan's trade with most GMS members is now considerably greater than would be predicted. In other words, the GMS cooperation has significantly promoted trade between Yunnan and most GMS members. To assess the impact of the GMS cooperation on poverty reduction in Yunnan, the pro-poor products that are traded between Yunnan and GMS members were identified before conducting the field survey. This part focuses only on pro-poor export products because those products have direct and indirect impacts on the lives of the poor. For example, export of labour-intensive agricultural products directly contributes to the income growth of the poor, and export of labour-intensive manufactured products provides more job opportunities for the poor. Import is not considered since the raw materials and tropical fruits which are the main products that Yunnan imports from the GMS countries have no impact on the poor.

Jenkins and Edwards (2004) looked at the impact of China's growth on poverty reduction in a group of countries in Asia, Africa and Latin America by identifying the pro-poor products which China traded with these countries. To apply the same methodology, here the first step was to identify the export structure of Yunnan to the GMS-4 and select the main pro-poor products at the 3-digit SITC level. The effects of Yunnan's

FIGURE 3.5
Ranking of Poverty-stricken Rural Population in Yunnan's Cities and Prefectures (10,000 persons), 2008

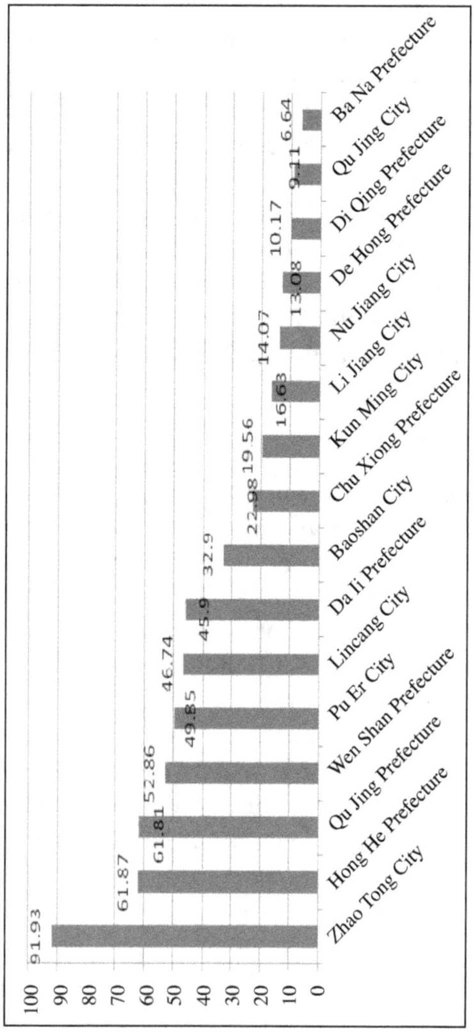

Source: Yunnan Provincial Investigation Corps of the National Bureau of Statistics.

FIGURE 3.6
Distribution of People Living Below the Poverty Line in Yunnan, 2008

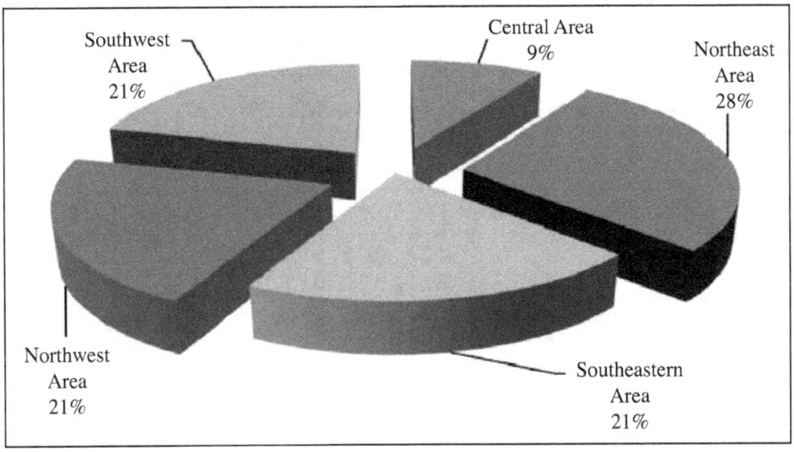

Source: Yunnan Provincial Investigation Corps of the National Bureau of Statistics.

exports on poverty reduction were classified as direct and indirect impacts: direct impact on the income of farmers and farm-based workers who temporarily work in the factories; indirect impact on the employment of unskilled workers.

Table 3.10 shows the main export products of Yunnan to the GMS-4 — manufactured and chemical products such as iron and steel, non-ferrous metals, fertilizer and phosphorus chemicals. Agricultural products such as fruit and vegetables are also main items for export to the GMS-4. In fact, significant shares of Yunnan's total export in 2008 comprised machinery and transport equipment (SITC Section 7), 12.5 per cent to Vietnam, 40.4 per cent to Laos and 47.2 per cent to Cambodia. However, interviews with officers from Kunming Customs revealed that most of the exported machinery and transport equipment is made in northeast China, not in Yunnan. Therefore, Section 7 is not considered in our study.

3.5 Field Survey and Case Studies

The next step was to conduct field surveys of the companies that produced the selected pro-poor products. Given time constraints and availability

TABLE 3.10
Yunnan's Main Pro-Poor Export Products to GMS-4, 2005 and 2008 (% of total)

	Export products and standard international trade classification codes											
	Fruit and vegetables 054, 057		Tobacco 122		Fertilizer 562		Phosphorus Chemicals 522, 523		Iron and steel 671, 672, 673, 676 677, 679		Non-ferrous metals 681, 685 687	
	2005	2008	2005	2008	2005	2008	2005	2008	2005	2008	2005	2008
Vietnam	6.1	6.5	—	—	31.3	16.0	9.0	13.2	18.3	4.8	2.2	1.3
Thailand	3.8	18.4	—	—	3.8	9.0	15.6	18.5	1.9	1.4	64.4	37.1
Laos	—	—	3.1		—	1.9	—	—	4.8	16.8	—	—
Cambodia	—	—	82.8	14.7	—	—	—	—	—	—	—	—

Source: Yunnan Yearly Statistics Book.

of resources, only two items were selected for the case study and field survey — iron and steel, and vegetables. Iron and steel represent labour-intensive manufactured products which have an indirect impact on poverty reduction since their production provides job opportunities for unskilled labourers. Vegetables represent labour-intensive agricultural products which relate directly to farmer's income. Two companies were selected, namely Kunming Steel and Iron Holding Co. Ltd and Kunming Chennong Green Products Co. Ltd.

Case-study: Kunming Steel and Iron Holding Co. Ltd

Founded in February 1939, Kunming Iron and Steel Holding (KIS) is a state-owned company with its headquarters in Anning city on the southwestern outskirts of Kunming. It is one of the largest industrial enterprises in China, one of the 500 Top Chinese Enterprises, and the largest iron and steel production base in Yunnan. It currently has an annual steel production capacity of 7,000,000 tonnes, and has become the largest enterprise group running businesses in steel metallurgy, coal chemical industry, mining, heavy equipment manufacturing, cement, real estate, modern logistics, engineering design and overseas business. In 2009, it had sales revenue of RMB41billion, profit and tax of RMB2.8 billion, and industrial added value of RMB5.7 billion. Of this, steel sales amounted to

5,454,400 tonnes with sales revenue of RMB18.089 billion (excluding tax). In 2009, the volume of steel sold within Yunnan province stood at 4.6951 million tonnes, a leap of 74.73 per cent or an increase of 2,008,100 tonnes compared with the previous period, which accounted for 86.1 per cent of the total, while its steel sales to other provinces numbered 744,600 tonnes, a drop of 89,600 tonnes.

By the end of 2009, KIS boasted twenty wholly owned subsidiaries, eight holding subsidiaries, and two shares subsidiaries, with total assets of RMB37 billion and about 28,000 workers. Its products are not only sold within and outside of Yunnan, but are also exported to Germany, Japan, Korea, Singapore, Vietnam, Indonesia, Thailand, Myanmar and others. Kunming Iron and Steel Holding is now working with Vietnam and Laos to develop iron ore mining and construct steel plants.

Export Situation. It is worth noting that exports came to a halt in 2009 because of the shrinking demand brought on by the financial crisis. Moreover, the joint announcement of the reduction and elimination of the export tax refund for pollution-inducing high energy or natural resource-consuming products, as well as the low-value-added products by the Ministry of Finance and the State Administration of Taxation were other important reasons for the zero export of KIS. Steel products are considered to be pollution-inducing high energy-consuming products. Hence, the tax refund for most types of manufactures was reduced significantly from 15 per cent to 5 per cent and some even reached zero. In addition, KIS had to pay 5–10 per cent export tax on its main export products such as steel sheets and bars. All these factors explain the sharp decline of export in 2008 and the zero export in 2009.

Figure 3.7 shows the fluctuation of KIS's steel exports from 2000 to 2008. Table 3.11 shows the main export destinations of KIS steel products. The main export markets are located in Asia and Vietnam. Vietnam seems to be the main importer of KIS products and export volume to Vietnam accounts for 16.8 per cent of KIS's total exports in 2004 and 85.7 per cent 2007. The year 2004 witnessed diversification of export destinations as evidenced by the increasing number of export markets. From 2004 and for the next three years, KIS' exports experienced stable and continuous growth.

Figure 3.8 shows KIS's export to the GMS countries over the period 2000–08. Vietnam has clearly been an important importer for KIS since 2002 and the export volume to Vietnam reached its peak in 2007 with KIS's

FIGURE 3.7
KIS Steel Exports (tonnes), 2000–08

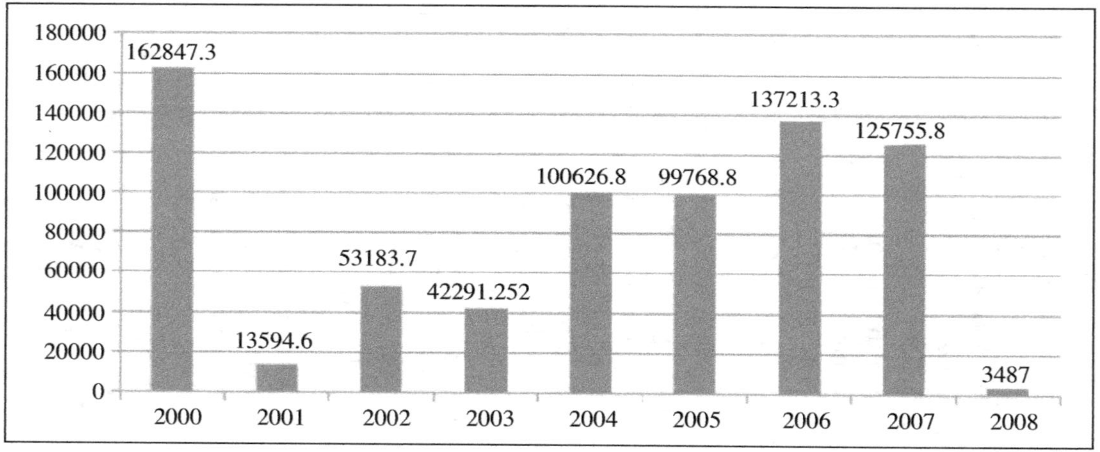

Source: Kunming Iron and Steel Holding Co. Ltd.

TABLE 3.11
Main Export Destinations of KIS Products in 2000, 2004 and 2007 (%)

Share of total KIS exports (%)					
2000		2004		2007	
Myanmar	35.45	Hong Kong	24.09	Vietnam	85.69
Indonesia	22.36	Vietnam	16.78	Hong Kong	4.20
Hong Kong	22.10	Korea	8.44	Kazakhstan	2.46
Korea	8.02	Taiwan	8.85	USA	2.42
Malaysia	3.61	Thailand	8.81	Other	5.22
Japan	3.52	Myanmar	7.77		
Other	4.94	Netherlands	7.15		
		USA	9.74		
		Japan	4.65		
		Other	4.95		

Source: Kunming Iron and Steel Holding Co. Ltd.

steel exports going to Vietnam in 2008. The KIS export sales person said that most of the products exported to the GMS countries were used as construction materials. Given Vietnam's rapid economic growth, it has a huge demand for steel sheets and cables. Myanmar was another important export market for KIS before 2006. Laos imported a small quantity of steel products for a few years.

Employment of Unskilled Labour from the Rural Areas. An interview with the director of KIS Human Resource Department found that the company provided 5,600 job opportunities to rural labourers in 2009. However, it is very difficult to trace the origins of these farm-based workers because of the changes in employment patterns. With the implementation of the National Labour Law in 2008, the employment of temporary workers has since been outsourced to labour recruitment agents in order to reduce costs and avoid risks. KIS is responsible for setting the job requirements and the base pay. Most of the outsourced jobs are labour-intensive, such as loading and unloading and packing. Some are skilled-based such as welders and maintenance workers. In this case, KIS had no record of the temporary workers' origins. The interview also found that the majority of temporary workers were hired by the mining company located in Yuxi city and Honghe prefecture where 30 per cent of the workers were hired

FIGURE 3.8
KIS Iron and Steel Exports (tonnes) to GMS, 2000–08

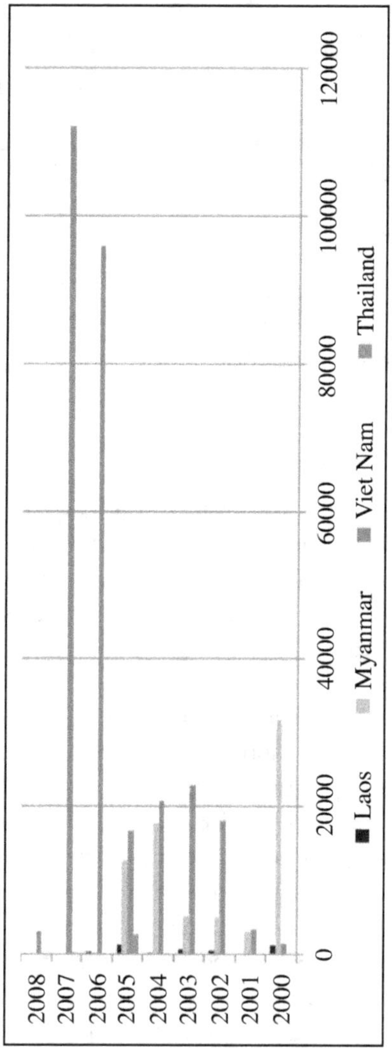

Source: Kunming Iron and Steel Holding Co. Ltd.

by local recruitment agents. Meanwhile, payment to temporary workers had doubled in 2009 compared to 2005. As a result, the development of the company does provide job opportunities and makes some contribution to the income growth of the local rural population.

Case-study: Kunming Chennong Enterprise Group

Kunming Chennong Enterprise Group (KCEG) was founded in 2005 after years of gradual development from its first company Kunming Chennong Green Products Co. Ltd which was founded in 1992. Presently, KCEG is managing thirteen affiliated companies and claims to be becoming a modern agriculture-related enterprise group running businesses in growing vegetable seedlings, cultivation, agri-product processing (keeping-fresh, quick-freezing, freeze-drying), packaging materials, logistics, marketing and sales. It covers an area of 180 square kilometres, has total assets of RMB320 million and employs over 1,200 staff. It has a vegetable production capacity of 100,000 tonnes and an annual vegetable seedlings production of 800 million plants.

In recent years, the annual processing and sales of all kinds of vegetables by the Kunming Chennong Group has averaged over 5 million tonnes, and the logistics service companies have transported more than 15,000 tonnes of vegetables and flowers. With its rapid development, the average annual household income of the 60,000 rural families who have been part of KCEG's supply chain is at least RMB2,500 higher compared to pre-2005 period. Meanwhile, KCEG has provided about a thousand job opportunities to rural labourers.

Trade Situation. More than 100 products, such as freeze-dried green onions, garlic, bitter gourds, aloe powder, quick-frozen sweet corn, fresh broccoli, lettuce, sweet peas, and sweet peppers are exported to Canada, Australia, South Korea, Japan, Singapore, Malaysia, Thailand, Bangladesh, the United Arab Emirates and Vietnam among others. These products are also sold to domestic markets in more than twenty cities such as Beijing, Shanghai, Hangzhou, Nanjing, Zhengzhou, Guangzhou, Shenzhen, Wuhan and Changsha. Approximately 58 per cent of the total production is sold through domestic markets and 42 per cent goes to foreign markets.

In 2009, KCEG realized a sales income of RMB350 million and a foreign trade turnover of US$4.8 million. The main export destinations included Singapore with 45 per cent share of the total export, Canada 25 per cent, Malaysia 10 per cent, and Korea 10 per cent. When interviewed, a representative from export sales explained that the main export products are sugar beans and peapods and that 99 per cent of the transport methods are land transport plus sea transport. Products exported to Thailand are usually transported down the Mekong River from Guan Lei port in Xishuangbanna to Chiangseng port in Thailand, taking about 2.5 days. The completed Kunming-Bangkok highway has not been used as yet because of the high cost, complicated formalities for customs clearance and longer transportation time.

Direct Impact on the Income Growth of the Rural Population. The company successfully implemented the production pattern of "company + base + farmers" in 1999. This pattern was realized by two methods: (1) an organized cultivation base with orders given by KCEG at a fixed price; and (2) the individual rural households that supply vegetables based on the quality standards required by KCEG. The head of Yong Fa village in Malong County of Qujing city, said that the whole village has significantly benefited from cooperation with KCEG since 2009. The village has 300 households, a population of approximately 1,000 and about 1,000 *mu* of land.[2] The villagers used to grow wheat and tobacco. Compared to wheat and tobacco, vegetable production generates higher income from three to four harvests a year. In addition, KCEG is responsible for providing seed, fertilizer, technology guidance and assistance. Hence, the annual income per household almost doubled from RMB3,500 to RMB6,000.

The story of Mr Z, a rural resident, is an example of the pattern of individual suppliers. Based on cultivation instructions and the product varieties advised by KCEG, he receives seed, fertilizer and technology assistance from the company and supplies the required quality of vegetables at the market price to KCEG. Any products that fail to meet KCEG's standards are rejected. The advantage of this pattern of cooperation is that the market risks are shared by both KCEG and the individual household. The market price of vegetables fluctuates frequently and it has happened before that the products could not be sold because of oversupply in the market. Also, the production area has been expanded from 3 *mu* to 40 *mu* and Mr Z's income had significantly increased by two or three times compared to four years ago when he first became one of KCEG's suppliers.

3.6 Summary

Interviews with representatives of the enterprises found that trade development and production expansion do have a direct and indirect impact on income growth in rural areas. However, there is little evidence to show that the income growth of poor people in the poverty-stricken areas is significantly related to trade expansion. As mentioned, most of the poverty-stricken areas are located in remote areas with poor natural conditions where the environment is not suitable for growing agricultural export products such as fruit and vegetables. Additionally, it is difficult for poor people living in poverty-stricken areas to benefit from working in the export-oriented factories because of their low educational level and lack of work-related skills.

4. CONCLUSIONS AND POLICY RECOMMENDATIONS

Macro level analysis shows that Yunnan's participation in GMS cooperation has significantly promoted trade between Yunnan and other GMS member countries. Additionally, micro level analysis shows that the development of regional trade has a positive impact on the income growth of the poor. Hence, it is very important for Yunnan to pay more attention to the further development of Yunnan-GMS trade.

First, further efforts should be made to promote Yunnan's import from the GMS countries in order to maintain trade balance in the subregional areas. In 2008, the trade surplus between Yunnan and the GMS member countries reached US$832.93 million. Reducing the trade surplus and maintaining the trade balance would lead to a long-term trade relationship between Yunnan and the GMS member countries. As the import model shows, GMS cooperation has significantly improved Yunnan's imports from Laos, Myanmar and Vietnam, and it would be helpful for Yunnan to adopt further measures to expand its import of raw materials from these countries. Such measures include import tariff reduction, expansion of government and enterprises procurement, establishment of factories in GMS countries and development of overseas cooperation.

Second, more preferential policies should be in place to support border trade. As the gravity model suggests, regional cooperation has significantly promoted border trade between Yunnan and its neighbouring countries. This reflects the fact that border trade has played an important role in mutual trade between Yunnan and its neighbours including Laos, Vietnam and Myanmar. Preferential policies include industrial policy, management policy, and investment policy. Other supportive measures should be taken to:

- improve and simplify border trade import and export procedures;
- expand bartering of characteristic products and products with advantages through further mutual discussion between Yunnan and its neighbouring countries, and relax the limits on the import-export operation rights;
- speed up logistical infrastructure construction and establish complete supporting facilities such as storage, reloading and packing, at the border check points; and
- implement export tax refund (to be settled in renminbi) policies for small-scale border trade.

Third, local government should be innovation-oriented to enhance the efficiency of trade cooperation. Local government plays a marked role in facilitating trade between Yunnan and the GMS countries. In the border regions, local governments of prefectures and cities play an important role in administration and coordination. Their impacts on coordination and trade promotion will be proved by the effective conduct of foreign trade via land routes. Under the framework of GMS cooperation, local governments need to update and enrich their concepts of traditional administration and adjust their services to meet public demand. Meanwhile, local governments and different administrative departments of Yunnan province should fully understand trade facilitation policies in order to address the concerns raised through in-depth consultation with enterprises. This would help enterprises to understand the macro-level policy information and facilitate the smooth development of foreign trade and avoid unforeseen obstacles and losses due to insufficient understanding of the policies. At the same time, local governments should take the initiative to maintain dialogue with enterprises, keep abreast of their problems and needs, and communicate in a timely manner with various functional departments of central government to keep higher-level departments informed about the implementation of trade facilitation.

Finally, recommendations for individual GMS countries are given according to the different trade situations.

4.1 Yunnan-Myanmar

Yunnan-Myanmar trade enjoys complementarities resulting from their different levels of economic development. The continuing upgrading of the industrial structure, the development of related export-import industries and the expanded capacity of export-import market in Yunnan are prerequisites for the further expansion of bilateral trade between Yunnan and Myanmar. The trade trend between Yunnan and Myanmar is promising and provides a successful example for Yunnan to build trade exchanges with other GMS countries.

It is believed that the sustainable and steady development of Yunnan-Myanmar bilateral trade depends on two aspects. First, the adjustment of industrial structure in Yunnan and industrial transfer from the eastern area will contribute to promote Yunnan's industrial structure optimization and enhance its industrial competitiveness; consequently, the upgrading of industrial competitiveness will expand the demand for raw materials in other countries, which would guarantee the continuity of trade between Yunnan and Myanmar. Second, Myanmar needs to maintain a sound momentum of economic development, improve its level of industrialisation and increase the demand for its manufactured goods from other countries in order to ensure steady economic and trade exchanges between Yunnan and Myanmar.

4.2 Yunnan-Vietnam

As a country with robust economic development, Vietnam is enjoying rapid economic growth. Consequently, the product structure of its foreign trade will adjust gradually and the tradable range between Vietnam and Yunnan will expand, indicating a promising future for Yunnan-Vietnam trade. Therefore, the product mix must be expanded and trade scope further tapped to avoid centralization of the product mix in import-export. The expansion of tradable scope between Yunnan and Vietnam implies new requirements for both sides. Increasing the diversity of the industrial sector and establishing the sound credibility and core competitiveness of key industries are viable strategiesfor maintaining the current trade trend and further optimizing the development of future trade.

4.3 Yunnan-Laos

The analysis reveals that Yunnan-Laos trade also significantly exceeds the levels predicted by distance, relative economic size and development. To maintain this positive trend, Yunnan should fully understand the status of Laos' economic development via mutual communication. Hence, those industries and enterprises that have close trade links with Laos will be adjusted properly. In addition, Yunnan's small and medium size enterprises should be encouraged to invest in building factories in Laos to make use of the abundant cheap labour force and increase intra-industry trade.

4.4 Yunnan-Thailand

Sustainable trade development between Yunnan and Thailand necessitates expanding the trade scope and enriching the product mix. However, the Kunming-Bangkok Highway (which is open to traffic but with some cut-off) seems to be the key obstacle to the further expansion of bilateral trade. Only if the cost advantage of land transportation via the Kunming-Bangkok highway is tangible, can the tradable scope between Yunnan and Thailand be enlarged. The effective utilization of the Kunming-Bangkok highway demands not only the collaboration of China and Thailand, but also the participation of Laos. Such full-scale cooperation among China, Thailand and Laos would guarantee the implementation of trade facilitation, accommodate the differences in policies and deliver benefits to all three countries.

In terms of Yunnan, the central government's support would be a prerequisite and guarantee to resolve this problem. According to Yunnan Provincial Communications Department, permission for Thai commercial trucks to enter China is related to the traffic rights of national sovereignty and is subject to the approval of the Chinese State Ministry of Communications rather than the Yunnan Provincial Communications Department. Such problems call for local government to make greater efforts to coordinate different aspects and broaden their outlook to find policy resolutions so as to resolve issues concerning trade and transportation enterprises in realistic and pragmatic terms.

4.5 Yunnan-Cambodia

As the gravity model shows, the trade momentum between Yunnan and Cambodia is not impressive when compared with the other GMS countries. In the past ten years, Yunnan imported hardly any products from Cambodia, while it exported small quantities of certain products to Cambodia. The trade connection and trade complementarities between Yunnan and Cambodia are still at a rather lower level. This situation is largely due to geographical distance, plus the traffic barrier. Although the trade between Cambodia and Yunnan is not clear at this stage, it does not mean that there is no potential to be tapped.

Government departments and enterprises in Yunnan province should carry out in-depth study of Cambodia and get to know its industrial structure and economic development level so as to open more trade channels for Yunnan's enterprises and their counterparts in Cambodia and to gradually expand the trade scope between the two countries.

Notes

1. On 19 June 2007, the Ministry of Finance and the State Administration of Taxation jointly issued a circular named "Notice Regarding the Adjustment in Export Reform Rate for Certain Commodities" (Caishui [2007] No. 90) to announce the reduction and elimination of the export tax refund of pollution-inducing, high energy or natural resource-consuming products (as well as low value-added products).
2. One *mu* is approximately equal to 0.07 hectare.

References

Chai Zhengmeng. "The Comparative Empirical Analysis of the Relationship between Import-export Trade and Economic Growth in Guangdong and Yunnan". *Journal of Market Modernisation* 9 (2009).

Chatterjee, S. "Poverty Reduction Strategies-Lessons from the Asian and Pacific Region on Inclusive Development". *Asian Development Review* 22, no. 1 (2005): 12–44.

Chen Lizhong. "The Influence of Income Growth and Distribution on Rural Poverty Reduction in China". *Journal of Economy* 1 (2009): 53–59.

Dollar, D. and A. Kraay. "Trade, Growth and Poverty". *Economic Journal* 114, Issue 493 (February 2004): F22–F49.

Edmonds, C. and M. Fujimura. "Impact of Cross-border Infrastructure on Trade and Investment in the Greater Mekong Sub-region". Paper presented at LAEBA conference, ADBI-IDB Seoul, November 2007. ADB Institute, Tokyo.

Jenkins, Rhys and Chris Edwards. *How Does China's Growth Affect Poverty Reduction in Asia, Africa and Latin America?* Norwich: Overseas Development Group, University of East Anglia, 2004.

Li Shixin, Zhou Xinyue and Guo Xinhua. "Trade Liberalisation and Poverty Reduction in Rural China". *Journal of China Soft Science* 10 (2005).

Linder, S.B. *An Essay on Trade and Transformation*. Stockholm: Almqvist & Wicksell, 1961.

Mao Hui. "The Great Vitality of Regional Economic Cooperation". *Journal of China Statistics* (2006).

Poncet, S. "Economic Integration of Yunnan with the Greater Mekong Sub-region". *Asian Economic Journal* 20, no. 3 (2006): 303–17.

Roemer, M. and M.K. Gugerty. *Does Economic Growth Reduce Poverty?* CAER II Discussion Paper No. 4. Cambridge, MA: Harvard Institute for International Development, 1997.

Shen Chengxiang. "Empirical Analysis on China's Export-oriented Economic Growth". *Journal of World Economy* 8, no. 2 (1999): 26–30.

Wang Wei and Zhu Huibo. "Analysis of China's Foreign Aid Since the Reform and Opening-up". *Mao Zedong and Deng Xiaoping Theories Studies* 8 (2008).

Wilson, John S., Catherine Mann and Tsunehiro Otsuki. *Trade Facilitation and Economic Development Measuring the Impact*. Washington, D.C.: World Bank, 2003.

Xiang Guo-chun, Zhu Jinq-iu and Yan Zheng-min. "Research on the Definition of the Poverty Standard". *Chinese Health Resources* 2009-06.

Xiao Shuo, Zhi Yu and Li Bin. "Co-integration Analysis of the Relationship between Trade and Economic Growth of Yunnan". *Journal of Economic Issues* No. 2 (2006): 100–102.

Xue Baoshe. "Reflections on the Issue of Rural Poverty Reduction after China Practiced Opening-up Policy for Three Decades". *Inner Mongolia University Journal*, No. 2 (2009): 2–4.

Zhang Tianjia. "Trade Effect of China's Participation in the Greater Mekong Sub-region". *Journal of Economic Research Guide*, No. 25 (2009): 168–74.

Zhou Xiaoli. "Retrospect and Prospect of China's Participation in the Greater Mekong Sub-region Economic Cooperation". *Inner Mongolia University Journal*, No. 5 (2008): 112–13.

4

CHINA'S CAPITAL OUTFLOWS AND THE GMS-4

Wen Shuhui and Tu Xinquan

The research theme of this chapter is devoted to the influence of China's economic growth on its investment outflow and overseas development assistance (ODA) to the GMS-4 countries, namely Thailand, Vietnam, Laos and Cambodia. In this chapter we deconstruct China's foreign direct investment (FDI) outflow and ODA with a view to establishing past and current trends, and identifying possible future trends. Principally, China's FDI and ODA are looked at from the perspective of China and those of the GMS-4.

The first part of the chapter deals with the issues that relate to FDI outflow from China to the GMS-4, beginning by identifying where China's FDI outflow goes to and how China's FDI flow to the GMS has varied over space and time in terms of total volume, and sectors and enterprises invested in. The second section looks at the agreements that have facilitated this movement of FDI and discusses how these may influence future FDI outflows. The third section provides an analysis of the sources, their geographical distribution and the motivations underlying China's FDI outflows. Finally, the conclusion provides a summary of the key points and possible future policy directions.

The second part focuses on issues concerning China's ODA to the GMS-4. The first section provides a brief background to ODA from China and looks at a selection of literature on this topic. The second section considers motives and goals of China's development assistance to the GMS countries. The third section looks at the main forms of China's ODA to GMS countries while section four discusses the issues that relate to the future prospects for China's foreign aid policy towards GMS countries. Section five looks at the organizational and institutional arrangement of China's ODA. Section six concludes the discussion and provides some policy recommendations.

1. FDI TO THE GMS-4

1.1 Background

Current research on the issue of China's outward investment in the GMS still constitutes a piecemeal literature and lacks a systematic framework or much in-depth empirical or theoretical research and analysis. However, it can be said that countries in the GMS have outstanding advantages in attracting China's outward capital. The economic integration facilitated by ASEAN and the consolidation of regional economies in the GMS have led to China's increasing outward investment in this region. Given the trend of growing economic cooperation, Chinese FDI outflows to the GMS may increase even further in the future. Chinese scholars Du and Song (2004) constructed an analytical framework to predict the likely FDI effect of the China-ASEAN Free Trade Area and concluded that this agreement would facilitate increased Chinese investment in GMS countries.

Because of the geographical proximity of the GMS and southern China, many argue that GMS countries have a unique advantage in attracting China's FDI. Gao (2005) holds that in vertical FDI, the shorter the distance between the host country and the investing country, the lower the cost of transportation and the greater the information available to the investing country. Because the markets in the less well-off GMS-4 countries are not so developed, most FDI flowing to this area is of a vertical pattern, thus the GMS is extremely well placed to benefit in this regard. The economic integration of ASEAN and the consolidation of regional economies in the GMS have boosted China's outward investment in the region.

In the literature, there is controversy concerning the influence of China's economic growth on the GMS countries' (and to a larger extent ASEAN's)

FDI inflow profiles. The theoretical discussions of such literature give some meaningful insights into the present research. Some scholars argue that China has a positive influence on GMS countries' investment profile. For example, Wang (2007) points out that the benefits of international investment come from the increased welfare standards brought about by changes in the worldwide distribution of capital. Wang (ibid.) employs two gap models to describe the changing investment profiles of developing countries. Given that China and the GMS countries are both "developing", these two models could be employed to analyse the possible effect of China's investment in the GMS.

In fact, most literature concerning the influence of FDI on GMS countries focuses on its positive effects. In 2004, Kanta Marwah and Akbar Tavakoli utilized an empirical method based on time series data and found that FDI and exports in Indonesia, Malaysia, the Philippines and Thailand had positive effects on their economic growth and productivity. This finding concurs with the research findings of Jeffrey Sachs (2000), i.e., that imports and free inflow of FDI are the two main channels for absorbing advanced foreign technologies. On the basis of data concerning FDI in eighty-four countries from 1970 to 1999, Li and Liu (2005) assessed whether FDI impedes economic growth or not, and their research findings indicate that there is a high degree of correlation between FDI and economic growth.

Other scholars believe that China's FDI exerts negative influences on host countries. Chinese scholar Gong (2003) points out that as far as FDI is concerned, ASEAN could benefit in some respects, but there is also the possibility that the development of its own emerging industries could be stunted. Chia (1996) has elaborated on this issue, arguing that FDI tends to concentrate on mining natural resources and importing related substitutes which can have negative impacts on host countries' industrial development. Further, industries heavily reliant on FDI are vulnerable as the interests of domestic producers take second place to the protection of foreign producers' interests. Yan (2008) argues that though FDI in the GMS countries is increasing, the disparity among member countries in terms of investment and environmental policies has to some extent resulted in uneven capital distribution within each country and, in some cases, resulted in negative socio-economic and environmental impacts that damage prospects for sustainable development.

In practice, there is much controversy over the influence of FDI on economic growth: while many believe that FDI has positive effects, some researchers conclude that FDI has a profoundly negative impact. One reason for such controversy could be inadequate data availability. Borensztein, Gregorio and Lee (1998), however, point out that the varied abilities to absorb technologies could account for FDI's varying influence on economic growth in different countries. When FDI is fixed, a host country's high human resources investment could generate a high-yield growth rate. Bengoa and Sanchez-Robles (2003) state that the inflow of FDI is positively correlated with economic growth, but the precondition for this is that the host country must have related human resources, a stable economic environment and free markets. That said, other empirical research shows that FDI's positive effects are not always positively correlated with the ability to absorb technologies. For instance, Bende-Nabende et al. (2003) found that the long-term direct influence generated by FDI on production is bigger in the Philippines and Thailand than in Japan and Taiwan, even though the Philippines and Thailand evidently have poorer abilities to absorb technologies.

The impact of FDI on a host country's economic development hinges on a variety of factors including the nature of its economy and level of technological expertise as well as its cooperation with other countries. Kohpaiboon (2003) shares this view and states that the positive influence of FDI on economic growth is not generated automatically, but is related to the measures taken by different countries. He took Thailand as an example to illustrate the relationship between foreign trade policies and the influence of FDI on economic growth, that is, the positive influence of FDI on export-prompt countries is bigger than on import-prompt countries. She (2003) summarizes the issues around FDI inflows thus: "To utilise FDI to resolve the technological gaps depends on whether the host country boasts well-trained human resources and whether the enterprises of the host country could effectively utilise the acquired technologies to bring about reform and innovation without stop."

Those who hold to the "China threat theory" think that China's economic growth poses threats to its neighbouring countries' development, and while China's FDI enables host countries to become familiarized with and master advanced production technologies and management know-how, the host countries have many challenges to absorbing this knowledge. Moreover, if FDI results in a scale of foreign debt that becomes too large and exceeds the capacity of the national economy, debt expansion will trigger hyperinflation and eventually bring on an economic crisis. On this issue, Sun and Zhang (2008) found this to be the root cause of Vietnam's economic crisis: the huge influx of foreign investment pushed up asset prices in Vietnam and formed a bubble and when the bubble burst foreign capital flight took place as a consequence.

In some cases, China's FDI outflow to the GMS is characterized as being damaging to the natural environment. Specifically, China's continual investment in such sectors as mining, energy, tourism and agricultural development has led to the influx of pollution-intensive industrial projects in many GMS countries. Further environmental and ecological damage has occurred as China has developed the upper reaches of the Mekong River. However, environmental protection is of great and increasing importance in subregional cooperation. On this point, Wang Gucheng and Li Peng (2009) assert the importance of the environment and people's overall quality of life as key factors influencing the functional evolution of economic corridors. Therefore, all cooperation within the framework of the GMS should also attach great importance to both economic operations and crucially, the defining role of ecological systems in economic development. From this perspective, Chinese scholars Long Feng et al. (2009) come to this conclusion: China's increased national strength would deliver enormous benefits to its neighbouring countries and developed countries rather than pose a threat to any of them.

1.2 Distribution and Characteristics of Chinese FDI

This section analyses China's current FDI flow to the GMS-4. First a general overview and periodical analysis of China's FDI to the GMS-4 is provided. Then in order to gain a comprehensive picture of China's FDI in the GMS, the FDI in each of the GMS host countries, the sectoral distribution of China's FDI and the characteristics of recipient enterprises are analysed.

Figure 4.1 illustrates sharp fluctuations in China's annual aggregate FDI outflow to the GMS-4 between 2003 and 2008. China's FDI declined from 2003 to 2005, with 2005 registering the lowest point at US$51.27 million, and then it recovered dramatically from 2006 to 2008. The fluctuations were partially caused by the domestic political environment of some ASEAN countries from 2003 to 2005; for example, Myanmar witnessed intense conflicts and struggles among its military personnel, Union of Democratic League and ethnic groups; southern Thailand was plagued by frequent riots; the terrorism situation in Indonesia became more severe; and the Philippines was riddled with armed conflicts between government and

FIGURE 4.1
China's Aggregate FDI Outflow to GMS-4, 2003–08 (US$ million)

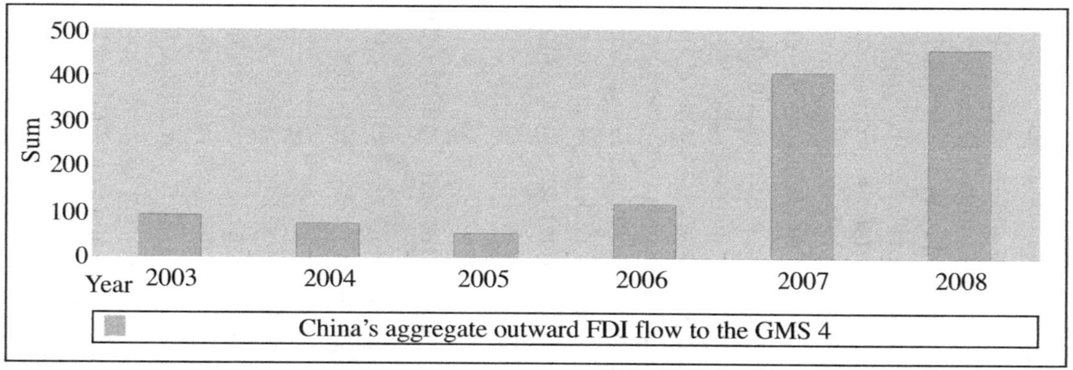

Source: Ministry of Commerce of China 2008; Statistical Bulletin of China's Outward Foreign Direct Investment <www.moftec.com.cn>.

anti-government troops. These instabilities not only affected local economic development, but also undermined investors' confidence. However, these countries attach great importance to improving the domestic political environment, for political stability is an important component of a country's environment. Affected by the slowdown in world economic growth in 2005 in particular, the influence of political stability in economic investment becomes more significant. As shown in Table 4.1, while China's annual outward FDI to the GMS-4 between 2003 and 2008 fluctuated sharply, overall it demonstrated a considerable increase. The annual rate of increase in 2006 and 2007 even exceeded the rate of China's total outward FDI to ASEAN at some points. However, 2008 saw a slowdown in the growth of FDI outflow due to the international financial crisis.

Looking at China's outward FDI to the GMS as a per centage of total Chinese FDI outflow, it can be seen from Figure 4.2 that 2003 registered as the highest point in the past six years, with China's total outward FDI to the GMS-4 representing 7.8 per cent of China's total outward FDI to ASEAN and about 0.03 per cent of China's total outward FDI. Since 2004, this ratio has increasingly declined, which indicates that China expanded its outward FDI to other countries and regions. According to the gradient of cross-border transfer of capital-exporting business rules, the export of capital is generally from developed countries to newly industrialized countries, to developing countries that have a relatively long history of development, and then to developing countries that have a relatively short history of development. It is easy for those countries in proximate stages of development to "team up" in terms of technologies, human resources and management, and to profit from their investments. For countries that are further apart in their development, it is difficult for the host countries' factors of production to meet the demands of investing countries, and difficult for investors to derive huge profits from their investment. Cambodia, Laos and Vietnam are countries with relatively low-level economic development in the GMS; from the theory of the gradient of the transfer of capital, they are the areas that receive a larger share of China's FDI. Thailand — the most developed of the GMS-4 — receives the least.

Even considering the above, from an aggregate perspective, China's FDI outflow to the GMS-4 has increased from US$92.81 million in 2003 to US$456.95 million in 2008: a fourfold increase in just six years, making China the most active investor in this region. As the figures for China's FDI in the GMS-4 were only systematically recorded from 2003, this research

TABLE 4.1
Chain Relative Ratio (CRR) of China's Outward FDI Flow by Country and Region, 2003–08 (US$ million)

Index Country/ region	2003	2004		2005		2006		2007		2008	
	Sum	Sum	CRR %	Sum	CRR %	Sum	CRR %	Sum	CRR %	Sum	CRR %
Total	2854.65	5497.99	92.60	12261.17	123.01	17633.97	43.82	26506.09	50.31	55907.17	110.93
Asia	1498.95	3000.27	100.16	4374.64	45.81	7663.25	75.17	16593.15	116.53	43547.50	162.44
ASEAN	119.32	195.56	63.90	152.56	–21.99	335.75	120.08	968.08	188.33	2484.35	156.63
Cambodia	21.95	29.52	34.49	5.15	–82.55	9.81	90.49	64.45	556.98	204.64	217.52
Laos*	0.80	3.56	345.00	20.58	478.10	48.04	133.43	154.35	221.29	87.00	–43.63
Thailand	57.31	23.43	–59.12	4.77	–79.64	15.84	232.08	76.41	382.39	45.47	–40.49
Vietnam*	12.75	16.85	32.16	20.77	23.26	43.52	109.53	110.88	154.78	119.84	8.08

Source: Ministry of Commerce of China: 2008 Statistical Bulletin of China's Outward Foreign Direct Investment <www.moftec.com.cn>.

FIGURE 4.2
Ratio of China's Total Outward FDI to GMS-4 and ASEAN

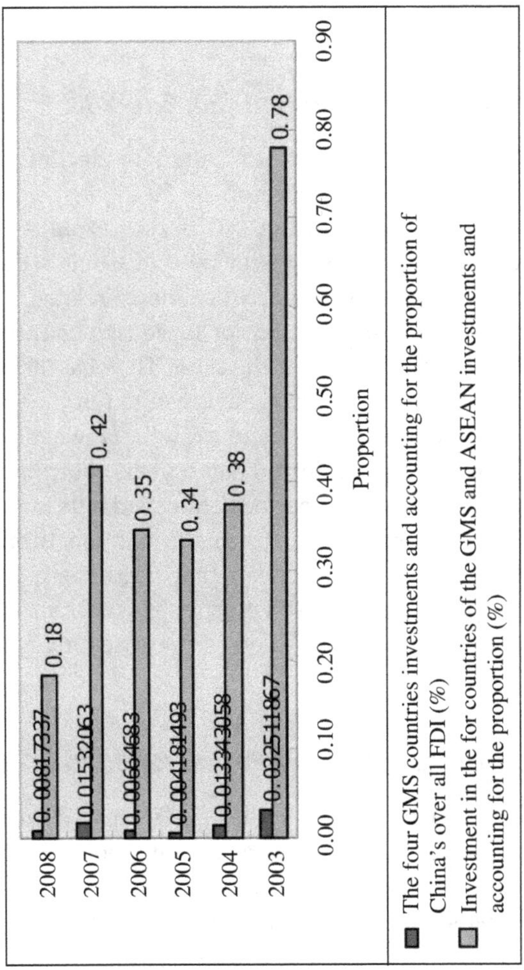

Source: Ministry of Commerce of China: 2008 Statistical Bulletin of China's Outward Foreign Direct Investment <www.moftec.com.cn>.

could only use the data from that time. According to the available figures, China's FDI in the GMS-4 has been on the increase, but it shows evident signs of fluctuations and trends. From 2003 to 2005 China's total FDI in the GMS-4 fluctuated heavily, and from 2006 it began to recover rapidly. From this perspective, China's FDI in these GMS countries can be divided into two periods.

Sluggish Period for Investment (2003 to 2005)

China's FDI in the GMS countries began to decline from US$92.81 million in 2003 to US$51.27 million in 2005. To be specific, China's FDI in Thailand and Cambodia during this period experienced the biggest drop and ended with the lowest ever flow of China's FDI in these two countries. The reason for the sharp decline is related not only to the economic and political environment of these two countries, but also to the state of the world economy at the time. The year 2005 saw oil prices on the international market soar, which resulted in a negative influence on international trade and investment growth. However, China's FDI in Vietnam and Laos increased in the same years, both in aggregate and proportional terms. During this period, China had little interest in investing in the GMS-4 but had small investments in manufacturing, mining and even a few hi-tech industries. Given that Laos has a lot of untapped mineral resources, many Chinese enterprises went there to explore and research their future potential. These enterprises invested in technical services and geological surveys.

Recovery and Stable Growth Period (2006 to 2008)

Generally speaking, China's FDI in the GMS increased during this period. As indicated in Figure 4.2, 2006 was the turning point as China's total FDI in the four countries had been in decline until then; from 2006 China's FDI increased rapidly. Although the overall investment was increasing, China's FDI in each of these four countries was significantly different. That in Laos continued to decline after 2007 because the country was plagued by severe natural disasters and epidemics during this period. Also, the changed international situation made Laos less attractive to FDI than other countries. However, China maintained its FDI flow to Vietnam during this period, and its FDI in Vietnam was hardly affected by Vietnam's worsening domestic economic crisis and hyper-inflation. China's FDI in Thailand increased but was still smaller in quantity in comparison with the other three GMS countries. China's FDI in Cambodia grew steadily during this period, both in amount and in proportion, in 2008. China's FDI in Cambodia accounted for 44.78 per cent of its total FDI in the GMS-4. All the statistics show that China's recognition of Cambodia's market potential has become ever greater in the past few years largely due to Cambodia's rapid economic development and its increasing attractiveness to investors. From 2006 to 2008, China's FDI in the GMS-4 was mainly in industries such as manufacturing, construction and mining. In addition, some FDI went to the hi-tech sector. For example, due to the low rate of telephone use and the untapped development of Internet use in Laos, many enterprises have already realized the potential of the hi-tech sector in Laos, and more and more Chinese enterprises are going there to set up and run local television networks, engaging in information transmission, services and the software industry.

FDI by Country

Thailand: China's outward FDI in Thailand has experienced sharp fluctuations, and from 2003 to 2008, the ratio of China's FDI in Thailand was in decline in comparison with that of the other three GMS countries. The lowest point of US$4.77 million was registered in 2005, while 2007 saw some recovery in China's FDI which dropped again in 2008. The reasons for China's FDI in Thailand falling to the lowest recorded level are: the tsunami in Thailand's six southern provinces at the end of 2004, the recurrence of bird flu, the widespread violence in three of the southern provinces, the drought in early 2005 as well as the continued high prices of world oil. In 2005, the Thai Government pursued a tight monetary policy, and Thailand's Monetary Policy Committee (MPC), in the face of inflationary pressures and the negative rate of actual savings, raised the benchmark repurchase rate seven times. Consequently, the high inflation and high interest rates greatly reduced the world's investment in Thailand. In 2008, Thailand's "People's Democratic Union" organized supporters to besiege government offices and stage large-scale demonstrations which seriously disrupted social order, undermined the economic development of Thailand and affected regional development and cooperation to some extent. Coupled with the global financial crisis, Thailand's instabilities significantly dampened any further FDI from China, and most Chinese enterprises adopted a wait-and-see approach.

Vietnam: China's FDI in Vietnam has been steadily growing, with a relatively high flow among the GMS-4, from US$12.75 million in 2003 to US$119.84 million in 2008. By the turn of the millennium, Vietnam had achieved a lot in terms of economic development, and its people have seen their income increase. Accordingly, Vietnam's domestic consumer demand grew and its domestic market potential has been further tapped. Many Chinese companies have realized the trend and prospects of this development, and have increased their investment in resources development and market exploration. In this context, Chinese companies have already seen Vietnam's potentially advantageous economic prospects in maintaining rapid economic growth given its low labour costs and abundant labour resources.

Cambodia: China's FDI in Cambodia has also fluctuated sharply in past years, with a low flow from 2003 to 2006. In 2005 China's FDI in Cambodia dropped to its lowest level of US$5.15 million and then rose only slightly to US$9.81 million in 2006. In 2005, the Cambodian riel depreciated many times; consequently the prices of commodities rose rapidly and Cambodia's internal inflation hindered China's investment and business activities to some extent. After the quotas on textile products were abolished in 2005, some Chinese enterprises presumed they could export textile products in large quantities and spent huge amounts of money buying production equipment to mass produce textile products. However, the United States and the European Union applied a variety of restrictions on importing China's textile products. Due to these factors, many Chinese enterprises had to set up factories and transit markets in Southeast Asia in a bid to circumvent restrictions from the United States and Europe, and Cambodia became China's first choice for overseas investment at that time. Since 2007, China's FDI in Cambodia has increased in leaps and bounds, including Jiangsu province which established Yangguang (Cambodia) Garment Co. Ltd in Cambodia in 2006. Shenzhou Knitting Group Co. Ltd of Ningbo (Zhejiang province) invested US$33.8 million in setting up textile factories in Cambodia so as to directly export textile products to U.S. markets, and the Red Bean Group, the star enterprise of China's clothing industry which is engaged in garment production and sales, also established Red Bean International Garment Co Ltd in Cambodia.

Laos: Due to its economic, industrial and resource characteristics, China's FDI flow to Laos grew quickly from US$0.8 million in 2003 to US$154.35 million in 2007. In addition, China's FDI flow to Laos peaked from 2004 to 2006, approaching 40 per cent of China's total outward FDI in the GMS-4, but then declined in 2008. In 2008, Laos was struck by its largest natural disaster since 1973, and some provinces were also plagued by epidemics of bird flu and dengue fever. In the first half of 2008, Laos was forced to raise gasoline prices eleven times because of rising gasoline prices in the international market, which led to inflation. Given the impact of the international financial crisis and the plummeting external demand, China cut back its FDI in Laos.

FDI by Sector

As can be seen from Table 4.2, China's established overseas enterprises fall into the categories of manufacturing, which share 31.3 per cent of China's total outward FDI, followed by wholesale and retail with 19.7 per cent, and leasing and business services with 14.5 per cent. The leasing and business services sector is for market surveys and information feedback, and investors have gradually realized the significance of investing in this sector and its role in directing enterprises by means of market demands and information collection. On the other hand, the sectors with the lowest shares of FDI are power and gas with 0.7 per cent, water production and supply with 0.9 per cent, and finance and real estate at 1 per cent.

Focusing on ASEAN, Table 4.3 shows that the three sectors receiving the greatest share of China's FDI outflow in 2008 are power and other utilities, manufacturing, and leasing and business services. Power and other utilities attracted the largest amount of China's total FDI flow to ASEAN, while the high-tech industries of IT, science research and services, and geo-survey had just a small share of the total flow, which shows that China's FDI in ASEAN is mainly used for natural resources exploitation.

As far as China's FDI in the GMS-4 is concerned, the distribution of China's FDI across all industries varies between different countries in different years. Generally speaking, Chinese enterprises mainly invest in

TABLE 4.2
Major Sectoral Categories of Chinese Overseas Enterprises by 2008-end

Industry	Share %
Residential services and other services	3.1
Agriculture, forestry, land husbandry, fishing	4.8
IT	2.4
Power and other utilities	0.7
Science research , services and geo-survey	3.1
Construction	6.8
Real estate	1.0
Manufacturing	31.3
Transport, warehousing and postal services	4.1
Mining	6.2
Wholesale and retail	19.7
Finance	0.9
Leasing and business services	14.5
Others	1.4
Total	100

Source: Ministry of Commerce of China: 2008 Statistical Bulletin of China's Outward Foreign Direct Investment <www.moftec.com.cn>.

TABLE 4.3
Major Sectors Receiving China's FDI in ASEAN, 2008 (US$ million)

Industry	Flow	Share %	Stock	Share %
Power and other utilities	1,175.71	47.3	1,385.46	21.4
Transport, warehousing, postal service	279.75	11.3	600.58	9.3
Leasing and business services	161.32	6.5	867.26	13.4
Wholesale and retail	92.07	3.7	704.30	10.9
Construction	162.86	6.6	489.88	7.6
Mining	241.75	9.7	438.38	6.7
Science research, services and geo-survey	23.07	0.9	120.60	1.9
IT	21.69	0.9	35.21	0.5
Agriculture, forestry, land husbandry, fishing	42.24	1.7	191.43	3.0
Real estate	0.59	0.0	24.45	0.4
Residential services and other services	5.13	0.2	13.44	0.2
Residential and catering trade	0.02	0.0	12.44	0.2
Manufacturing	237.15	9.5	1,141.48	17.5
Finance	41.00	1.7	454.00	6.9
Others	0.00	0.0	8.08	0.1
Total	2,484.35	100.0	6,486.99	100.0

Source: Ministry of Commerce of China: 2008 Statistical Bulletin of China's Outward Foreign Direct Investment <www.moftec.com.cn>.

manufacturing, power and other utilities, wholesale and retail, leasing and business services. We can employ the "Marginal Industry Expansion Theory" of Kiyoshi Kojima (1975) to account for this phenomenon. This theory asserts the potential for positive outcomes to result from FDI, especially for those countries that have the smallest relative gaps in technology, and that investing in enterprises with a similar level of technology would make it easier for Chinese overseas enterprises to find a starting point in a host country and also have a share of their foreign market. Kiyoshi Kojima posits the theory that even though China and the GMS-4 have disparities in their economic resources, such as physical assets, technological level, labour force, prices and so on, they could create a win-win result as long as China targets its FDI at industries that enable both sides to form a more rational combination of production factors and make full use of their complementarities.

As the world's largest developing country, China has a long way to go to develop its economy and gain many advantages in high-tech industry; however, it has higher international competitiveness in technologies related to manufacturing, petrochemicals, mining, and road and bridge construction. Meanwhile, a lot of second-hand equipment and a number of relatively mature and standardized technologies in China could find their market in the GMS-4. Given that the small-scale production techniques of China have matured, to transfer said techniques to the market demands would create complementarities for all parties concerned, not only in prioritizing the industrial mix of China and boosting domestic enterprises' profit margins, but also in facilitating the technologies of host countries.

For a long time, China has been committed to regional economic development and its foreign policy of "making its neighbouring countries prosperous and peaceful". As indicated in Kiyoshi Kojima's theory, such FDI could revitalize and promote the comparatively advantageous industries of host countries. Special accommodation must be made, however, for the host countries' needs, transplanting new industries and transferring new technologies in such an order as to promote their economic development step by step. FDI should play the "role of teaching" to bring about positive effects for local enterprises, enable local enterprises to improve labour productivity, teach and spread technologies and operational techniques to local enterprises, and enable local entrepreneurs to carry out their production independently. After fulfilling its role of teaching, FDI should transfer its ownership in phases. Being the neighbouring country of Cambodia, Laos, Thailand and Vietnam and one of the GMS developing country members, China has an obligation and responsibility to help these countries develop their economies and realize win-win outcomes.

FDI by Enterprise Characteristics

Having analysed the investment scale, periodical shifts, regional composition, investment flows and industries of the GMS-4 that received China's FDI from 2003 to 2008, here we analyse the types of enterprise that Chinese FDI manifests in the GMS-4. From this we hope to identify investment trends and predict which Chinese enterprises could become the main investors and in which country.

Among the Chinese enterprises investing in Thailand, the proportion of state-owned enterprises and group companies is small, while that of various privately owned limited companies is quite large. As shown in Table 4.4, Chinese enterprises investing in Thailand in 2004 were all limited companies, and from 2005 onwards, Thailand saw the entry of different investors such as state-owned enterprises and group companies. However, the proportion of privately owned limited companies is still the largest, and that of state-owned enterprises and group companies the smallest. Compared with limited companies and privately owned companies, group companies and state-owned companies have greater advantages in terms of technologies, capital and innovation. Consequently, they have higher competitiveness in FDI. Their occurrence in Thailand is a result of the country having a higher level of economic development, and thus being more suited to FDI outflows in the form of state-owned or group company enterprises than the other three countries, which are lagging behind in economic development and are poor in innovation, infrastructure, technological development, capital, human resources and industrial structure.

For Cambodia in particular, agriculture remains the largest pillar of its economy, and the overall structure of its industry is simple with the garment industry as the main player. Cambodia lacks enterprises that have their own research and development and manufacturing ability.[1] Therefore, investing in even small- and medium-sized enterprises, such as the limited companies of privately owned enterprises which have lower competitiveness in China, can achieve a competitive edge in Cambodia's economic landscape. Integrating FDI from state-owned Chinese enterprises and group companies into a country with an economic landscape such as

TABLE 4.4
China's FDI Enterprises in Thailand by Type and Share, 2004–08

Type of enterprise	2004		2005		2006		2007		2008	
	No.	Share %	No.	Share %	No.	Share %	No.	Share %	No.	Share %
State-owned enterprise	0	0.00	2	11.11	0	0.00	1	5.00	0	0.00
Limited company	0	0.00	9	50.00	11	73.33	14	70.00	12	60.00
Group company	2	100.00	3	16.67	3	14.00	3	15.00	7	35.00
Company limited by shares	0	0.00	4	22.22	1	6.67	2	10.00	1	5.00
Total	2	100	18	100	15	100	20	100	20	100

Source: Ministry of Commerce of China; 2008 Statistical Bulletin of China's Outward Foreign Direct Investment.

Cambodia's can be problematic as they have higher requirements from host countries. Limited domestic market capacity, talent pool and innovative capacity of this kind of host country would need to be reconciled with the needs of bigger, more advanced companies.

Further, in line with Kiyoshi Kojima's theory of comparative advantage, small- and medium-sized enterprises have advantages over large enterprises in investing in manufacturing industry because the technologies transferred by small- and medium-sized enterprises can be better suited to local factors of production, create more job opportunities for host countries, and optimize the industrial mix of host countries. Besides, small- and medium-sized enterprises have comparatively low-volume production, flexible operation and high adaptability. In order to develop their economies, the GMS-4 have eliminated various restrictions and further opened their markets to provide foreign investors with a variety of preferential policies, including tax reductions and low threshold market access to attract foreign investment. For instance, in a bid to attract FDI the Board of Investment (BOI) of Vietnam has lifted its restrictions on the ownership ratio of foreign investors and, regardless of the location of the factory, allowed foreign investors to hold the majority or all of the shares of the factory they invest in. The BOI also divided the seventy-six prefectures of Vietnam into three zones in line with economic development factors such as income and infrastructure, and granted differentiated investment incentives to different zones.[2] These policy measures practised by the GMS-4 have provided small- and medium-sized enterprises, which have difficulty surviving by investing in their own economically developed countries, the opportunity to find outlets in other countries. Consequently, more and more Chinese enterprises come to invest in the GMS-4.

1.3 Agreements Facilitating China's FDI in the GMS-4

As a member of the GMS, China regards strengthening its integration with other member countries and facilitating regional economic integration as an important foreign policy. Since China's FDI is under the management of the Ministry of Commerce of China, the policies for overseas investment issued by this ministry in the past few years are reviewed.

The bilateral agreements detailed in Table 4.5 facilitate Chinese enterprises "going out of China" in many aspects. Examples of such agreements that are seen as key in this regard include the "Agreement on Avoiding Double Taxation and Forestalling Tax Evasion" reached between China and Thailand in October 1986, the "Agreement on Avoiding Double Taxation and Forestalling Tax Evasion" signed between China and

TABLE 4.5
Signed Investment Agreements between China and GMS-4

	Related Agreements
Thailand	China and Thailand Agreement on the Promotion and Protection of Investment Agreement on Avoidance of Double Taxation and Prevention of Tax Evasion Twenty-first Century Partnership Joint Statement Joint Communiqué between China and Thailand
Vietnam	Encouragement and Reciprocal Protection of Investment Agreement with regard to the avoidance of double taxation and prevention of tax evasion
Laos	China and Laos Agreement on the Encouragement and Reciprocal Protection of Investment China and Laos Agreement to Avoid Double Taxation
Cambodia	Cambodia on the Promotion and Protection of Investment Agreements

Vietnam in May 1995, and the three "Agreements on Avoiding Double Taxation" reached between China and Laos in order to avoid and forestall double taxation.

The "Joint Communiqué between the People's Republic of China and the Kingdom of Thailand on Cooperation in the 21st Century" signed in 1999 highlights the fact that close cooperation through consultation and technical cooperation, particularly in the macro-economic and finance sectors, is necessary. Both sides committed to encourage and support the growth of two-way investment and fulfil current obligations in accordance with the investment agreement, utilize the raw materials and technologies of both sides to co-produce and co-develop industrial zones and industrial harbours, and cooperate closely in human resources development, giving priority to the development of small- and medium-sized enterprises. In the "Joint Communiqué between China and Thailand" signed in 2001, both sides are of the view that their cooperation in various fields, such as in politics, economy, culture, education, health, science and technology, have delivered benefits to both countries and peoples. Both sides agreed that the tariff rates of the ASEAN Free Trade Area should either be abolished or dropped to 5 per cent before 2002 and completely abolished by 2010. The Thai side hoped China would take this investment and trade opportunity to transfer its manufacturing industry to Thailand and other ASEAN countries. These agreements have played a guiding role in Chinese enterprises' FDI in the GMS countries, accelerated the "going out of China" pace of Chinese enterprises and expanded these enterprises' investment in the GMS-4.

Aside from bilateral agreements, China has also cooperated with and integrated into regional institutional frameworks, most notably in the construction of the China-ASEAN Free Trade Area. The Eighth China-ASEAN Economic and Trade Ministerial Meeting was held in Bangkok on 15 August 2009. During this meeting, Chen Deming, Chinese Minister of Commerce, signed the Investment Agreement of China-ASEAN Free Trade Area with the Ministers of Commerce from the ten ASEAN countries, marking the successful completion of the main aspects of the Agreement on China-ASEAN Free Trade Area, and this area is expected to be fully completed on schedule by 2010.

The Investment Agreement includes twenty-seven Articles and aims to promote investment liberalization and facilitation on both sides by granting national treatment, most favoured treatment and fair and equitable treatment for investors, improving the transparency of investment-related laws and regulations, creating a liberal, facilitative, transparent and fair investment environment for both sides, and providing adequate legal protection for investors.

The signing of this agreement sent a clear signal to the outside world that China and the ASEAN countries wish to help one another, work together to combat the international financial crisis, continue to promote trade and investment liberalization, oppose protectionism in trade and investment, and contribute to the economic recovery and development of the region and of the world at large. Also, the signing of this agreement built a new platform for constantly expanding investment and cooperation between China and ASEAN countries, created a more stable and open investment environment under the framework of the China-ASEAN Free Trade Area, reduced unreasonable restrictions and controls on mutual investment and created more investment and trade opportunities for enterprises on both sides and achieved mutual benefits and win-win results. This agreement provided institutional back-up for mutual investment between China and ASEAN countries and helped deepen and strengthen bilateral investment cooperation so as to complement each other with their own advantages, enhance competitiveness and promote the development of related industries on both sides.

China and the GMS-4 are members of China-ASEAN 10+1 Free Trade Area, and the above mentioned policies concerning investment agreements would definitely be employed in China's FDI in the GMS-4. In addition to these policies, the Chinese government is committed to promoting FDI in other respects. The Ministry of Commerce of China promulgates "The Management Approach on Overseas Investment" signed on 16 March 2009, which aims to decentralize the authority to approve the setting up of overseas enterprises, simplify the approval procedures and further implement the decision-making power of investment enterprises. This approach took effect from 1 May 2009. Thanks to cooperation among different departments, a co-management framework for FDI has been formed, which is characterized by "macro-management of the Ministry of Commerce, coordination among various departments, local management of local government, the linear supervision of industrial organisations, overseas Chambers of Commerce funded by China and its embassies, and co-management of inter-government".[3] After issuing the "Regulations on Projects Contracted with Other Countries" in 2008, China's Ministry of Commerce formulated "Regulations on Labour Cooperation with Other Countries and Regulations on Investment Cooperation with Other Countries" and established a more rational and effective management system. On 3 November 2009, Zhang Xiaoqiang, deputy director of the National Development and Reform Commission, stated that the Chinese Government would encourage qualified enterprises to carry out mutually beneficial FDI cooperation with other countries, and that China's overall foreign investment policy was to strengthen multilateral and bilateral cooperation, improve the legal and policy system, establish and complete the service system and improve enterprises' behaviour. These new policies on FDI could be employed in China's FDI in the GMS-4, further strengthening the structural framework for deploying FDI in the region.

1.4 Sources of FDI to the GMS-4

Sources of FDI from China

FDI sourced from China's provinces is mainly engaged in industries closely related to the utilization of natural resources such as mineral exploration, agriculture, forestry, animal husbandry, fishing and manufacturing. However, the geographical source of FDI depends on various factors. For example, figures from 2003 to 2008 indicate that Yunnan province had the largest proportion of FDI in Laos, mainly due to its geographical proximity. Provinces such as Hunan, Hebei and Shandong also invested in Laos, specifically in mineral exploration and extractive industries, agriculture, forestry, animal husbandry, fishing and manufacturing; their manufactured products are also closely related to natural resources. Laos has tin, lead, potassium, copper, iron, gold, coal, salt and other minerals, and only tin, gypsum, potassium, salt and coal have been explored. Additionally, Laos' forests are at a low altitude and abound with valuable timber. Therefore, the FDI of China's provinces has been focused on the development and utilization of natural resources in Laos.

When it comes to FDI destined for labour-intensive industry in Cambodia, apart from Dalian city and Zhejiang province which were sources of FDI in 2005, FDI comes from economically developed provinces and municipalities such as Hunan and Chongqing in the central and western regions of China. From 2006 onwards, an increasing number of coastal cities and provinces such as Ningbo city and Jiangsu and

Shandong provinces have FDI in Cambodia; Jiangsu province in particular, is the biggest investor. These provinces and cities are mainly engaged in manufacturing industry, with garment production accounting for a large proportion. There is also FDI in mineral research and in the development of various other enterprises.

Similarly, when it comes to total FDI in Vietnam, Jiangsu province and Shanghai city are its biggest investors, and their investment goes largely to the manufacturing industry with a wide range of products, and involves a large number of categories like mining, mineral exploration and the export-import trade of mining products, manufacturing and processing of hardware, and the production and sales of rubber rollers, rubber products, rubber machinery, plastic products, plastic machinery and raingear.

Provinces and cities of China that have FDI in Thailand are mainly from more developed coastal areas like Jiangsu and Shanghai, and most of their investment goes to the manufacturing industry, ranging from machinery to household items. In addition, the construction industry, led by Ningbo city, has a wide scope of engineering contracts from basic housing construction projects and decoration to large-scale projects such as the design and construction of water conservation infrastructure, cable and fibre optic cable installation. All this indicates that the development of China's construction industry in Thailand is relatively mature.

From this analysis, the location of the sources of Chinese FDI varies depending on the economic and geographical attributes of the city or province and the location and sectoral attributes of the host country or industry. Shanghai, Jiangsu, and Shandong, for example, focus on FDI outflows to the manufacturing industry, whereas Yunnan looks to mineral extraction in Laos.

The reason for the changing nature of China's FDI outflows stems from the (uneven) development of the country. China's coastal provinces and cities are the generators of China's economic growth. The top seven cities and provinces in 2008 in terms of per capita GDP were Shanghai, Beijing, Tianjin, Zhejiang, Jiangsu, Guangdong and Shandong, all with per capita GDP above US$4,000 (national average = US$2,000).[4] These cities and provinces are in the fourth phase of the investment cycle, so the growth of their FDI flow is faster than that of their foreign capital inflow, and their net FDI amounts to an increasing and positive figure. Some central and western areas, such as Guizhou, Gansu, Yunnan and Tibet are in the second phase of the investment cycle, and the rest of the provinces and regions are in the transformation period between the second and third phase. Therefore, it is not difficult to understand why the eastern coastal provinces of China are the major investors in the GMS countries.

1.5 Motives behind China's FDI Disbursement

The common motive for developed countries and developing countries alike is to derive socio-economic and political benefits from their FDI. The GMS-4 are rich in natural resources, abundant low-cost labour and have favourable foreign investment policies, which could lead to win-win results for both sides. Therefore, resources, market and efficiency of investment are the vital factors among China's motives and patterns for investing in the GMS countries, and China's policies and the appreciation of the renminbi are two driving factors that cannot be ignored.

Resource-oriented FDI

With its rapid economic development in recent years, China needs ever-more strategic resources. In today's world of economic globalization, a country's economic development increasingly hinges on its ability to integrate a global range of natural resources to expand the scope of its economic development and provide long-term and reliable resources for the region. In order to develop their own economies sustainably, the six GMS countries are expected to cooperate so that their economic development will not be hampered by insufficient resources, and resources will not be wasted because of inadequate techniques of resource extraction.

Among the GMS countries, China has advantages of capital, technologies, human resources and management expertise in natural resource exploitation. However, much of the GMS-4's natural resources still await exploitation, and to this end, China is expected to grant these countries more financial and technological assistance, which would not only fuel China's economic development, but also improve the resource exploitation abilities of the four countries. Consequently, countries could complement each other with their own resource advantages which would lead to a win-win situation. For example, in 2009 China and Laos co-invested and set up Nam Ngum hydropower station in northern Laos, an underdeveloped area, which now provides cheap but high-quality electricity and plays a vital role in promoting resource exploitation and coordinating the development of industries in related areas, thus optimizing the industrial structure and boosting the rapid development of the Lao economy.

Market-oriented FDI

Market-oriented FDI accounts for a large proportion of China's FDI in the GMS. Although the economic development of the countries in the GMS is in its infancy, the pace of development is relatively fast. Taking 2008 as an example, Cambodia had the highest economic growth rate in the GMS at 14.5 per cent, followed by China at 9.9 per cent, Thailand at 9.8 per cent, Laos at 7.9 per cent and Vietnam at 6.2 per cent.[5] The rapid development of the GMS-4 has created a huge demand for capital, technologies, human resources, machinery, and equipment, and the development prospects of such industries as manufacturing, mining, construction, leasing and business services in the four GMS-4 are bright. Some of the key industries in the GMS-4 suffer from overproduction in China; therefore, it is the best foreign location for Chinese enterprises to tap into their hosts domestic and export market. In this case, both China and the GMS-4 will win from China's FDI outflow.

The GMS-4 countries have a combined population of 170 million which constitutes a huge potential market for consumer goods. Taking Vietnam as an example, its total sales of commodities and services amounted to US$58.63 billion in 2008, an increase of 31 per cent over previous years. Such market demand would bring Chinese enterprises a lot of benefits if they were to invest in wholesale and retail industries in Vietnam. The GMS-4 will also benefit from a huge market in the near future. On the basis of such development, more and more Chinese enterprises pursue similar market-oriented FDI. During our surveys and interviews, we found that Chinese enterprises are committed to seeking markets with investment potential, whether these markets are large or small.

Efficiency-oriented FDI

Like transnational companies in developed regions, Chinese transnational companies also seek areas of geographical proximity that have lower labour and transportation costs in which to invest. For China, the least developed countries in the GMS are undoubtedly its best choice. On the one hand,

China could reduce the cost of transporting large-scale machinery when investing in setting up factories because of geographical proximity. On the other hand, even if the cost of labour in China is low, wages in the GMS countries are even lower. As indicated in Table 4.6 (data taken from the field investigation of FDI in developing countries conducted by the Multinational Investment Guarantee Agency of the World Bank), a comparison of Vietnam (the host country receiving the largest amount of FDI inflow in the GMS) with Thailand (the country with the largest amount of FDI outflow in the GMS) shows that there are huge salary gaps between the two countries, and in particular, there is a double salary gap in the management sector. Such salary gaps made it possible for efficiency-oriented FDI to develop in the GMS. Taking Yunnan province (the main and front practitioner of China's FDI in the GMS) as an example, the average salary in this province was US$243.8 in 2007, which exceeded the average salary of a technician in Vietnam. In such cases, Chinese companies would reduce the cost of production if they were to carry out production and provide services in these low-salaried countries. Therefore, China's efficiency-oriented FDI has a bright future in the GMS-4, and such efficiency-oriented FDI would deliver benefits to China as well as to the GMS-4. China could not only reduce its production costs by employing cheap labour in the four countries, but also help these countries resolve their employment problem.

Policy-oriented FDI

At the GMS Economic Cooperation Ministerial Meeting in 2003, Chinese Minister Tang Jiaxuan stated that China practises a nation-friendly approach and vowed to be the best neighbour, friend and partner to other ASEAN countries. This is a vital part of Chinese foreign policy. Additionally,

TABLE 4.6
Comparison of Salary Rates in Thailand and Vietnam (monthly wages US$)

Country	Unskilled labour	Specialized worker	Technician	Manager	Insurance proportion (%)
Thailand	118	162	315	889	20
Vietnam	84	135	206	393	20

Source: Multilateral Investment Guarantee Agency, World Bank Group.

Tang put forward the concept of "stabilizing neighbouring countries and enriching them", which shows that China would not only like to boost the economic development and revitalization of the GMS, but also wants to closely link its development with that of the GMS countries. Such a foreign policy outlook is one of the driving forces which strengthen China's FDI in the GMS-4. As a big country in the GMS, China finds that its relationship with neighbouring countries is significant to its own foreign strategy. As the GMS member country with the highest level of economic development and the largest potential for development, China has large foreign exchange reserves, while the GMS-4 countries need capital to improve their industrial capability. In its role as a neighbouring country of the GMS-4, and as a responsible developing country in the international community, China would like to shoulder its obligation to help other GMS countries develop their economies and increase its economic assistance to these countries. Over the years, while accepting assistance from the international community to develop its own economy, the Chinese government has insisted that its foreign policy is committed to developing the regional economy and granting help to the economically less developed countries in the GMS, including transferring capital and technologies, the training of labour and high-level management personnel by investing and establishing factories, and cooperating in various sectors. In the future, with China's economic development, the Chinese government intends to increase its development assistance to the governments of the GMS countries and carry out more aid projects in these countries.

Exchange Rate-oriented FDI

In the past few years, under pressure from Western countries headed by the United States, the renminbi exchange rate continued to appreciate against the U.S. dollar, which made China's exported products relatively expensive and created huge pressure on China's export companies. Such companies faced ever increasing challenges to their business due to reduced profits. Under such circumstances, these companies might consider leaving China and investing in other countries and setting up factories there. Such a practice would not only avoid negative impacts generated by the appreciation of renminbi on China's exports, but would also reduce the costs of the payroll, purchase of raw materials, machinery and equipment, and upgrading equipment. Indeed, when the Japanese yen appreciated sharply in the 1980s, Japan's FDI in other countries increased rapidly at the same time. In the preceding analysis, we saw that China's FDI increased by a large margin in 2005, but its FDI flows to Thailand, Laos, Vietnam and Cambodia were on the decline before 2005. After 2005, China's FDI flow to these countries increased significantly. This phenomenon indicates that a country's FDI is related to its currency exchange rate against the currencies of host countries.

1.6 Conclusion and Policy Recommendations

The discussion in the first section illustrates that China's FDI flow to the GMS-4 has fluctuated widely and increased rapidly in recent years, yet it still accounts for only a small fraction of China's total FDI outflow. Although the absolute flow of China's FDI grew rapidly, as a percentage of China's total investment in ASEAN, China's total FDI has actually declined. The destinations of China's FDI have also changed. Thailand is strategically located in the centre of Southeast Asia and is the most economically developed of the GMS-4. Statistics show that the share of China's FDI in Thailand in recent years has been smaller than in the other three GMS countries. While being the most developed of the GMS-4, with relatively sound infrastructure and higher degrees of transparency and trade liberalization, the cost of investment in Thailand is relatively high and recent political turmoil has increased investment risks. Although Thailand's economic development level is higher than that of the second most developed of the GMS-4, Vietnam, its overall ability to attract FDI is relatively small. Vietnam's competitiveness in the investment environment lies mainly in its political stability, sound economic development prospects, huge market potential, transparent policies, and improved market access. Also, Vietnam has geographical advantages in ASEAN, relatively low costs of labour and land, and high-quality human resources (Vietnam has the highest literacy rate among ASEAN countries), which would bring more benefit to its investors.[6] Consequently, Thailand is second to Vietnam in attracting the FDI of other countries. By the end of 2008, China's FDI stock in Vietnam was the largest among the four countries.

Laos and Cambodia are among the world's least developed countries as identified by the World Bank. Cambodia in particular, has a poor industrial foundation and infrastructure, low-capacity technologies, a poor pool of talent and funds and no enterprises with independent research development and innovation capability. Therefore, its attraction to FDI is poor.[7] China's FDI flow and stock in Cambodia was not large in 2003; but from 2003 to 2008 great changes occurred in China's FDI in the GMS-4 countries in that its FDI flow to Laos peaked in 2007 and that to Cambodia reached its highest level in 2008. All these changes give credit to the economic development of these two countries. Laos has rich natural resources, abundant untapped mineral and agricultural resources, as well as rich hydropower capability. In recent years, the Lao government has been increasing infrastructure improvement.[8] Since 2004, Cambodia's economy has developed rapidly, and its government has implemented open market economy policies which have enhanced the liberalization of its economic operation. According to the "Ranking of Economic Freedom Index in 2006" of the Heritage Foundation in the United States, Cambodia was second to Singapore among ASEAN countries, and its index of "non-government interference in, or restriction of, economic activities" ranked ninth among the thirty-two countries in Asia.[9] All of these factors increased Cambodia's attraction to foreign FDI, and China's FDI in Cambodia increased by a large margin.

In terms of the sectoral distribution of China's FDI to the GMS-4, we have found a preference to invest in primary commodity extraction and manufacturing rather than hi-tech industry. China has a greater advantage in the manufacturing industry because of its knowledge of production processes. Although it has recently strengthened its ability in innovation and scientific research in hi-tech industries, China is still at a disadvantage when it comes to the fierce competition in the global hi-tech industry. Therefore, it is wise for China to benefit from its investment in the industries in which it has advantages. However, from a long-term perspective, it is far from enough for a country to depend on its own manufacturing industry if it wants to optimize its domestic industrial structure and get an upper hand in the competition for international markets. In addition, the GMS-4 are still poor in their hi-tech industry and need the technology and information of investing countries to raise their technological level and the quality of their human resources so as to optimize their own domestic industrial structure.

In recent years, with the growth of China's economy, the improved investment environment in the GMS as well as the boosted economic development of countries in this region, a lot of Chinese enterprises have realized the broad development prospects and untapped business opportunities in the hi-tech industry of the GMS-4. For instance, in 2006 Guangda Electronic Telecommunications Technology Development Co. Ltd of Chengdu in Sichuan province set up Savannakhet Cable TV Co. Ltd, a local cable TV network engaged in information transmission, computer services and software services, in Laos. However, the overall pattern of China's FDI in the GMS countries has not changed, and FDI in the hi-tech industry is in the minority. Therefore, in its future investment China should take the development of the whole region into consideration, invest in such industries as scientific research, computer services and software in the GMS-4, promoting and optimizing the industrial structure in this region.

In terms of China's FDI enterprise characteristics in the GMS-4, we found that limited companies rather than group companies and state-owned companies are the main routes of investment. In terms of China's total FDI outflow from 2004 onwards, as the objects of China's FDI became more diversified, group companies and state-owned companies, especially state-owned enterprises and enterprises whose stocks are held by the state, increasingly lost their share of total FDI outflows to privately owned enterprises and joint-stock enterprises. Statistics from the Ministry of Commerce in 2008 indicate that limited liability companies ranked first among China's FDI investors, state-owned enterprises ranked second and had declined by 3.6 per cent and privately owned enterprises had increased to 9.4 per cent.[10] When it comes to China's FDI in the GMS countries, however, the situation is even more exaggerated with a larger share of FDI coming from limited companies and privately owned enterprises. This is because of the economic structure, level of development and market capacity of the GMS-4.

Looking at the geographical sources of the FDI bound for the GMS, a large proportion of the total originates in the east coast provinces and cities. FDI flow from the central and western provinces has been relatively small, leading to regional imbalance. Due to historical factors, poor infrastructure and an insufficient pool of talent, the economic development of central and western provinces and regions of China has been uneven for a long time, and their GDP has had great gaps. The economically developed east coast provinces and regions not only have plentiful financial resources to develop their economy, but also have sufficient funds to go out of their own provinces or regions, or China, to invest and optimize their industrial structure. Conversely, some central and western provinces and regions, until now, have been the core subjects of China's financial support. Their economic development greatly needs funding, and so their FDI in other countries is still in its infancy.

The section has identified a large number of motivating factors underlying China's FDI outflows to the GMS, all of which are complementary to the interests of both the GMS and China. Raw material exploration will secure resources for China and enable GMS countries to benefit from Chinese knowledge, resulting in more efficient resource extraction. China's FDI to the GMS is also driven by market incentives: first, a desire to find access points to new markets; and second, to exploit the wage gap between itself and the GMS-4 (possibly with the exception of Thailand) and benefit from lower production costs in general. GMS countries benefit through higher rates of employment and skill and knowledge transfer, which hastens industrial development. Similarly, the appreciation of the renminbi has resulted in Chinese companies locating industry elsewhere to remain competitive. Finally, from a policy point of view, China's interest in and commitment to a thriving GMS strategically contributes to its own economic health through potentially providing a large market with a complementary industrial structure that will enhance China's own long-term growth.

Policy Recommendations

China should increase investment to the GMS-4. In the past six years, China's total outward FDI to the GMS-4 peaked in 2003, representing 7.8 per cent of China's total outward FDI to ASEAN and about 0.033 per cent of China's total outward FDI to the world. However, since 2004 this ratio has become increasingly smaller. Although China's outward FDI to the GMS-4 has been increasing rapidly, it still represents less than 10 per cent of China's total outward FDI to ASEAN and less than 0.1 per cent of China's total outward FDI. This indicates the broader country and regional range of China's total outward FDI; meanwhile it shows that there is great potential for China's outward FDI to the GMS-4.

China should expand the range of industries which its outward FDI to the GMS-4 represents at present. China's FDI in industries varies between different countries in different years. However, China's established overseas enterprises in the GMS-4 fall into the categories of manufacturing, which shares 31.3 per cent of China's total outward FDI, followed by wholesale and retail with 19.7 per cent, and leasing and business services with

14.5 per cent, which shows that China's FDI mainly targets the exploration of natural resources and labour intensive manufacturing industries and thus could make a greater contribution to local employment and technology transfer by diversifying from these core areas. In the future, China should put more effort into investing in high-tech industries like IT, science research and services, and geo-surveying.

China should consider encouraging large state-owned enterprises and group companies to invest in the GMS-4. Among the Chinese enterprises investing in the GMS-4, the proportion of state-owned enterprises and group companies is small, while that of various privately owned limited companies is quite large. Compared with limited companies and privately owned companies, group companies and state-owned companies have greater advantages in terms of technologies, capital and innovation. Therefore, with the rapid economic growth in the GMS-4, the Chinese government should consider taking certain measures to encourage large state-owned enterprises and group companies to invest in these countries both in the future and in response to their development trajectories.

2. ODA TO THE GMS-4

2.1 Background

Since the early 1950s, more than 160 countries and regions have received aid from China in various forms. The outcomes of Chinese aid are partly dependent on how the recipient countries utilize it, and partly on its deployment and the underlying policy goals. While Africa continues to be the largest recipient of Chinese aid, Southeast Asia, in particular the less developed countries in the GMS, has been receiving more development assistance from China in recent years. This chapter reviews China's development assistance policy towards the GMS countries, with a view to helping them better understand and utilize China's aid.

Only in recent years has China, as a donor of development assistance, begun to attract more attention. A number of papers and reports on China's development assistance or foreign aid have been published both by Chinese and international scholars. Among them, Chinese researchers pay much attention to the principles and strategies and the implementation of Chinese foreign aid from the Chinese perspective, while foreign scholars are more concerned about the motives and impacts of China's foreign aid.

However, only a few studies touch upon the poverty reduction effects of China's development assistance to the GMS countries.

Zhang (2006) has made the most comprehensive investigation so far of the historical evolution of China's foreign aid. She divides China's foreign aid experience into five phases: 1950–63, 1964–70, 1971–78, 1979–94, and 1995 to the present. She puts all the major changes of China's foreign aid policy and activities into specific historical context, showing that shifts in China's economic and political situations ultimately determine the priorities and objectives of its foreign aid. Qiu (2006) reviews China's foreign aid before the reform, principally looking for factors explaining why pre-reform China provided external assistance in such difficult economic circumstances. While claiming that this policy had its relevance and values, he also highlights several shortcomings and mistakes of China's foreign aid during that period. Zhou (2008) reviews the development of China's foreign aid since the reform and opening up in the early 1980s. The study pays much attention to Deng Xiaoping's thoughts on China's foreign aid policy and the resulting shift in China's role from an aid recipient to an aid donor. She describes the changes in the guiding principles, policy tools, and decision-making process of China's foreign aid during the reform era. Wang and Zhu (2008) study the same themes, highlighting very similar issues. Chin and Frolic (2007) also briefly overview the evolution of Chinese foreign aid policy, noting that the eight principles[11] are still the main guiding values while China has not issued a formal foreign aid policy.

With regard to China's foreign aid principles or strategies, Zhang (2006) concludes that China's foreign aid is rooted in its traditional culture, internationalist spirit, external extension of a united front theory, and mutual benefits values. However, she points out that since the reform, China's foreign aid has prioritized its own national interests over ideological considerations, and put more emphasis on economic returns than political support. Li and He (2008) argue that China should adjust its strategic goals, administrative mechanism and monitoring system in the field of foreign aid because of the great changes in international political and economic arenas. They believe that China should take "a harmonious world" and "mutual development" as the guiding principles of its foreign aid policy and prioritize strategic goals such as supporting China's overall diplomacy, assuring steady supply of energy and commodities, assisting Chinese companies' foreign investment, and disseminating China's developmental model and values. Zhang (2008) puts China's foreign aid in the context of China's overall diplomatic strategies. He states that foreign aid is the important component of China's peaceful diplomacy strategy and that China should develop foreign aid in a more active way.

While Chinese scholars use terms like strategies and principles as shaping aid distribution, foreign scholars use a different lexicon, one that stresses China's self-serving motives and objectives behind its foreign aid activities. Although Chinese and foreign scholars might discuss the same issue, they often have different perspectives and observations. Chinese scholar, Lum (2009), while accepting that China's foreign assistance during the past several years has been driven to a large extent by Beijing's desire to secure and transport natural resources, does not necessarily see this as a negative. Rather, he argues that even though access to natural resources plays a prominent role in China's engagement in Southeast Asia, for example, long-term strategic interests are likely to influence China's activities to a greater extent in Asia than they do in Africa and Latin America. Many of China's aid activities in the region appear to provide relatively greater long-term diplomatic benefits and comparatively few short-term economic ones.

While Lum (ibid.) highlights that Chinese aid destined for development projects can yield long-term benefits for the recipient country, Davies (2008) sees China's aid as more parasitic in nature; he argues that it pays little attention to the long-term development of the recipient country and is geared only to extracting resources. Based on his research on China's foreign aid to Africa, Davies (ibid.) concludes that the main motive underlying China's interest in Africa is to secure energy and resource assets. In order to hedge against immediate rises in commodity prices and possible long-run supply shortages, the Chinese government has encouraged its companies to secure a wide range of commodity assets. The Chinese government's aid policy plays an important role in supporting these companies (largely state-owned enterprises) to outbid foreign companies so as to secure these resource assets. Also, political factors continue to play an important part in the relationship. In Laos, for example, The China Development Brief (2006) argues that China's emphasis has shifted from political gain to economic gain through exploiting the country's natural resources. To this end, along with its aid, China has also paid more attention to technical and human resources assistance to Laos. Hubbard (2007) suggests that the purpose of Chinese concessional lending is more to do with promoting the export of Chinese products than the economic development of recipient countries.

On the administration of China's foreign aid, scholars share many common criticisms. Lack of inter-agency coordination is the most concerning aspect of China's foreign aid administration. Chin and Frolic (2007) notice that China's development assistance programming is scattered across a number of government units. Zhou (2008) suggests that there is no government agency responsible for the general coordination of foreign aid, resulting in China not having formulated a consistent and coordinated foreign aid policy. Davies (2008) also finds that aid spending is quite disorganized and lacks effective coordination in China. Li and He (2008) propose that China should establish a unified decision-making mechanism for foreign aid and clarify the division of labour among relevant ministries. Also, the development of an evaluation and supervision mechanism that builds on the experiences of other aid-giving countries is suggested. Huang (2007) reviews China's foreign aid administrative system, in particular, pointing out five problems and putting forward some suggestions on how to reform this system. Hubbard (2007) focuses on the concessional loans of China Exim Bank, explaining the operational procedures, the main borrowers, and the quantity of concessional loans. Xu (2008) discusses operational issues in China's foreign aid, describing how projects are decided and carried out. He finds some problems with the process and makes some suggestions as to possible reforms.

When evaluating the success of China's foreign aid, two different sets of criteria are used. One is from the Chinese perspective, focusing on whether foreign aid fulfils China's objectives. The other is the foreign perspective, focusing on whether China's foreign aid is good for the recipient countries. From the Chinese perspective, Zhang (2006) claims that China's foreign aid has enhanced China's international influence, promoted bilateral relations with recipient countries, gained significant political support and economic returns as well as supported the economic and political development of recipient countries. Zhu (2008) notes foreign concerns about the impacts and intentions of China's foreign aid and analyses the reasons for these concerns. For example, China's principle of non-interference is viewed by some Westerners as a threat to their efforts towards democratization in Africa. Zhu defends China's policy, but also suggests that China should cooperate with and learn from Western countries to achieve better results from aid to Africa. However, due to the lack of relevant data and clear policy statement, these evaluations are rather primary, some of which are even biased. So enhancing transparency in foreign aid is desirable for the Chinese government to eliminate misunderstanding and criticism.

2.2 Motives and Goals of China's Development Assistance to the GMS Countries

In its official statements, the Chinese Government never explicitly identifies its own goals with regard to its provision of foreign aid. Officially, the eight principles proposed by Premier Zhou Enlai in 1964 are still considered the guidelines for Chinese foreign aid policy. The fourth principle claims the "purpose" of Chinese foreign aid is to help the recipient countries develop by themselves. What China wants from the recipient remains unsaid.

In general, analysts agree that China's foreign aid has always been a foreign policy tool. The provision and allocation of foreign aid is mostly determined by China's overall diplomatic agenda. More specifically, in the early years, ideological reasons such as internationalism and the external extension of the united front theory once played a great role in the decision making of Chinese foreign aid. By providing aid to poor friends in the world, China established something of a bond or relationship with them. These Cold War alliances, in particular with African countries, greatly helped China get back into the international arena. Since the reform at the end of the 1970s, China's foreign aid policy has adapted to changing circumstances. China no longer needs ideological allies because it has eased its tension with the West since taking a more market-oriented economic development approach. Geopolitical and economic benefits have become the most important factors affecting Chinese aid policy.

Since aid and development assistance are tools used as part of a broader strategy to meet China's strategic long-term objectives, it is necessary to see its foreign aid policy in the context of the broader drivers of the country's engagement with the GMS or the wider Southeast Asian region. In its diplomatic strategy, China always puts the relationship with its neighbouring countries first. Although the wording of Chinese diplomatic policy is somewhat confusing, the government is seriously exercising so-called "Good Neighbour" diplomacy to maintain a peaceful and stable regional environment in which China can pursue its goal of economic development, and to promote Chinese leadership and influence within the context of an East Asian community. So, strategic and geopolitical interests are likely to influence China's foreign aid to Southeast Asia to a greater extent than they do in Africa or Latin America, which are now major providers of natural resources to China.

Although political factors dominate China's foreign policy towards the GMS, economic reasons are playing a more important part in the relationship. The Chinese government tends to use aid as part of a package of tools to support Chinese companies in expanding their export markets and business scope overseas. China's "Go Out" Strategy, launched in 2002, aims to create a number of "national champions" — globally competitive enterprises which will act as foreign commercial policy vehicles for China. Government aid provides Chinese companies with a distinct advantage in overcoming protectionism and regulatory red tape. In recent years, the government has financed many infrastructure, energy-related (especially hydropower), agricultural, and other high-profile development projects around the world which also rely upon Chinese construction materials, equipment, technical expertise, and labour. The rapid development of the GMS countries, especially Vietnam, presents a great commercial opportunity for many Chinese companies.

China's increasing foreign aid to Africa has aroused concerns and anxieties in the West, with the fear that the non-conditionality of China's loans will encourage poor policies and increase debt burdens for recipient countries. In comparison, Chinese aid to the GMS has been paid less attention since China's motivations are not so obviously oriented to its self-interest. For the GMS recipients, China's aid is helpful to them regardless of whether it is politically or economically motivated. A good political and economic relationship with China is beneficial for their development.

2.3 Main forms of China's ODA to the GMS Countries

According to the OECD Development Assistance Committee's (DAC) definition, grants or loans that are extended to developing countries constitute ODA when they are undertaken by the government or government bodies with the promotion of economic development and welfare as their main objectives at preferential financial terms. In the OECD statistics, bilateral ODA includes grants (including debt cancellation), interest subsidy, loans, equity investment, technical cooperation, and humanitarian aid. In China, the term "foreign aid" is more often used than "official development assistance". Chinese interpretations of foreign aid do not fully correspond to the DAC definition of ODA. In particular, equity investment and humanitarian aid are usually excluded from the coverage of foreign aid. FDI is considered as commercial cooperation rather than official assistance, though it has significant development connotations. Humanitarian aid is run by the Ministry of Social Welfare with the intention of preventing excessive suffering rather than providing support for sustainable development. For the convenience of research, discussion in this chapter is structured along the lines of China's ODA mechanisms. In general, there are three modes of delivery with respect to China's bilateral aid: grant aid, interest-free loans, and concessional loans.

Grant Aid and Technical Assistance

Grants awarded by the Chinese government tend to be disbursed in kind through various projects, rather than in cash. This is viewed as preferable, since the Chinese government can monitor utilization of the aid more closely. China has also provided technical assistance to GMS states across a wide spectrum. A regular influx of teachers, medical personnel and agricultural experts has provided core expertise in the fields of education, health, agriculture and environmental conservation. According to China's Ministry of Commerce (MOFCOM), up to the end of 2008, China had trained 6,760 people in the GMS in areas such as administration, economy, agriculture, energy and IT.

Concessional Finance and Interest-free Loans

Preferential or concessional loans are extended by the Chinese government, provided by the EXIM Bank, and given an interest subsidy by MOFCOM. (MOFCOM approves this process and the funds for the interest subsidy are taken from the budget allocated to foreign aid that sits with the Ministry of Finance.) These are medium- to long-term loans with an emphasis on the profitability of projects. Technically, only the subsidized portion of the interest rate is "aid", as given by the Chinese government. For example, if a concessional loan with an interest rate of 3 per cent is granted, and the commercial interest rate is 8 per cent, the remaining 5 per cent is paid out of the pot of funds designated as "foreign aid" by the Ministry of Finance.

Interest-free loans used to be a major form of Chinese foreign aid. However, the government has reformed its aid since 1995, sharply decreasing the amount of interest-free loans in preference for concessional loans. Given that interest-free loans are run directly by the aid agency under MOFCOM, they are undoubtedly considered as foreign aid. The China EXIM Bank, in charge of concessional loans, is a trade promotion agency rather than a traditional foreign aid provider. Consequently, although concessional loans are subsidized by the Chinese government as a kind of foreign aid, not all recipient countries take them as governmental aid, but as commercial activities with an obvious benefit purpose. Normally, loans are officially extended to the recipient country, though the recipient government may never actually receive the funding. Instead, the funding may be directly transferred to the approved implementing company as soon as they have won the tender, even though the recipient country will be invoiced as the official payee of the loan.

Given that the Chinese government still considers foreign aid data a state secret, there are no detailed statistics on its aid to the GMS countries. It is therefore impossible to identify how much aid China has given to the GMS or the geographical distribution of that aid. This chapter gathers relevant information from the *Yearbook of China's Foreign Economic Relations and Trade* and the *China Commerce Yearbook* which are semi-official publications. During 2000–07, about eleven projects were completed and sixteen new projects approved in Cambodia, Laos and Vietnam (see Table 4.7). In general, the GMS is not a priority region for Chinese foreign aid, especially compared to Africa, and has only a few projects, accounting for a small portion of Chinese aid.

The statistics in the aforementioned publications only cover projects funded by grants and interest-free loans. According to other informal sources, a dozen projects financed by concessional loans from the EXIM Bank are being implemented in Vietnam. The total value of these loans is reportedly over US$1.0 billion. All of these projects are related to power generation or transmission. It seems that China is trying to play a greater role in the infrastructure development of the GMS. However, as noted before, concessional loans provided by EXIM Bank are not always considered as governmental aid. As a result, there are discrepancies between China's "aid offered" statistics and recipients' "aid received" statistics. For example, according to Vietnamese information, the total aid from China between 1989 and 2008 was only US$300 million. Apparently,

TABLE 4.7
China's Aid to GMS Countries, 2000–07

Year	Completed projects	New projects	Technical assistance
2000	Cambodia 2	Cambodia 2 Laos 1	Cambodia 1 Laos 1
2001	Cambodia 1 Vietnam 1	Cambodia 5	
2002	N/A	N/A	N/A
2003	Laos 1 Vietnam 1	Laos 1	Vietnam 2
2004	Laos 2	Cambodia 1 Laos 2	Laos 2
2005	Laos 1	Cambodia 2 Thailand 1	
2006	Laos 2	Laos 1	
2007	N/A	N/A	N/A
GMS	11	16	6
World	225	272	266

Source: Yearbook of China's Foreign Economic Relations and Trade China Commerce Yearbook, 2000–07.

concessional loans by China EXIM Bank are not included in the figure. It seems that the Vietnamese side views these loans as commercial lending rather than a benevolent offer. Therefore, the political result of these loans does not meet the initial intention of the Chinese government of showing generosity and friendship.

2.4 Organizational and Institutional Arrangement of China's Foreign Aid

From our research, the main official institutions that govern China's development assistance programme are as follows:

- *State Council* is the highest executive organ of the state administration, essentially the regulatory body that oversees all aid programmes of the Chinese State. The State Council as a whole decides on the portion of the national budget that will be designated as foreign aid at the beginning of every budgetary year.

• *Ministry of Finance* is responsible for drawing up the foreign aid budget in consultation with the Ministry of Commerce. Multilateral aid through the International Financial Institutions (World Bank and IMF) also falls under the jurisdiction of this ministry.

• *Ministry of Commerce (MOFCOM)* is the lead agency governing China's aid programme — both incoming and outgoing. Under MOFCOM, two departments are in charge of aid. The Department of International Co-operation manages incoming aid (i.e., for China) while the Department of Aid to Foreign Countries (DAFC) supervises China's outgoing aid. Within the DAFC, sits the Executive Bureau of International Economic Cooperation, a policy-executing body which administers the delivery of aid, executing MOFCOM's policies at project level. MOFCOM and, more specifically, the DAFC, coordinate China's foreign aid policy including negotiating inter-government agreements, reviewing requests that come from the Ministry of Foreign Affairs (MOFA) that require approval, conducting feasibility studies for aid projects, choosing aid implementers and conducting project reviews. MOFCOM is also responsible for managing the foreign aid fund, concessional loans and special funds of the Chinese government, as well as facilitating reform on foreign aid provision modalities. Several internal directorates within MOFCOM are also involved in playing an advisory role on aid and economic co-operation within the GMS. MOFCOM is essentially in charge of all aid disbursements to the GMS countries, including grant aid, technical assistance, and all interest-free and concessional loans. Although EXIM Bank is involved in the evaluation process of concessional loans, MOFCOM is the decision-making body.

• *Ministry of Foreign Affairs (MOFA)* is in charge of institutionalizing China's foreign policy, such as drafting China's policy toward the GMS, and shaping the announcements of aid packages and commitments. In terms of aid, MOFA plays an advisory role to MOFCOM. It is involved to a greater extent in the negotiation and provision of humanitarian assistance, but as mentioned previously, this does not come under the category of "foreign aid" as disbursed from the pot of funds set aside by the Ministry of Finance.

• *Embassies*: The embassies, especially through the Economic and Commercial Councillor's Offices which are staffed by MOFCOM officials, play a significant role in terms of determining recipient countries' needs and the type of aid required. In addition, the embassies serve as the agency within the recipient country, assisting with reporting on the monitoring and evaluation of projects as they are implemented. While individual embassies may not be well-informed of regional developments, each is tasked with monitoring the projects and disbursements within its own country, and is generally quite knowledgeable regarding these.

• *Other Ministries:* Ministries such as Agriculture, Education and Health are also involved in the provision of China's aid programme. These include the deployment of medical teams, scholarships and educational projects as well as agricultural programmes for rural development. In terms of science and technology, the Ministry of Science and Technology oversees this sphere of China's aid process. These ministries play a consultative role in the aid disbursement process up to the point that MOFCOM is allocated the funds, when they assist to a greater extent in terms of administration and implementation of any foreign aid that falls under their jurisdiction and expertise.

• *Export-Import Bank of China (EXIM Bank):* EXIM Bank is the sole administrative body of concessional loan financing. Established in 1994, EXIM is a government policy bank that is exclusively managed by the State Council. It is the third largest export credit agency (ECA) in the world and has been a vital cog in the rapid expansion of Chinese global trade and investment. The Bank is playing an increasingly important role in promoting the development of China's export-oriented economy and has taken on the role of trade financing, previously executed by the Bank of China. China EXIM Bank carries out three major functions: (1) it is the official export agency looking after trade and investment guarantees, (2) it provides aid administration (i.e. evaluating projects) and, (3) it acts as the policy bank that deals with foreign aid that comes to China. There are two divisions within the bank that oversee financial outflows: commercial and concessional. The Bank performs a number of financing roles and, as mentioned above, is also the sole provider of government concessional loans. While it is difficult to distinguish between the concessional and non-concessional loan financing of the Bank, total loan approvals reached US$20 billion in 2005. The Bank's role within the Chinese aid process has been greatly informed by the 1995 reorganization of aid disbursement mechanisms and an attempt to increase the number of preferential loans. The Bank's lending practices are closely tied to China's foreign policy, with package deals that tend to focus *inter alia* on projects in the construction industry and the exploration of resources abroad, and concessional loans mainly targeted towards infrastructure development.

• *Grants:* In line with their mantra of aid for development, grant aid is specifically extended for social welfare projects (like hospitals, schools and housing), material assistance, technical assistance and personnel training. Interest-free loans are primarily granted for infrastructure projects, while concessional loans largely focus on the profitability of projects. The first three forms of aid disbursement are administered by the Executive Bureau of International Economic Cooperation within the DAFC. In all cases, the preferred method of disbursing aid is in kind, rather than in cash. This essentially ensures that money stays within the Chinese system. It also ensures that aid-financed projects, as much as they are developed in consultation with the recipient country, still remain at the discretion of the Chinese government, especially in terms of the contract tendering process. The grant-awarding process, from inception to implementation, generally follows this procedure:

1. The recipient government makes a request to the Chinese diplomatic mission in their country. This request will generally go through the Economic Councillor's office.
2. The embassy screens the request and, if it appears viable, it is passed onto MOFA and MOFCOM in Beijing.
3. MOFCOM appoints a technical team to be dispatched to the recipient country to evaluate the viability of the proposal and develop a preliminary budget.
4. The technical team makes its assessment of the proposal. This takes place in discussions with both the local Chinese Embassy, and the relevant ministries or departments of the recipient country.
5. The technical team returns to Beijing and submits their detailed report to MOFCOM, and specifically, to the Department of Aid to Foreign Countries.
6. MOFCOM circulates the proposal, evaluation, and budget to various parties to garner their opinions on the project. This consultative process includes the embassy in the recipient country, MOFA, and

the relevant ministry or ministries on the Chinese side (for example, if it is a proposal for a housing project, the Department of Housing in Beijing will be involved).

7. If the project is deemed viable and worthwhile, MOFCOM submits the proposal and the results of the consultative process to the State Council.
8. The State Council makes the final decision regarding whether the project will go ahead. If the project is to be implemented, the State Council then instructs the Ministry of Finance to release the relevant funds to MOFCOM.
9. Once the funds are released, MOFCOM then initiates the tendering process. This may involve provincial governments lobbying for their own firms to win contracts.
10. Once the tendering process is complete, the companies who have won the contracts will begin project implementation, under agreement with MOFCOM. There will always be more than one contract awarded per project, as another company will always be appointed to supervise the project, and act as "quality control".
11. After the project has been awarded, the Executive Bureau of International Economic Cooperation, a unit within MOFCOM, executes the policies at project level when the actual construction of the project begins. The bureau has no overseas staff and therefore has to rely on the input of the Chinese Embassies in specific countries. The bureau, however, does make mid-term site visits as well as upon completion of the project, and this is done in conjunction with the DAFC. This entire process usually takes at least one year to complete, from inception to implementation. Generally, the aid-financed projects are of a turnkey nature.

It is often assumed that this system provides an entry point for Chinese labour to gain employment on such projects. However, during the in-market research, it was noted on several occasions that the use of Chinese labour was for reasons of operational pragmatism and dependent on the level and availability of skills in the local market. In instances where the requisite skills were available locally, the preference was to only use Chinese labour in the capacity of supervision, engineering, design or at a more senior level with tasks involving technical expertise, such as the grading of roads and the operation of sophisticated machinery. Chinese companies have no automatic preference for Chinese labour, but given the lack of specialized skills in local markets where aid projects are being implemented, the import of Chinese skilled labour is sometimes required. This is partly also to ensure that project deadlines are met and that the project is delivered within budget. Interestingly, what has become increasingly apparent is that as much as Chinese labour employed on projects may be skilled, they also engage in manual tasks, working with local labourers. In these cases it is easy to note where misconceptions around the employment practices of Chinese companies may have arisen, as it may appear that Chinese companies are importing manual labour, when in reality, Chinese labourers are brought in for their skills.

Loans

In cases where a concessional loan is extended from China EXIM Bank — the only provider of Chinese government concessional loan financing — the following constitutes the process:

1. The government of the borrowing country (represented by its Ministry of Finance) submits an application to China EXIM Bank for no less than RMB20 million (US$2.4 million).
2. The Bank evaluates the application and the intended project in the form of a feasibility assessment report and submits a recommendation to the Ministry of Commerce.
3. The Chinese Government signs a framework agreement with the borrowing country, given that the recommendation is accepted.
4. The borrowing country (represented by a minister of the borrowing government) signs a project loan agreement with EXIM Bank (represented by a president or vice-president of the bank). The loan interest rate and grace period are separately negotiated, with repayment due semi-annually following loan negotiations. Each agreement provides an occasion for a high-profile signing ceremony, often reported in public news sources and on official government websites.
5. According to contractual terms, the Chinese contractors and exporters invoice the foreign executing agency requesting payment.
6. The foreign executing agency submits the invoice and progress report to the borrowing country's government.

7. The foreign government submits a drawing application, invoice and progress report to China EXIM Bank.
8. China EXIM Bank then disburses the funds to the exporter.
9. The foreign government pays the principal, interest, fees and loan repayments to China EXIM Bank.

As much as the above outlines how China conducts its aid processes, it still remains a complicated procedure. For instance, in the case of concessional loans from EXIM Bank, it is difficult to know whether these conform to the ODA definition of promoting economic development and welfare as the main objective, as very little information on the maturity, interest rate and grace period affecting the grant element of the loan is disclosed. A better understanding of Chinese concessionary financing is required. In comparison to English news and media sources, publicly available Chinese sources can present more information on the terms of loan agreements, based on the official signing ceremony between the borrowing government and EXIM Bank. These Chinese sources at times report both the size of the loan and its proposed purpose. Generally, loans must be utilized for infrastructure (energy, transportation telecommunications), social (health, housing) or industrial (manufacturing, mining) projects.

According to EXIM Bank's concessional loan requirements, Chinese contractors must be awarded the infrastructure contract financed by the loan. This is similar to the concessionary finance of traditional donors and provides these companies with an entry point to set up a presence in host markets where they can bid for commercial contracts, independent of projects under the concessional loan agreements. In principle concessional loans are used for procuring equipment, materials, technology and services, with no less than 50 per cent of the contract's procurement coming from China. The loan is denominated in Chinese renminbi and has a maximum maturity of twenty years. A grace period of three to seven years may be granted to the borrower, during which the borrower will only repay interest and not the principal sum. The interest rate which ranges between 2 and 4 per cent is subsidized by the Chinese government. The loans are seen as a foreign policy tool, especially by those with major infrastructure needs, who can use their proven resource reserves as collateral.

While China EXIM Bank is the lead financial institution in concessional loans, other banks are also engaged, providing other forms of finance. These financial institutions have positioned themselves to become suppliers of non-concessionary finance, predominantly in the sphere of facilitating trade and investment opportunities for Chinese companies wishing to invest abroad.

Project Monitoring

A number of different bodies play a role in monitoring the roll-out of various projects after implementation begins. For all projects, a second company is appointed by contract, purely to monitor the practices and implementation policies of the first company that actually carries out the project. These companies have no link to one another. In addition, the local embassy, the economic councillor's office, and visiting DAFC staff also provide some supervision.

In the case of loans, obviously EXIM Bank, as the financier of the project, maintains a close eye on proceedings along with the local country embassy, the economic councillor's office, and visiting MOFCOM officials.

2.5 Future Prospects for China's Foreign Aid Policy

China's foreign aid policy has been gradually evolving over the past six decades. In particular, its major goal has changed from building ideological alliances to assuring economic and political partnership. Establishing a so-called harmonious world and expanding the markets for Chinese products and companies will be the most important targets of China's foreign aid, as well as its overall diplomatic strategy. Therefore, China's current aid policy puts more emphasis on mutual benefit rather than selfless bestowal. This largely reflects the market-oriented economic reform of China. However, China will not follow the approach of the Western countries' ODA, but, instead, commit to its Chinese-style foreign aid, which means China will not attach conditions to its loans and will focus on promoting Chinese trade and investment relations with the recipient through foreign aid.

With the rapid development of the Chinese economy and the increasing relevance of the international market to China, China will have an increased capability and greater momentum to provide more foreign aid. Recently, some observers have proposed that China should initiate a Chinese-version Marshall Plan to use its huge foreign exchange reserves to help developing countries in Asia, Africa, and Latin America. The proposal was criticized by many foreign affairs scholars and ignored by the Chinese government because they are concerned that the ambitiousness of this plan will raise fears in the West and even in the recipient countries about China's intentions of a new hegemony. Besides, China is still a developing country itself with a lot of domestic economic and social difficulties to address. Therefore, China does not seem to be in the mood to take on the responsibility of a major donor in international development assistance. Actually, foreign aid's share of the total budget since 2000 has remained at less than 1 per cent, even lower than in the 1990s; but in absolute terms, the amount of Chinese foreign aid has kept growing. See Table 4.8.

Partly because no single entity is responsible for constructing an overall foreign aid strategy, China has no evaluation mechanism with

TABLE 4.8
Foreign Aid Expenditure as Share of Total Central Expenditure (100 million yuan)

Year	(A) Expenditure on foreign aid	(B) Total central expenditure	(A/B) Share (%)
1990	15.62	1,004.47	1.56
1991	16.82	1,090.81	1.54
1992	16.61	1,170.44	1.42
1993	18.50	1,312.06	1.41
1994	28.86	1,754.43	1.64
1995	29.00	1,995.39	1.45
1996	32.20	2,151.27	1.50
1997	35.45	2,532.50	1.40
1998	37.20	3,125.60	1.19
1999	39.20	4,152.33	0.94
2000	45.88	5,519.85	0.83
2001	47.11	5,768.02	0.82
2002	50.03	6,771.70	0.74
2003	52.23	7,420.10	0.70
2004	60.69	7,894.08	0.77
2005	74.70	8,775.97	0.85
2006	82.37	9,991.40	0.82
2007	111.54	11,442.06	0.97
Total	794.01	83,872.90	0.95

Source: Expenditure on foreign aid (1990–2004) from Zhang (2006), 2005–07 from *China Statistical Yearbook 2006 to 2008*, total expenditure of the central government from *China Statistical Yearbook 2008*.

regard to its foreign aid. At present, China has not published any official documents on its foreign aid strategy and so outside observers, and even "inside" stakeholders, have no clear understanding of China's foreign aid policy and possible future patterns. That said, in the coming years, it can be expected that China's foreign aid expenditure will increase rapidly. The preferred form of aid would be concessional loans which could be reviewed in commercial terms and provide market access and investment opportunity for Chinese enterprises. With this increase in aid it is hoped that the GMS could benefit from China's past development experience, for example its successes in physical infrastructure construction, and with technical assistance, "leap frog" stages of development.

2.6 Conclusions and Policy Recommendations

ODA donor countries like to claim that the motivations underlying their aid giving are altruistic and selfless. However, this is rarely true. In fact, it is not shameful to expect some rewards from the recipient. Mutual benefit is much more reliable and sustainable than unilateral almsgiving. Mutual benefit does not mean that ODA is a kind of cost in exchange for something. This is not trading. China, though still a developing country itself, has become an important donor of ODA to other developing countries, like those in the GMS. What China wants from the provision of ODA is the recipient's gratitude and goodwill, which will improve the quality of their bilateral relationship and broaden the scope of future cooperation. This is readily demonstrable in the non-conditionality of Chinese foreign aid.

Nevertheless, there are still some problems with Chinese foreign aid policy and its implementation which cause some misunderstandings of the intentions and outcomes of China's ODA. One problem is that Chinese aid projects do not have enough local involvement during their implementation. Some recipient countries complain that some Chinese contractors prefer to use labour and materials from China. These finished projects will finally bring considerable benefits to local communities, but their presence and perception is discounted. Another problem is the lack of transparency of Chinese aid project implementation. Some observers from the GMS claim that, during the whole process of project implementation, the borrowing country only takes part in the initial and the end stages, i.e. borrowing money and repaying money; there is a little scope for participation in design and planning, bidding, construction, and quality monitoring. Although the reputation of Chinese foreign aid projects is fairly good, the recipient countries tend to resent being excluded from the process.

For China, the most important consequence of these problems is that China does not fully get what it wants from the recipient by delivering ODA to them, namely gratitude and goodwill. While the Chinese side is wondering why the recipient countries do not show their appreciation, the recipient side is suspecting that China's real intention is just to export its products and extract resources. Although the Chinese government is trying to explain its good intentions, there are still a lot of misunderstandings in the borrowing countries.

Considering the concerns of recipient countries, the Chinese government should take some actions to reform and improve the current foreign aid system and policy to meet the needs of both sides. First of all, China should enhance the involvement of local communities in aid projects. The Chinese contractors could work with other institutes to train local workers in Chinese language and necessary techniques. More involvement would make the local community feel the benefits of Chinese aid more directly. With the rising costs of Chinese labour, it would also be economically viable to hire more local workers. Second, China should further improve the transparency of its foreign aid system. More information and statistics on foreign aid should be publicly disseminated. An official policy statement on Chinese foreign aid should be developed and announced. More foreign stakeholders should be allowed to take part in the implementation of foreign aid projects. Of course, these reforms could not take place overnight, but a clear strategy of Chinese foreign aid is urgently needed. With the predictable increase of Chinese foreign aid, a kind of neutral project evaluation should be introduced to improve the implementation quality of aid projects.

Notes

1. Ministry of Commerce of China; *Guidelines for Investing in Cambodia* <http://fec.mofcom.gov.cn/gbzn/gobiezhinan.shtml> (accessed 15 October 2009).
2. Ministry of Commerce of China, *Guidelines for Investing in Vietnam* <http://fec.mofcom.gov.cn/gbzn/gobiezhinan.shtml> (accessed 15 October 2009).
3. Ministry of Commerce of China, "The Management Approach on Overseas Investment on 16 March 2009" <http://www.mofcom.gov.cn/> (accessed 9 October 2009).

4. National Bureau of Statistics website <http://www.stats.gov.cn/> (accessed 16 September 2009).
5. Secretarial website of the Ministry of Commerce of China and ASEAN <http://www.mofcom.gov.cn/> (accessed 12 October 2009).
6. Ministry of Commerce of China; *Guidelines for Investing in Cambodia* <http://fec.mofcom.gov.cn/gbzn/gobiezhinan.shtml> (accessed 15 October 2009).
7. Ibid.
8. Ministry of Commerce of China, *Guidelines for Investing in Laos* <http://fec.mofcom.gov.cn/gbzn/gobiezhinan.shtml> (accessed 15 October 2009).
9. Ministry of Commerce of China, *Guidelines for investing in Cambodia* <http://fec.mofcom.gov.cn/gbzn/gobiezhinan.shtml> (accessed 15 October 2009).
10. Ministry of Commerce, *Statistics of China's FDI in 2008* <http://www.mofcom.gov.cn/> (accessed 15 October 2009).
11. Chinese Premier Zhou Enlai announced the eight principles in January 1964 during a speech in Mali. They are: (1) Emphasize equality and mutual benefit; (2) Respect sovereignty and never attach conditions; (3) Provide interest-free or low-interest loans; (4) Help recipient countries develop independence and self-reliance; (5) Build projects that require little investment and can be accomplished quickly; (6) Provide quality equipment and material at market prices; (7) Ensure effective technical assistance; (8) Pay experts according to local standards.

References

Bende-Nabende, A., J. Ford, B. Santoso and S. Sen. "The Interaction between FDI, Output and the Spillover Variables: Co-integration and VAR Analyses for APEC 1965–99". *Applied Economics Letters* 10, no. 3 (2003): 165–72.

Bengoa, M. and B. Sanchez-Robles. "Foreign Direct Investment, Economic Freedom and Growth: New Evidence from Latin America". *European Journal of Political Economy* 19, no. 3 (2003): 529–45.

Borensztein, E., J. Gregorio and J. Lee. "How Does Foreign Direct Investment Affect Economic Growth". *Journal of International Economics* 45, no. 1 (1998): 115–35.

Chin, Gregory T. and B. Michael Frolic. *Emerging Donors in International Development Assistance: The China Case*. Ottawa: International Development Research Centre, 2007.

China Development Brief. "Communist Capital Flows Downstream: China's Aid to Laos". 2006. <http://www.chinadevelopmentbrief.com/node/454>. Accessed 3 November 2009.

Davies, Martyn. *How China Delivers Development Assistance to Africa*. Stellenbosch, SA: Centre for Chinese Studies, University of Stellenbosch, 2008.

Du Qunyang and Song Yuhua. "FDI Effect of China-ASEAN Free Trade Economic Area". *International Business Issues*, no. 3 (2004): 51–54.

Gao Ting. "Foreign Direct Investment from Developing Asia: Some Distinctive Features". *Economics Letters* 86, Issue No. 1 (January 2005): 29–35.

Gong Zhankui, Meng Xia and Liu Chengyang. *The Economic Integration of China and ASEAN: Patterns Comparison and Policies Option*. Beijing: University of International Business and Economics Press, 2003.

Hardin, G. "The Tragedy of the Commons". *Science* 162 (1968): 1243–48.

Huang Meibo. "China's Foreign Aid: Current Situation and Prospects". *International Economic Cooperation*, no. 6 (2007): 12–26.

Hubbard, Paul. *Aiding Transparency: What We Can Learn about China EXIM Bank's Concessional Loans*. Washington, D.C.: Centre for Global Development, 2007. <http://www.cgdev.org>. Accessed 25 November 2009.

Kanta Marwah and Akbar Tavakoli. "The Effect of Foreign Capital and Imports on Economic Growth: Further Evidence from Four Asian Countries (1970–1998)". *Journal of Asian Economics* 15 (2004): 399–413.

Kiyoshi Kojima. "A Macroeconomics Approach to Foreign Direct Investment". *Hitotsubashi Journal of Economics* 14 (1973): 1–20.

———. "International Trade and Foreign Direct Investment: Substitutes or Complements". *Hitotsubashi Journal of Economics* 16 (1975): 1–12.

Knickerbocker, F.T. *Oligopolistic Reaction and Multinational Enterprise*. Boston: Harvard University School of Business Administration, 1973.

Kohpaiboon, Archanun. "Foreign Trade Regimes and the FDI-Growth Nexus: Case Study of Thailand". *Journal of Development Studies* 40, no. 2 (December 2003): 55–69.

Li Diao and He Fan. "Reflections on China's Foreign Aid Strategy". *Journal of Contemporary Asia-Pacific Studies* 6 (2008): 120.

Li Xiaoying and Liu Xiaming. "Foreign Direct Investment and Economic Growth: An Increasingly Endogenous Relationship". *World Development* 33, Issue 3 (March 2005): 393–407.

Long Feng, Guo Chazhong, Zhong Xiaohong and Yang Qijia. "The Environmental Protection Issue of China's Outward FDI and ODA". *Environmental Protection* 1 (2009): 66–68.

Lum, Thomas. *China's Foreign Aid Activities in Africa, South America, and Southeast Asia*. Washington, D.C.: Congressional Research Service, 2009.

Qiu Guilin. "China's Foreign Aid between 1950s to 1970s". Master thesis. Xiangtan University, 2006.

Rawls, J. *A Theory of Justice*. Cambridge, MA: Belknap Press, 1971.

Sachs, J.D. "Globalisation and Patterns of Economic Development". *Weltwirtschaftliches, Archive* 136, no. 4 (2000): 579–600.

She Minghua. "The Influence of FDI on the Developing Host Countries and the Related Controversies". *Financial Economics*, no. 1 (2003): 409–11.

Sun Zhao Dong and Zhang Zhiqian. *Vietnam in the "Crisis"*. Beijing: China Economic Press House, 2008.

Wang Gucheng and Li Peng. "Research on the Functional Transformation of Sub-regional Economic Corridor under the GMS Framework". *Journal of Zhengzhou College of Aviation Industry Management*, no. 4 (2009): 18–21.

Wang Zhongbao. *Economic Globalisation with Its Impact on Chinese Interests Changing*. Shanghai: Fudan University Press, 2007.

Wang Wei and Zhu Huibo. "Analysis on China's foreign aid since the reform and opening up". *Mao Zedong and Deng Xiaoping Theories Studies*, no. 8 (2008): 45–49.

Xu Liang. "The Management of China's Foreign Aid Projects: A Case-study on Aid to Laos". Master thesis. Kunming University of Science and Technology, 2008.

Yan Fang. "The Strategies of the GMS to Attract FDI on the Basis of Sustainable Development of Regional Economy". *Journal of Guangxi University, Philosophy and Social Sciences Version*, no. 5 (2008): 5–11.

Zhang Xiaomin. "China's Foreign Aid in the Perspective of Its Foreign Policy for Peace". *International Forum*, no. 3 (2008): 38–43.

Zhang Yuhui. "Research on China's Foreign Aid". Doctoral dissertation. Central Communist Party School, China, 2006.

Zhou Hong. "Chinese Foreign Aid and the Reform and Opening-up in 30 years". *World Economic and Politics*, no. 11 (2008): 33–43.

Zhu Ming. "A Brief Analysis of 'Chinese Aid Threat': Challenges and Pressures Facing China's Diplomacy". Sixth Annual Conference of Shanghai Social Sciences Association. 2008.

PART III

The GMS-4 and China

5

IMPACTS OF CHINA ON POVERTY REDUCTION IN VIETNAM

Nguyen Thi Kim Dung, Nguyen Manh Hai and Tran Trung Hieu

1. INTRODUCTION

1.1 The Context

Emerging as a major driver of regional growth, China is currently presenting Vietnam with enormous business opportunities and challenges. On the one hand, rapid expansion of China's industries, exports and consumer goods markets has led to a surge in demand for raw materials, energy, intermediate products, manufactured goods and services. On the other, China and Vietnam are said to be competing in their domestic and the third-country markets, particularly with regard to labour-intensive products.

Vietnam, over the last few decades, has made remarkable improvements in enhancing per capita income and in reducing poverty. Poverty and hunger incidence in the country has been significantly reduced (Table 5.1). In comparison with the standard poverty measurement of US$1 per capita per day, Vietnam has well exceeded the millennium development goal (MDG) of halving the proportion of people whose income is less than US$1

TABLE 5.1
Poverty Incidence (%)

	1993	1998	2002	2004	2006
General poverty rate	58.1	37.4	28.9	19.5	15.97
Poverty rate based on standard of US$1 per person per day	39.9	16.4	13.6	10.6	4.9
By urban/rural area:					
Urban	25.1	9.2	6.6	3.6	3.9
Rural	66.4	45.5	35.6	25.0	20.4
By ethnic group:					
Kinh and Chinese	53.9	31.1	23.1	13.5	10.3
Other	86.4	75.2	69.5	60.7	52.3
By region:					
Northern Mountains	81.5	64.2	43.9	35.4	30.2
Red River Delta	62.7	29.3	22.4	12.1	8.8
North Central	74.5	48.1	43.9	31.9	29.1
South Central Coastal	47.2	34.5	25.2	19.0	12.6
Central Highlands	70	52.4	51.8	33.1	28.6
Southeast Region	37	12.2	10.6	5.4	5.8
Mekong Delta	47.1	36.9	23.4	19.5	10.3

Source: MPI (2008*a*).

a day by 2015. This proportion was cut eightfold from 39.9 per cent in 1993 to 4.9 per cent in 2006. Poverty incidence as measured by the standard food poverty of Vietnam also declined sharply from 24.9 per cent in 1993 to 10.9 per cent in 2002, 7.4 per cent in 2004 and 6.7 per cent in 2006.

With a view to achieving the standards set by other developing countries in the region, the prime minister issued Decision No. 170/QĐ-TTg dated 8 April 2005, promulgating updated national standards for a new period of development. Measured by the new poverty line, approximately 3.9 million households were still living in poverty in 2005, accounting for 20.2 per cent of total households. The rate then reduced to 15.5 per cent in 2006 and to 14.8 per cent in 2007. At the same time, GDP per capita, measured based on purchasing power parity (PPP), increased from US$402 in 2001 to US$492 in 2003, US$553 in 2004, US$639 in 2005, US$723 in 2006 and to US$834 in 2007. Living conditions for all levels of society in Vietnam improved, and poverty indicators were successfully reduced across the board. By all measurement standards and methods of calculation, Vietnam achieved poverty alleviation over and above the corresponding MDG.

However, challenges remain despite impressive achievements in poverty alleviation across the country. There is a large gap between urban and rural areas, including high poverty incidences in mountainous areas and among ethnic minority groups. As shown in Table 5.1, the highest national poverty incidence in 2006 was in the Northern Mountains (30.2 per cent), followed by the North Central region (29.1 per cent), Central Highlands (28.6 per cent), South Central Coastal area (12.6 per cent), Mekong Delta (10.3 per cent), Red River Delta (8.8 per cent) and the Southeast region (5.8 per cent). At the same time, a widening poverty gap between Kinh-Chinese and minority groups has emerged. The pace of poverty reduction among minority groups is slower than that of the Kinh and Chinese people. In 2006, poverty incidence among ethnic minority people was 52.3 per cent, much higher than the rate among Kinh and Chinese groups (10.3 per cent). While they amount to one-eighth of the total population, ethnic minority people make up over 50 per cent of the poor, especially in terms of food poverty (MPI 2008*a*).

Moreover, if seen in broader terms, the definition of poverty can move beyond this single income and consumption dimension to a utility and capacity-based concept. For example, poverty can be looked at from a much larger number of other "non-material" dimensions, such as: *lack of opportunities*, for example, lack of opportunity to sustain livelihood includes access to market information, lack of cultivation land or access to other natural resources; *lack of capacity* as capacity is vital for the poor to move out of poverty when it includes health, nutrition, mortality rates, education attainment, access to safe drinking water, hygiene and sanitation; *social exclusion* that is defined as the barriers preventing the poor from fully participating in mainstream society; and *vulnerability* which is related to food security, being exposed to natural disasters, or physical isolation in remote areas. In this chapter, poverty is defined in broader terms when assessing how China's growth can influence poverty in Vietnam.

Jenkins and Edwards' (2004) study *How Does China's Growth Affect Poverty Reduction in Asia and Latin America* examines the impact of China on the trade of third countries at the 3-digit SITC level with analysis of trade-poverty linkages based on Winters' analysis framework. Applicable to Vietnam, the research points out that four types of direct impact are usually identified namely: (1) growth of Vietnam's exports to China; (2) increased competition from China for exports to third markets; (3) increased competition by China in Vietnam's home markets; and (4) effects on foreign direct investment (FDI) flows either through the diversion of FDI from Vietnam to China, or through the growth of outward investment from China to Vietnam. The study also indicates that trade and FDI can impact on poverty through their effects on production and factor markets, or through changes in the prices of consumer goods, or via effects on government revenues and expenditure.

Vietnam's exports to China are mainly primary products (for example, minerals and petroleum). As Jenkins and Edwards (2004, p. 14) point out, "Vietnam has very limited exports of labour intensive products to China, apart from some agricultural exports". According to their study, Vietnam has been facing stiff competition from China's exports of manufactured products to third countries: the share of labour-intensive products threatened by Chinese competition in exports to third countries is around 50 per cent, mainly in textile and garment production. Thus the textile and garment sectors will be most affected from Chinese competition in third markets. While Vietnam's imports from China are reported to be overwhelmingly of manufactured goods, it appears that manufactured imports from China do not threaten Vietnamese industries, which employ a high level of unskilled labour. This implies directly that the negative effect on the poor in Vietnam is likely to be small. Moreover, Jenkins and Edwards (2004, p. 24) find that in Vietnam "there is much potential for the poor to benefit significantly from imports of consumer goods from China". In terms of FDI, the study points out that even in the short run, the poverty effect of China's FDI diversion is very small as is that of outward FDI from China as so far the country has played a much smaller role in exporting FDI than importing it. However, this study was completed in 2004. All the calculations are based on World Bank and IMF aggregate data collected before 2002. Since then, the world has changed substantially, as has Vietnam's trade with China and its foreign economic relations.

A more recent study in late 2008 by Rutherford, Lazarus and Kelley (2008), provides a useful and updated overview of investment, trade and aid flows from China to the three selected Mekong countries (Cambodia, Laos and Vietnam), with a particular focus on agribusiness, hydropower and mining industries. The study also analyses their policies, regulatory and institutional frameworks and determines specific policy recommendations for further improvements. Nevertheless, the main objective of this study is to get insight into Chinese investment in natural resources and its impact on the region's ecology and environment. Therefore, not much attention is given to pro-poor impact analysis or assessment of improvement of income, employment or other aspects of local people's well-being. A more detailed and meaningful picture of how China's growth could currently affect workers and poor households in neighbouring countries in general and in Vietnam in particular is still lacking.

In Vietnamese academic and policy circles there are many anecdotal discussions on the positive and negative effects of China's growth.[1] With regards to the former, China's growth could lead to an increase in demand for products exported to China from sectors such as agriculture, aquaculture, food processing and handicrafts. This is often said to increase demand for labour, thus expanding employment opportunities and raising income for some groups of workers. Raw materials, agricultural and aquacultural products are currently ranked among the most popular commodities traded from Vietnam to China. Geographical proximity and mutual complementarities of farming seasons substantially contribute to strengthening the competitiveness of Vietnam's agricultural exports in China's markets (Nguyen, Nguyen and Luu 2008). For example, Vietnam is often seen as a large net exporter of tropical agricultural products to China. New jobs created in export industries are reported to be an attractive opportunity for workers, especially young people, from rural areas.

On the other hand there have also been discussions as to possible negative consequences of China's rise. China's increased competitive threat in Vietnam's domestic and export markets, its expanded export volume, its competition in services and foreign direct investment could all, in principle, have negative impacts on employment and labour earnings. A common argument that is highlighted by Nguyen, Nguyen and Luu (2008) is that mass penetration of the domestic market by cheap products imported from China might be the downside of trade liberalization for Vietnam as it could sweep aside the demand for domestic unskilled labour. At the same time, as in many other studies, very little attention is paid to estimating how much extended commercial and other economic relations with China could affect the income and living standards of the local populace.

1.2 Research Questions and Analytical Framework

This chapter takes an in-depth look at the magnitude and main characteristics of the actual impact of China's current economic growth on poverty in

Vietnam and also attempts to suggest ways to both promote positive effects and mitigate or totally avoid any negative impacts. Towards achieving its aims, the study posits the main research question: What is the overall impact of China's economic growth on poverty reduction in Vietnam? While this is the overarching subject for investigation, several specific questions are addressed within the research implementation including:

- How good are current China-Vietnam economic relations?
- How significant are trade, investment and other types of capital flows between Vietnam and China?
- Which industrial sectors and/or products are most affected by China's growth?
- To what extent do the poor participate in the sectors and/or products traded to and from China?
- How significant is the impact of China's trade and investment on poverty reduction in these sectors and regions?
- How significant is China's development assistance in bridging the development gap in general and maximizing benefits from economic cooperation in particular?
- What is the way forward for Vietnam to reap the greatest benefits from China's rapid development?

In order to properly address these questions, this study makes direct use of Jenkins and Edwards' (2004) research framework in which three major channels for assessing the impact of China's growth are identified: trade development; investment, particularly FDI; and official development assistance (ODA). Through these channels, both challenges and opportunities for poverty reduction as a result of China's growth are closely examined.

Three main research methods were utilized for conducting the study, including desk review, key informants interview and quantitative analysis. These methods are not used separately, but in combination throughout the study.

Desk review comprises library research which included scanning through existing strategic documents and related research literature to see what has been done so far with the aim of consolidating and comparing the findings and results of previous research. This is also to consider whether the existing policies of both China and Vietnam (for example, Vietnam's foreign trade and investment policy, labour market policy or policy measures on expansion of labour-intensive agricultural or manufactured exports) have direct and/or indirect implications for the investigation of pro-poor impact, as well as to ascertain to what extent China's "outgoing policy", policy on cooperation with ASEAN and GMS, could effect Vietnam's economy.

Key informant interviews were conducted to derive information from relevant policy makers (e.g. from the Ministry of Planning and Investment (MPI), Ministry of Trade and Industry (MTI), General Statistics Office (GSO), and General Customs Office (GCO), donors and/or business representatives, and local authorities in those provinces that have border gates with China (such as Lang Son and Lao Cai provinces) for the most significant (in terms of Chinese export and import) production sectors and products. Through direct conversation, information from various representatives of respective government agencies and major donors on the recent and potential impact of China, and on how China's engagement in the country could fit well with Vietnam's development programme, was obtained.

Quantitative analysis utilized a gravity model, computable general equilibrium (CGE) model and other econometric approaches to examine the impact of trade with China. Detailed descriptions of the models are given in the next sections where they are explicitly applied.

This chapter is divided into five main sections. Section 2 focuses on trade, providing a general picture of Vietnam-China trade, its magnitude and trends and also presents an empirical analysis of the impact of trade exchange on the poor in Vietnam. Sections 3 and 4 are devoted to the analysis of the status of capital inflows from China to Vietnam (including FDI, ODA and technical cooperation) and also take a good look at the pro-poor effects of these flows. Finally, section 5 draws out the salient points of the research and makes some policy recommendations with a view to improving trade and other economic transactions between the two countries, as well as towards improving the livelihoods of the poor.

2. TRADE WITH CHINA AND ITS PRO-POOR IMPACT IN VIETNAM

2.1 Vietnam's General Policies on Bilateral Trade with China

A dozen treaties and agreements on bilateral trade and trade promotion have recently been ratified by the Vietnamese and Chinese governments. The most important ones include the bilateral agreements on trade (1991) and the establishment of the inter-governmental committee for economic and commercial cooperation (1994), and agreements on: commodity exchange across border lines; payment; mainland border lines (1999); ocean border lines (2000); communication and railway transport; communications and road transport; communications and sea transport; communications and air transport; transit transport; cross-border trade; and tourism cooperation. These agreements have laid a solid legal foundation for accelerated economic cooperation and cross-border trade between enterprises and localities of the two countries.

Indeed, outside these agreements various policy initiatives have aimed at boosting trade between the two nations. For example, some of Vietnam's provinces that border China have been granted preferential policies on cross-border commodity exchange and import-export taxes from some informal goods have been removed. Financial incentives such as export bonuses, subsidies for trade promotion costs, and preferential loans to enterprises producing goods for export have been given. As part of the Early Harvest Programme, Vietnam has cut import-export tariffs on a series of more than 480 commodities, the majority of which are agricultural and fisheries products.

The Vietnamese government had set a target to increase bilateral trade transactions with China to US$15 billion in 2010. However, actual bilateral trade between the two countries had already reached roughly US$20 billion by the end of 2009. Towards this, Vietnam has made a strong commitment to economic cooperation and promotion of peace and friendship with China. All of the six provinces (Quang Ninh, Lang Son, Cao Bang, Ha Giang, Lai Chau and Lao Cai) that border China have established a good economic relationship with their counterparts in the two Chinese provinces of Yunnan and Guangxi. Favourable relations for economic cooperation extend to the lower administrative levels (district and border cities). A number of working delegation exchanges to China have taken place.

Vietnam has made very strong efforts to simplify and coordinate its administrative procedures for financial and commercial transactions, and for entrance visas at international border gates. The opening of bank branches at the international border gates to China and the simplification of administrative procedures on imports from and exports to Chinese southern provinces have proved very attractive to Vietnamese enterprises and gradually led to increases in the share of formal trade.

Vietnam's Policy Response to ASEAN–China Free Trade Area (ACFTA)

Scheduled to take effect as of 1 January 2010, the ASEAN-China free trade area (ACFTA) includes China and ten Southeast Asian countries. It is expected to become the world's third largest free trade area with a combined population of 1.9 billion and a GDP close to US$6 trillion. This new framework is expected to be a strong lever for regional trade and faster economic integration.

The ACFTA could benefit Vietnam in many ways. Tariff reductions, simplification of administrative procedures such as customs and investment licensing, and the application of the zero (0 per cent) tariff on around 90 per cent of exchanged goods, mean that Vietnamese products will have better access to the Chinese market. Under the scheme, tariffs will be lowered, thus helping to reduce illegal trading to China along the borders. The ACFTA will also enhance economic cooperation between China and Vietnam as equal members and facilitate collaboration in the production process. Moreover, cooperation in the manufacturing process will not only help Vietnamese entrepreneurs tap the markets of China and ASEAN, but also pave the way for them to enter other markets such as the European Union and Africa.

At the same time, Vietnam is expected to face numerous challenges. Anecdotal evidence suggests that ACFTA will bring tougher competition to Vietnamese companies in third markets, as there are many similarities in the manufactured products produced by the two countries. Further, there is the risk that with the removal of import tariffs, Vietnam's domestic markets will be inundated with cheap Chinese consumer goods. Surprisingly, however, very little attention is being paid to such an eventuality, and policy responses, from either government or business, have been altogether absent. Delay in the implementation of the ACFTA schedule for the four new members (Cambodia, Laos, Vietnam and Myanmar) until 2015 is often taken as a "good explanation" for this policy gap.

Vietnam–China Trade: Magnitude and Changes

A steady increase is clearly evident in both the volume and value of trade between Vietnam and China during the last decade. The total value of trade in commodities has risen from only US$32 million in 1991 to more than US$20 billion in 2009. This figure is much higher than the target set by the two governments of increasing total bilateral trade to US$15 billion by the end of 2010. So far, Vietnam's total trade with China accounts for around 12 per cent of the country's total foreign trade.

Vietnam's Exports to China

Table 5.2 shows a steady increase in Vietnam's exports to China from 2001 to 2009. Ranked the third largest destination for exports from Vietnam, China's markets presently absorb around 10 per cent of the total value of the country's commodity exports (ranking behind the United States and Japan). Vietnam has recently exported more than 100 commodities to Chinese markets, which can be primarily classified into four categories as follows:

- *Raw production materials*: crude oil, rubber, coal, metal minerals, oil grains, medicinal herbs;
- *Agricultural products*: food (rice, dried cassava), vegetables, fruit (especially tropical fruit such as banana, mango, dragon fruit), tea, rubber and cashew nuts;
- *Aquacultural products*: fresh and frozen produce, some specific tropical items such as snakes and turtles from aquaculture production;

TABLE 5.2
Trade with China, 2001–09 (US$ million)

Year	Total exchange	% Change	Exports	% Change	Imports	% Change	Exports – imports
2001	3,023.6	14.1	1,417.4		1,606.2		–188.8
2002	3,677.1	21.6	1,518.3	7.1	2,158.8	34.4	–640.5
2003	5,021.7	36.6	1,883.1	24.0	3,138.6	45.4	–1,255.5
2004	7,192.0	43.2	2,735.5	45.3	4,456.5	36.8	–1,721.0
2005	8,739.9	21.5	2,961.0	8.2	5,778.9	29.7	–2,817.9
2006	10,420.0	19.2	3,030.0	19.2	7,390.0	27.9	–4,360.0
2007	15,858.0	52.19	3,356.0	10.76	12,502.0	69.17	–9,146.0
2008	17,810.0	12.31	4,010.0	19.49	13,800.0	10.38	–9,790.0
2009*	20,000.0	13.30	4,600.0	14.70	15,400.0	11.59	–10,800.0

Note: * Data for 2009 is estimated.
Source: GSO Yearbooks (various issues); Annual Reports on Imports and Exports, 2001–09.

- *Consumer goods*: handicraft products, footwear, high-quality furniture, detergents, bakery produce.

Table 5.3 shows that major exports from Vietnam to China comprise agricultural commodities (seafood, fruit and vegetables, rubber, tea, coffee, rice). These items account for a relatively high proportion of the total value of exports. In 2006, due to rapidly increasing demand in China's market, rubber alone brought around US$852 million (more than 28 per cent of total exports to China) to Vietnam.

Vietnam's Imports from China

Owing to some favourable factors such as larger production size, geographical proximity and cheaper prices (leading to higher price competitiveness), China has recently become one of the biggest sources of capital and consumer goods to Vietnam. As seen from Table 5.2, the total value of imports from China has increased rapidly from US$1.6 million in 2001 to US$15,400 million in 2009. Chinese exports to Vietnam include about 200 commodities that can be classified into five categories, including:

- *Complete industrial plants and equipment*: for example, plants for cement and sugar production;
- *Machinery:* such as for textiles and agriculture, transport vehicles, medical equipment, equipment for precise measurement;
- *Energy, fuel, production materials:* such as refined oil, fertilizer, cement, steel and iron, construction glass and other materials, chemical products, parts for textiles, garments and foot wear manufacturing;
- *Agricultural products:* such as temperate climate seeds, fruit and vegetables such as pears, apples, plant oils, wheat flour, sugar;
- *Consumer goods and pharmaceuticals:* such as motorbikes, motorbike parts, electronics, watches, clothes, toys, medicinal herbs (Table 5.4).

It is noticeable from Table 5.5, that since 2001, the steadily increasing value of exports from China to Vietnam has made the trade balance between the two countries uneven. China is now the third largest country (after South Korea and Taiwan) with which Vietnam has a trade deficit. The trade

TABLE 5.3
Main Export Commodities to China, 2001–06

Year	2001		2002		2003		2004		2005		2006	
Units	US$ million	%	US$ million	%	US$ million	%	US$ million	%	US$ million	%	US$ million	%
Total trade	1,417.4	100.0	1,518.3	100.0	1,883.1	100.0	2,735.5	100.0	2,961.0	100.0	3,030.0	100.0
Agriculture, forestry and fishery												
Rubber	51.6	3.6	89.8	5.9	160	8.5	358.0	13.1	519.2	18.0	851.8	28.1
Cashew nuts	30.3	2.1	38.3	2.5	53.5	2.8	70.2	2.6	97.4	3.3	94.5	3.1
Seafood	253.0	18.0	173.6	11.4	174.0	9.2	48.2	1.8	62.0	2.1	65.0	2.1
Fruit & vegetables	145.0	10.0	77.8	5.1	86.6	4.6	137.6		34.9	1.2	24.6	0.8
Coffee	2.6	0.2	3.9	0.3	6.9	0.4	5.9	0.2	7.6	0.3	15.9	0.5
Rice	0.5	0.0	1.7	0.1	0.3	0	19.2	0.7	12.0	0.4	12.4	0.4
Tea	0.8	0.1	0.6	0.0	0.8	0	3.5	0.0	6.0	0.0	7.6	0.3
Pepper	6.6	0.5	3.3	0.2	0.7	0	0.4	0.0	0.0	0.0	0.8	0.0
Industrial												
Coal	17.3	1.2	44.3	2.9	51.2	2.7	134.0	4.9	370.2	13.0	594.8	19.6
Crude oil	559.0	39.0	686.8	45.2	863.0	46.0	1,471	53.8	1,160.0	39.0	399.9	13.2
Furniture	9.3	0.7	13.3	0.9	1.3	0.1	30.1	1.1	60.3	2.0	94.1	3.1
Computers	2.7	0.2	3.6	0.2	21.1	1.1	21.6	0.8	74.6	2.5	73.8	2.4
Footwear	5.1	0.4	7.3	0.5	10.9	0.6	19.2	0.7	28.3	0.9	42.0	1.4
Textiles & garments	7.8	0.6	2.1	0.1	7.3	0.4	14.0	0.5	8.1	0.3	29.7	0.9
Electrical cable and wire	0.2	0.0	0.6	0.0	1.6	0.1			7.7	0.3	11.6	0.4
Others	325.6	23.4	371.3	24.7	443.9	23.5	402.6	19.8	522	16.7	711.5	23.6

Source: GSO (various issues): Annual Reports on Exports, 2001–06.

TABLE 5.4
Main Import Commodities from China, 2001–06

Year	2001		2002		2003		2004		2005		2006	
Units	US$ million	%	US$ million	%	US$ million	%	US$ million	%	US$ million	%	US$ million	%
Total trade	1,606	100	2,159	100	3,139	100	4,457	100	5,779	100	7,391	100.0
Steel and iron	54.7	3.4	69.6	3.2	109.4	3.5	409.6	9.2	718.1	12.4	1,296.2	17.5
Machinery	284.0	15.4			515.0	16.4	827.0	18.6	817.6	14.4	1,200.1	16.2
Cloth	48.9	3.0	183.3	8.5	324.0	10.3	447.3	10.0	661.2	11.4	895.6	12.1
Oil	231.7	14.4	473.5	21.9	720.6	23.0	739.8	16.6	884.3	15.3	555.3	7.5
Chemicals	51.5	3.2	95.5	4.4	108.1	3.4	123.8	2.8	169.9	2.9	347.3	4.7
Parts for footwear	51.3	3.2	109.8	5.1	147.0	4.7	290.3	6.5	323.6	5.6	304.8	4.1
Fertilizer	62.6	3.9	58.0	2.7	243.2	7.7	392.0	8.8	264.3	4.6	298.7	4.0
Computers	9.9	0.6			50.8	1.6			155.4	2.7	243.2	3.3
Motorbikes	401.9	25.0	95.5	4.4	47.7	1.5					120.8	1.6
Pesticides	19.3	1.2	26.8	1.2	26.0	0.8	62.4	1.4	76.1	1.3	119.0	1.6
Electronics	3.2	0.2	3.0	0.1	6.4	0.2	51.2	1.1	99.9	1.7	107.4	1.5
Wood and wood products	12.6	0.8			8.0	0.3	25.6	0.6	54.8	0.9	79.6	1.1
Fibres	18.8	1.2	28.4	1.3	43.3	1.4			51.5	0.0	71.9	0.9
Plastics	6.8	0.4	10.5	0.5	14.8	0.5	22.4	0.5	35.2	0.6	59.7	0.7
Pharmaceuticals	6.8	0.4	7.2	0.3	7.9	0.3	6.8	0.1	39.6	0.7	46.9	0.6
Rubber& products		0.7				0.7		0.7		0.5	39.3	0.5
Animal feed	7.4	0.5			27.7	0.9	2.6	0.6	24.4	0.4	37.6	0.5
Tobacco ingredients	22.0	1.4			34.9	1.1	20.8	0.5	30.6	0.5	19.0	0.3
Glass	5.4	0.3	7.2	0.3	3.6	0.1	2.6	0.1	4.9	0.1	5.9	

Source: GSO Annual Statistics on Imports, 2001–06.

TABLE 5.5
Vietnam-China Trade Deficit, 2006–09 (US$ billion)

Year	Vietnam-China trade deficit	Change	Total trade deficit	Percentage
				5
2006	4.36	54.7	5.37	81.1
2007	9,145	109.7	14,000	65.3
2008	11,116	21.5	18,028	61.6
Nov 2009	9,206	4.64	8,447	108

Source: GSO (various issues).

deficit increased from only US$189 million in 2001, to US$4,360 million in 2006 (more than 23 times larger than in 2001). This trend has continued with Vietnam's trade deficit to China reaching US$10,800 million in 2009 (more than 57 times larger than in 2001).

Vietnam–China "Informal" Cross-border Trade

As well as formal trade, informal cross-border trade between the two countries has also developed rapidly during the last two decades. In narrow terms, cross-border trade implies merely a form of consumer goods exchange between inhabitants living in the frontier areas. In broader terms, this form of bilateral trade activity has gradually evolved to become a more effective and comprehensive form of economic cooperation, including not only the transactions of goods, but also of technical equipment and machinery, and import and export of services.

In China, cross-border trade was actively encouraged during the 1980s and 1990s and became a specific form of subregional economic integration policy, specifically applicable towards its neighbouring countries (UNESCAP 1997). With the purpose of accelerating economic development in the southwestern less developed regions of the country, the Chinese government created a package of preferential policies for cross-border trade. Generally, the policy entails a sharp 50 per cent reduction of general tariffs and VAT on the commodities exchanged at some of the identified Chinese remote mainland border areas. The preferential treatment was granted only to local people and enterprises operating in these identified regions.

In Vietnam, cross-border trade activities have become increasingly lucrative since the early 1990s, and since then, have been officially recognized as an important part of the national economy (CDRI 2005). At first, cross-border trade activities were limited to just a few local border gates or forest tracks and thus could not make much of an economic impact. Some years later, with the purpose of "revitalizing" the border areas, the government of Vietnam decided to pilot new policy mechanisms on the promotion of trade activities across the border gate area in Quang Ninh province (Mong Cai border gate). The new mechanism included a broad array of policy incentives ranging from tariff reduction or tax preferences and other economic special treatment. Preference was granted to producers, exporters and importers in the cross-border economic areas. The positive experience from the pilot then was extended to other border provinces, especially those neighbouring China (Quang Ninh, Lang Son, Cao Bang, Ha Giang, Lai Chau and Lao Cai).

In the 1990s, informal cross-border trade activities made up a dominant share, almost 90 per cent, of the total value of the Vietnam-China bilateral trade transactions (this implied that almost all trade transactions at that time were made through informal channels, in a form of cross-boundary trade). Moreover, it was reported that cross-border economic areas as a new form of regional cooperation were highly effective in helping border provinces revitalize their natural potentials and human resources for the sake of social and economic development (CDRI 2005). Although the absolute total trade value was not so large, it was still highly meaningful for the localities given that no international commercial activities were undertaken in these areas before the implementation of this preferential policy.

However, results from the research team's interviews with cross-border exporters reveal several constraints and problems that have recently emerged in the practical implementation of the policies. First, in order to enjoy the preferential treatment granted by the Chinese government, Vietnamese exporters have to transport their goods to the border gates and sell them to Chinese collectors only. Very often, these transactions are made in the form of direct barter trade exchanges, without formal contracts, and in many cases, in implicit ignorance of general international trade rules. These practices are usually at the expense of the Vietnamese side. Second, being bound by trade preferences, the Vietnamese exporters cannot penetrate the Chinese mainland's more competitive and thus more attractive markets.

Moreover, since 2005, due to the requirements of WTO membership and the formation of the ACFTA, the preferential policy on cross-border trade in China was formally dismantled by the central government. Informal cross-border trade between the two countries, therefore, declined to around 10 to 15 per cent of total value of bilateral trade transactions. In practice, however, some forms of the policies remain applicable in Yunnan and Guangxi provinces. Particularly, the province of Yunnan still grants its local people and businesses border trade preferences (such as 50 per cent VAT reduction). At the same time, Guangxi province keeps implementing a "half-preferential trade policy" to partners from other countries. This half-way preferential trade policy implies that cross-border transactions of particular importance for Guangxi goods and materials (such as minerals or natural rubber) are still given preferential tariffs. This "favourable treatment" is very often communicated to the trade partners in informal (i.e., verbal) terms that can be changed quickly without any warning, or trade sanctions. As gleaned from the interviews, the informality of such policy implementation often leads to market uncertainty. Given that a major part of Vietnam's agricultural produce export to China is traded through these two provinces, it becomes obvious that this market uncertainty poses a high cost to Vietnamese trade partners.

2.2 Methodology

This section outlines the approach used to analyse how China's rise has affected the poor of Vietnam through trade.

To test the effects that exports to China have on Vietnam's economy this study uses the gravity model specified by Bergstrand (1985), represented in the equation:

$$EX_{ij} = \beta_0 (Y_i)\beta^1 (Y_j) \beta^2 (D_{ij}) \beta^3 (A_{ij}) \beta^4 u_{ij} \quad (1)$$

where EX_{ij} is exports from country i to country j; Y_i is the GDP of country i and Y_j is the GDP of country j; D_{ij} is distance between country i and country j; A_{ij} is preferential trade factors.

There are six assumptions for this model: (1) country i is a small open economy, "which implies that the foreign price level, the foreign interest rate and foreign income can be treated as exogenous" (Berstrand 1985, p. 477); (2) "identical utility and production functions across countries" (ibid., p. 477) ensures that price and aggregate quantity demanded for manufactured goods export are the same "across all country pairings" (ibid., p. 477); (3) "perfect substitutability of goods internationally in production and consumption"; (4) "perfect commodity arbitrage"; (5) "zero tariffs" and (6) "zero transport costs" (ibid., p. 477).

The triple-index gravity model specification for Vietnam's exports is:

$$Ex_{ijt} = \beta_0(Y_{it})\beta^1(Y_{jt})\beta^2(D_{ij})\beta^3(Brd_{ij})\beta^4(ER_{ijt})\beta^5 u_{ijt} \quad (2)$$

Taking the natural log of equation (2), we have the gravity equation in the log-linear form:

$$lnMex_{ijt} = \beta_0 + \beta_1 lnY_{it} + \beta_2 lnY_{jt} + \beta_3 D_{ij} + \beta_4 Brd_{ij} + \beta_5 lnER_{ijt} + u_{ijt} \quad (3)$$

where Ex_{ijt} is Vietnam's exports of one specific product to country j at time t; Y_{it} is the GDP of Vietnam at time t and Y_{jt} is the GDP of for country j at time t; D_{ij} is the distance between Vietnam and country j; Brd_{ij} is a dummy variable capturing border effects (Brd equals 1 if country j shares the same border with Vietnam and 0 otherwise); ER_{ijt} is the foreign exchange rate between Vietnam's currency and country j currency (VND per unit of foreign currency) at time t; and u_{ijt} is unobserved factors that affect the export. It is assumed to have standard normal distribution. See also Table 5.6.

From this model, we derive the following hypotheses:

- GDP of an economy determines its production capacity. Thus, a rise in Vietnam's GDP is expected to increase its exports ($\beta_1 > 0$).
- Y_j is income of country j, which captures its demand for Vietnam's products. Vietnam is expected to export more to country j when Y_j increases ($\beta_2 > 0$).

TABLE 5.6
Description of Specific Variables

Variables	Description	Sources
EX_{ij}	Vietnam's exports of one specific product to country j	GSO
Y_i	GDP of Vietnam	GSO
Y_j	GDP of country j	UNSTAT
$Dist_{ij}$	Distance between Vietnam and country j	WRI
Border	Dummy variable (1 if Vietnam shares the same border with country j and 0 otherwise)	GSO
ER_{ij}	Exchange rate (VND per unit of foreign currency)	UNSTAT

- The greater the distance between Vietnam and its trading partner, the smaller Vietnam's exports as lower distance reduces transaction cost ($\beta_3 < 0$).
- Border reflects the adjacent effect on trade flows between two countries. If country *j* shares the same border with Vietnam, trade will be encouraged ($\beta_4 > 0$).
- Marshall-Learner condition holds to ensure that depreciation of Vietnam's currency would promote Vietnam's exports ($\beta_5 > 0$).

A key facet of this investigation is its specifically pro-poor focus. To measure the impact of China on poverty we want to highlight sectors that make the most significant contribution to reducing poverty and quantify their impacts. To identify these we first estimate the elasticity of GDP of the importing country, in this case China, to Vietnamese exports and project the absolute values of Vietnam's exports to China. This data is used to identify an export item which, by function of China's GDP growth, has a large impact on poverty reduction in Vietnam. We assume that the higher the value of one specific export item is to China the larger effect this product has on poverty reduction in Vietnam.

The study uses Vietnam Living Standard Survey (VLSS) data for 1992, 1997 and 2004 to estimate the poverty rate in sectors where China's GDP growth is expected to have the largest impact (GSO 1993, 1998, 2004). Moreover, we aim to identify if there is any correlation between the volumes of these export products and the poverty rate in these sectors. These calculations are conducted on the assumption that the poverty rate in a given sector is determined by the poverty rate of a member of an average household who derive their primary source of income from this sector. The leader or main worker of household, and the income of this person, is viewed as the average income among family members. Empirical evidence from a specific product, the export of which to China is expected to impact on poverty reduction in Vietnam, is also provided to support the link between China's growth and poverty reduction in Vietnam.

2.3 Analysis

In order to examine how trade with China has impacted on poverty in Vietnam, this study uses data on Vietnam's fruit and vegetable and fishery exports, as the poor are believed to participate actively in the production processes of these sectors. Data for the year 2005 on sixty-two countries and for 2007 on fifty-four countries was used. To estimate these gravity models, panel data on the GDP of Vietnam and the volume of exports were collected from General Statistics Office of Vietnam. The statistics website of the United Nations (UNSTAT 2010) provides data on Vietnam's trading partners and exchange rates. Distance data was collected from the World Resource Institute (WRI 2010) website. Table 5.7 presents a summary of the statistics for fruit and vegetable exports: the total number of observations is 186. Table 5.8 presents a summary of the data statistics for fishery exports: the total number of observations is 162.

This section reports the estimation and test results using different approaches to specify the most appropriate model for Vietnam's exports. Panel data were estimated by pooled ordinary least square (OLS), first difference (FD), fixed effects (FE) and random effects (RE) (Wooldridge

TABLE 5.7
Summary of Statistics for Fruit and Vegetable Exports

Variables	Obs	Unit	Mean	Standard Deviation	Min	Max
ve_{ij}	186	US$	3843158	1.17e+07	1000	9.43e+07
y_i	186	US$	1.44e+11	1.13e+10	1.31e+11	1.58e+11
y_j	186	US$	2.92e+12	7.33e+12	7.81e+08	5.32e+13
$dist_{ij}$	186	km	7523.5	3976.795	482	16643
br_{ji}	186		0.048387	0.215162	0	1
$lner_{ij}$	186	VND per US$	9706.58	12114.22	1.488378	56554.52

Source: Authors' summary.

TABLE 5.8
Summary of Statistics for Fishery Exports

Variables	Obs	Unit	Mean	Standard Deviation	Min	Max
$fish_{ij}$	162	US$	57817.02	142791.9	3	846146
y_i	162	US$	1.44e+11	1.13e+10	1.31e+11	1.58e+11
y_j	162	US$	3.33e+12	7.77e+12	7.81e+08	5.32e+13
$dist_{ij}$	162	km	7628.593	3785.45	869	16643
br_{ji}	162		.037037	.1894382	0	1
er_{ij}	162	VND per US$	9670.597	11707.16	1.634141	56554.52

Source: Authors' summary.

2006). STATA 10 is used to estimate these gravity models by three methods: OLS, FE and RE. The details are in Appendix 5A. Table 5.9 compares the results of pooled OLS, FE and RE estimations for fruit and vegetable exports, and Table 5.10 compares the results of pooled OLS, FE, and RE estimations for fishery exports.

Tests of Estimation Method Selection and Model Specification

A number of tests were conducted to select the estimation method. The summary of the tests is shown in Tables 5.11 and 5.12. First, OLS could not be used to estimate the model as it is believed to produce inconsistent estimators. Panel data were collected from the same cross-sectional unit over time. Therefore, observation was not independently distributed across time, and unobserved factors could be serially correlated over time. This

TABLE 5.9
Determinants of Fruit and Vegetable Exports, 2005–07

Dependent variable: *lnveij*

Independent Variables	Coefficients (standard error)		
	Pooled OLS	FE	RE
Lnyi	3.7096 (1.48)	1.6267 (1.4926)	3.7062 (0.7061)
Lnyj	0.6779 (0.0559)	2.2049 (1.8484)	0.6805 (0.0915)
Lner	0.0395 (0.049)	2.7547 (1.7737)	0.0441 (0.0803)
Dist	–0.0001 (0.00003)	Dropped*	–0.0001 (0.00006)
Border	2.5465 (0.5983)	Dropped*	2.5638 (0.9807)
_cons	–100.1849 (38.0188)	–108.9745 (27.8410)	–100.1916 (18.1249)
Observations *R-squared*	186 0.5505	186 0.0959	186 0.5505

Note: *Variables: border and distance dropped in FE because of no variation across time.
Source: Authors' calculation.

TABLE 5.10
Determinants of Fishery Exports, 2005–07

Dependent variable: *lnfishij*

Independent Variables	Coefficients (standard error)		
	Pooled OLS	FE	RE
Lnyi	4.0893 (2.0031)	4.5470 (1.8696)	4.0896 (0.8260)
Lnyj	0.7517 (0.0818)	1.7014 (2.3627)	0.7553 (0.1367)
Lner	0.1552 (0.068)	–2.2119 (2.3493)	0.1497 (0.1137)
Dist	–0.0001 (0.00005)	Dropped*	–0.0001 (0.00008)
Border	1.6901 (0.8842)	Dropped*	1.6850 (1.4800)
_cons	–110.3972 (51.4569)	–130.5752 (36.8190)	–110.4739 (21.2038)
Observations	162	162	162
R-squared	0.5505	0.0559	0.4343

Note: *Variables: border and distance dropped in FE because of no variation across time.
Source: Authors' calculation.

TABLE 5.11
Test Results of Gravity Model for Fruit and Vegetable Exports

Null hypothesis	χ^2 – Statistics	χ^2 – Critical value	Decision at 5% significant level
1. Hausman test: H_0: difference in coefficients not systematic	3.27	12.59	Fails to reject H_0
2. BP test: H_0: Var(u) = 0	109.54	3.84	Rejects H_0

Source: Authors' calculation.

caused OLS standard errors and statistics to be misleading though the coefficients were still consistent. Therefore, we focused on FE and RE as the appropriate estimation method.

TABLE 5.12
Test Results of Gravity Model for Fishery Exports

Null hypothesis	χ^2 – Statistics	χ^2 – Critical value	Decision at 5% significant level
1. Hausman test: H_0: difference in coefficients not systematic	1.13	12.59	Fails to reject H_0
2. BP test: H_0: Var(u) = 0	110.88	3.84	Rejects H_0

Source: Authors' calculation.

The Hausman test was implemented to select the estimation method between RE and FE. Details of the test are in the Appendices. The null hypothesis that RE estimators are appropriate could not be rejected as chi^2 statistics are smaller than critical values for two estimations. Therefore, RE is the appropriate method to estimate these gravity models.

Breusch and Pagan Lagrange multiplier (BP) tests were conducted after the RE estimation was designed to check the homoscedasticity assumption of the error terms. The results in Tables 5.11 and 5.12 show that the null hypothesis is rejected, and there is the problem of heteroscedasticity in the model. Therefore, the generalized least square (GLS) RE estimation with robust option was used to correct the standard errors and other statistics of the gravity model on Vietnam's exports.

Parameter Estimates of the Gravity Model for Vietnam's Exports

Parameters of the gravity model for Vietnam's exports were identified using GLS random effect estimation with robust option. Tables 5.13 and 5.14 show the estimated results and that signs of the coefficients of the main explanatory variables are hypothesis robust. The GDP of Vietnam and its trading partners, exchange rate and border effect have positive effects on Vietnam's exports. Conversely, distance has negative impact on exports. Except for the effect of the exchange rate variable in the model for fruit and vegetable exports, all other effects are statistically significant at 5 per cent level. Therefore, we estimate that if China's GDP increases by 1 per cent, Vietnam's export value of fruit and vegetables to China increases by 0.68

TABLE 5.13
Results of the GLS-RE Estimation of the Gravity Model for Fruit and Vegetable Exports, 2005–07

Variables	Coefficients	Standard errors	z – ratio
$\ln Y_i$	3.709653	1.455984	2.55
$\ln Y_j$	0.6779685	0.055021	12.32
$\ln ER_{ij}$	0.0395656	0.048258	0.82
$dist_{ij}$	–0.0001196	0.000034	–3.46
border	2.546499	0.588611	4.33
Constant	–100.1849	37.40061	–2.68

Source: Authors' calculation.

TABLE 5.14
Results of the GLS-RE Estimation of the Gravity Model for Vietnam's Fishery Exports, 2005–07

Variables	Coefficients	Standard errors	z – ratio
$\ln Y_i$	4.089395	1.96569	2.08
$\ln Y_j$	0.751789	0.0802806	9.36
$\ln ER_{ij}$	0.155191	0.066751	2.32
$dist_{ij}$	–0.000108	0.0000484	–2.24
border	1.690158	0.8677395	1.95
Constant	–110.3972	50.49499	–2.19

Source: Authors' calculation.

per cent and that of fishery produce by 0.75 per cent, keeping other factors constant. In order to project the export value of fruit and vegetables and fishery produce to China in the period 2010–15, we assume that China's GDP will increase 8 per cent annually while keeping other factors constant. As can be seen from Figure 5.1, upward trends are projected for Vietnam's fruit and vegetable and fishery exports to China in the period 2010–15. Exports of fruit and vegetables, however, are larger than fishery exports in this period. Thus, we can conclude that fruit and vegetable exports to China have larger effects on Vietnam than fishery exports.

In order to link China's growth with poverty reduction in Vietnam, poverty rate by sector was estimated. The details are given in Appendix 5B. Table 5.15 shows the estimation results and Vietnam's fruit and vegetable and fishery exports to China in 1992, 1997 and 2004. The correlation ratio

FIGURE 5.1
Projection of Fruit and Vegetable and Fishery Export to China, 2010–15

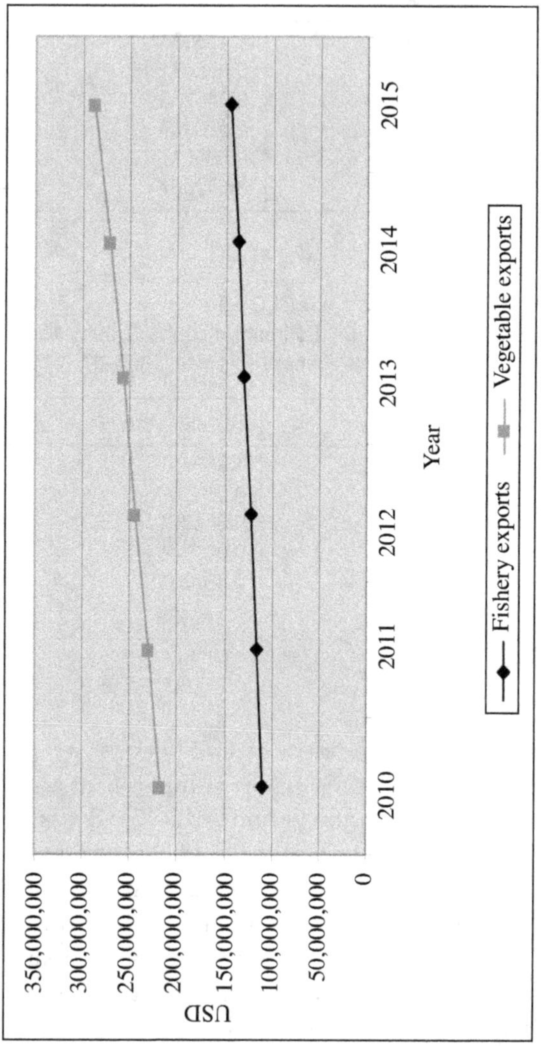

Source: Authors' calculation.

TABLE 5.15
Fruit, Vegetable and Fishery Exports to China and Sectoral Poverty Rate in 1992, 1997 and 2004

Indicators/Year	1992	1997	2004
Fruit and vegetables (US$ million)	0.50	24.50	75.00
Poverty rate in fruit and vegetable sector (%)	67.50	46.00	29.27
Fisheries (US$ million)	4.80	28.80	38.20
Poverty rate in fisheries sector (%)	54.50	37.30	17.08

Source: GSO 1993, 1998, 2004; authors' calculation.

between exports of fruit and vegetables and fishery produce, and the sectoral poverty rate was calculated. The results show that the correlation ratio between fruit and vegetable exports to China and the poverty rate in this sector is –0.9626 while that for fishery exports is –0.9572. This implies that fruit and vegetable exports to China have a slightly stronger effect on poverty reduction than fishery exports.

2.4 Case study of the Fruit and Vegetable Sector: Trade and Poverty in the Banana Industry

The banana industry is a good example of how growth in certain sectors can yield more "bang for their buck" with regards to poverty reduction. Although not a major export product of Vietnam to China, banana exports have nevertheless made a significant contribution to poverty reduction in certain areas. Thus future policies aimed at enhancing growth in this sector have the potential to pay high dividends as a poverty reduction mechanism. This section looks at the case of the banana industry in more detail.

Bananas are grown in all three main regions of Vietnam, with stable producing areas of around 100,000 ha since 1996, accounting for nearly 17 per cent of all fruit producing areas. Bananas are grown on large fields or in small gardens. Some provinces in the Central and Southern regions have large areas from 3,000 ha to 8,000 ha planted with banana trees such as *thanh hoa, nghe an, dong nai, soc trang* and *ca mau* varieties. Recently, banana cultivation has increased mainly in the Northwest and the Central Highlands. However, the area of banana production in the Mekong River Delta — the largest banana production area in Vietnam — has been shrinking over the last ten years as farmers have turned to growing other more profitable crops.

The Centre for Agricultural Policy's (CAP) 2008 survey shows that collectors and wholesalers play a critical role in the local Vietnamese supply chain. Most growers are small-scale producers and they lack research and investment. Overall, Vietnam does not have large intensive banana farms. Bananas are often grown in places with poor soil and intercropped with other crops. Technologically, post-harvest and storage techniques are not sophisticated. Fried and dried bananas are the most common processed products. As the size of this industry is small, collectors and wholesalers play an important role because they are responsible for connecting the growers to processors and markets. This is the largest difference between Vietnam and the Philippines — the largest banana exporter in the ASEAN region — as the absence of collectors in the Philippines helps to cut production costs by one-third. Almost all bananas produced in Vietnam are consumed domestically where retailers are the main sellers in the market. China is the main market for Vietnam's banana exports where wholesalers and processors export directly.

In terms of competitiveness, Vietnam has the lowest production level compared to its main ASEAN competitors such as the Philippines, Indonesia and Thailand. In terms of yield, Vietnam is not particularly competitive as its yield is also lower than that of other countries, except for Thailand. In addition, banana production costs in Vietnam are high. For example, fresh bananas produced for export in the Mekong River Delta cost from US$115 to US$120 per tonne while the freight on-board price of Philippine fresh bananas is US$110 to US$115 per tonne. Vietnam's banana exports also have some quality problems such as skin blemishes and the fruits are not uniform in size and shape. Lack of refrigerated transport results in high spoilage rates and limits access to distant markets. Trade policies also affect Vietnam's competitiveness in the international banana market. For example, Thailand's banana exports to China enjoy a bilateral trade agreement without import tax while a tax of 5 per cent is levied on bananas imported from Vietnam.

Although the banana industry in Vietnam is less competitive than in other ASEAN member countries, CAP's survey shows that Cavendish varieties (especially for export) and processed bananas have the greatest potential for a pro-poor impact. Table 5.16 shows that Cavendish varieties have a strong impact on poverty reduction because they fetch a higher retail price and yield better. This effect is even stronger if this type of banana is exported because returns are higher.

TABLE 5.16
Comparison of Pro-poor Impacts of Fresh and Processed Banana Production

Variety and type of banana	Total income (VND per ha)	Pro-poor income (VND per ha)	Employment creation (FTE per ha)	Total beneficiaries (farmers and workers per ha)
		Fresh		
Su, mat moc, cau	48,000	37,711	2.5	4.5
Cavendish varieties (domestic market)	91,685	66,325	4.0	7.0
Cavendish varieties (export)	134,608	75,380	6.0	9.5
		Processed		
Bom (plaintain)	82,500	70,661	10.0	14.0

Source: CAP (2008).

CAP's survey also shows that though banana production provides lower incomes and profits to farmers than other crops such as cashews or pepper, it helps to reduce poverty as banana production requires lower investment, provides daily income and the trees can be grown on marginal soils as Table 5.17 shows. *Tieu*, a type of Cavendish banana, earns the highest profit and is comparable to cashews. Clearly then, the rapid growth in trade with China during the last decades has had a strong impact on poverty.

2.5 Pro-poor Impact of Imports from China

Previous studies on the impact of trade with China on Vietnam have highlighted the importance of textiles and garments from China in reducing poverty.[2] Therefore, this study has chosen to focus on this sub-sector for a more detailed investigation. The difference here is that this assessment pays attention not only to the direct impact generated by imports from China, but also to possible indirect effects that Chinese imports could generate through Vietnam's garment exports to international markets. Impacts could be significant as China is the largest exporter of garments to Vietnam. As seen from Figure 5.2, China accounted for nearly 34 per

TABLE 5.17
Comparison of Cost, Income and Profit for Banana Varieties, Cashews and Pepper (VND1,000 per ha)

	Bananas			Cashews	Pepper
	Bom (plantain)	*Cau* and *Su*	Cavendish		
	Processing	Worship, eating, processing	Eating, worship, export		
Cost	7,000	7,000	23,835	7,050	120,057
Yield (kg per ha)	15,000	12,000	16,670	1,660	3,000
Income	17,250	18,000	36,674	19,517	215,500
Profit	10,250	11,000	12,840	12,467	95,443
Soil adaptation	Gravel soils	Gravel soils	Light gravel soils + irrigation	Basalt oil	Basalt oil + irrigation
Feasibility	Daily income	Daily income	Daily income (half year)	Once a year	Once a year

Source: CAP (2008).

cent of total imports of garments to Vietnam in 2007, while South Korea — the second largest exporter — accounted for only 19 per cent.

China's garment exports to Vietnam are an important source of affordable consumer goods for the poor. With an income of around US$2 per day, poor people in Vietnam only have access to lower priced products, the cheaper the prices of imported products, the more the poor will be able to access them. Therefore, the bigger the supply of these cheap products is, the larger the benefit to the poor will be. Imported garments and textiles from China are said to be not only cheap in price, but also in plentiful supply, and thus poor people in Vietnam enjoy more benefit from widened access to them.

Another aspect of Chinese exports to Vietnam relates to the potential impacts they have on the Vietnamese garment industry. Vietnam is a large exporter of garments to the global market. Growth in this sub-

FIGURE 5.2
Major Exporters of Garments to Vietnam in 2007

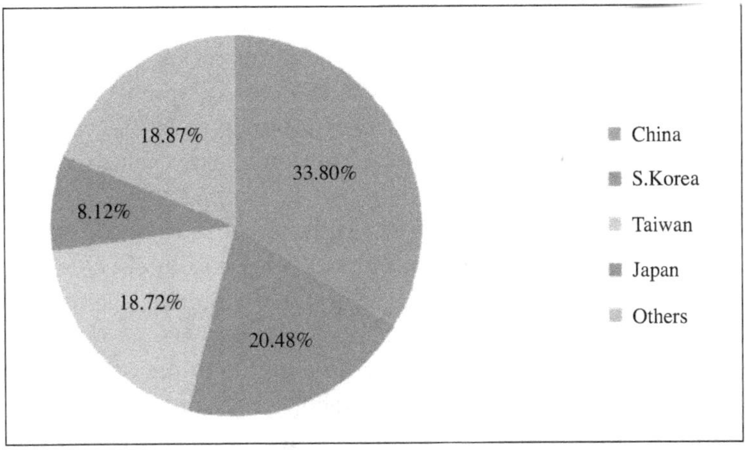

Source: GSO (2009).

sector is believed to help reduce poverty as the majority of workers in this industry are low skilled and poor. At the same time, Vietnam still has to import most of the necessary materials and machinery for textile production. For example, in 2007, Vietnam imported US$6.6 billion of machinery and textiles in order to export over US$7 billion of garments (GSO 2009) in which imports from China accounted for around 35 per cent of Vietnam's total imports. It is therefore highly likely that a decrease in the price of textiles and machinery imported from China would lead to an increase in Vietnam's garment exports. In this way, cheap imports of machinery and materials for textile manufacturing from China could indirectly help reduce poverty in Vietnam through the growth of Vietnam's commodities exports.

A computable general equilibrium (CGE) model was chosen to evaluate this assessment as it captures both direct and indirect impacts of imported textiles and garments from China on poverty reduction. Here we apply the IFPRI/TMD Standard CGE Model developed by Lofgren, Harris and Robinson, with the assistance of Moataz El-Said and Thomas. GAMS software is used to run the model. Data is from SAM 2007 for Vietnam on sixteen commodities, sixteen activities, four factors and four types of households.

In order to assess the impact, the study assumes the shock that the price of imported clothes, textiles and machinery from China declines by 10 per cent and thus, the price of Vietnam's garment exports also decreases by 7 per cent as Vietnam's imports of textiles and garments amounted to 70 per cent of Vietnam's exports of these products in 2007. Each scenario will have its own impact on the poor. The combined scenario is expected to provide a general assessment.

Empirical evidence shows that results are consistent as WALRASX parameter (savings — investment imbalance) is absolutely close to zero. Table 5.18 shows the impact on poverty reduction in Vietnam under different scenarios.

All four types of households benefit when the prices of imports from China decline. In contrast, they lose when the price of Vietnam's garment exports decreases. In the combined scenario, the income of all types of households increases from 0.16 per cent to 0.21 per cent. However, the poor benefit more than the non-poor, particularly the poor in rural areas. Indeed, the rural poor receive the largest benefit as their income increases by 0.21 per cent while that of the non-poor in rural areas increases by 0.16 per cent. These figures in urban areas are 0.19 for the poor and 0.17 per cent for the non-poor. Therefore, we can conclude that the lower price of imported textile materials and machinery from China has a significant impact on the poor.

TABLE 5.18
Changes in Income by Type of Household, percentage (comparison to base scenario without shock)

Type of household	Scenario		
	Price of imports from China declines by 10%	Price of Vietnam exports to China declines by 7%	Combined scenario
Poor in rural areas	1.05	–0.80	0.21
Non-poor in rural areas	1.08	–0.85	0.16
Poor in urban areas	0.83	–0.57	0.19
Non-poor in urban areas	0.85	–0.57	0.17

Source: Authors' calculation.

3. FOREIGN DIRECT INVESTMENT FROM CHINA AND ITS IMPACT ON THE POOR

3.1 Trends and Characteristics of China's FDI

Since the late 1980s, Vietnam's policy-makers have been actively encouraging inflows of FDI. The ability to attract FDI and effectively utilize foreign inflows of capital is considered to be one of the key elements for the success of Vietnam's long-term development strategy.

The country's liberal policy on FDI has been clearly reflected in legal and regulatory frameworks. The first Law on Foreign Investment in Vietnam was passed in 1987, immediately after the announcement of *Doi Moi*, and has been amended several times in 1992, 1996 and 2000, to steadfastly respond to the increased requirements of attracting FDI. Moreover, in order to create "equal ground" for both foreign and domestic investors, the Law on Foreign Investment was integrated with the Law on Domestic Investment to create one unified Investment Law in 2005. The changes and amendments were made to remove obstacles and discrimination against foreign investors and to improve the general investment climate. In practice, a number of incentives have been given to international investors.

A key mechanism in attracting FDI comes in the form of *tax incentives* from the Vietnamese government; tax exemptions, accelerated depreciation, investment allowance and reduced tax rates, have been extended to FDI inflows. In particular, a generous financial incentive package has been offered including tax holidays of two years followed by tax reduction of up to half the regular rate for two years. A preferential corporate income tax of 10–15 per cent has been set for FDI projects in priority sectors (against the regular rate of 21–25 per cent). To encourage reinvestment, Vietnam also offers a refund of profit tax to foreign companies against capital reinvestment over a period of three years. Moreover, foreign companies are exempt from all duties on imported machinery, equipment, raw materials, spare parts and other inputs used either in manufacturing goods for re-export or as a contribution to the total capital of the company. Further, land rental and levies for using infrastructural facilities have been reduced for foreign investments made in poor, mountainous or remote areas or disadvantaged sectors.

There have also been *non-tax incentives*, which have come through Vietnam's commitment not to nationalize or revoke foreign investors' ownership rights and not to restrict their right to undertake appropriate management policies. Vietnam is open to FDI in all sectors with the only exception of defence-related industries. High priority and preferential treatment is given to investment in infrastructure, industry supporting sectors, and high technology projects. At the same time, there is no requirement for minimum investment capital, nor are restrictions imposed on the share of foreign investment in the total equity of investment: foreign investors can own up to 100 per cent of their business. Vietnam also allows maximum investment duration of up to seventy years. Moreover, no limits or restrictions on remittance of earnings, profits or dividends are imposed. Foreign investors can freely repatriate the earnings and profit derived from their business.

In addition to active involvement in the regional and international multilateral cooperation programme, the government of Vietnam has negotiated a number of bilateral agreements with more than fifty countries and territories on investment promotion and protection. These commitments are all made towards the common goals of market opening and investment liberalization.

In order to further fulfil its commitment towards an improved investment climate, Vietnam has recently accelerated public administration reforms through implementing the comprehensive Programme on Public Administration Reform (PAR). The simplification of investment licensing procedures is seen as one of the key outcomes of the reform. A "One Stop Shop" mechanism is widely implemented by many respective local authorities to ease administrative procedures for foreign investors and to reduce their operational costs.

Vietnam has also simplified its visa application procedure, and has adopted some new policies such as the twelve entry-exit measures, one of which exempts Chinese citizens from filling in the entry-exit registration record and another improves entry-exit inspection services. At the Friendship Border Pass (Langson–Guangxi), one of the key ports in the south-north economic corridor, customs clearance information services have been launched, providing and disseminating a range of information to the public through a computerized service and exhibition of free printed materials. Although Vietnam and China do not have a bilateral investment treaty, the "Comprehensive Cooperation Treaty" recently signed by senior leaders of the two governments contains important provisions on investment. These provisions greatly contribute towards a more favourable investment climate for Chinese investors while remaining in line with international standards.

Magnitude and Change

In the twenty-year period 1988–2007, China was ranked the twelfth largest investor in Vietnam, with total registered capital of US$1,792.2 million and implemented capital of US$253.2 million in 550 projects distributed unevenly across various industries (FIA 2009). However, the relative share of China's FDI in total FDI to Vietnam was still very modest, accounting for only 1.46 per cent of registered and 0.86 per cent of implemented capital, for the period 1988 to 2008. A big interval can be observed in the investment amounts between China and other top foreign investors (Table 5.19).

More recently, the size of China's FDI in Vietnam has increased from almost zero to US$2.742 billion of registered capital in 2009 (though the corresponding implemented capital was just US$386.3 million). New FDI inflows to Vietnam in 2009 were US$210 million (registered), a reduction of 37 per cent compared to 2008 due to the global financial crisis.

As can be seen from Table 5.19, in terms of registered capital, China's FDI is about 12–13 per cent of the corresponding figure for South Korea which was the top investor in Vietnam up to 2008. The gap is even larger in terms of implemented capital which counts for less than 10 per cent; even compared with Singapore and Taiwan, the second and the third biggest investors in Vietnam, China's FDI counts for a far smaller amount. In the two decades of 1988–2007, FDI from both of these two largest investors was six times higher than that of China in terms of registered capital and just over ten times higher in terms of implemented investment.

TABLE 5.19
Ranking of FDI by Country, 1988–2007

Rank	Country	Number of projects	Registered capital (US$)	Implemented capital (US$)
1	South Korea	1,857	14,398,138,655	2,738,114,393
2	Singapore	549	11,058,802,313	3,858,078,376
3	Taiwan	1,801	10,763,147,783	3,079,209,610
4	Japan	934	9,179,715,704	4,987,063,346
5	British Virgin Islands	342	7,794,876,348	1,375,722,679
6	Hong Kong	457	5,933,188,334	2,161,176,270
7	Malaysia	245	2,823,171,518	1,083,158,348
8	USA	376	2,788,623,488	746,009,069
12	China	550	1,792,264,711	253,214,212

Source: FIA (2008).

In 2008, new registered capital from China to Vietnam was just US$334 million accounting for a very small 0.5 per cent of total registered FDI in Vietnam.

A very clear pattern emerges if one looks at China's FDI outflows to Vietnam over time. Chinese investment counted for a very minor share of total FDI in the 1990s, both in terms of capital volume and project scale. The largest new inflow of implemented Chinese FDI reached only US$24.2 million[3] in 1995. However, the volume increased faster during the 2000s to reach almost US$1.2 billion during the period 2000–07. China's total FDI to Vietnam during the last eighteen years is shown in Figure 5.3. The sharp increase in 2006–07 was mainly due to implementation of the new Investment Law (2005) which provides more favourable conditions for foreign investors. The second reason is the accelerated implementation of China's "going global" strategy.

Geographical proximity and the opening up of land borders have shaped both the volume and nature of Chinese FDI to Vietnam. Indeed, investments to Vietnam mainly originated from southeastern provinces such as Guangxi, Guangdong, Sichuan, Hepei, Jiangxu, Shandong and Shanghai (Ha Thi Hong Van and Do Tien Sam 2009). The proximity to

FIGURE 5.3
New Chinese FDI Flows to Vietnam, 1990–2008

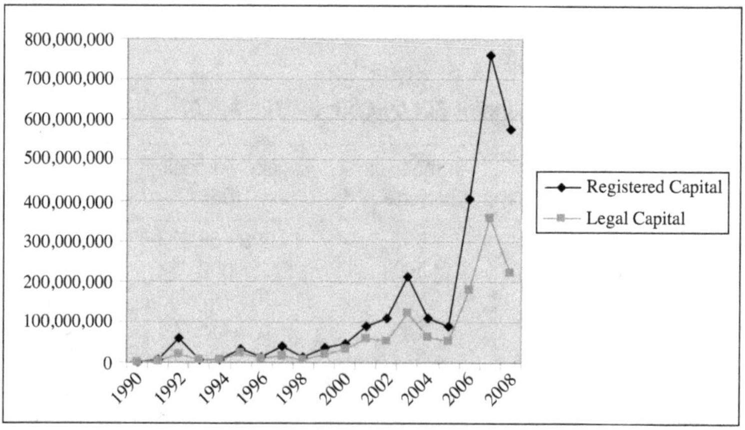

Source: FIA (2009).

the border of Yunnan and Guangxi provinces is said to make them a "champion" of investments to Vietnam in the near future. A number of projects, including infrastructure and special economic zones, are underway. Fuco Steel Ltd in Ba Ria Vung Tau province — the largest project in the first quarter of 2010 with a total investment capital of US$180 million is one example. The next largest projects are Vietnam–China Mineral and Metallurgy Ltd in Lao Cai province and Tham Viet Investment Ltd in Hai Phong, both with investment capital of US$175 million (FIA 2010). Among CLMV (Cambodia, Laos, Myanmar and Vietnam), Vietnam is the top FDI recipient from China accounting for about 41.1 per cent of the total amount of China's investments in the region between 2003 and 2006.

Sectoral Composition of China's FDI

In terms of sectoral composition (Figure 5.4) the statistics show that the manufacturing and construction sector dominates, accounting for 71 per cent of China's total registered FDI during the period 1990–2008. However, the service sector's share is increasing and now counts for around 25 per cent of the total investment. Meanwhile, the total share of Chinese FDI in the agriculture, forestry and fisheries sector remains very minor. In the

FIGURE 5.4
China's Registered FDI Sectoral Composition, 1990–2008

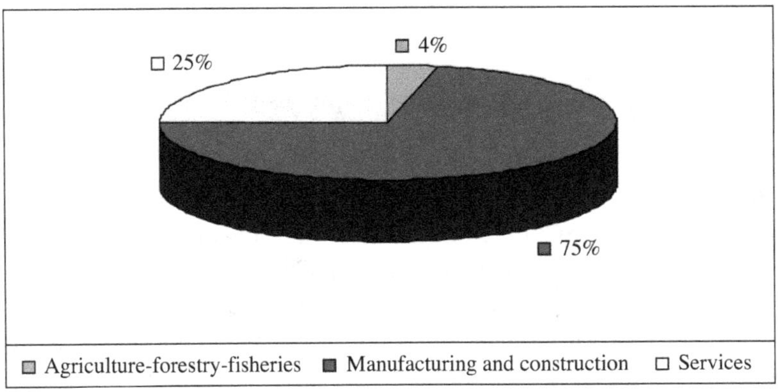

Source: Authors' estimation based on FIA (2009) data.

service sector, real estate is the largest sub-sector accounting for about 14 per cent of the total investment capital by the end of the first quarter of 2010 (FIA 2010). Although Chinese investments in natural resource extraction are not large, certain pursuits like mineral exploitation are particularly harmful to the environment, making China's impact more serious than the figures might suggest (Rutherford, Lazarus and Kelley 2008).

A visible change in China's investment profile has become discernable during the last few years. Hotel and restaurant services, real estate business, manufacturing, construction and mining have become the major industries attracting China's investment. In 2009, total new FDI inflows and incremental FDI capital from China for hotel and restaurant services reached US$8,794.2 million accounting for 41 per cent of the total investment. The corresponding figure for real estate services is 37 per cent, making it the second largest recipient of China's FDI. The third largest share of China's FDI goes to the manufacturing sector, accounting for 14 per cent of the total. These figures show a strong trend of China's FDI moving to the service sector. Mining and construction are the next destinations of China's FDI. For the time being, investment in these sectors is still modest compared to that in the top three invested sectors (i.e. hotel and restaurants, real estate and manufacturing). For example, China's investment in construction in Vietnam was just US$487.4 million by December 2009, equating to 5.5 per cent of total FDI in the hotel and restaurant sector. During the same period, only six projects were implemented in the mining sector; Chinese investment in this sector was only US$397 million, accounting for 4.5 per cent of that in the top invested sectors. The general picture of Chinese FDI to Vietnam in 2009 can be seen in Table 5.20.

Geographical Distribution of China's FDI

Although Chinese FDI projects are found in many provinces throughout Vietnam, their geographical distribution is uneven. The most highly attractive provinces to China's FDI are those which have better infrastructure or are geographically close to China. Hai Phong province in the north, which has the largest port, received the largest share of China's FDI with a value of US$329.3 million, accounting for 12.05 per cent of the country's total in March 2010. Lao Cai is ranked second with twenty-seven projects and total registered investment capital of US$307.9 million, followed by Ba Ria-Vung Tau province with seven projects and total registered investment

TABLE 5.20
Top Ten Sectors of China's FDI to Vietnam in 2009

Rank	Industry	Number of new projects	Newly registered capital (US$ million)	Incremental registered capital (US$ million)	Total newly registered and incremental registered capital (US$ million)
1	Hotel and restaurants	32	4,982.6	3,811.7	8,794.2
2	Real estate	39	7,372.4	236.1	7,608.5
3	Manufacturing	245	2,220.0	749.3	2,969.2
4	Construction	74	388.3	99.2	487.4
5	Mining	6	397.0	0.0	397.0
6	Arts and entertainment	12	291.8	0.0	291.8
7	Wholesale, retail distribution and repairing	115	191.7	46.5	238.2
8	Transportation and warehouses	26	109.8	74.8	184.6
9	Electricity, gas, water and air-conditioners	16	129.0	27.9	156.9
10	Scientific and specialist contracts	148	89.0	10.9	99.9

Source: FIA (2009).

capital of US$189.8 million, accounting for accounting for 11.2 per cent and 6.9 per cent of China's total FDI in Vietnam, respectively. The next largest localities are Binh Duong province, Ho Chi Minh City and Tien Giang province (FIA 2010).

Form of Foreign Investment

The 2005 Foreign Investment Law provides high flexibility in the choice of the form of foreign investment. The policy change is recognized to be facilitating FDI flows including those from China. The number of 100 per cent foreign-owned companies increased, overtaking the earlier dominance of joint-ventures. The composition of China's FDI in Vietnam by form of investment is shown in Table 5.21.

As seen from Table 5.21, the 100 per cent foreign-owned projects outnumber the other three forms of investment. A similar pattern is also reflected in total registered investment and in terms of legal capital. The total registered capital of China's 100 per cent foreign-owned projects is more than double that of its counterpart, joint venture projects. The number of projects and their registered capital in the forms of business cooperation contracts and shareholding companies are minor. The capital sizes of these two last forms account for just 2.8 per cent and 1.2 per cent of China's total FDI registered capital, respectively.

3.2 Impact of China's FDI on the Economy and Poverty Reduction in Vietnam

Possible Competitive and Complementary Attributes of China's FDI

An impact that can be expected from China's FDI to Vietnam is increased market competition. Indeed, a certain level of competition is observed between Chinese FDI businesses and Vietnamese counterparts such as in the hotel and restaurant, and real estate services. In these services, the level of competition seems higher than in the manufacturing sector. However, even in these service sectors, clear complementarities are also observed. For example, Chinese cuisine tends to serve the hotel and restaurant sector

TABLE 5.21
China's FDI in Vietnam by Form of Investment as of March 2010

Order	Form of investment	Number of projects	Total investment (US$ million)	Legal capital (US$ million)
1	100% foreign owned capital	463	1,773	852
2	Joint venture	171	845	366
3	Business cooperation contracts	38	76	48
4	Shareholding companies	9	33	28
	Total	681	2,727	1,294

Source: FIA (2010).

and thus becomes more complementary than competitive. This is also true of the manufacturing sector: Chinese investments often take place where Vietnamese companies do not have enough expertise, technology or investment capacity. Projects such as Fuco Steel Ltd in Ba Ria and China Mineral and Metallurgy Ltd in Lao Cai are two such examples. Hence, competitive pressure from Chinese FDI has so far proved to be not very strong.

A further possible competitive impact could be investment diversion from third countries, but this is reported to be small. The evidence is that FDI to Vietnam has been growing parallel with that to China over the same time period. With respect to foreign investing countries, Vietnam and China share some large common investors such as Hong Kong, Taiwan, Japan and Singapore. However, the level of investment of these countries in both Vietnam and China has simultaneously increased during the last ten years. This implies that China and Vietnam so far are not big competitors in attracting FDI. Some of the largest investors to Vietnam are not going to China as much. For instance, though South Korea has been the top foreign direct investor to Vietnam for a long time, its share in China is very moderate (though it is still in the country's top ten). South Korea's FDI to China decreased by 13.8 per cent in 2009 compared to 2008 (US-China Business Council Website 2010).

Another reason for the low level of FDI diversion effects from third countries to China is that Vietnam has lower labour costs compared to China. The average wages of workers in China's FDI sector was 32,653 yuan per year in 2008 (National Bureau of Statistics of China 2009), equivalent to almost US$400 per month which is much greater than the average corresponding figure of US$140 per month in Vietnam.[4]

Moreover, in terms of the sectoral distribution of FDI, there are large differences between China and Vietnam that further limit the potential of FDI diversion. The top FDI destination in China is the manufacturing sector, which accounted for 59 per cent of total FDI in China in 2008, while real estate took up 22 per cent and the leasing and business services sector accounted for 6 per cent. This structure is different in Vietnam, where the top FDI sector is hotels and restaurants, accounting for 41 per cent of total FDI in 2009. This explains why the level of foreign investment diversion from the country is still not so high.

However, the picture for the real estate sector may be slightly different as FDI in this sector is ranked second largest in both countries. Also, geographical proximity and similar socio-economic conditions between China and Vietnam could result in possibly larger investment diversion effects. Some real estate investors may go to China instead of Vietnam. Moreover, the diversion effects could be much more obvious in the near future given the anticipated greater growth and further diversification of China's economy. That China is becoming increasingly attractive to FDI is evidence of this. Since China joined the WTO in 2001, the pace of FDI has increased sharply, reaching US$60.3 billion in 2005 and US$92.4 billion in 2008 (Ministry of Commerce of People's Republic of China 2009). Therefore, Vietnam, as any country in Southeast Asia, should take heed of the possible effects of foreign direct investment diversion to China.

A complementary impact could be technology transfer and skills upgrading of the Chinese FDI projects' labour force. Although little evidence has been found, some transfer of skills can be observed in a number of service sectors such as restaurant, hotel and sports services. Also, China's FDI has contributed to technology transfer and human capital formation in the manufacturing and construction sectors. Chinese investment companies sub-contract Vietnamese counterparts, and technology and skills are transferred through mutual operational cooperation. Entrepreneurs and local labour skills have increased due to cooperation with Chinese counterparts. In this sense, China's FDI has visible positive impacts. The Vietnamese poor who work for China's FDI enterprises and projects have certainly benefited from improving and upgrading their work skills which in turn help them to earn more income. On the other hand, it is true that most of the technologies brought into Vietnam are outdated and bring little technological progress (such as the technology used in Chinese constructed sugar mills).

At the same time, very little employment has been created by Chinese FDI compared to total employment in the economy and the total number of workers in the FDI sector as a whole. By 2008, a total of 10,782 Vietnamese labourers had been recruited by China's FDI projects. Although the sector contributes to increased employment in Vietnam, the number is still very modest, accounting for only 0.6 per cent of total employment in the FDI sector.[5] The employees in China's FDI enterprises were concentrated in a small number of provinces such as Dong Nai, HCM City, Quang Ninh, Bac Giang and Tay Ninh for the period 1990–2008. However, it seems that this employment creation has not made a real difference in the economy. The provinces that have most benefited in terms of employment from China's FDI are presented in Figure 5.5.

FIGURE 5.5
Employment by China's FDI Projects in 2008

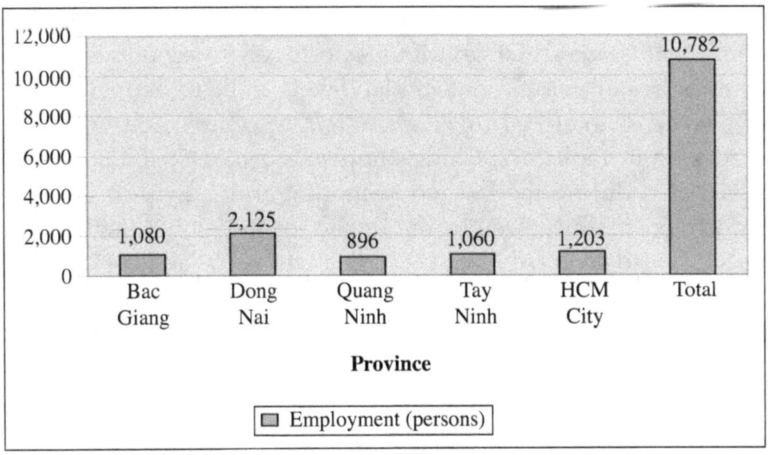

Source: FIA (2009).

China's FDI is also reported to have a direct environmental impact. A new tendency of China's FDI is the move towards mining and mineral extraction industries which have a negative impact on the environment and the living conditions of the poor, especially in the mountainous areas where the poor ethnic minority groups live (Rutherford, Lazarus and Kelley 2008).

FDI, Growth and Poverty Reduction

China's FDI could affect poverty reduction in Vietnam by enhancing the country's economic growth rate, but there are also a variety of other potential mechanisms. Blomstrom, Lipsey and Zejan (1996) and Tran Trong Hung (2004) suggest Vietnam's poverty incidence may be affected by, among other factors, Vietnam's GDP growth, the ratio of FDI over Vietnam's GDP, employment statistics, and government expenditure (in addition to a number of dummies in their regression models[6]). Due to the limited number of observations in the case of China's FDI in Vietnam, the regressions may not be appropriately applied. However, direct comparisons of these factors can certainly reflect the extent to which China's FDI could impact on the country's poverty reduction.

Growth has played a large role in reducing Vietnam's poverty figures over the past twenty years. As part of the total FDI in Vietnam, there is no doubt that China's FDI contributes positively to economic growth in Vietnam as its partner. Its contribution level can be measured both in its relative share of total FDI to Vietnam, and in comparison with its total GDP. As seen in Table 5.22, China's implemented FDI capital in Vietnam has fluctuated during the last ten years though it has been showing an upward trend recently. Due to the impact of the global financial crisis, China's FDI also decreased in 2009 compared to 2008 and 2007. However, Vietnam's GDP has been increasing constantly, albeit at a slower pace. Vietnam's economy still grew at the rate of 5.32 per cent in a crisis-affected 2009 reaching US$91,764 million in value.

Indeed, China's FDI in Vietnam as part of the country's GDP is minor, accounting for only 0.02 per cent in 2000. The figure improved slightly by 0.08 per cent in 2003, 0.15 per cent in 2007 and 0.09 per cent in 2008. However, all these figures are very small meaning that China's FDI, up to now, has contributed only modestly to Vietnam's economic growth. That economic growth is the major driving force for poverty reduction leads to the argument that China's FDI does not strongly affect poverty reduction in Vietnam.

Another critically important factor that has contributed directly to poverty reduction in Vietnam is the huge effort by the Vietnamese government through various poverty reduction programmes. For example, the targeted Socio-economic Development Programme for Extremely Difficult Communes in the Mountainous and Ethnic Minority Regions (called Programme 135) which has been implemented over the last ten years, and many other programmes supporting disadvantaged regions and ethnic minority peoples. This kind of government intervention is realized through increasing government expenditure in the identified areas. Given that a considerable share of government expenditure is utilized for socio-economic service programmes such as healthcare, education, sports and culture and especially poverty reduction programmes as indicated above, government expenditure is often considered as a supporting indicator for poverty reduction. The share of budget for socio-economic service programmes in total government expenditure is always around more than half in the case of Vietnam (for example, 53.06 per cent in 2007). Other

TABLE 5.22
China's FDI in Vietnam as a Proportion of GDP and Government Spending

Year	GDP growth (%)	China's implemented FDI (US$ million)	GDP (US$ million)	China's FDI/GDP (%)	Government spending (US$ million)	China's FDI/Vietnam government's spending (%)
2000	6.79	6.44	31,207.89	0.02	7,699.477	0.08
2001	6.89	12.77	32,259.43	0.04	8,698.207	0.15
2002	7.08	15.52	35,079.65	0.04	9,704.095	0.16
2003	7.34	29.90	39,801.39	0.08	11,755.51	0.25
2004	7.79	15.65	45,362.93	0.03	13,582.49	0.12
2005	8.44	12.62	53,105.15	0.02	16,623.43	0.08
2006	8.23	57.29	60,828.52	0.09	19,233.67	0.30
2007	8.46	107.23	71,035.02	0.15	24,806.47	0.43
2008	6.18	81.69	89,140.62	0.09	29,634.62	0.28
2009	5.32	30	91,764	0.032		

Note: The ratio between registered FDI capital and implemented FDI capital is assumed to be equal to that of the period 1988–2007 as a whole; official exchange rate is used to convert figures from VND into US$.

Source: Authors' estimate based on GSO (2009): FIA (2009).

donor programmes such as those of the World Bank (Northern Mountains Poverty Reduction Project), ADB (Supporting the Implementation of Poverty Reduction Programme II (SIPRP II) approved in 2005), and UNDP are also seen as being of great help in poverty reduction.

The estimated figures in Table 5.22 show that China's implemented FDI as a per centage of Vietnamese government spending is also very small. In 2000, China's implemented FDI capital in Vietnam was just 0.08 per cent of the corresponding government spending in Vietnam and the corresponding figure for 2008 was only 0.28 per cent. For all other years during the last nine to ten years, the figures are all smaller than 0.5 per cent, showing the possible minor impact of China's FDI on poverty alleviation in Vietnam. When China's FDI is compared with government spending for socio-economic development and service programmes only, these figures double. However, even in these cases, China's FDI takes up just a very minor share with all figures less than 1 per cent for this part of government spending, which has effective and direct impact on poverty reduction in Vietnam. Therefore, it can be seen that even though the comparison is made simply in absolute terms, the impact of China's FDI on poverty reduction in Vietnam would be minor because the volume is too small to have a meaningful impact.

Even if the volume of China's FDI was the same as government spending, it would have a much smaller impact on poverty in Vietnam in comparison. This is because poverty reduction *per se* is not a motive for FDI, capital accumulation is. Thus, FDI reduces poverty through enhancing economic growth, is indirect in nature and its exact effects are debatable in both theory and practice. In contrast, Vietnamese government spending is used for infrastructure construction and poverty reduction programmes. Both of these investments help the poor directly by improving their livelihoods in different regions in Vietnam, especially in rural and remote areas.

4. CHINA'S ODA TO VIETNAM AND ITS IMPACT ON POVERTY REDUCTION

4.1 Vietnam's Policy on ODA

The Roundtable organized by the World Bank in Paris in November 1991 has been cited as the beginning of international official development assistance to Vietnam. Since then, commitment of ODA to the country has increased rapidly. The donor community has extended to include fifty-one international donors (twenty-eight bilateral and twenty-three multilateral) that have regular operations in Vietnam. Apart from the traditional donors from OECD-DAC, new members such as India, Czech and China have joined the community. The amount of ODA committed to Vietnam from 1993 to 2008 totals US$35.217 billion, of which around 80 per cent is in the form of preferential loans, and 20 per cent in grants.

During this period, five development areas have been identified as pro-poor priorities for ODA, namely:

- Agricultural and rural development (including agriculture, irrigation, forestry and fishery) with the aim of poverty reduction and hunger alleviation;
- Modernization of economic infrastructure;
- Construction of social infrastructure (health, education and training, population and development);
- Protection of environment and natural resources;
- Institutional capacity strengthening and human resources development, technology transfer, enhancing R&D capacity.

4.2 China's ODA to Vietnam

In the past, especially during the Vietnam–American war, a large package of official assistance from China was extended to the Vietnamese people. Among others, the civil support from China included a number of projects focusing on the construction of manufacturing factories, such as Ha Bac fertilizer factory and Thai Nguyen Iron and Steel complex. Most of these projects have since become outdated, obsolete and subject to either comprehensive upgrading or closure.

The last decade has seen the renewal of development cooperation between Vietnam and China. As reported by the Ministry of Planning and Investment (MPI), China's ODA to Vietnam largely concentrates on development sectors and areas such as industry, mining, railway construction, energy, textiles, chemicals, and physical infrastructure. These ODA flows are largely in the form of preferential loans. The provision of ODA grants has more of a political focus and is often made to areas such as culture and human resource development.

TABLE 5.23
Chinese ODA to Vietnam, 1993–2008

	ODA (US$ million)	Loan (US$ million)	Grant (US$ million)
Chinese ODA to Vietnam	358.91	329.63	29.28
Chinese ODA as a percentage of total ODA to Vietnam	1.09%	1.20%	0.53%

Source: MPI (2008*a*).

In fact, China's recent ODA to Vietnam is rather modest in both total amount and its per centage share of Vietnam's total ODA. As shown in Table 5.23, the total of both soft loans and grants from China between 1993 and 2008 is just over US$358 million, (almost 1.1 per cent of the total ODA inflows to Vietnam), of which more than US$328 million is preferential loan (1.2 per cent of total soft loans provided to Vietnam) and only around US$29 million is in the form of grants (0.55 per cent of total grants to Vietnam).

4.3 China's Preferential Loans to Vietnam

Since 1997, following renewal of the formal relationship between the two countries, preferential loans from China to Vietnam have steadily increased, focusing mainly on the reconstruction and upgrading of China's former projects. Table 5.24 shows the actual loans including both completed and ongoing projects. The capital provided through such various ODA has enabled recipient enterprises to remarkably improve their operational capacity. For example both the Thai Nguyen Iron and Steel Complex and the Ha Bac fertilizer factory are now in regular operation as a result of preferential loans from China.

At the 2006 ASEAN–China conference, the Chinese Premier said that China was willing to provide a preferential loan of US$500 million to Vietnam if Vietnam could make a good proposal for its implementation. Based on this high level commitment, the Vietnamese government called for investment project proposals which were then short-listed by the Ministry of Planning and Investment before being submitted to the prime minister for official approval. The final approved list put to China for its consideration includes three big high priority projects, namely:

TABLE 5.24
Projects Supported by Preferential Loans from China

No.	Projects	Loan amount (yuan million)	Remarks
	A. Completed projects		
1	Reconstruction of 8th March textile factory	17.5	
2	Upgrading Star rubber factory	12.5	
3	Upgrading Hai Phong iron plating factory	11.2	
4	Purchasing equipment for small-scale hydropower plants in Vietnam's five northern border provinces	15.0	
5	Upgrading Hai Duong poultry factory	11.2	
6	Upgrading Thai Nguyen plywood factory	40.0	
7	Upgrading Vinh Phu textile company	41.5	
8	Reconstruction and extension of Nam Dinh textile factory	233.3	
9	Investment in 19th May textile company	6.0	
10	Purchasing work equipment for Transportation Construction Company No-6	52.0	
11	Reconstruction of Thai Nguyen iron and steel complex and Ha Bac fertilizer factory	55.2	
12	Construction of Cao Ngan thermo power factory	710.0	
	B. Ongoing projects		
13	Construction of Sin Quyen copper ore screening factory	US$40.5 million	3% interest rate, payback in 15 years
14	Construction of railway signal system for the lines Hanoi–Dong Dang; Ha Noi–Thai Nguyen; Hanoi–Lao Cai; and in Hanoi	530 million yuan	3% interest rate, payback in 15 years
15	Modernisation of Thong Nhat Railway signal system; line Vinh city–Ho Chi Minh City	50 million yuan	3% interest rate, payback in 15 years

Source: MPI (2008*a*).

- Construction of a chemical fertilizer factory in Ninh Binh province by Vietnam Chemical Cooperation (US$400 million).
- Construction of the urban Hanoi-Ha Dong railway line, by the Railway Authority, Ministry of Transport (US$150 million).

- Rural telecommunication project, under Vietnam's General Electricity Corporation (EVN) (US$100 million).

So far only the project for construction of the Ha Noi–Ha Dong urban railway line has been approved by the Chinese government, the other two are still under official consideration.

4.4 China's Grants to Vietnam

As shown in Table 5.25, the number of grants provided by China during the period 1993–2008 is not significant. Moreover, the grants are largely focused on projects of a political nature.

Major projects currently supported by grants from the Chinese government include:

(i) Sino-Vietnamese Friendship Palace: this project is expected to be implemented with an initial grant of RMB150 million. The Chinese embassy in Hanoi recently announced that an additional grant

TABLE 5.25
Chinese Grant Projects to Vietnam, 1993–2008

No.	Projects	Amount (US$ million)	Recipients
1	Construction of the hostel in Ho Chi Minh Political Academy	1.21	Ho Chi Minh Political Academy
2	Construction of the hostel in Ho Chi Minh Political Academy	2.41	Ho Chi Minh Political Academy
3	Construction of China-Vietnam Friendship House	6.04	
4	Grant committed (60 million yuan) within the China-Vietnam Treaty on Technical Cooperation	7.24	
5	Grant committed (50 million yuan) within the China-Vietnam Treaty on Technical Cooperation	6.25	

Source: MPI (2008*a*).

of RMB50 million will be made, bringing the total to RMB200 million;

(ii) The project to construct a 15-storey residence for Ho Chi Minh Political Academy was completed in October 2009;

(iii) A grant of RMB20 million is committed to support study tours to China for Vietnamese government officials to gain experience from exchange trips;

(iv) As informed by the Chinese Embassy in Hanoi, China will provide financial support (in grant form) to developing countries, including Vietnam, for 100 "clean energy" projects. Eligible projects include small-scale hydropower, solar energy and gas. Currently, Vietnamese and respective Chinese partners are working to fulfil this plan.

Clearly, economic cooperation in the form of ODA between Vietnam and China has been increasing during the last decade. However, there is not much evidence to suggest that these projects are pro-poor. Indeed, very little of the assistance is designed to focus on Vietnam's prioritized pro-poor areas and sectors.

4.5 Vietnam–China Technical Cooperation

Since the mid-1990s, several key fields of technical cooperation, where specialists from both China and Vietnam work together towards a common goal, have emerged:

Cooperation in transport and communication: At a meeting of the Chinese and Vietnamese prime ministers in Beijing in May 2004, the idea of building "Two Corridors and One Economic Circle" by 2020 was proposed. In November 2006, Vietnam and China signed a Memorandum of Understanding on the said strategy. In July 2008 the Vietnamese government approved the development plan to build the Lao Cai–Hanoi–Hai Phong–Quang Ninh Economic Corridor, and Lang Son–Hanoi–Hai Phong–Quang Ninh as an important section of the "Two Corridors". It was agreed that the "Two Corridors and one Economic Circle" project should be put under the auspices of the Working Group on Economic Cooperation of the two countries.

Cooperation in healthcare provision: Utilizing the Special Fund for Regional Cooperation in Asia and the China-ASEAN Cooperation Fund, Vietnam and China have actively cooperated in the prevention and control of livestock disease epidemics and the promotion of cross-border epidemic prevention and control in the subregion. China provided some training sessions on bird flu diagnosis, and trained technicians from Vietnam in combating the virus. Close collaboration has been initiated to substitute green opium cultivation in the border provinces with other crops. Many solid efforts have been made to strengthen technical cooperation between the two countries in law enforcement on drug prohibition and to crack down on a number of major transnational cases of making and trafficking drugs.

Cooperation in tourism: Substantial progress has been achieved through cooperation in border tourism, especially the area between Vietnam's northeastern provinces and Guangxi province, China. Vietnam has actively cooperated with China in planning large-scale natural-setting performance programmes, for example the "Impression–Ha Long Bay" programme. Tremendous efforts have also been made recently to promote cooperation in maritime tourism between Bei Hai in China and Ha Long Bay in Vietnam.

Cooperation in human resource development: Vietnam and China have actively collaborated in human resource development. Through holding various workshops and technology training classes since 2005, China has provided training to a large number of Vietnamese officials and technical staff. The two countries have undertaken a number of joint research studies and seminars on prevention and control of the trafficking of women and children, and the promotion of safety for immigrants.

Cooperation with Guangxi and Yunnan provinces: Cooperation projects in agricultural development, environmental protection, tourism, health and human resource development have been comprehensively implemented between Vietnam and the two southern provinces of China, Guangxi and Yunnan. Along with the accelerated trade and investment, Guangxi has signed agreements with Quang Ninh province of Vietnam on agricultural cooperation. Yunnan has been active in training various Vietnamese technicians.

5. MAIN FINDINGS AND POLICY RECOMMENDATIONS

5.1 Main findings

Trade with China and its Impact on Poverty in Vietnam

China's impact on Vietnam is most clearly observed in rapidly growing bilateral trade. China has become Vietnam's third largest trade partner, with a rapidly increasing total trade value from around US$32 million in 1991 to more than US$20 billion in 2009. Imports from China have increased steadily from US$1.6 billion in 2001 to around US$16 billion in 2009. China today is one of the biggest providers of production and consumer goods to Vietnam. Vietnam's exports to China have also increased, but to a lesser extent.

Accelerated trade, especially cross-border trade with China, has had both positive and negative impacts on poverty reduction in Vietnam. In particular, increased agricultural exports to China have had a direct positive impact on poverty in Vietnam. With a large number of poor households involved in production processes, the agriculture sector (including crop and livestock farming, fishery and forestry) is identified as one of the most visible pro-poor "gainers" from trade with China. Trade is especially important in this sector given that Vietnam exports many agricultural, aquatic and forestry products to China.

This study has found that GDP growth in China will result in increased agricultural exports to China, which in turn will reduce poverty in Vietnam. As pointed out, if China's GDP increases by 1 per cent, Vietnam's export value of fruit and vegetables to China increases by 0.68 per cent and that of fisheries by 0.75 per cent. This implies that China's growth has direct and positive effects on Vietnam's exports of these products. In fact, a direct correlation has been found between increased fruit and vegetables and fishery exports to China and reduced poverty rate in Vietnam. Even export of bananas, the agro product that returns lower income and profit margin to farmers than other vegetable crops (such as cashew or pepper), can provide poor people with opportunity to escape deep poverty. Fruit and vegetable exports to China have a stronger effect on poverty reduction than fishery exports.

In addition to exports, China is highly important to Vietnam as an import source. Imports from China have grown rapidly, from US$1.6 billion in 2001 to more than US$15 billion in 2009. Despite the lack of empirical evidence, it can be said that rapid penetration of Chinese products to Vietnam's markets has helped address the shortage of many types of consumer goods in the country. Poor people in Vietnam are proved to benefit significantly from the low prices of garments and textiles imported from China.

Moreover, strengthened trade with China has brought about a significant improvement in the livelihoods of the poor in remote border areas. Cross-border trade is commonplace in frontier areas which are otherwise lagging behind other regions of the country. Circulating goods and services across the borders has helped resolve the problem of meeting urgent production and consumption requirements. Through different forms of commodity trade, the inhabitants of border areas can import machinery, production materials and industrial products for their own production and consumption needs. In addition, the demands of trade partners on the other side of the border are also stimulus to Vietnam in that local inhabitants are motivated to exploit natural potentials more effectively. Some kinds of goods, which would not be easily sold in Vietnam's domestic market, now can find their market niches in China's provinces.

Many inhabitants in border areas have seen yields increase as new technology has diffused across the border. Such technology includes fertilizers, water pumps, agricultural machinery, pesticides, seeds and breeds. New cultivation techniques and seed varieties transferred to Vietnam's agriculture and forestry have significantly contributed to increased productivity in these sectors. It is widely recognized that the productivity of crops such as rice and sugar cane has risen remarkably in many provinces as a result of new seed varieties imported from China. For poor peasants living in the remote areas, increased yield directly means alleviation of hunger and food shortage. The new cultivation techniques imply also a change from traditional self-sufficient production to commercial agricultural practices: Lao Cai and Lai Chau provinces have started to export tea and cardamom to China and other markets.

It is proved that cross-border economic transactions have also created jobs for labourers both in and outside the area. Poverty is reported to be reduced by the increase in income from non-agricultural activities. Cross-border trade transactions have helped to familiarize borderland inhabitants with market economic relations. Due to the increased economic exchange with domestic as well as foreign partners, borderland inhabitants can escape subsistence economic relations, which have long been the tradition in these areas. Now they produce not only to meet their own direct needs, but also produce surplus to sell at the markets (CDRI 2005).

The impacts of trade with China on local budget income and expenditure are also noteworthy. Provinces such as Quang Ninh, Lang Son and Lao Cai, which had earlier reopened their border gates, can significantly increase their budget revenues through trading activities. Larger and more stable budget revenues as a source for development financing allow local authorities to extend public expenditures to meet the local population's needs. Interviews with representatives of the Lang Son Provincial People's Committee found that at least half of locally collected revenues are retained for investment in local infrastructure and local social development.

The rise of trade with China has laid the initial foundations for establishing new economic centres in the previously poor border provinces. Today, Mong Cai (Quang Ninh province), Dong Dang (Lang Son province) and Lao Cai (Lao Cai province) have become main focal points for flows of goods, services, currencies and transport from and to Vietnam. Some of them have become transit destinations or commercial centres of national importance, where domestic and international companies choose to locate their branches, representative offices or trade agents. A number of rural communities, communes and districts located along the borders have now become new urban centres, conveniently located for commercial transactions, storage of goods, money exchange and service suppliers to the cross-border economic areas. Ethnic minority groups have greater opportunity to gain better understanding of the rules of market economy.

Trade with China has also brought a number of constraints and challenges. Increased smuggling has become one of the most serious concerns since the strengthening of cross-border trade activities. The long borders and difficult mountainous landscape make it relatively easy for smugglers to evade security and customs forces. While smuggling is sometimes argued to be "good" for the poor as it involves direct participation of many poor local people, thereby increasing their cash income,[7] results from the interviews show that smuggling also has negative impacts. First, smuggling results in loss of local budget revenue from taxes and tariffs that otherwise could have been allocated to improving local people's standard of living. More seriously, the commodities smuggled across the frontier lines often include illegal or toxic consumer goods, rare wood and endangered animals. Consumption of these goods can be either dangerous to human health, or cause damage to the environment and natural resources.

It was found by some researchers that the large amount of fertilizers, pesticides and chemicals imported from China are the main sources of water and soil degradation and contamination (though empirical evidence is yet to be provided). Anecdotal evidence suggests that the acceleration of cross-border trade with China has increased environmental problems in Vietnam.

Impact of FDI Flows from China

There is no clear evidence of FDI being diverted from Vietnam by China. As far as capital inflows from China are concerned, it seems that the impact is relatively minor. This is because the relative size of China's FDI to total FDI to Vietnam is still modest. More than that, China's projects are often small-scale and thus employ limited numbers of workers. This study has found that only around 12,000 Vietnamese workers are directly involved in China's FDI projects (less than 1 per cent of the total workforce engaged in FDI projects), though the pattern has improved substantially during the last few years.

China's FDI has positively impacted on economic growth in Vietnam, but not much competition has been brought about in the fields of their investments. However, with more FDI to come from China in the near future, this spillover effect could be both positive and negative. At best, direct inflows of investment would likely stimulate domestic enterprises to be more efficient. A new tendency of China's FDI moving to mining and mineral extraction industries in Vietnam is clearly observed. These investments will not necessarily have positive effects in terms of benefiting the poor. Moreover, such investment is reported to have very negative impacts on the environment, especially in the mountainous areas where poor ethnic minority groups mainly live. The environmental impact of China's investment in some sectors such as mineral and natural resource exploitation is, in principle, negative as in any other projects in this field. However, to have good evidence for that, it would be necessary to conduct further assessment of what effects these projects have on the environment.

The larger Chinese firms seem to bring in more technology and skilled labourers as they often operate in fields where domestic businesses do not have sufficient capacity to undertake the projects. The smaller Chinese firms may provide less modern technologies. In general, the technology used in

China's projects is often old and outdated with limited attention paid to research and development. This explains why Chinese investment projects are largely ineffective in terms of technology transfer and technological improvement for the host industries in Vietnam.

The impact of China's FDI with its direct and spillover effects may become greater as both the size of FDI flows and the size of FDI projects are expected to increase further in the near future.

Pro-poor Impact of ODA and Technical Cooperation

The impact of China's ODA on the poor is not visible either. Very little linkage can be found from China's implemented ODA projects to poverty alleviation priority areas such as education, health and employment creation. This is because the ultimate goal of the projects is either political or economic, not social improvement, i.e., enhancing people's living standards.

Vietnam's tourism is one of the sectors that has mostly benefited from technical cooperation. Since implementation of the accelerated cross-border economic exchange, the number of tourists visiting Vietnam through border gates has increased substantially. This spurt of tourism has not only contributed to increased income and job creation for a number of inhabitants in the local mountainous areas, but also brought intangible values to the local populace by expanding their worldview, enhancing their knowledge of and access to the market economy.

At the same time, the transport sector has also made acknowledged progress. A number of roads and local tracks connecting main border gates to mainland cities and centres have been either upgraded or newly built. Hanoi–Lang Son and Ha Noi–Lao Cai railways have been substantially improved. Construction under the "Two Corridors One Circle" programme will soon also contribute to boosting the local economy and this will implicitly affect the local poor.

Technical cooperation and trade with China has boosted the upgrading or new construction of physical infrastructure such as electricity, roads, bridges and communications in many of the northern mountainous areas. Direct impact on poverty is seen in that the process of building the infrastructure has created new jobs for the local poor. At the same time, improvement of the local infrastructure has enhanced access to and participation in market activities. Opening markets, in its turn, has altered the local economy as it leads to higher demand for more local products, consumer goods and services. In this way, improved transportation is a driver for poverty reduction in those localities involved.

5.2 Policy Recommendations for Vietnam

Vietnam Should Look for Market Opportunities in China to Expand Labour-intensive Agricultural Exports

Trade with China has grown rapidly in recent years but only those who are capable of effectively penetrating the Chinese market can benefit. Vietnam has long been well known as a large exporter of fruit and vegetables to China, especially tropical produce. This is largely due to the country's geographical proximity and high market demand. However, as indicated in a number of studies, despite remarkable achievements, Vietnamese fruit and vegetable producers and exporters encounter many difficulties and constraints.[8] Low labour productivity, lack of specialization, and low physical processing and storage capacity has made Vietnam less competitive at Chinese market. Exporters' inability to take advantage of the increased demand from China for high-quality fruits and vegetables (for instance the demand from newly established supermarkets as a new niche market) has prevented Vietnam from penetrating this highly promising market. At the same time, high labour costs in production have made the total production costs of these export items in Vietnam relatively high.

It is strongly recommended therefore, that these constraints should be removed by actors at every stage of the value chain. Apart from development of human resources for the agriculture sector as a whole, improvement of production technology can be a great help in replacing manual work and thus reducing labour costs. Moreover, in order to increase labour productivity and export efficiency, there is an urgent need to enhance specialization on one hand, and co-operation on the other.

The Government of Vietnam Is to Provide All Necessary Support to Poor Agricultural Producers

As human resources and labour capacity is seen to be weakest in the agriculture sector and rural areas, the government of Vietnam should give priority to supporting human capital development. In particular, the government should fund training for the poor producers of agricultural products for export to Chinese markets. Appropriate support and guidance should also be given to poor farmers in accessing other financial sources for their capacity building. The organization and implementation of thematic seminars and workshops with contributions from highly qualified international and domestic experts could be considered as a means to disseminate critical marketing skills and knowledge to agricultural producers Further support to strengthen the capacity of agricultural produce export enterprises could be provided through the implementation of some economic instruments such as tax incentives or special fund/ financial facility for training at enterprise level.

The role of agricultural producers and exporters associations should be enhanced. These organizations could take an active part in the collection, processing and analysis of data and statistics on Chinese markets, as well as being a catalyst in disseminating the new achievements of technological progress. Support should be given to businesses and producers/exporters in seeking trade partners, market opportunities or even new market niches.

As the revenue from tax on primary product exports increases, the government of Vietnam could also seek to use the tax revenues to better fund pro-poor initiatives. In doing so, the government should assess existing policies or redistributive measures aimed at poverty reduction (such as Programme 135[9] and Programme 134,[10] or other national targeted poverty reduction initiatives) in order to see if they still remain just as relevant in light of China's growth. At the same time, other policies, such as emphasizing the expansion of labour-intensive manufactured exports as a means of poverty reduction, may need to be qualified in light of increasing competition and falling prices for many such products.

To reduce the challenge caused by extended exploitation and export of primary products to China, the Vietnamese government should better monitor its impact on the poor and local communities and seek appropriate measures to mitigate negative effects.

Recommendations to Producers of Vegetables, Fruits and Other Agricultural Products

In order to know what types of vegetables and fruits suit the taste and consumption habits of Chinese consumers, agricultural producers in

Vietnam should focus more on marketing and market investigation. The same efforts are needed also for vegetable and fruit production planning to clearly identify what and how much to produce. The establishment of a network involving producers, collectors and exporters is highly recommended. In this network, a double role should be given to vegetable exporting/processing enterprises. In particular, such enterprises should act as both vegetable producer and collector of produce for export from small individual farmers. These enterprises could also provide technical assistance to farmers (with support from MARD Agricultural Extension Unit), as well as formal contracts for purchasing produce for primary processing. Stable purchase contracts for agricultural products are very important for both farmers and processors/exporters.

The establishment of technical centres for seed/seedling production in all localities is necessary. The centres would be responsible for producing and supplying good quality seeds and seedlings for the whole locality. At the same time, it would be important to persuade farmers to use only those strains of seed and seedlings that have been certified by responsible authorities. To avoid unnecessary "surprises" at the Chinese market place, vegetable producers and exporters from Vietnam should have a thorough understanding of Chinese quarantine and sanitation regulations and market operation rules. Further, increased cooperation with Thailand in exploring the Chinese fruit and vegetable markets might be a good option to consider. Close collaboration between the two competitors may help in enhancing the value-added of exported commodities and reducing transaction costs.

With the visible trends of China's FDI expansion in mining and natural resources exploitation, Vietnam should strengthen its policy implementation on environment protection. At the same time, more efforts should be made to monitor the impact of the expansion of primary product exports on the poor and local communities which may be negatively affected.

It is also important to consider whether existing policies aimed at attracting FDI and ODA need to be changed in the light of China's expansion. Some policies such as preferential tax and cheap land rental in some environmentally sensitive areas, or those that emphasize the expansion of labour-intensive primary exports as a means of poverty reduction may need to be qualified.

6. CONCLUDING REMARKS

During the last decades, an advancement of trade, investment and other forms of economic cooperation between China and Vietnam has clearly been witnessed. Trade with China in particular has increased rapidly: the acceleration of cross-border trade has been key to making China one of Vietnam's biggest trading partners. Much of the achievement and improvement made in trade has manifested as positive outcomes for the poor, especially through the export of agricultural products. Capital flows from China to Vietnam have also increased making a positive (but to a lesser extent compared with trade) contribution to the improvement of Vietnam's economy. At the same time a number of challenges still remain. Much effort will have to be made if these are to be addressed.

One of the most important elements for the success of such efforts is a clearly articulated commitment by both governments to significantly strengthen bilateral cooperation and support in order to solve the problems (for example, trade deficit, trade fraud, smuggling). The government and export businesses can also be incorporated to promote better trade and investment between the two countries. As Vietnam faces the task of policy reforms due to both domestic and regional (international) circumstances, the findings of this short study on the impact of China's growth on poverty in Vietnam may become a useful guide for more targeted policy considerations.

APPENDICES

Appendix 5A

VLSS 92-93

```
do "C:\Documents and Settings\Administrator\My Documents\DAN 8\Mergefiles\Pover
> ty92.do"

cd "C:\Documents and Settings\Administrator\My Documents\DAN 8\Mergefiles"
C:\Documents and Settings\Administrator\My Documents\DAN 8\Mergefiles

use "C:\Documents and Settings\Administrator\My Documents\DAN 8\Mergefiles\me
> rgefile92.dta", clear
(Muc 4.E: Viec chinh 12 thang)

*Set total pov ln:
gen zt=1160.41

gen povtotal=1 if realpcex< zt
(6133 missing values generated)

replace povtotal=0 if realpcex> zt
(6133 real changes made)

svyset, strata (s4eq02)

      pweight: <none>
          VCE: linearized
  Single unit: missing
     Strata 1: s4eq02
         SU 1: <observations>
        FPC 1: <zero>
```

*Ty le doi ngheo trong nganh nong nghiep
svy: mean povtotal if s4eq02==111
(running mean on estimation sample)

Survey: Mean estimation

Number of strata	= 1	Number of obs	= 10106
Number of PSUs	= 10106	Population size	= 10106
		Design df	= 10105

	Mean	Linearized Std. Err.	[95% Conf. Interval]	
povtotal	.6745498	.004661	.6654132	.6836863

svy: mean povtotal if s4eq02==121
(running mean on estimation sample)

Survey: Mean estimation

Number of strata	= 1	Number of obs	= 11
Number of PSUs	= 11	Population size	= 11
		Design df	= 10

	Mean	Linearized Std. Err.	[95% Conf. Interval]	
povtotal	.5454545	.1574592	.1946137	.8962954

.
end of do-file

VLSS 97-98

```
. do "C:\Documents and Settings\Administrator\My Documents\DAN 8\Mergefiles\Poverty98.do"

cd "C:\Documents and Settings\Administrator\My Documents\DAN 8\Mergefiles"
C:\Documents and Settings\Administrator\My Documents\DAN 8\Mergefiles

use "C:\Documents and Settings\Administrator\My Documents\DAN 8\Mergefiles\me
> rgefile98.dta", clear

*Set total pov ln:
gen zt=1789.871

gen povtotal=1 if rlpcex1<zt
(11215 missing values generated)

replace povtotal=0 if rlpcex1>zt
(11215 real changes made)

svyset ,strata(s4dq02)

      pweight: <none>
          VCE: linearized
  Single unit: missing
     Strata 1: s4dq02
         SU 1: <observations>
        FPC 1: <zero>

svyset [pweight= wt]

      pweight: wt
          VCE: linearized
  Single unit: missing
     Strata 1: <one>
         SU 1: <observations>
        FPC 1: <zero>
```

*Ty le ho ngheo trong nganh nong nghiep
svy: mean povtotal if s4dq02==01
(running mean on estimation sample)

Survey: Mean estimation

Number of strata	= 1		Number of obs	= 10732
Number of PSUs	= 10732		Population size	= 3.1e+07
			Design df	= 10731

	Mean	Linearized Std. Err.	[95% Conf. Interval]	
povtotal	.4596237	.0050619	.4497014	.4695461

*Ty le ho ngheo trong nganh thuy san
svy: mean povtotal if s4dq02==05
(running mean on estimation sample)

Survey: Mean estimation

Number of strata	= 1		Number of obs	= 306
Number of PSUs	= 306		Population size	= 843668
			Design df	= 305

	Mean	Linearized Std. Err.	[95% Conf. Interval]	
povtotal	.3732914	.0294426	.315355	.4312277

.
end of do-file

VLSS 2004

```
do "C:\Documents and Settings\Administrator\My Documents\DAN 8\Mergefiles\Pover
> ty04.do"

cd "C:\Documents and Settings\Administrator\My Documents\DAN 8\Mergefiles"
C:\Documents and Settings\Administrator\My Documents\DAN 8\Mergefiles

use "C:\Documents and Settings\Administrator\My Documents\DAN 8\Mergefiles\me
> rgefile04.dta",clear

*Set total pov ln:
gen zt=2077.21

gen povtotal=1 if pcexp1rl<zt
(179373 missing values generated)

replace povtotal=0 if pcexp1rl>zt
(179373 real changes made)

svyset ,strata(m4ac5)

      pweight:  <none>
          VCE:  linearized
  Single unit:  missing
     Strata 1:  m4ac5
         SU 1:  <observations>
        FPC 1:  <zero>
```

svyset [pweight= hhwt]

pweight: hhwt
VCE: linearized
Single unit: missing
Strata 1: <one>
SU 1: <observations>
FPC 1: <zero>

*Ty le ho ngheo trong nganh nong nghiep
svy: mean povtotal if m4ac5==01
(running mean on estimation sample)

Survey: Mean estimation

Number of strata	= 1	Number of obs	= 13137
Number of PSUs	= 13137	Population size	= 2.4e+07
		Design df	= 13136

	Mean	Linearized Std. Err.	[95% Conf. Interval]	
povtotal	.1708583	.0041111	.166747	.174969

*Ty le ho ngheo trong nganh thuy san
svy: mean povtotal if m4ac5==05
(running mean on estimation sample)

Survey: Mean estimation

Number of strata	= 1	Number of obs	= 816
Number of PSUs	= 816	Population size	= 1.6e+06
		Design df	= 815

	Mean	Linearized Std. Err.	[95% Conf. Interval]	
povtotal	.1908599	.0140932	.1631967	.218523

.
end of do-file

Appendix 5B

*** Gravity model for Vegetable**

* OLS model

reg ln_veij_ ln_yi_ ln_yj_ ln_eij_ distij brij

Source	SS	df	MS		
				Number of obs	= 186
				F(5, 180)	= 44.09
Model	553.082323	5	110.616465	Prob > F	= 0.0000
Residual	451.607747	180	2.50893193	R-squared	= 0.5505
				Adj R-squared	= 0.5380
Total	1004.69007	185	5.43075713	Root MSE	= 1.584

ln_veij_	Coef.	Std. Err.	t	P>|t|	[95% Conf.	Interval]
ln_yi_	3.709653	1.480051	2.51	0.013	.7891701	6.630136
ln_yj_	.6779685	.0559305	12.12	0.000	.5676047	.7883323
ln_eij_	.0395656	.0490563	0.81	0.421	–.0572337	.136365
distij	–.0001196	.0000351	–3.40	0.001	–.000189	–.0000503
brij	2.546499	.5983408	4.26	0.000	1.365835	3.727164
_cons	–100.1849	38.01884	–2.64	0.009	–175.2048	–25.16491

* Panel data set

tsset id year, yearly

panel variable: id (strongly balanced)
time variable: year, 2005 to 2007
delta: 1 year

* Hausman test

xtreg ln_veij_ ln_yi_ ln_yj_ ln_eij_ distij brij, fe

```
Fixed-effects (within) regression          Number of obs        = 186
Group variable: id                         Number of groups     = 62

    R-sq: within   = 0.2449                Obs per group: min   = 3
          between  = 0.1020                avg                  = 3.0
          overall  = 0.0959                max                  = 3

                                           F(3,121)             = 13.08
corr(u_i, Xb)      =  -0.9741              Prob > F             = 0.0000

---------------------------------------------------------------------------
ln_veij_ |  Coef.      Std. Err.      t    P>|t|   [95% Conf. Interval]
------------+--------------------------------------------------------------
ln_yi_ |      1.626774  1.492665    1.09   0.278   -1.328351   4.581898
ln_yj_ |      2.204993   1.84842    1.19   0.235   -1.454442   5.864427
ln_eij_ |     2.754731  1.773796    1.55   0.123   -.7569654   6.266428
distij |     (dropped)
brij |       (dropped)
_cons |      -108.9745  27.84102   -3.91   0.000   -164.0932  -53.85588
------------+--------------------------------------------------------------
sigma_u |  9.4722504
sigma_e |  .75067955
rho |       .99375858 (fraction of variance due to u_i)
---------------------------------------------------------------------------
F test that all u_i=0:    F(61, 121) = 11.15       Prob > F = 0.0000

est store fixed
xtreg ln_veij_ ln_yi_ ln_yj_ ln_eij_ distij brij, re

Random-effects GLS regression              Number of obs        = 186
Group variable: id                         Number of groups     = 62

R-sq: within = 0.2246                      Obs per group: min   = 3
between = 0.5827                           avg                  = 3.0
overall = 0.5505                           max                  = 3

Random effects u_i ~ Gaussian              Wald chi2(5)         = 114.76
corr(u_i, X) = 0 (assumed)                 Prob > chi2          = 0.0000
```

ln_veij_	Coef.	Std. Err.	z	P>|z|	[95% Conf. Interval]	
ln_yi_	3.706201	.7061652	5.25	0.000	2.322142	5.090259
ln_yj_	.680497	.0915772	7.43	0.000	.5010089	.8599851
ln_eij_	.0440697	.0803358	0.55	0.583	–.1133855	.201525
distij	–.0001206	.0000576	–2.09	0.036	–.0002335	–7.75e-06
brij	2.563839	.980749	2.61	0.009	.6416059	4.486071
_cons	–100.1916	18.12496	–5.53	0.000	–135.7158	–64.66729
sigma_u	1.429549					
sigma_e	.75067955					
rho	.78385436	(fraction of variance due to u_i)				

hausman fixed

	---- Coefficients ----			
	(b)	(B)	(b-B)	sqrt(diag(V_b–V_B))
	fixed	.	Difference	S.E.
ln_yi_	1.626774	3.706201	–2.079427	1.315059
ln_yj_	2.204993	.680497	1.524496	1.84615
ln_eij_	2.754731	.0440697	2.710661	1.771976

b = consistent under Ho and Ha; obtained from xtreg
B = inconsistent under Ha, efficient under Ho; obtained from xtreg

Test: Ho: difference in coefficients not systematic

chi2(3) = (b–B)'[(V_b–V_B)^(–1)](b–B)
= 3.27
Prob>chi2 = 0.3523
(V_b-V_B is not posit4e definite)

```
* BP test
xttest0

Breusch and Pagan Lagrangian multiplier test for random effects

ln_veij_[id,t] = Xb + u[id] + e[id,t]

Estimated results:
                 |       Var       sd = sqrt(Var)
        ---------+-----------------------------
         ln_veij_ |   5.430757        2.330398
                e |   .5635198        .7506795
                u |    2.04361        1.429549

Test: Var(u) = 0
                         chi2(1)  =   109.54
                     Prob > chi2  =   0.0000


* GLS model

xtgls ln_veij_ ln_yi_ ln_yj_ ln_eij_ distij brij

Cross-sectional time-series FGLS regression

Coefficients:   generalized least squares
Panels:         homoskedastic
Correlation:    no autocorrelation

      Estimated covariances   = 1    Number of obs      = 186
  Estimated autocorrelations  = 0    Number of groups   = 62
      Estimated coefficients  = 6    Time periods       = 3
                                     Wald chi2(5)       = 227.79
                                     Prob > chi2        = 0.0000
```

ln_veij_	Coef.	Std. Err.	z	P>|z|	[95% Conf.	Interval]
ln_yi_	3.709653	1.455984	2.55	0.011	.8559771	6.563329
ln_yj_	.6779685	.055021	12.32	0.000	.5701293	.7858077
ln_eij_	.0395656	.0482586	0.82	0.412	–.0550194	.1341507
distij	–.0001196	.0000346	–3.46	0.001	–.0001874	–.0000519
brij	2.546499	.588611	4.33	0.000	1.392843	3.700156
_cons	–100.1849	37.40061	–2.68	0.007	–173.4887	–26.88101

*** Gravity model for Fishery**

* OLS model

reg ln_fishij_ ln_yi_ ln_yj_ ln_eij_ distij brij

Source	SS	df	MS			
				Number of obs	=	162
				F(5, 156)	=	23.95
Model	479.319008	5	95.8638016	Prob > F	=	0.0000
Residual	624.373064	156	4.00239144	R-squared	=	0.4343
				Adj R-squared	=	0.4162
Total	1103.69207	161	6.85523026	Root MSE	=	2.0006

ln_fishij_	Coef.	Std. Err.	t	P>|t|	[95% Conf.	Interval]
ln_yi_	4.089395	2.003135	2.04	0.043	.132628	8.046163
ln_yj_	.7517892	.0818099	9.19	0.000	.5901911	.9133874
ln_eij_	.1551917	.0680226	2.28	0.024	.0208275	.2895558
distij	–.0001087	.0000493	–2.20	0.029	–.0002061	–.0000112
brij	1.690158	.8842694	1.91	0.058	–.056528	3.436844
_cons	–110.3972	51.45688	–2.15	0.033	–212.0394	–8.755087

```
* Panel data set

tsset id year, yearly
  panel variable:  id (strongly balanced)
   time variable:  year, 2005 to 2007
           delta:  1 year

* Hausman test

. xtreg ln_fishij_ ln_yi_ ln_yj_ ln_eij_ distij brij, fe

Fixed-effects (within) regression          Number of obs        = 162
Group variable: id                         Number of groups     = 54

   R-sq: within  =  0.2365                 Obs per group: min   = 3
        between  =  0.0571                 avg                  = 3.0
        overall  =  0.0559                 max                  = 3

                                           F(3,105)             = 10.84
   corr(u_i, Xb) =  -0.9240                Prob > F             = 0.0000

------------------------------------------------------------------------------
ln_fishij_ | Coef.       Std. Err.      t    P>|t|   [95% Conf. Interval]
-----------+------------------------------------------------------------------
ln_yi_  |    4.54707     1.869642     2.43   0.017   .8399147    8.254225
ln_yj_  |    1.70142     2.362723     0.72   0.473   -2.983423   6.386263
ln_eij_ |    -2.211999   2.349396    -0.94   0.349   -6.870417   2.446418
distij  |    (dropped)
brij    |    (dropped)
_cons   |    -130.5752   36.81903    -3.55   0.001   -203.5806  -57.56991
-----------+------------------------------------------------------------------
sigma_u |  6.4639439
sigma_e |  .82295012
rho     |  .9840497 (fraction of variance due to u_i)
------------------------------------------------------------------------------
```

```
F test that all u_i=0:     F(53, 105) = 15.41          Prob > F = 0.0000

est store fixed

. xtreg ln_fishij_ ln_yi_ ln_yj_ ln_eij_ distij brij, re

Random-effects GLS regression                  Number of obs        = 162
Group variable: id                             Number of groups     = 54

R-sq: within          = 0.2283                 Obs per group: min   = 3
between               = 0.4532                 avg                  = 3.0
overall               = 0.4343                 max                  = 3

Random effects u_i    ~ Gaussian               Wald chi2(5)         = 72.43
corr(u_i, X)          = 0 (assumed)            Prob > chi2          = 0.0000

------------------------------------------------------------------------------
ln_fishij_ | Coef.        Std. Err.       z    P>|z|  [95% Conf. Interval]
-----------+------------------------------------------------------------------
ln_yi_ |     4.089635     .8260608     4.95   0.000   2.470585     5.708684
ln_yj_ |     .755382      .1367123     5.53   0.000   .4874309     1.023333
ln_eij_ |    .1497006     .1137251     1.32   0.188   -.0731966    .3725978
distij |     -.0001067    .0000825    -1.29   0.196   -.0002685    .0000551
brij |       1.685021     1.480023     1.14   0.255   -1.21577     4.585812
_cons |      -110.4739    21.20385    -5.21   0.000   -152.0327    -68.91512
-----------+------------------------------------------------------------------
sigma_u |    1.8795508
sigma_e |    .82295012
rho |        .83913215 (fraction of variance due to u_i)
------------------------------------------------------------------------------
```

```
hausman fixed

                ---- Coefficients ----
 |              (b)          (B)           (b-B)      sqrt(diag(V_b-V_B))
 |             fixed          .          Difference           S.E.
-------------+----------------------------------------------------------------
ln_yi_ |      4.54707     4.089635       .457435          1.677255
ln_yj_ |      1.70142      .755382      .9460377          2.358764
ln_eij_ |   -2.211999     .1497006       -2.3617          2.346642
------------------------------------------------------------------------------
b = consistent under Ho and Ha; obtained from xtreg
B = inconsistent under Ha, efficient under Ho; obtained from xtreg

Test: Ho: difference in coefficients not systematic

          chi2(3)   = (b-B)'[(V_b-V_B)^(-1)](b-B)
                    = 1.13
        Prob>chi2   = 0.7694

. * BP test
. xttest0

Breusch and Pagan Lagrangian multiplier test for random effects

ln_fishij_[id,t] = Xb + u[id] + e[id,t]

Estimated results:
                  |       Var        sd = sqrt(Var)
---------+-----------------------------------------
     ln_fish~_ |     6.85523        2.618249
             e |    .6772469        .8229501
             u |    3.532711        1.879551

Test: Var(u) = 0
        chi2(1)   = 110.88
    Prob > chi2   = 0.0000

.
```

```
. * GLS model

.

. xtgls ln_fishij_ ln_yi_ ln_yj_ ln_eij_ distij brij

Cross-sectional time-series FGLS regression

Coefficients: generalized least squares
Panels: homoskedastic
Correlation: no autocorrelation

Estimated covariances      = 1     Number of obs     = 162
Estimated autocorrelations = 0     Number of groups  = 54
Estimated coefficients     = 6     Time periods      = 3
                                   Wald chi2(5)      = 124.36
                                   Prob > chi2       = 0.0000

------------------------------------------------------------------------------
ln_fishij_ | Coef.       Std. Err.      z    P>|z|   [95% Conf. Interval]
-----------+------------------------------------------------------------------
ln_yi_   |   4.089395    1.96569      2.08   0.037   .2367141    7.942077
ln_yj_   |   .7517892    .0802806     9.36   0.000   .594442     .9091364
ln_eij_  |   .1551917    .066751      2.32   0.020   .0243621    .2860212
distij   |   -.0001087   .0000484    -2.24   0.025   -.0002036   -.0000138
brij     |   1.690158    .8677395     1.95   0.051   -.0105799   3.390896
_cons    |   -110.3972   50.49499    -2.19   0.029   -209.3656   -11.42887
------------------------------------------------------------------------------

.
end of do-file
```

*** Gravity model for Rubber**

```
* OLS model

reg ln_rubberij_ ln_yi_ ln_yj_ ln_eij_ distij brij
```

```
Source |       SS        df        MS          Number of obs  =   111
-------------+------------------------------   F( 5, 105)     =   37.47
Model |    354.609559     5   70.9219118       Prob > F       =   0.0000
Residual |  198.71392   105   1.89251353       R-squared      =   0.6409
-------------+------------------------------   Adj R-squared  =   0.6238
Total |     553.32348   110   5.03021345       Root MSE       =   1.3757

------------------------------------------------------------------------------
ln_rubberij_ | Coef.        Std. Err.      t     P>|t|    [95% Conf. Interval]
-------------+----------------------------------------------------------------
ln_yi_ |        2.575954   1.664457    1.55    0.125    -.724356     5.876265
ln_yj_ |        1.151271   .092515    12.44    0.000    .9678309     1.334711
ln_eij_ |       -.045273   .0717344   -0.63    0.529    -.1875091    .0969631
distij |        -.0001012  .000042    -2.41    0.018    -.0001845   -.0000178
brij |          3.423431   .6216022    5.51    0.000    2.190909     4.655954
_cons |         -82.9415   42.75543   -1.94    0.055    -167.7176    1.834606
------------------------------------------------------------------------------
```

```
* Panel data set

tsset id year, yearly
  panel variable:  id (strongly balanced)
   time variable:  year, 2005 to 2007
           delta:  1 year
* Hausman test

xtreg ln_rubberij_ ln_yi_ ln_yj_ ln_eij_ distij brij, fe

Fixed-effects (within) regression        Number of obs        = 111
Group variable: id                       Number of groups     = 37

   R-sq: within   = 0.2466               Obs per group: min   = 3
         between  = 0.1371               avg                  = 3.0
         overall  = 0.1327               max                  = 3

                                         F(3,71)              = 7.75
   corr(u_i, Xb)  = -0.9359              Prob > F             = 0.0002
```

ln_rubberij_	Coef.	Std. Err.	t	P>|t|	[95% Conf. Interval]	
ln_yi_	1.051012	1.746686	0.60	0.549	–2.431781	4.533805
ln_yj_	2.364279	2.235002	1.06	0.294	–2.092187	6.820746
ln_eij_	1.734332	1.914274	0.91	0.368	–2.082623	5.551287
distij	(dropped)					
brij	(dropped)					
_cons	–92.14839	34.75922	–2.65	0.010	–161.4563	–22.84047
sigma_u	5.8341999					
sigma_e	.578745					
rho	.99025551 (fraction of variance due to u_i)					

F test that all u_i=0: F(36, 71) = 14.51 Prob > F = 0.0000

.

. est store fixed

.

. xtreg ln_rubberij_ ln_yi_ ln_yj_ ln_eij_ distij brij, re

Random-effects GLS regression			Number of obs	= 111
Group variable: id			Number of groups	= 37
R-sq: within	=	0.2347	Obs per group: min	= 3
between	=	0.6654	avg	= 3.0
overall	=	0.6408	max	= 3
Random effects u_i	~	Gaussian	Wald chi2(5)	= 86.48
corr(u_i, X)	=	0 (assumed)	Prob > chi2	= 0.0000

ln_rubberij_	Coef.	Std. Err.	z	P>|z|	[95% Conf.	Interval]
ln_yi_	2.57133	.7035104	3.65	0.000	1.192475	3.950185
ln_yj_	1.154705	.1560317	7.40	0.000	.848889	1.460522
ln_eij_	–.0395602	.121032	–0.33	0.744	–.2767786	.1976582
distij	–.0001033	.000071	–1.45	0.146	–.0002425	.000036
brij	3.435643	1.050854	3.27	0.001	1.376006	5.495279
_cons	–82.94968	18.04873	–4.60	0.000	–118.3245	–47.57483
sigma_u	1.306378					
sigma_e	.578745					
rho	.8359371 (fraction of variance due to u_i)					

hausman fixed

	---- Coefficients ---- (b) fixed	(B) .	(b–B) Difference	sqrt(diag(V_b–V_B)) S.E.
ln_yi_	1.051012	2.57133	–1.520318	1.598745
ln_yj_	2.364279	1.154705	1.209574	2.229548
ln_eij_	1.734332	–.0395602	1.773892	1.910444

b = consistent under Ho and Ha; obtained from xtreg
B = inconsistent under Ha, efficient under Ho; obtained from xtreg

Test: Ho: difference in coefficients not systematic

chi2(3) = (b–B)'[(V_b–V_B)^(–1)](b–B)
= 1.13
Prob>chi2 = 0.7706

```
* BP test
xttest0

Breusch and Pagan Lagrangian multiplier test for random effects

ln_rubberij_[id,t] = Xb + u[id] + e[id,t]

Estimated results:
                 |       Var     sd = sqrt(Var)
       ---------+-----------------------------
       ln_rubb~_ |   5.030213       2.242814
               e |   .3349458        .578745
               u |   1.706623       1.306378

Test: Var(u) = 0
                        chi2(1)  =  74.21
                    Prob > chi2  =  0.0000

* GLS model

. xtgls ln_rubberij_ ln_yi_ ln_yj_ ln_eij_ distij brij

Cross-sectional time-series FGLS regression

Coefficients: generalized least squares
Panels: homoskedastic
Correlation: no autocorrelation

Estimated covariances       = 1     Number of obs       = 111
Estimated autocorrelations  = 0     Number of groups    = 37
Estimated coefficients      = 6     Time periods        = 3
                                    Wald chi2(5)        = 198.08
                                    Prob > chi2         = 0.0000
```

ln_rubberij_	Coef.	Std. Err.	z	P>|z|	[95% Conf. Interval]	
ln yi_	2.575954	1.618847	1.59	0.112	–.5969266	5.748835
ln_yj_	1.151271	.0899799	12.79	0.000	.9749138	1.327629
ln_eij_	–.045273	.0697687	–0.65	0.516	–.1820172	.0914712
distij	–.0001012	.0000409	–2.47	0.013	–.0001813	–.000021
brij	3.423431	.6045688	5.66	0.000	2.238498	4.608364
_cons	–82.9415	41.58382	–1.99	0.046	–164.4443	–1.438713

Notes

1. For example, Vietnam's Ministry of Trade commisioned a series of studies on the potential impact of China's accession to the World Trade Organization on Vietnam's economy and its specific sectors; for more details see Ministry of Trade (2007*a*, 2007*b*), Centre for Chinese Studies (2001), Institute of the World Economy and Politics (2000), Centre for Asia-Pacific Economic Studies (2004), and Ngo Vinh Long (2002).
2. See Introduction.
3. Authors' estimated results from FIA's data.
4. <http://www.qdnd.vn/QDNDSite/en-US/75/72/182/156/191/98633/Default.aspx>.
5. Authors' estimation based data from GSO (2009).
6. Their developed econometric model takes the following form:
   POVi = b1 + b2*lnGDPi + b3*ln(FD2/GDPi) + b4*lnEMPi + b5*lnGOV_SPENDi + DUMMIES + ui
   where: POV is poverty rate; GDP is gross domestic product; FDI/GDP is the ratio between FDI and GDP; EMP is employment; GOV_SPEND is government spending; and DUMMIES is relevant dummy variables.
7. A large number of local poor people including men and women are hired by smugglers to carry prohibited goods to and from China for very low (slave) pay.
8. For more details, see Nguyen, Nguyen and Luu (2008).
9. Programme 135 refers to the "Socioeconomic Development Programme for Extremely Difficult Communes in the Mountainous and Ethnic Minority Regions" launched and implemented by the government of Vietnam to target poverty reduction for ethnic minority groups since the early 2000s.

10. Programme 134 is the "Programme Supporting Ethnic and Poor Minority Groups in Access to Land for Production, Housing, and Clean Drinking Water" launched and implemented by the government of Vietnam since 2004.

References

Bergstrand, J. "The Gravity Model in International Trade: Some Microeconomic Foundations and Empirical Evidence". *Review of Economics and Statistics* 67, no. 8 (1985): 474–81.

Blomstrom, Magnus, Robert E. Lipsey and Mario Zejan. "Is Fixed Investment a Key to Economic Growth?". (MIT Press) *Quarterly Journal of Economics* 111, no. 1 (1996): 269–76.

Cambodia Development Resource Institute. *The Cross-border Economies of Cambodia, Laos, Thailand and Vietnam*. Phnom Penh: CDRI, 2005.

Centre for Agricultural Policy (CAP). "Short analysis of the banana sector as regards demand, competitiveness, impact and opportunities with the aim of helping to eradicate poverty in Vietnam through market forces". (2008). <http://prosperityinitiative.org/images/stories/Small-scale_Review_of_Bananas.pdf>. Accessed 18 April 2010.

Centre for Chinese Studies Hanoi. "China's Accession to WTO and ASEAN". Mimeographed, 2001.

Dong Dong Zhang. "The Impact of China's Growth on the ASEAN Countries". In *Japan's Future in East Asia and the Pacific*, edited by Mari Pangestu and Ligang Song. Canberra: ANU Press & Asia Pacific Press, 2007.

Foreign Investment Agency. *Report on Vietnam-China Investment*. Hanoi: Ministry of Planning, 2010.

Foreign Investment Agency. "Selected data on China's FDI in Vietnam." MPI, Hanoi, Vietnam, various issues, 2008, 2009, 2010.

General Statistical Office (GSO). *Vietnam Living Standard Survey 1992*. Hanoi: Statistics Publishing House, 1993.

———. *Vietnam Living Standard Survey 1997*. Hanoi: Statistics Publishing House, 1998.

———. *Vietnam Living Standard Survey 2008*. Hanoi: Statistics Publishing House, 2004.

Ha Thi Hong Van and Do Tien Sam. "Vietnam-China Trade, FDI and ODA Relations (1998–2008) and the Impact upon Vietnam". Research paper submitted to the Institute of Chinese Studies, Vietnam Social Science Academy, 2009. <www.ide.go.jp/English/Publish/Download/Brc/pdf/01_vietnamandchina.pdf>. Accessed 7 May 2010.

Hao Hongmei. "Chapter 6: China's Trade and Economic Relations with CLMV".

In *Development Strategy for CLMV in the Age of Economic Integration*, edited by Chap Socharith. 2008. <www.eria.org/research/images/pdf/PDF%20No.4/No.4-part2-6-China.pdf>. Accessed 15 May 2009.

Ikiara M.M. "Foreign Direct Investment, Technology Transfer and Poverty Reduction: Africa's Hopes and Dilemma". *Special Paper Series No. 16*. Nairobi: African Technology Policy Studies Network, 2003.

Institute of Development Studies. "China: Its Impact on Developing Asian Countries". *Working Paper 295*. Brighton: IDS, University of Sussex, 2008.

Institute of World Economy and Politics. "China's Accession to WTO and Lessons Learned for Vietnam". 2000. <http://www.rsis-ntsasia.org/people/members/member-iwep-vn.html>. Accessed 10 August 2009.

Jenkins R. and Chris Edwards. *How Does China's Growth Affect Poverty Reduction in Asia, Africa and Latin America?* Norwich: ODG, University of East Anglia, 2004.

Ministry of Commerce, People's Republic of China. <http://english.mofcom.gov.cn/>. Accessed 10 October 2009.

Ministry of Planning and Investment (MPI). *Vietnam Continues to Achieve the Millennium Development Goals*. Hanoi: MPI, 2008*a*.

———. *Results-based Mid-term Review Report for Implementation of the Five Year Socioeconomic Development Plan 2006–2010*. Hanoi: MPI and UNDP, 2008*b*.

Ministry of Trade (MoT). *Promotion of Commodity Trade Exchange with China in the Period 2007–2015*. Hanoi: MoT, 2007*a*.

———. *Current Status of the China-Vietnam Trade Relations, Period 2001–2006*. Hanoi: MoT, 2007*b*.

National Bureau of Statistics of China. China Statistical Yearbook, 2009. Beijing, 2009.

Ngo Vinh Long. "Who is Winner, Who is Loser in China's WTO Membership and Its Direct Implications for Vietnam". Mimeographed, 2002.

Nguyen Thi Kim Dung, Nguyen Manh Hai and Luu Duc Khai. *Agricultural Trade between Vietnam and China: Case Studies of Vegetables, Tea and Rubber*. Chiang Mai: Social Research Institute, University of Chiang Mai, 2008.

Rutherford, Jeff, Kate M. Lazarus and Shawn Kelley. "Re-thinking Investment in Natural Resources: China's Emerging Role in the Mekong Region". A scoping study submitted to Heinrich Boll Stiftung, WWF and ISD as a part of a research project on "Understanding China and An Actor in the Mekong Region", 2008. <http://www.iisd.org/publications/pub.aspx?id=1054>. Accessed 2 September 2010.

Tran Trong Hung. "Impacts of Foreign Direct Investment on Poverty Reduction in Vietnam", IDS Programme, GRIPS, 2004. <http://www.grips.ac.jp/vietnam/VDFTokyo/Doc/18TTHungPaper.pdf>. Accessed 20 September 2010.

UNCTAD. *Investment Policy Review: Vietnam*. Geneva: United Nations, 2008.

UN-ESCAP. *Border Trade and Cross-border Transactions of Selected Asian Countries*. Bangkok: UN-ESCAP, Trade and Investment Division, 1997.

UNSTAT. <http://unstats.un.org/unsd/economic_main.htm>. Accessed 20 September 2010.

US-China Business Council. <https://www.uschina.org/>. Accessed 20 September 2010.

Wooldrige, J.M. *Introductory Econometrics: A Modern Approach*. 3rd ed. Chichester, UK: John Wiley & Sons, 2006.

World Resource Institute. <http://www.wri.org>. Accessed 25 September 2010.

Xingmin Yin. "China's Trade and FDI to MRB Countries: An Advocacy Document". IDE-JETRO, 2008. <http://www.ide.go.jp/English/Publish/Download/Brc/pdf/01_chinastrade.pdf>. Accessed 10 November 2009.

6

IMPACTS OF CHINA ON POVERTY REDUCTION IN THAILAND

Wisarn Pupphavesa, Srawooth Paitoonpong, Montinee Chakrisinont and Siam Sakaeo

1. INTRODUCTION

Over the last three decades, China has witnessed dramatic economic transformation, rapid development and greater involvement in regional and global economic and political affairs. Because of the huge size of its economy, China's development is likely to have great impacts on other countries, both positive and negative. For example, its economic and political expansion may squeeze some small, poorer countries out of the world economy, while perhaps pulling others up — the effects may vary according to context-specific factors. Regionally, it can be said that the current increasing economic interdependency implies that China will likely have profound social, political and economic impacts on countries in ASEAN, GMS and Thailand in particular.

1.1 Overview

Thai-Chinese Economic Interactions

Thailand and China have a long-standing close relationship. Diplomatic relations between the two countries have been officially established since 1 July 1975. Economic cooperation began in 1978 when China opened its doors to the market economy. Trade between the two countries has increased from approximately US$25 million in 1978 to approximately US$31,062 million in 2007. In terms of investment, Thailand's investors started to invest in China as early as 1979 (THAI BIZChina.com). More recently, a Thailand-China Free Trade Area (TCFTA) was implemented in October 2003, under an early-harvest programme (EHP) that covered fruits and vegetables. The TCFTA follows an agreement on comprehensive economic cooperation called ASEAN-China Free Trade Area (ACFTA) signed by the leaders of ASEAN and China in Phnom Penh on 4 November 2002. The agreement with ASEAN-6 members (Thailand, Singapore, Malaysia, Indonesia, Philippines and Brunei) and China became effective in 2010 and will include new ASEAN members and China by 2015. In addition, an ASEAN-China Agreement on Trade in Services of the Framework Agreement on the Comprehensive Economic Cooperation was signed on 14 July 2007 in Cebu, the Philippines, and an ASEAN-China Investment Agreement of the Framework Agreement on the Comprehensive Economic Cooperation was reached on 9 November 2008.

The numerous agreements between the two countries have had direct implications on China-Thailand economic cooperation, which has increased over time. The extent and trend of trade and investment between Thailand and China during 2002–09 is depicted in Figures 6.1 and 6.2 and Table 6.1. With regards to trade, the value of trade between Thailand and China has been increasing, except for 2009 when Thailand's import from China declined from US$20,046 million in 2008 to US$17,232 million in 2009; Thailand ranked eleventh among China's trade partners. However, it should be noted that in the period 2002–09, Thailand's imports from China have been consistently greater than its exports to China. This situation is contrary to what most people would have anticipated — that export to China would be huge because of China's vast economy.

In 2009, the total value of Thailand's export to China was US$16,183 million whereas the total value of import from China stood at US$17,232

FIGURE 6.1
Trade between Thailand and China, 2002–09

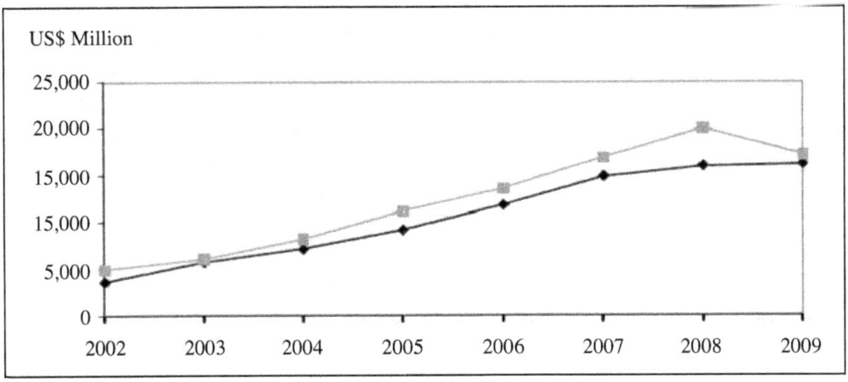

Source: <www.trademap.org> (accessed July 2010).

FIGURE 6.2
Investment between Thailand and China, 2002–09

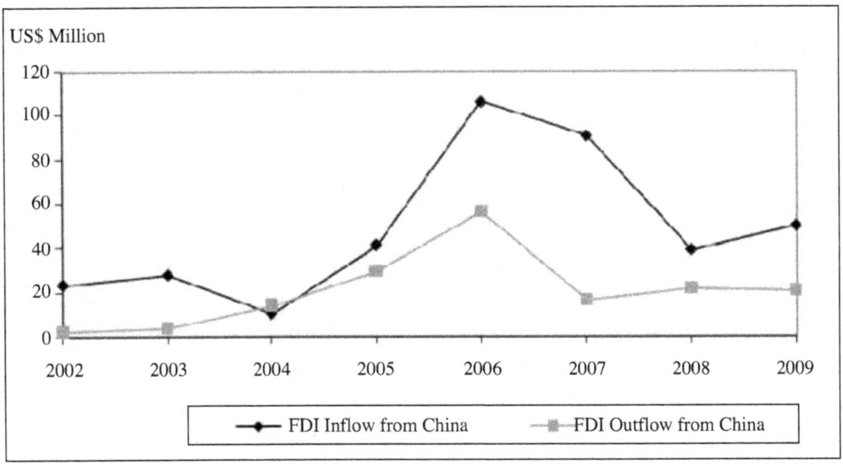

Source: Bank of Thailand <www.bot.or.th/english/Pages/BOTDefault.aspx> (accessed July 2010).

TABLE 6.1
Trade and Investment (US$ million) between Thailand and China, 2002–09

	Thailand's export to China	Thailand's import from China	Thailand's FDI outflow to China	China's FDI inflow to Thailand
2002	3,554	4,932	2.37	23.28
2003	5,701	6,065	3.92	27.76
2004	7,098	8,188	13.99	10.17
2005	9,134	11,158	29.51	41.07
2006	11,774	13,617	56.07	105.94
2007	14,873	16,980	16.50	90.50
2008	15,998	20,046	21.65	38.93
2009	16,183	17,232	20.44	49.64

Source: Trade data from <www.trademap.org> (accessed 2 August 2010); FDI data from the Bank of Thailand <www.bot.or.th/english/Pages/BOTDefault.aspx> (accessed July 2010).

million. Major exports were computers, parts and accessories (26.8 per cent), rubber (9.6 per cent), chemical products (8.4 per cent) and plastics (6.7 per cent). Thailand's major imports from China were computers, parts and accessories (16.2 per cent), electrical machines and parts (14.4 per cent), electrical appliances (9.7 per cent), machinery and parts (8.2 per cent), chemical products (6.7 per cent) (Department of Export Promotion).

During the period 2002–09, Thailand's FDI to China increased from US$2.37 million in 2002 to US$21.65 million in 2008 and then dropped to US$20.44 million in 2009. Thailand's FDI inflow from China has always been higher than its FDI outflow to China, increasing from US$23.28 million in 2002 to US$49.64 million in 2009. FDI from China peaked in 2006 with a value of US$105.94 million. However, investment between Thailand and China has fluctuated over the period with FDI inflow from China dominating Thailand's FDI outflow to China, except for 2004. Both countries' FDI peaked in 2006. China's FDI dropped in 2007 and again in 2008 before increasing in 2009 to US$49.64 million while Thailand's FDI dropped in 2007 but picked up slightly in 2008, dropping back to US$20.44 million in 2009.

Examples of China's investment in Thailand can be seen from the Board of Investment Promotion (BOI) data on requests for investment promotion by Chinese investors. In 2008, twenty-seven projects from China with a total value of US$105 million were approved by the BOI. The first five projects were electricity generation by Jinjiang International Development Co. Ltd, electricity production from waste by Golden Trues Co. Ltd, and the manufacture of airconditioner parts by Duman Metals (Thailand) Co. Ltd, gypsum board by Xin Yuan (Thailand) Co. Ltd., and metal parts for automotive products by Mint Aapico (Thailand) Co. Ltd. (Office of Foreign Investment Cooperation 2009).

Structure of Poverty in Thailand

Against this backdrop of increased Thai-China cooperation and economic integration, poverty has persisted as one of Thailand's most serious problems, particularly after the financial crisis in 1997. Prior to this crisis, high economic growth rates had brought poverty incidence (percentage of the population with per capita consumption below the poverty line) down from 42.2 per cent in 1988 to a mere 14.8 per cent in 1996, equating to a reduction in the total number of the poor from 22.1 million in 1988 to 14.75 million in 1996 (NESDB 2010). At the same time, average incomes were growing rapidly, migration from the poor areas northeast of Bangkok and the Central region helped keep poverty rates in the Northeast below what they might otherwise have been, the construction boom accelerated demand for low- and semi-skilled workers, and school enrolments increased significantly as the poor were provided better access to primary and lower secondary education. Poverty reduction was underway and at a fast pace.

With the financial crisis in 1997, much of the development came to a halt and poverty incidence increased sharply over the next two years, reaching 17.5 per cent in 1998 and 21 per cent in 2000. However, poverty incidence declined to 14.9 per cent in 2002 and 8.5 per cent in 2007. In 2007 the poverty line was 1,443 baht per person per month and the number of the poor had decreased to 5.4 million (NESDB 2010).

The global financial crisis, triggered in 2007 by the bursting of the housing bubble in the United States, affected Thailand considerably because of the country's export orientation and reliance on external demand. As always, the poor were hit the hardest by the economic downturn. The poverty incidence in Thailand rebounded to 8.9 per cent in 2008 but decreased to 8.1 per cent in 2009 (NESDB 2010). The role of China in Thailand's recovery from impacts of the crisis cannot be overlooked.

Although several studies have been conducted to identify the impacts of China on Thailand's development, this study re-examines these impacts using a different approach and with a focus on poverty reduction. A gravity model is applied to identify the impact of China on trade (and investment) in Thailand by commodity. Then the commodities found to be affected by China are linked with poverty reduction through their labour input structure. A commodity, positively affected by China, which employs a larger proportion of unskilled or semi-skilled workers than would be expected (the average) is considered pro-poor and vice versa. Similarly, foreign direct investment (FDI) in Thailand will be examined to see whether it is affected by China. Investment that is affected by China will be examined further to see whether that type of investment is pro-poor.

This study aims to assess the potential impact of China on Thailand. It includes China's impact on trade and investment in Thailand and the corresponding impact on the poor and marginalized people. Through the type of trade or commodities and investment affected by China, the study aims to suggest ways to avoid or mitigate the negative impacts and promote the positive ones so that poverty reduction and sustainable, equitable development in Thailand can be achieved. In addition, the study seeks to highlight opportunities for trade and poverty reduction in Thailand.

The remainder of this study comprises a literature review in section 2; methodology for measuring the impact of China on Thailand's poverty in section 3; section 4 discusses the empirical findings; and section 5 gives policy recommendations, summary and conclusion.

2. LITERATURE REVIEW

There is a wide literature discussing the impacts of China's rise on Thailand's economy. In the main, this literature consists of policy and research papers published within Thailand and the Southeast Asian region, which have focused on the case of Thailand in detail; and second, internationally published academic papers that have included Thailand as part of a comparative analysis of China's rise on developing countries in general, and or ASEAN in particular.

With regards to the former, a pioneering study by Felt and Pupphavesa (1995) looks at the effect of China's rise on Thailand, and analyses whether China's economic growth creates opportunities or presents a competitive threat for Thailand's economic development. The focus of the study is merchandise exports, the respective comparative advantages of each country and how these facets of the Thai economy have been affected by China's growth. The methods used in the study are the Revealed Comparative Advantage (RCA) and Intra-Industry Trade Index (IIT).

While the former was used to measure competitiveness between China and Thailand, the latter was used to quantify the degree to which these two nations are engaged in intra-industry trade, using trade data from 1985 and 1992. The RCA analysis finds that though Thailand and China have similarity in export structure, Thailand's comparative advantage has diverged from labour-intensive production to more capital- and skilled labour-intensive production, while China's comparative advantage is shown to be in raw materials and primary products export combined with an increasing specialization in labour-intensive production. The result shows that, first, both countries have succeeded in expanding their export; and second, the growth of China's economy need not be at the expense of Thailand's, and, indeed may be complementary, increasing market opportunities for Thai exports and investments.

Following on from this, a study by Pupphavesa (2008) examines the effects of increasing economic cooperation facilitated through the ASEAN-China Free Trade Agreement (ACFTA), emphasizing the effect of the ASEAN Early Harvest Programme (AEHP) on Thailand's economy. The methodology is a combination of trend and market share analysis, RCA, Trade Intensities Index (TII) and field surveys. Looking at the outcome of exporting AEHP produce, it is apparent that some important products might have competition from China in domestic and third markets after implementation of AEHP (for example, fresh and frozen durian, fresh longans). On the other hand, AEHP may help increase the export of some products to China (mangoesteens, lychees) as China was the biggest fruit and vegetable importer from Thailand even before the AEHP. The results of Pupphavesa's (2008) analysis highlight a variety of impacts. First, the highest volume product exported to China is cassava, which is not significantly affected by AEHP. Second, AEHP tends to shift and diversify Thailand's imports away from Chinese sources to markets further afield. Third, from these diverse sources, Thailand is importing many more products, such as apples, pears, mandarin oranges, dried mushrooms, cabbages and broccoli, as well as the traditional staple imports of onions and garlic, which have maintained the high growth seen before AEHP.

While AEHP impacts heavily on Thailand's exports and imports, it does not directly affect exports and imports between Thailand and China. Nevertheless, China's impact on Thailand's economy remains visible: Pupphavesa (2008) surveys the social costs for onion and garlic farmers who were affected by the very large supply and lower prices of agricultural products imported from China (even though a large proportion of said imports did not qualify for tariff preference since the volumes exceeded import quotas). He finds that the source of the problem is not AEHP or ACFTA, but production cost factors: Thailand's agricultural production costs are much higher compared to China's. Another interesting issue is that China would like to import a lot of fruit from Thailand. However, most of Thailand's local exporters are small and their capacity cannot meet the huge demand. The benefits might accrue to giant-sized businesses that have far greater capacity than small- and medium-sized businesses.

In a similar vein, other studies have analysed the potential impacts of increased economic cooperation between Thailand and China. Chayodom Sabhasri et al. (2005) conducted a study on the impact of the China-ASEAN FTA for the Department of Trade Negotiation, Ministry of Commerce, Bangkok. The study uses Global Trade Analysis Project (GTAP) Version 6 and qualitative analysis to assess the impact of both ongoing and upcoming ACFTA (ASEAN-China Free Trade Agreement) agreements. Products included in the analysis are tea, raw silk, flowers, rubber, cassava, and manufactured goods, which include garments, electrical and electronic products, shoes and leather products, vehicles and parts, furniture, iron and products, primary plastics, petrochemical products and oil, jewellery and ornaments, and paper and products. Quantitative analysis shows that ACFTA does not significantly affect Thailand's economic variables. However, the agreement will eventually positively affect Thailand's GDP growth by 0.13 per cent. After ACFTA, Thailand's export to China is likely to increase by 23.62 per cent but trade with ASEAN will decrease by 0.62 per cent and with the rest of the world by 0.26 per cent. Somkiat Tangkitvanich et al. (2008) conducted a policy study titled "Reaping Benefits from Free Trade Agreements (FTAs) (Phase II)" for the Ministry of Industry. The authors applied tariff preference and utilization rates to measure how much the country will benefit from a free trade agreement. It found that although Thailand is expected to gain from ACFTA, Thai enterprises have accrued quite low benefits. In 2006, Thailand's exports to China had average tariff preference of 4.94 per cent, while the average utilization rate was 38.02 per cent; Thailand's imports from China had average tariff preference of 11.91 per cent and utilization rate of 8.33 per cent.

International literature does not offer a specific analysis of economic interactions between Thailand and China. However, the relationship has been addressed in numerous regional comparative studies. For instance,

Eichengreen, Rhee and Tong (2004) conducted a study on the impact of China on the exports of other Asian countries concerning the effect of the growth of China's export on other Asian countries' exports. The study used a gravity model with data on thirteen Asian export countries and 180 destination countries from 1990 to 2002. China's exports are included as an additional variable; the volume of China's export to the same destination country is added to identify the effect of China's export on that of other Asian countries. The study indicates a crowding-out effect of other Asian countries' export to third markets from the growth of China's exports. However, the growth of China's export is limited to consumer goods — at least in 2004 — while China's imports from other Asian countries are increasingly made up of capital goods. These findings could imply that China's growth has a negative effect on low-income Asian countries that export mainly consumer goods, and that the brunt of Chinese competition is felt in third markets. In contrast, high-income Asian countries get positive benefits from exporting capital goods since China has a voracious appetite for importing machinery and equipment. The study also estimates the impact of China's income growth on the exports of other Asian countries, including Thailand. The estimate results show that a 10 per cent increase in Chinese income will lead to 0.7 per cent decline in Thailand's exports, increased export volume in capital and intermediate goods and decreased export volume in consumer goods. This could have implications for poverty reduction if we link categories of export commodities to the benefits generated for the poor.

Again analysing economic impacts of China's rise on other countries through changing trade structures, Yumiko Okamoto (2005) finds a mixture of competitive and complementary outcomes. He analyses the impact of China and India by using RCA and IIT to examine how the rise of a country affects other countries and specifically how the rise of China could create challenges and opportunities for ASEAN. The study uses RCA to calculate Spearman's rank correlation coefficient between ASEAN and China, while using IIT calculation and the market share analysis to examine whether there is a competitive or complementary trade structure. For Thailand, the high scores of Spearman's rank correlation coefficient between Thailand and China mean that Thailand and China are competing with each other in export markets, while high IIT index scores indicate that the two countries may benefit from intra industry specialization. Similarly, Chia and Sussangkarn (2006), studying the impact of China on ASEAN by analysing trade data using the trend and market share analysis, also found that intra-industry trade in electronic products and components, which is growing rapidly, has shown signs of a complementary emerging economy. Further, their trade analysis indicates that ASEAN has received benefits in both the consumption and production side as a result of China's rise. Consumers have cheaper goods while producers are able to use cheaper raw materials from China. Unfortunately, the domestic markets, especially small and medium enterprises, are in competition with these cheap labour-intensive Chinese goods.

A further mechanism through which China could affect other countries and Thailand in particular, is through influencing the distribution of FDI. Indeed, Chia and Sussangkarn (2006) note that China's FDI inflows have grown rapidly from US$53.5 billion in 2003 to US$60 billion in 2004, raising the question as to whether China has been attracting investment flows away from other developing countries, especially ASEAN. This theme is addressed in Eichengreen and Tong's (2005) study "Is China's FDI Coming at the Expense of Other Countries", which raises the important question of whether China's emergence as a low-cost production and export platform and its growing attraction as an FDI destination have made it more difficult for other countries to attract FDI. The gravity model is again employed[1] to analyse the flow of FDI with other variables which are GDP, GDP per capita, distance between countries including land area, number of islands, common language, common colonizer, past colonial relationship(s) (if any), and political, economic and financial risk. The significant difference in this gravity model is that China's and other countries' FDI inflow from the same source country is a variable which has been added to the model. The analysis is based on twenty-nine investment countries (such as the principal European countries, the United States, Canada, Australia, New Zealand, Mexico, South Korea and Turkey) and sixty-three investment destination countries between 1988 and 2003.

The result of the gravity model follows the general hypothesis, that: larger countries send and receive more FDI; higher labour costs in the originating country and lower labour costs in the destination country (as captured by per capita GDP) are associated with larger FDI flows; distance between the sending and receiving countries has a negative impact; while common language, common land border, common colonizer, past colonial relationship, access to sea lanes, and the existence of a currency union all have a positive impact. The time-varying measure of institutional quality enters positively for both the sending and receiving countries. This makes sense, since higher values of this variable imply lower risk. The key coefficient of this study is that on Chinese FDI. In the instrumental-variables regressions, the coefficient on this variable is negative but not significantly different from zero at the 95 per cent confidence level. With the exclusion of the time-fixed effects, the coefficient remains negative and becomes significantly different from zero. Thus, in general there is a tendency for China's FDI inflows to divert FDI flows from other countries, though the robustness of the effect is not clear. However, due to cross-country regional production networks, the estimated results show that if the FDI inflows in China increase by 1 per cent, the FDI inflows in Asia will increase by 0.74 per cent.

Adopting a more holistic approach, Jenkins and Edwards (2004) review four approaches to analysing the links between trade and poverty: cross-country regression, partial equilibrium or cost of living analysis, Computable General Equilibrium (CGE) modelling, and Winter's approach. They note that one limitation of all these approaches to analysing the impact of trade on poverty is that they are based on a narrow income or consumption definition of poverty. The methodology used in their study is a combination of the disaggregated approach to analysing the impact of China on national economies, and Winter's approach to tracing the effect on poverty, with some recognition of broader issues of vulnerability, exclusion and conflict. The Winter's approach identifies three channels through which trade shocks can affect poverty: enterprise, distribution, and government. The approach corresponds to the impacts on the poor as producers, consumers and beneficiaries of government expenditure. The four types of direct impacts of China's growth which Jenkins and Edwards identify as having implications for poverty reduction are: (1) growth of developing country exports to China (complementary effect), (2) increased competition from China for developing country exports to third markets (competitive effect), (3) increased competition from China in the home markets of developing countries (competitive effect), and (4) effects on FDI (competitive or complementary effect). The study found that the growth of China has implications for other countries through its impact on their exports to China itself (positive) and to third countries (negative), and through their imports from China. It may also have implications for FDI flows either through the diversion of FDI from other countries to China, or through the growth of outward investment from China.

3. CHINA'S IMPACT ON TRADE

The measurement of China's impact on poverty reduction in Thailand focuses on three major transmissions, namely, trade, FDI and overseas development assistance (ODA). With regards to trade, the study applied a gravity model to evaluate China's impact on poverty in Thailand. This was conducted in two major steps. First, China's impact on Thailand's trade and investment was identified and assessed. Then, the impact of the identified trade on poverty in Thailand was analysed.

3.1 Key Issues

A key route of China's impact of the Thai economy is trade. Bilateral trade with China could induce a greater demand for Thailand's exports. The potential for the expansion of Thailand's exports to China varies from product to product, depending both on the demand from China and the capacity of Thailand to supply these goods. Further, the nature of export expansion would also depend on the supply elasticity of each given export product. Increase in export value might be due to increase in export volume if the supply was relatively elastic, or increase in price if the supply was relatively inelastic.

In the case of imports from China, it should be noted that China's economic growth might be due to improvement in productivity, resource allocation and production efficiency and hence competitiveness in Thailand's and world markets. Consequently, competition from China's exports could substitute Thailand's products in its domestic market as well as its export markets and, in turn, reduce Thailand's production of those products. In other words, China's trade liberalization and facilitation policy could reinforce the induced increase in demand for Thailand's exports as well as the substitution for Thailand's products in the domestic and world markets. It should also be noted that growing production networking through FDI by Thai or Chinese investors and or third country investors could further increase intra- as well as inter-industry trade between Thailand, China and the rest the world.

The key idea about the trade effect on poverty is that it will vary from product to product depending on specific characteristics associated with each product, such as income elasticity of demand, elasticity of substitution or complementarily vis-à-vis other relevant products, the extent of trade liberalization and facilitation and the poor's involvement in the production network. As such, the trade effect would in turn affect poverty levels through various channels. A product that enjoyed export expansion as a result of China's rise would increase income to its factor owners and thus help reduce poverty, but the economic and productive attributes of the product would influence the degree to which this impacted on rates of poverty. For example, it is likely that the product using intensive unskilled labour and/or poor owners of factor inputs would have a more favourable poverty reduction effect. On the other hand, the income of factor owners of a product that is substituted with a Chinese product would suffer and production would decline. This would increase poverty, especially if the affected product made intensive use of factor inputs owned by the poor.

The trade effect might also impact on poverty through consumption. If the product that enjoys export expansion is a major item in the poor's consumption basket and if the export expansion is accompanied by rising price, the poor would suffer from rising cost of living (falling real income). On the other hand if the increasing import was a major item in the poor's consumption basket, the poor might benefit from better choice of product varieties and lower price.

3.2 Methodology

To quantify China's impact on Thailand's trade, we applied Roses's (2005) modified gravity model to estimate determinants of Thailand's trade at commodity level classified at 6-digit Harmonized System (HS) of product classification. Here the model is specified in two separate functions (export and import) as:

$$
\begin{aligned}
LN\,(EXPORT^{k}_{ij}) &= \beta_0 + \beta_1 LN(RGDP^{t}_{i}) + \beta_2 LN(RGDP^{t}_{j}) + \beta_3 LN(RFEX^{t}_{ij}) \\
&\quad + \beta_4 LN(DIST_{ij}) + \beta_5 (TARIFF_{ij}) + \beta_6 CHINA + \varepsilon_{ij} \\
LN\,(IMPORT^{k}_{ij}) &= \beta_0 + \beta_1 LN(RGDP^{t}_{i}) + \beta_2 LN(RGDP^{t}_{j}) + \beta_3 LN(RFEX^{t}_{ij}) \\
&\quad + \beta_4 LN(DIST_{ij}) + \beta_5 (TARIFF_{ij}) + \beta_6 CHINA + \varepsilon_{ij}
\end{aligned}
$$

where: $EXPORT^{k}_{ij}$ = export value (FOB) of product k from country i to country j in year t

$IMPORT^{k}_{ij}$ = import value (CIF) of product k from country j to country i in year t

$RGDP^{t}_{i}$ = real gross domestic product of country i in year t

$RGDP^{t}_{j}$ = real gross domestic product of country j in year t

$RFEX^{t}_{ij}$ = real bilateral exchange rate of currencies i/j in year t

$DIST_{ij}$ = distance between country *i* and country *j*
$TARIFF_{ij}$ = simple average applied tariff rate on export (import) product *k* (defined at 2-digit HS from country *i*(*j*) to country *j*(*i*) in year *t*
$CHINA$= dummy variable equals one in the case of China, otherwise zero.

The above gravity model postulates the trade (export or import) as log functions of scale of the economy of the trading partner, comparative commodity prices, transportation or logistics costs and tariff rates as follows:

Scale of the economy of the trading partner, represented by the trading partner's GDP, reflects the demand for export or the demand for import of the trading partner. A positive relationship can be expected if the increase in GDP means an increase in national output which in turn results in the propensity to increase export. In the case of import, GDP increase can imply increasing propensity to import more both for increasing consumption and increased import of inputs from abroad. On the other hand, a reverse relationship is also possible when the increased GDP, for some reasons, reflects higher consumption of local (import-substituted) goods and services.

Comparative commodity prices are usually captured by real exchange rate. Increased real exchange rate means the depreciation of baht (in comparison with the trading partner). If the demand for export (or import) is elastic with respect to prices, it (export) will increase with depreciated exchange rate. Import will decrease when exchange rate depreciates as depreciated exchange rate means the price of imported product increases.

Transportation/logistics costs reflect the distance between Thailand and its trading partner. The further away the trading partner is, the higher the costs of transportation and in turn, the higher the price of import or export. Thus, the relationship in both export and import should be inverse.

Tariff rates clearly reflect trade barriers which directly positively affect the prices of export products and import products. It can be expected that the higher the tariff rate, the larger the decrease in export or import; in other words, it should be an inverse relationship. The time coverage of available data differs between export and import. Export data cover the period 1996 to 2008 and import data cover the period 2002 to 2008.

Measuring the Impact of Trade on Poverty

The impact of China on poverty reduction is traced through the poverty effect of trade on the employment of unskilled workers in Thailand. In the case of trade, the poverty effect is based on the extent that the commodity in question employs unskilled and semi-skilled workers with the implicit assumption that the majority of these classes of workers are poor. To see how trading with China affects poverty in Thailand, ideally we would identify product *k* that is found to be significantly affected by China factors, then we would identify the gainers and losers from the China effect and whether they are absolutely or relatively poor and where they are. One way this could be done is by visiting some selected area where the poor gainers or losers are concentrated and interviewing them to verify the effect and gain insight on transmission of the impact from China (to the poor). However, due to time and resource constraints, we use a simpler approach, examining secondary data and existing studies as described below.

The first step is to identify commodities imported from and exported to China from Thailand and examine them to see whether they are affected by China's trade with Thailand using the gravity model detailed above. The next step is to identify whether the affected commodities of import and export are pro-poor or contra-poor by using employment criteria. In brief, whether a commodity is pro-poor or not is defined according to the proportion of unskilled labour in each affected commodity. The methodology to select significant import and export commodities is as follows:

1. Selected lists of commodities that show significant relationship between the variable China and the value of import and export between Thailand and China: (a) import commodities — the commodities that have significant relationship with the China dummy variable are selected; (b) export commodities — the commodities that have significant relationship with tariffs and the China dummy variable are selected.
2. For each selected commodity, a simulated trade volume is calculated[2] under the following assumptions: (a) for import,

simulated Thailand's import volumes are calculated under the assumption that the increase of China's GDP is associated with the increase of China's export to and the corresponding increased volume of Thailand's import from China; (b) for export, simulated Thailand's export volumes are calculated with the assumption that an increase in China's GDP and a decrease in China's import tariff rate will increase Thailand's export volume to China.

The simulated, exchange rate adjusted, import and export volumes are used to estimate poverty effect based on the proportion of unskilled employment input of the commodity in question. Since the simulated import and export volumes, the so-called trade effect, are estimated, the employment effect can be found by using Output:Employment ratio or O:E ratio.[3] The O:E ratio is calculated from the domestic output value of each commodity divided by total labour employed in the commodity in question:

$$\text{Output/Employment Ratio}_i = (\text{Value of domestic output in commodity}_i)/(\text{Employment used in commodity}_i)$$

However, due to data constraints, the proxy of output value and employment are used. Because of different data classification, the value of output data is from input-output (I-O) table classification, employment data is in International Standard International Classification) classification (ISIC), while trade data is in HS code. The value of output is obtained by converting each HS code into I-O table classification and uses the output value of that I-O code as a proxy of each HS code.

The value of employment is obtained by converting each HS code into ISIC classification (4 digits), and uses the employment volume under the ISIC code as a proxy of each HS code. The employment effect can then be derived from the estimated O:E ratio using the formula below:

$$\text{Employment effect of commodity} = (\text{simulated import or export volume of the commodity})/(\text{O:E ratio of the commodity})$$

The employment effect of a commodity is the estimated employment volume either generated from an increase in Thailand's export volume or lost in the case of an increase in Thailand's import volume. After obtaining estimated employment, the next step is to find the proportion of unskilled labour used in each commodity, so-called unskilled labour index (ULI). The ULI is the ratio of unskilled labour employed in the production of commodity i to total employment of the same commodity:

Unskilled labour index$_i$ = (unskilled labour employment in commodity)/(total employment in commodity)

According to ISIC and for the purpose of this study, unskilled labour includes plant and machine operators, assembly workers and elementary occupation workers for all commodities except for agricultural commodities in that the definition includes skilled agricultural and fishery workers. The ULI for each commodity is calculated based on national data and is used as a reference for the calculation of employment of the commodities exported or imported. The unskilled labour employed in an export or import commodity can be derived by multiplying the volume of the employment effect of said commodity by the corresponding ULI:

Unskilled labour used in commodity = (employment effect *i*) × ULI$_i$ export or import *i*

Since unskilled workers are generally low-income earners or poor, trade effect can be traced to see whether it trickles down to the poor (making the poor better or worse off). Figures 6.3 and 6.4 show the poverty effect of commodity trade, Thailand's export to China (or China's import from Thailand) and Thailand's import from China. On Thailand's import from China, if import volume impacts on a large amount of unskilled labour and the commodities have a tendency to be unskilled labour-intensive products, then higher import volume has a tendency to make the poor worse off. On Thailand's export to China (or China's import from Thailand), the export volumes that have greater effect on unskilled labour tend to be unskilled labour-intensive products. The increase in China's import has a tendency to be pro-poor.

4. FINDINGS

4.1 China's Impact on Thailand's Economy

Table 6.2 presents the results of two regression estimates of China's impact on Thailand's trade using aggregate export and aggregate import as

FIGURE 6.3
Poverty Effect of Thailand's Export to China

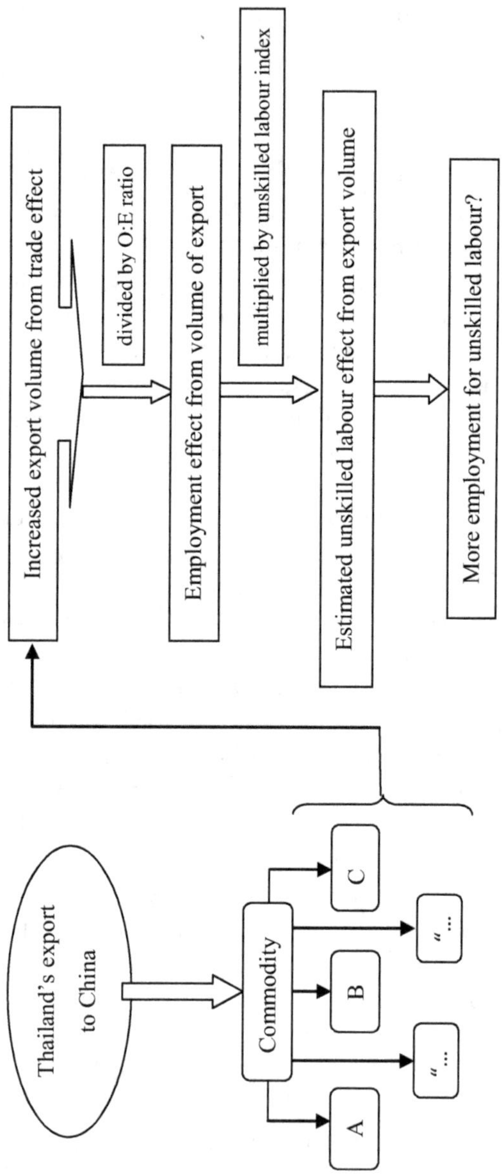

FIGURE 6.4
Poverty Effect of Thailand's Import from China

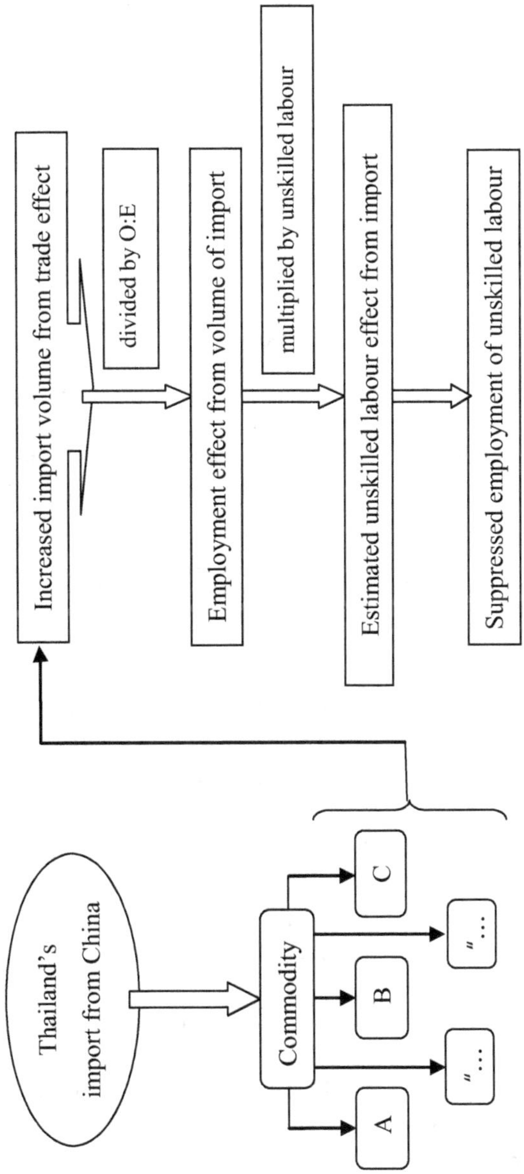

TABLE 6.2
Regression Estimates of China's Impact on Thailand's Trade
(Aggregate export and import are dependent variables)

Variable	LNEXPORT$_{ij}$		LNIMPORT$_{ij}$	
LNRGDP$_i$	1.8030	***	8.3424	
	(0.2219)		(17.6365)	
LNRGDP$_j$	1.0377	***	1.0802	***
	(0.0488)		(0.0800)	
LNRFEX$_{ij}$	–0.0361		0.0523	
	(0.0482)		(0.0660)	
LNDIST$_{ij}$	–0.9634	***	–1.4904	***
	(0.1798)		(0.2454)	
TARIFF$_{ij}$	0.0080		6.5011	
	(0.0101)		(16.2585)	
CHINA	–0.2107		0.1551	
	(0.2242)		(0.3379)	
Constant	–52.0594	***	–271.0593	
	5.8399		587.6588	
Obs	759		521	
Countries	159		175	

Note: *** denotes 1 per cent, ** 5 per cent, * 10 per cent significance levels; robust standard errors are in parentheses.

dependent variables. In general, the results are consistent with theoretical expectations with respect to the direction of the relationship. For the export equation, the result of the postulated relationship is impressive with R^2 of 0.44. The relationship between both GDP of Thailand and of its trading partners and export are positive and significant at 1 per cent level. According to the estimate, a 1 per cent increase in Thailand's GDP will result in a 1.803 per cent increase in its export, whereas a 1 per cent increase in trading partners' GDP will result in a 1.0377 per cent increase in Thailand's export. For the distance between Thailand and its trading partners, the estimate indicates that increased distance will result in decreased Thai export: a 1 per cent increase in distance reduces Thai export by 0.9634 per cent. However, it is found that exchange rate, tariff rate, and dummy variable (China) do not have any significant relationship with Thai export.

The result of import is much less satisfactory, with a very low R^2. However, two variables are found to have significant (at 1 per cent level) relationship with Thai import. They are GDP of trading partners and distance between Thailand and its trading partners. According to the estimate, a 1 per cent increase in the trading partners' GDP will increase Thailand's import by 1.0802 per cent and a 1 per cent increase in distance between Thailand and its trading partners will reduce Thailand's import by 1.4904 per cent.

The results of the regression estimates of China's impact on Thailand's export using export products classified at 6 digits HS code as dependent variables are shown in Appendix Table 6C.1. The results of regression estimates of China's impact on Thailand's import using import products classified at 6 digits HS code as dependent variables are shown in Appendix Table 6C.2. By and large, the results are consistent with the findings of the aggregate export and aggregate import equations. In addition, it was found that an increase in the tariff rate in trading partner countries will reduce a number of export and import items. It is also found that the relationship of the dummy variable China and trade becomes more significant.

4.2 China's Impact on Poverty through Trade

From the results of the import and export commodities regression we can now calculate the employment effect of import and export commodities. Regarding imports from China, seventy-seven commodities were found to be significantly affected by China's exports to Thailand during 2003–08. With regards to their scale of impact, nine import commodities have substituted domestic products which provided employment for more than 1,000 unskilled workers, three have effects on 500–999 unskilled workers, twenty-one on 100–499, and forty-four on less than 100 unskilled workers. The top nine import commodities, each with impacts on more than 1,000 unskilled workers, come under several types of commodities.

Table 6.3 illustrates that the import commodity that has the largest negative impact on unskilled Thai workers is the Skipjack/stripe-bellied bonito (tuna) industry, which replaced production processes that employed 128,094 unskilled workers during 2003–08. The calculation and number of unskilled labour effect of Skipjack/stripe-bellied bonito (tuna) imports are shown here.

Based on the regression results of selected commodities, we calculate the total employment effect of Chinese imports on Thailand's labour markets, information on which is summarized in Table 6.4. During 2003–09, Thailand

TABLE 6.3
Employment Effect from Skipjack/Stripe-bellied Bonito (Tuna) Import

Year	Simulated trade effect (US$1,000)	Exchange rate (THB/US$)	Simulated trade effect (THB1,000)	O:E ratio (THB1,000 per person)	Employment effect (persons)	Unskilled labour index (%)	Unskilled labour use (persons)
(1)	(2)	(3)	(4) = (2)*(3)	(5)	(6) = (4)/(5)	(7)	(8 =(6)*[(7)/100]
2002	–	42.96	–	907.04	–	43.96	–
2003	300,818.00	41.48	12,479,319.42	907.04	13,758	43.96	6,048
2004	475,104.00	40.22	19,109,830.22	907.04	21,068	43.96	9,261
2005	904,410.00	40.22	36,375,487.96	907.04	40,104	43.96	17,629
2006	1,234,048.00	37.88	46,748,185.63	907.04	51,540	43.96	22,656
2007	2,012,788.00	34.52	69,477,779.68	907.04	76,599	43.96	33,672
2008	2,404,970.00	33.31	80,117,488.64	907.04	88,329	43.96	38,828
Total	7,332,138.00	–	264,308,091.55	–	291,398	–	128,094

Source: Based on regression results.

TABLE 6.4
Total Employment Effect from Import

Year	Total simulated trade effect (US$ '000)	Total employment effect No. of persons	Unskilled labour used	
			(No. of persons)	% to total employment
2002	0	0	0	–
2003	478,370.76	17,660	8,542	48.37
2004	854,110.80	28,639	14,019	48.95
2005	1,476,709.27	49,847	23,685	47.52
2006	2,032,931.15	64,332	30,596	47.56
2007	11,159,847.09	178,836	80,204	44.85
2008	13,659,135.46	209,664	94,091	44.88
Total	29,663,994.74	548,967	251,137	45.75

Source: Summarized from regression results.

lost about 251,137 unskilled jobs through imports from China. This may be considered an opportunity cost of import in terms of employment. That is, if Thailand had not imported (from China), the production of seventy-seven commodities in Thailand would have created 251,137 jobs for unskilled workers.

Regarding the impacts of exports to China on poverty and unskilled employment, from the gravity model estimate, sixteen export commodities are found to have been significantly affected by China during 2003–08. Out of this number, three export commodities have effects on more than 1,000 unskilled workers, and five have effects on less than 1,000 unskilled workers. One export commodity, natural rubber, has an extraordinarily large effect on 465,836 unskilled workers. The calculation procedure is illustrated in Table 6.5. Of total exports to China during the seven-year period, natural rubber alone employed 465,836 unskilled workers. The remaining fifteen export commodities employed only 4,562 unskilled workers giving the total employment of 470,398 unskilled workers by the sixteen export commodities (Table 6.6).

The net impact of trade with China is obtained by comparing the employment effect of export and the employment effect of import. During the seven years between 2003 and 2008, Thailand gained approximately 219,261 jobs for unskilled workers, with an average gain of 31,323 unskilled

TABLE 6.5
Employment Effect from Natural Rubber Export

Year	HS 400129 US$ '000	Exchange rate THB:US$	Trade effect THB '000	O:E ratio THB '000 per person	Employment effect (persons)	Unskilled labour index (%)	Unskilled labour used (persons)
(1)	(2)	(3)	(4) = (2)*(3)	(5)	(6) = (4)/(5)	(7)	(8)=(6)*[(7)/100]
2002	0	42.96	0	25.32	0	98.99	0
2003	13,414.73	41.48	556,443.00	25.32	21,975	98.99	21,752
2004	27,817.70	40.22	1,118,827.89	25.32	44,185	98.99	43,736
2005	44,110.55	40.22	1,774,126.32	25.32	70,064	98.99	69,353
2006	61,080.02	37.88	2,313,711.16	25.32	91,373	98.99	90,446
2007	81,041.38	34.52	2,797,548.44	25.32	110,481	98.99	109,360
2008	100,749.80	33.31	3,355,975.84	25.32	132,534	98.99	131,189
Total	328,214.10	–	11,916,632.65	–	470,612	–	465,836

Source: Appendix C.

TABLE 6.6
Total Employment Effect from Export

Year	Total trade effect (US$ '000)	Total employment effect (No. of persons)	Unskilled labour used	
			No. of persons	% to total employment
2002	0	0	0	–
2003	58,399.40	22,206	21,896	98.60
2004	121,562.06	44,579	43,976	98.65
2005	349,670.25	70,919	69,850	98.49
2006	435,614.24	92,360	91,018	98.55
2007	1,473,189.95	113,123	110,806	97.95
2008	1,790,183.16	135,590	132,855	97.98
Total	4,228,618.72	478,777	470,398	98.25

Source: Based on regression results.

jobs per year which is almost negligible compared to the size of the unskilled labour pool in Thailand of more than 20 million. In fact, when considering skilled and high level workers, the net employment effect in some years (2007 and 2008), as shown in Table 6.7, was negative.

4.3 China's Impact on Capital Inflows to Thailand

China can also affect investment flow to and from Thailand through various channels. China's economic growth could generate higher saving rates and, therefore, a larger amount of investable funds. Part of the funds might flow into Thailand and other countries in the forms of FDI, portfolio investment and loans. This study focuses only on FDI because it has more direct implications on factor uses and hence on factor owners' income. As with trade, the analysis comprises both a macro level and a poverty centered evaluation of the rise of China and its FDI flows to Thailand.

4.4 Key Issues

China's economic growth could have both positive and negative effects on FDI flow to Thailand. First, it may increase the amount of capital from China available for investment in Thailand, resulting in an increased flow

TABLE 6.7
Net Employment Effect from Export and Import

Year	Total export employment effect	Total import employment effect	Net employment effect gain	Total export unskilled labour used	Total import unskilled labour used	Net unskilled labour used gain
	(1)	(2)	(3)=(1)–(2)	(4)	(5)	(6)=(4)–(5)
2002	0	0	0	0	0	0
2003	22,206	17,660	4,546	21,896	8,542	13,354
2004	44,579	28,639	15,940	43,976	14,019	29,957
2005	70,919	49,847	21,072	69,850	23,685	46,165
2006	92,360	64,332	28,028	91,018	30,596	60,422
2007	113,123	178,836	(65,713)	110,806	80,204	30,602
2008	135,590	209,664	(74,074)	132,855	94,091	38,764
Total	478,777	548,967	(70,190)	470,398	251,137	219,261

Source: Based on regression results.

of FDI from China to Thailand. On the other hand, China's economic growth could also divert FDI from other countries including Thailand, perhaps at the expense of investment opportunities in Thailand. There is also a possibility that increased investment in China would induce more FDI in Thailand because of its role in regional production networks. The direction of the relationship of investment between China and Thailand will vary from industry to industry depending on the extent to which they are integrated in to global production and supply networks.

Investment liberalization and the nature and effectiveness of the relevant policy frameworks would also affect the flow of FDI and the character of FDI flows between the two countries. Liberal and facilitator investment and trade policies of the host and home countries would be more conducive to production networking FDI and hence encourage FDI between the two countries rather than diverting FDI from one to another.

4.5 Methodology

To quantify China's impact on FDI in Thailand, we applied the modified gravity model of Sudsawasd and Chaisrisawatsuk (2006) to estimate determinants of FDI as follows:

$$Ln(FDI)^t_{ij} = \beta_0 + \beta_1 Ln(FDI^t_{CHN}) + \beta_2 Ln(RGDP^t_i) + \beta_3 Ln(RGDP^t_j) + \beta_4 Ln(RGDPPC^t_i) + \beta_5(RGDPPC^t_j) + \beta_6(DIST_{ij}) + \beta_7 Landl_{ij} + \varepsilon_{ij}$$

where $(FDI)^t_{ij}$ = bilateral FDI outflow from country i to country j
FDI^t_{CHN} = bilateral FDI outflow from country i to China
$RGDP^t_i$ = real GDP of country i in year t
$RGDP^t_j$ = real GDP of country j in year t
$RGDPPC^t_i$ = real GDP per capita of country i in year t
$RGDPPC^t_j$ = real GDP per capita of country j in year t
$DIST_{ij}$ = distance between home (i) and host (j) countries
$Landl_{ij}$ = land locked countries.

The above equation postulates FDI as a log function of the scale of the economy of the trading partner (represented by income — RGDP and RGDPPC), and the distance between home and host countries.

Increased income (RGDP) in home countries implies increasing resources, including factors of production; as a consequence, the propensity to invest abroad increases. The relationship of this variable is therefore positive, as expected. On the other hand, increased GDP in host countries implies their increased demand for consumption. As such, FDI to the host countries would consequently increase.

Per capita income (RGDPPC) is used in this model to capture labour costs in the home countries and the host countries. Increased labour cost in the home countries will push up FDI abroad. On the contrary, increased labour cost in the host countries will reduce FDI from abroad.

Distance between countries (DIST) and being land-locked countries (Landl) reflect transportation costs. The relationship of these variables with FDI can be either positive or negative. If transportation costs are higher, investors from home countries may decide to relocate to host countries. Thus, increased transportation costs will increase FDI from home countries to host countries. It is also possible that the long distance between home countries and host countries will reduce incentive to invest in the host countries because of management difficulties due to different time zone, travel time, higher cost of management. As such, the relationship of these two variables with FDI is an empirical question.

The data used in this study covers the period 1985 to 2007 (see Appendix Table 6A.1 for sources of data). For FDI data, this study uses FDI flows from OECD countries (home countries) to Thailand and China (host countries). To estimate the model, this model includes a variable which is constant over time (DIST); therefore, the pooled OLS regression and random effect can be estimated. Also, the Lagrange Multiplier test (Breuch and Pagan 1980) is performed to see which estimator is more appropriate. The results suggest that the random effect estimator is more appropriate than pooled OLS regression. The random effect with White's robust standard error estimators was used to correct the problem of heteroscedasticity.

From the results of the gravity model, commodities that have significant relationship with China's economic cooperation are identified and linked with poverty through their employment structure. It has been assumed, based on wage structure in Thailand unskilled and semi-skilled workers earn much less than their higher skilled counterparts,[4] hence they can represent the majority of the poor. Trade or investment with China will affect the poor more if the commodities in question employ a large proportion of unskilled workers. For example, if commodity A produced in Thailand employs a large proportion of unskilled workers, the more that Thailand imports commodity A, the worse will be the situation of the poor in Thailand (because their employment is taken away by import).

This analogy is applied to import and export as well as Thailand's FDI to China and China's FDI to Thailand.

To measure the effect of FDI on poverty, as in the case for trade, first, FDI inflows (in U.S. dollar) from China to Thailand are simulated from the FDI regression result of the gravity model. Second, the FDI inflows are converted into Thai currency. Third, the FDI inflows are divided by machine value-employment ratio (M:E ratio) to find the proportion of machine and employment of the FDI inflows in various years, in terms of value.

The M:E ratio is calculated from the total machine value used in Thailand divided by the total labour employed in Thailand:

$$\text{M:E ratio}_i = \text{(total machine value used in Thailand)/(employment in Thailand)}$$

Data on machine value is obtained from the Department of Factories (December 2009) and data on employment is from the Labour Force Survey (Round 3,2009). From this we can derive the number of jobs created as a result of FDI.

$$\text{Total FDI Employment} = \text{(total FDI)/(M:E ratio)}$$

Next employment generated by China's FDI is classified by industry to trace the number of unskilled workers employed by China's FDI industries. After obtaining estimated employment by industry, the next step is to find the proportion of unskilled labour used in each industry by using the industrial unskilled labour index (IULI). This index is the ratio of unskilled labour employed in each industry to total employment of the same industry.

$$\text{IULI}_i = \text{(unskilled labour employment in industry } i\text{)/(total employment in industry } i\text{)}$$

5. FINDINGS

5.1 The Impact of FDI on Thailand's Economy

Table 6.8 shows a regression estimate of the determinants of FDI inflows from OECD countries to Thailand. According to the estimate, an increase of 1 per cent in OECD countries' GDP will result in 0.8878 per cent increase in FDI inflow to Thailand, while an increase of 1 per cent in Thailand's GDP

TABLE 6.8
Regression Estimate of China's Impact on Thailand's FDI (dependent variable is FDI)

Variable	$LNFDI_{ij}$	
$LNFDI_{chn}$	0.2151	***
	(0.0732)	
$LNRGDP_{i}$	0.8878	***
	(0.1403)	
$LNRGDP_{j}$	8.3001	*
	(4.4315)	
$LNRGDPPC_{i}$	1.0062	***
	(0.2559)	
$LNRGDPPC_{j}$	–6.7922	*
	(3.6365)	
LNDIST	–1.0092	***
	(0.3452)	
LANDL	0.8033	**
	(0.3807)	
Constant	83.5808	
	(59.4323)	
Obs	306	
Countries	29	
R^2	0.8506	

will result in a 8.3001 per cent increase of FDI into Thailand. For GDP per capita, which reflects labour costs, it was found that OECD countries' FDI outflows will increase if their labour costs increase (a 1 per cent labour cost increase in OECD countries will result in a 1.0062 per cent increase in FDI outflow), whereas if the labour costs in Thailand increase, FDI inflow to Thailand will decrease (a 1 per cent increase in Thailand's labour costs will reduce FDI inflow to Thailand by 6.7922 per cent). It is interesting to note that the regression results indicate that a 1 per cent increase of FDI to China will result in a 0.2151 per cent increase of FDI in Thailand.

5.2 Impact of FDI from China on Poverty Reduction in Thailand

The estimated total employment created by FDI from China to Thailand is shown in Table 6.9. During 2000–07, FDI flow from China to Thailand

TABLE 6.9
Employment Effect of FDI Inflows from China to Thailand

Year	Simulated FDI (US$)	Exchange rate (THB: US$)	FDI (THB)	M:E ratio (THB per person)	Employment (No. of persons)
	(1)	(2)	(3)=(1)*(2)	(4)	(5)=(3)/(4)
2000	6,852,078.00	40.11	274,849,205.16	41,636.73	6,601
2001	7,560,977.00	44.43	335,948,573.97	41,636.73	8,069
2002	6,668,524.00	42.96	286,480,346.75	41,636.73	6,880
2003	9,098,456.00	41.48	377,445,959.42	41,636.73	9,065
2004	12,347,580.00	40.22	496,649,485.99	41,636.73	11,928
2005	12,487,930.00	40.22	502,266,170.63	41,636.73	12,063
2006	14,402,930.00	37.88	545,611,552.60	41,636.73	13,104
2007	15,134,250.00	34.52	522,406,774.62	41,636.73	12,547
Total	84,552,725.00	–	3,341,658,069.14	–	80,257

Source: Authors' calculation.

resulted in the generation of about 80,257 jobs. Of these, the total number of unskilled workers is estimated at about 27,678 (Appendix Table 6D.2).

The impact of Thailand's FDI outflows to China on the employment of unskilled labour in Thailand is difficult to estimate because the FDI outflows from Thailand do not necessarily mean that investment has been diverted from Thailand. That is, the investors may choose to invest in China or otherwise not invest; in such cases, Thailand does not forgo investment. Nevertheless, for illustrative purposes we shall assume that Thailand's FDI to China (as well as to other countries) are investments foregone from Thailand. Under this assumption, we can estimate the impact of FDI outflows on the employment of unskilled labour in Thailand: estimated forgone employment is approximately 42,365 workers; detailed calculation is given in Appendix D.

The net impact of FDI between Thailand and China is ambiguous, given the weak assumption that all FDI outflows from Thailand to China are investment foregone from Thailand. That said, the net impact of FDI between Thailand and China during 2000–07 on the employment of unskilled labour is around 14,687 workers. When this number is combined with the net impact of China-Thailand trade of 219,261 workers (Table 6.7), it is clear that there are still considerable net gains from the China-Thailand economic cooperation.

5.3 ODA and its Effect on the Economy and Poverty

Quantitative assessment of official development assistance (ODA) is impossible due to the negligible quantity of China's ODA to Thailand. In this section, a conceptual framework on ODA is briefly presented to illustrate its possible impacts.

Definition of ODA

The Development Assistance Committee (DAC) of the Organization for Economic Cooperation and Development (OECD) defines ODA as aid flows to developing countries and multilateral organizations, provided by donor government agencies (Ministry of Foreign Affairs 2005). Only aid provided to countries on the DAC List (Part 1) is classified as ODA: aid to countries not on this is not counted as ODA. The aid must be concessionary in character and be provided for "the promotion of economic development and welfare of developing countries" (Ministry of Foreign Affairs 2005). "Concessionary" is defined as grants, and the full face value of loans that have a grant component of at least 25 per cent at a discount rate of 10 per cent (ibid.).

Grants to countries on the DAC List (Part 1) to promote economic development and welfare and grants to multilateral organizations are straightforward and counted as ODA, with one exception. However, only a proportion of some grants to some UN agencies are counted as ODA because not all of their activities are in developing countries on the Part 1 List. For example, only 3.3 per cent of grants to the World Meteorological Organization are counted as ODA, while 100 per cent of grants to UNDP are counted.

On the other hand, whether a loan to a country on the DAC Part 1 List qualifies as ODA requires two calculations of the present value of the loan. The first is done using the term (number of years) and the interest rate of the loan. The second uses the same term (number of years) but a discount rate of 10 per cent. Hence, if the interest rate on the loan is 10 per cent, the two calculations would yield the same present value of the loan. There would be no concessionary component and the loan would not count as ODA. But if the difference between the first calculation of present value using the loan interest rate, and the second using the 10 per cent rate, is equal to or greater than 25 per cent, then the full face value of the loan is counted as ODA. When the interest rate charged is significantly below 10 per cent and or the term of the loan is long, the loan will always be found to have a grant component far in excess of 25 per cent. The use of a fixed 10 per cent discount rate for this calculation is criticized in many papers on ODA.

A final component of the definition is net ODA. This is calculated by subtracting any loan repayments to a donor country received in a given year from the total ODA provided for that country in that year..

ODA is usually associated with foreign aid and is normally targeted to the very poor countries. ODA can be divided into bilateral and multilateral components. Bilateral assistance is administered by donor governments' agencies. Multilateral assistance is funded by contributions from wealthy countries and administered by agencies such as the United Nations Development Programme and the World Bank. Multilateral ODA accounts for about one-third of all ODA (Dollar and Pritchett 1998).

It is acknowledged that some bilateral aid is tied — that is, it must be used to procure goods and services from the donor country. Such tied aid reduces the value of that assistance by about 25 per cent, and there is widespread agreement that untying bilateral aid would make ODA more effective. There has been a clear trend away from tied aid among OECD countries (ibid.).

ODA and Its Effect on the Economy and Poverty

A conceptual framework of the impact of ODA on poverty reduction is based solely on a World Bank Policy Research Report on "Assessing Aid: What Works, What Doesn't and Why" (Dollar and Pritchett 1998).

Does ODA affect economic growth? Yes and no, depending on whether countries have sound management such as stable macroeconomic environments, open trade regimes, and protected property rights, as well as efficient public bureaucracies that can deliver education, health, and other public services. According to the World Bank study, when developing countries have this kind of sound management, financial aid has a big effect on growth and poverty reduction, improving social indicators over and above what good management itself induces. Equally, aid has little effect on the development of countries with poor management. Financial aid will have a lasting effect only in a healthy climate for efficient investment and human capital development. This observation is based on three sources; cross-country studies, research into the success and failure of investment projects financed by the World Bank, and case studies of aid effectiveness (ibid.).

BOX 6.1
Impact of ODA on Growth and Poverty

If countries are distinguished according to their economic management, aid generally has a large effect in good-management environments: 1 per cent of GDP in assistance translates to a sustained increase in growth of 0.5 percentage points of GDP. Some countries with sound management have received only small amounts of aid and have grown at 2.2 per cent per capita. The good-management, high-aid group, however, grew much faster — 3.7 per cent per capita. There is no such difference for countries with poor management. Those receiving small amounts of aid have grown sluggishly (if at all), as have those receiving large amounts. Introducing other variables does not change the picture.

The effect of aid goes beyond growth. In a country with sound management, 1 per cent of GDP in assistance reduces poverty by 1 per cent. Aid has a similar effect on infant mortality, but again only if there is good management.

A final lesson from cross-country studies is that, with sound country management, aid works in partnership with private capital. Specifically, 1 per cent of GDP in aid draws in another 1.9 per cent of GDP in private investment. Put another way, assistance to well-managed countries increases private sector confidence and supports important public services. It hardly needs to be said, but in poorly managed countries aid crowds out private investment.

China's ODA to Thailand

Data on ODA from China to Thailand is not available, but ODA from China is not significant enough to affect poverty in Thailand. Compared to other GMS countries, Thailand does not rely as much on ODA. In 2008, total ODA from all sources was US$39.093 million. Out of this, only 0.31 per cent (US$120,400) was from Asian countries, including China (Table 6.10). Moreover, as shown in Figure 6.5, over the period 1997–2008 the amount of ODA declined consistently from US$520,300 in 1997 to US$120,400 in 2008.

TABLE 6.10
ODA to Thailand by Donor, Fiscal Year 2006–08 (US$ '000)

Donor	2006		2007		2008	
	Total	%	Total	%	Total	%
NGOs	9,369.4	17.49	13,781.1	28.94	12,999.7	33.25
Japan	8,259.3	15.42	8,794.3	18.47	6,539.1	16.73
France	6,284.5	11.73	7,206.8	15.13	6,830.6	17.47
U.S.A.	6,480.9	12.10	5,136.2	10.79	2,742.2	7.01
Volunteers	4,436.1	8.28	4,447.1	9.34	3,934.3	10.06
United Nations	10,110.1	18.87	3,070.0	6.45	3,025.0	7.74
Germany	2,047.4	3.82	1,999.0	4.20	1,191.4	3.05
European Union	1,096.9	2.05	1,975.7	4.15	1,530.3	3.91
Denmark	3,185.5	5.95	837.2	1.76	26.7	0.07
Asian Countries	65.6	0.12	140.3	0.29	120.4	0.31
Netherlands	–	0.00	94.4	0.20	52.8	0.14
Sweden	1,571.2	2.93	55.6	0.12	24.3	0.06
SEAMEO	28.5	0.05	43.6	0.09	53.6	0.14
Australia	493.4	0.92	26.8	0.06		0.00
CPS	26.6	0.05	7.5	0.02	7.7	0.02
Egypt	2.5	0.00	5.1	0.01	8.9	0.02
New Zealand	–	–	–	–	–	–
Canada	105.7	0.20	–	–	–	–
Spain	–	–	–	–	6.0	0.02
Total	53,564	100.00	47,621	100.00	39,093.0	100.00

Note: Fiscal year is from 1 October to 30 September.
Source: Ministry of Foreign Affairs.

6. CONCLUSION AND POLICY IMPLICATIONS

This study is limited to identifying the impact of China's economic cooperation with Thailand on poverty reduction in Thailand. It reviews the literature on the current situation of economic cooperation between China and Thailand and applies a modified gravity model to evaluate the impact of China on trade and investment between the two countries. The results from the gravity model were then used to find the impact of China on the employment of unskilled and semi-skilled labourers in Thailand, who usually suffer the highest incidences of poverty.

Through detailed analysis, this chapter identifies various modes of impact of China's rise in the case of Thailand. First, it should be noted

FIGURE 6.5
ODA from Asian Countries to Thailand, 1997–2008

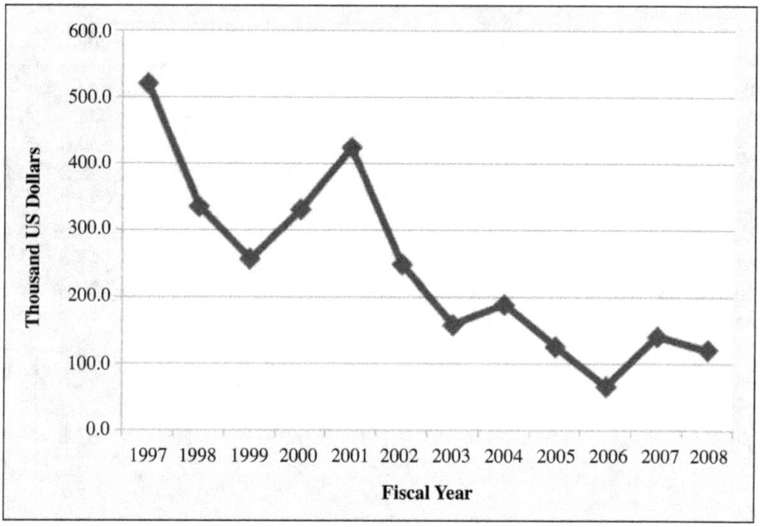

Source: Ministry of Foreign Affairs.

that the growth of China's economy, while presenting challenges, has also generated complementary trading structures between the two nations that have benefited Thailand. Principally, the rapid growth of China's economy helps increase the market opportunities for Thailand's exports and investments. Second, regional and bilateral trade agreements have not benefited Thailand because of supply-side constraints, the main problem being that Thailand's agricultural production costs are much higher compared to China's. It has also been found that China would like to import a lot of fruit from Thailand, but most of Thailand's local exporters are small and their capacity cannot meet the huge demand. Such benefits might accrue to the giant size businesses that have much more capacity compared to small and medium enterprises.

Gravity models have been used to quantify the impacts of China's rise through the mechanisms of trade and FDI. First, they were applied to examine the economic impact of China in the context of imports, exports and FDI between Thailand and China. Second, the regression results of the models were translated into the effects on the employment of unskilled and semi-skilled labour in Thailand with the assumption that these groups of workers represent the poor in Thailand because they have the lowest wages.

With regards to trade, three sets of regression were estimated, using dependent variables of: aggregate export and aggregate import, export products classified at 6 digits, and import products classified at 6 digits. Seventy-seven import and sixteen export commodities are found to be significantly affected by China.

With regards to investment, FDI flow from OECD countries to Thailand is used as a dependent variable. The estimate shows that a 1 per cent increase in OECD countries' GDP will result in 0.89 per cent increase in FDI flow to Thailand, while a 1 per cent increase in Thailand's GDP will result in an 8.3 per cent increase of FDI to Thailand. For GDP per capita, which reflects labour costs, it was found that if labour costs in OECD countries increase, their FDI outflow will increase: a 1 per cent increase of labour costs in OECD countries will increase FDI outflow by 1.01 per cent. However, if the labour costs in Thailand increase, FDI inflow will decrease: a 1 per cent increase in labour costs in Thailand will reduce FDI inflow by 6.79 per cent. It is interesting to find that a 1 per cent increase in FDI from OECD to China will result in a 0.22 per cent increase in FDI in Thailand. In other words, China has an indirect impact on OECD's FDI to Thailand since the attractiveness of China to OECD's FDI will also attract FDI from OECD to Thailand.

China's impact on poverty reduction in Thailand was identified by examining the impact on unskilled and semi-skilled labour employed to produce the commodities' or by the investment in question. In the case of trade, it is found that Thailand lost about 251,137 unskilled jobs through import from China from 2003 to 2009. This may be considered an opportunity cost of import in terms of employment. On the other hand, the export of sixteen commodities to China during the same period created employment for around 470,398 unskilled workers; natural rubber alone employed 465,836. In the case of investment, FDI inflows from China over 2000 to 2007 generated about 80,257 jobs. The impact of Thailand's FDI outflow to China is less straightforward because it does not necessarily mean this investment was foregone from Thailand. Nevertheless, the estimated employment effect of such "foregone" FDI is approximately 42,365 unskilled workers.

In conclusion, China's impact through trade and FDI on Thailand's economy is mixed and diverse, though marginal relative to the size of the Thai economy. The marginal and structural net impacts of China on trade and FDI in Thailand are favourable to unskilled employment and thus poverty reduction in Thailand. However, the qualitative socio-economic impact on the Thai economy appears to be to the detriment of the relatively poor. To ensure maximum benefits, policy measures to compensate the losers from the economic cooperation between the two countries must be effectively implemented. We propose the following recommendations:

1. Encourage and facilitate greater participation and timely effective absorption of relatively poor farmers and unskilled workers in export and FDI expansion through capacity building, i.e., better access to information, education, training, finance, relevant to meet and take advantage of emerging opportunities.
2. Simplify rules, regulations and bureaucratic process related to cross-border and domestic trade and investment to enable and facilitate equitable access and exploitation of emerging trade and investment opportunities.
3. Strengthen SPS (sanitary and phytosanitary) measures with regards to local and foreign sources of products to protect consumer health and welfare.
4. Enforce the competition policy to ensure a fair and transparent competitive market based on Most Favoured Nation and National Treatment principles.

These measures, if effectively introduced and implemented, are likely to enhance any impact that economic interaction with China or any other country may have on poverty reduction in Thailand. It is important to emphasize that if the poverty problem in Thailand is to be addressed effectively, the government should design and implement direct measures towards inclusive growth that systematically distributes income and enables the poor rather than relying on the trickle-down effects of trade and investment intervention.

APPENDICES

Appendix 6A

Table 6A.1 Definition and Source

Variable	Definition and Source
Export	Export Value (defined 6 digits) *Source*: <www.trademap.org>
Import	Import value (defined 6 digits) *Source*: <www.trademap.org>
RGDP	Real Gross domestic product in constant prices 2000. *Source*: <World Development Indicator>
RGGPPC	Gross domestic product per capita in constant prices 2000. *Source*: <World Development Indicator>
RFEX	Real bilateral foreign exchange rate *Source*: <World Development Indicator>
DIST	Distance between two countries *Source*: Rose (2005).
Tariff	Simple apply tariff rate *Source*: The Customs Department of Thailand.
FDI	Foreign Direct Investment *Source*: <www.sourceoecd.org>
Landl	Number of landlocked countries *Source*: Rose (2005).

Appendix 6B

Export Product

Table 6B.1
Major Product Thailand Export to China

Order	Product Code (HS)	Product label	Value (Thousand $, 2008)	Percentage	Sum
1	'847170	Computer data storage units	3,870,761	24.20	24.20
2	'271019	Light petroleum distillates nes	1,070,474	6.69	30.89
3	'847330	Parts&accessories of automatic data processg machines&units thereof	728,132	4.55	35.44
4	'270900	Petroleum oils and oils obtained from bituminous minerals, crude	551,565	3.45	38.89
5	'291736	Terephthalic acid and its salts	457,835	2.86	41.75
6	'854231	Electronic integrated circuits as processors and controllers, whether	322,045	2.01	43.76
7	'854239	Electronic integrated circuits (excl. such as processors, controllers,	311,559	1.95	45.71
8	'400110	Natural rubber latex, whether or not prevulcanised	297,366	1.86	47.57
9	'400599	Compounded rubber, unvulcanised in primary forms nes	249,022	1.56	49.12
10	'390740	Polycarbonates	246,280	1.54	50.66
11	'400129	Natural rubber in other forms nes	230,652	1.44	52.11
12	'071410	Manioc (cassava), fresh or dried, whether or not sliced or pelleted	209,220	1.31	53.41
13	'853400	Printed circuits	197,231	1.23	54.65
14	'850110	Electric motors of an output not exceeding 37.5 W	183,645	1.15	55.79
15	'100630	Rice, semi-milled or wholly milled, whether or not polished or glazed	156,779	0.98	56.77
16	'850440	Static converters, nes	122,338	0.76	57.54
	[illegible]	[illegible]	[illegible]	[illegible]	

Import Product

Table 6B.2
Major Product Thailand Import from China

Order	Product Code	Product label	Value (Thousand $, 2008)	Percentage	Sum
1	'847330	Parts & accessories of automatic data processg machines & units thereof	1,357,694	6.77	6.77
2	'852990	Parts suitable f use solely/princ w the app of headings 85.25 to 85.28	617,604	3.08	9.85
3	'847130	Portable digital computers <10kg	567,068	2.83	12.68
4	'732690	Articles, iron or steel, nes	335,909	1.68	14.36
5	'721391	Hot rolled bar/rod, irregular coils, <14mm diam	225,683	1.13	15.48
6	'392690	Articles of plastics or of other materials of Nos. 39.01 to 39.14 nes	197,534	0.99	16.47
7	'270900	Petroleum oils and oils obtained from bituminous minerals, crude	184,392	0.92	17.39
8	'850110	Electric motors of an output not exceeding 37.5 W	122,828	0.61	18.00
9	'853690	Electrical app for switchg/protec elec circuits, not exced 1,000 V, nes	120,104	0.60	18.60
10	'730429	Casings, tubing, drill pipe, for oil drilling use	118,967	0.59	19.19

continued on next page

Table 6B.2 — cont'd

Order	Product Code	Product label	Value (Thousand $, 2008)	Percentage	Sum
11	'853710	Boards, panels, includg numerical control panels, for a voltage <=1000 V	118,322	0.59	19.79
12	'310530	Diammonium phosphate, in packages weighing more than 10 kg	116,829	0.58	20.37
13	'280469	Silicon nes	110,669	0.55	20.92
14	'720719	Semi-fin prod, iron or non-alloy steel, cntg by wght <.25% carbon, nes	104,665	0.52	21.44
15	'841430	Compressors of a kind used in refrigerating equipment	101,026	0.50	21.95
16	'720838	Hot roll iron/steel nes, coil >600mm × 3-4.75mm	96,090	0.48	22.43
17	'850450	Inductors, electric	94,833	0.47	22.90
18	'722990	Wire of alloy steel, o/t stainless	93,815	0.47	23.37
19	'850440	Static converters, nes	91,539	0.46	23.82
20	'852580	Television cameras, digital cameras and video camera recorders	89,273	0.45	24.27
21	'721049	Flat rolled prod,i/nas,plated or coated with zinc, >/=600mm wide, nes	87,288	0.44	24.70
22	'847180	Units of automatic data processing equipment nes	83,901	0.42	25.12
23	'854442	Electric conductors for a voltage <= 1.000 V, insulated, fitted with c	83,788	0.42	25.54

24	‘852190	Video recording or reproducing apparatus nes	80,661	0.40	25.94
25	‘310540	Monoammonium phosphate&mx thereof w diamonium phosphate, in pack</=10kg	80,387	0.40	26.34
26	‘760120	Aluminium unwrought, alloyed	79,847	0.40	26.74
27	‘852290	Parts and accessories of apparatus of heading Nos. 85.19 to 85.21, nes	77,324	0.39	27.13
28	‘848180	Taps, cocks, valves and similar appliances, nes	75,877	0.38	27.51
29	‘280920	Phosphoric acid and polyphosphoric acids	75,092	0.37	27.88
30	‘851770	Parts of telephone sets, telephones for cellular networks or for other	=73,502	0.37	28.25
31	‘382490	Chemical/allied industry preparations/prods nes	70,667	0.35	28.60
32	‘847160	Computer input/outputs, with/without storage	69,810	0.35	28.95
33	‘850431	Transformers electric power handling capacity not exceeding 1 KVA, nes	69,618	0.35	29.30
34	‘310559	Fertilizers containg nitrogen & phosphorus, nes, in pack weighg</=10kg	69,497	0.35	29.64
35	‘854011	Cathode-ray television picture tubes, inc video monitor tubes,colour	69,267	0.35	29.99
36	‘080810	Apples, fresh	65,302	0.33	30.31
37	‘853120	Indicator panels incorporatg liquid crystal device/light emittg diode	64,497	0.32	30.64
38	‘310210	Urea,wthr/nt in aqueous solution in packages weighg more than 10 kg	61,960	0.31	30.94

continued on next page

Table 6B.2 — cont'd

Order	Product Code	Product label	Value (Thousand $, 2008)	Percentage	Sum
39	'590210	Tire cord fabric made of nylon or other polyamides high tenacity yarns	60,738	0.30	31.25
40	'844399	Parts and accessories of printers, copying machines and facsimile mach	60,542	0.30	31.55
41	'283620	Disodium carbonate	60,541	0.30	31.85
42	'847170	Computer data storage units	57,898	0.29	32.14
43	'720839	Hot roll iron/steel nes, coil >600mm × <3mm	57,354	0.29	32.43
44	'520812	Plain weave cotton fabric, >/=85%, >100 g/m2 to 200 g/m2, unbleached	56,526	0.28	32.71
45	'401699	Articles of vulcanised rubber nes, other than hard rubber	56,048	0.28	32.99
46	'551611	Woven fabrics,containg>/=85% of artificial staple fibres, unbleached/bl	56,022	0.28	33.27
47	'721499	Bars & rods, iron/nas, forged etc., nes	55,517	0.28	33.54
48	'761699	Articles of aluminium, nes	54,969	0.27	33.82
49	'722830	Bars & rods, alloy steel, o/t stainless nfw thn hot rolld/drawn/extrud, nes	53,295	0.27	34.08
50	'850140	AC motors, single-phase, nes	53,025	0.26	34.35
51	'690790	Tiles, cubes and sim nes, unglazed ceramics	52,886	0.26	34.61
52	'731100	Containers for compressed or liquefied gas of iron or steel	52,658	0.26	34.88

53	'720917	Cold rolled iron/steel, coils >600mm × 0.5-1mm	52,488	0.26	35.14
54	'841940	Distilling or rectifying plant	52,452	0.26	35.40
55	'720230	Ferro-silico-manganese	50,435	0.25	35.65
56	'720711	Semi-fin prod,i/nas,rect/sq cross-sect cntg by wgt <.25% c, wdth<2X thk	50,103	0.25	35.90
57	'852340	Optical media for the recording of sound or of other phenomena (excl.	49,133	0.25	36.15
58	'380891	Insecticides	48,522	0.24	36.39
59	'847190	Automatic data processing equipment nes	47,649	0.24	36.63
60	'900190	Prisms, mirrors & other optical elements of any material, unmounted, nes	46,117	0.23	36.86
61	'030343	Skipjack or stripe-bellid bonito, frozen ex headg No. 03.04, livers & roes	45,679	0.23	37.08
62	'741110	Pipes and tubes, refined copper	45,623	0.23	37.31
63	'380850	Goods containing one or more of aldrin ISO, binapacryl ISO, camphechlo	44,853	0.22	37.54
64	'760719	Foil, aluminium, not backed and not exceeding 0.2 mm thick, nes	44,339	0.22	37.76
65	'853650	Electrical switches for a voltage not exceeding 1,000 volts, nes	43,931	0.22	37.98
66	'280300	Carbon (carbon blacks and other forms of carbon, nes)	43,861	0.22	38.19
67	'950300	Tricycles, scooters, pedal cars and similar wheeled toys; dolls' carr	43,754	0.22	38.41

continued on next page

Table 6B.2 — cont'd

Order	Product Code	Product label	Value (Thousand $, 2008)	Percentage	Sum
68	'720916	Cold rolled iron/steel, coils >600mm × 1-3mm	43,740	0.22	38.63
69	'853669	Electrical plugs and sockets, for a voltage not exceeding 1,000 volts	43,524	0.22	38.85
70	'481029	Paper, fine, woodcontaining, in rolls or sheets, clay coated, nes	41,190	0.21	39.05
71	'854110	Diodes, other than photosensitive or light emitting diodes	40,814	0.20	39.26
72	'871499	Bicycle parts nes	39,208	0.20	39.45
73	'840991	Parts for spark-ignition type engines nes	38,287	0.19	39.64
74	'847290	Office machines, nes	37,228	0.19	39.83
75	'848210	Bearings, ball	37,172	0.19	40.01
76	'842810	Lifts and skip hoists	37,119	0.19	40.20
77	'640610	Uppers and parts thereof, other than stiffeners	36,614	0.18	40.38
78	'710691	Silver in unwrought forms	35,853	0.18	40.56
79	'850511	Permanent magnets&art intendd to become permanent magnets, of metal	35,599	0.18	40.74
80	'441299	Panels, 1 outer ply coniferous wood nes	34,562	0.17	40.91
Total		All products	20,045,768	40.91	

Appendix 6C

Table 6C.1
Regression Estimates of China's Impact on Thailand's Export
(Dependent variables are export products classified at 6 digits)

Variable	*LNRGDP*$_i$		*LNRGDP*$_j$		*LNRFEX*$_{ij}$		*LNDIST*$_{ij}$		*TARIFF*$_{ij}$		*CHINA*		*Constant*		Obs	Countries	R^2
HS 847170	17.0764	***	0.4686	***	0.3401	***	–0.6277	**	-0.8704	***	1.0816	***	–436.62	***	81	11	0.6387
	(1.6798)		(0.1223)		(0.0917)		(0.2979)		(0.1755)		(0.3061)		(42.36)				
HS 271019	6.4521	***	0.6023		–0.1122		–3.0420	**	–0.0964		2.0327	**	–148.09	***	65	11	0.1543
	(1.5623)		(0.4388)		(0.1922)		(1.5369)		(0.0940)		(0.9336)		(38.72)				
HS 847330	–1.9752		0.4600		0.2728		–1.3527	***	–0.0425		0.8788		60.84	*	78	10	0.0920
	(1.4852)		(0.3927)		(0.1895)		(0.4345)		(0.0273)		(0.7492)		(32.47)				
HS 270900	26.2968		–9.9016		–1.2327		11.1770		0.4112		21.8888		–496.18		38	5	0.3401
	(21.6960)		(13.5172)		(1.5699)		(11.8381)		(0.6485)		(25.8568)		(303.12)				
HS 291736	17.8242	***	–0.4150		–0.6709	*	–2.2152		–0.0449		6.8210	**	–422.71	***	100	14	0.4235
	(2.7732)		(0.7426)		(0.3455)		(1.3491)		(0.3307)		(3.1221)		(77.26)				
HS 854231	30.8089	***	0.1174		–0.0032		–0.2702		0.0985		–0.1952		–791.17	***	80	10	0.5016
	(1.4010)		(0.1185)		(0.0519)		(0.2453)		(0.4565)		(0.9000)	***	(37.32)				
HS 854239	29.5233	***	0.1442		0.0024		–0.1961		0.0865		–0.1476		–759.54	***	80	10	0.5012
	(1.4271)		(0.1360)		(0.0531)		(0.2927)		(0.4292)		(0.8655)	***	(37.71)				
HS 400110	1.7573	**	0.1848	**	0.1585		–1.1761	*	–0.0091	**	1.0593		–30.48		54	7	0.4726
	(0.8129)		(0.0934)		(0.1028)		(0.6176)		(0.0041)		(0.7225)		(19.07)				

continued on next page

Table 6C.1 — cont'd

Variable	$LNRGDP_i$		$LNRGDP_j$		$LNRFEX_{ij}$		$LNDIST_{ij}$		$TARIFF_{ij}$		*CHINA*		*Constant*		Obs	Countries	R^2
HS 400599	12.6865	***	–0.5135	*	0.1918	***	–0.4404		–0.1799	*	2.9960	***	–301.56	**	47	6	0.4946
	(4.4948)		(0.3090)		(0.0658)		(0.5448)		(0.1017)		(0.6214)		(118.18)				
HS 390740	2.4809	***	0.8590	**	0.0096		–1.8179	**	–0.1804	***	1.3296	**	–62.26	***	86	11	0.3678
	(0.8609)		(0.3993)		(0.0840)		(0.8175)		(0.0296)		(0.6507)		(22.58)				
HS 400129	0.2162		0.6899	***	–0.0323		–0.3404		–0.0091		1.3567	***	–11.11		55	7	0.0610
	(1.7302)		(0.2600)		(0.1170)		(0.7148)		(0.0063)		(0.5179)		(46.53)				
HS 071410	5.1401		1.3185		0.6031		0.2321		0.0036		4.1681	***	–164.30		61	8	0.0733
	(4.2039)		(0.8258)		(0.6618)		(0.7675)		(0.0039)		(1.2157)		(104.11)				
HS 853400	0.8909		0.5822	***	–0.0296		–0.8413	***	–0.0329		–0.5585	**	–20.96		88	11	0.0889
	(1.2955)		(0.1298)		(0.0888)		(0.1913)		(0.0245)		(0.2445)		(33.45)				
HS 850110	–0.2959		0.2584		–0.0572		–1.0717	***	–0.1137	**	1.9856	**	19.94		86	11	0.1212
	(0.6496)		(0.2731)		(0.0799)		(0.3552)		(0.0447)		(0.7999)		(20.09)				
HS 100630	2.3034	***	0.2313		–0.1911		–0.3737		0.0023		0.5746		–51.61	***	85	16	0.3174
	(0.5993)		(0.3382)		(0.3538)		(0.3089)		(0.0032)		(0.8707)		(14.88)				
HS 850440	0.3959		1.2643	***	0.0891		–1.4403	**	–0.0682	**	0.6859	**	–24.29		65	10	0.1143
	(1.6238)		(0.2080)		(0.1997)		(0.6846)		(0.0335)		(0.3618)		(41.76)				

Note: *** denote 1 per cent, **5 per cent, * 10 per cent significance levels; robust standard errors are in parentheses; the List of HS products accounted for 57.54 per cent of the value of trade that occurred in 2008.

Table 6C.2
Regression Estimates of China's Impact on Thailand's Import
(Dependent variables are import products classified at 6 digits)

Variable	*$LNRGDP_i$*		*$LNRGDP_j$*		*$LNRFEX_{ij}$*		*$LNDIST_{ij}$*		*$TARIFF_{ij}$*		*CHINA*		*Constant*		Obs	Countries	R^2
HS 847330	–0.2751		0.9280	***	0.0255		–1.3415	***	–0.0029		6.4277	***	–1.2526		882	130	0.0116
	(0.5996)		(0.1156)		(0.0742)		(0.4697)		(0.0026)		(0.8246)		(15.2147)				
HS 852990	–0.6757		0.9216	***	–0.0133		–1.1799	***	–0.0032		5.0977	***	7.3083		809	120	0.0155
	(0.6714)		(0.1193)		(0.0564)		(0.3944)		(0.0031)		(0.7397)		(16.7554)				
HS 847130	0.3773		0.5974	***	0.0975		–0.9428	***	–0.0025		7.1503	***	–14.6271		681	100	0.0296
	(0.6427)		(0.1010)		(0.0603)		(0.3600)		(0.0033)		(0.6576)		(16.3508)				
HS 732690	0.9272	**	1.0250	***	0.1476	***	–1.0453	***	–0.0052	*	3.2082	**	–36.2123	***	1086	162	0.0856
	(0.4313)		(0.0794)		(0.0553)		(0.2822)		(0.0030)		(0.5541)		(11.4789)				
HS 721391	–3.5902		1.4438	***	0.0418		–1.7634	*	0.0315		4.2262	***	72.3679		213	31	0.0346
	(3.2044)		(0.3744)		(0.1904)		(0.9159)		(0.0306)		(1.3230)		(82.9173)				
HS 392690	0.2493		0.9466	***	0.0911	*	–1.1381	***	0.0001		3.4773	***	–16.1978		1133	169	0.0235
	(0.4207)		(0.0772)		(0.0522)		(0.2746)		(0.0012)		(0.5504)		(10.8819)				
HS 270900	4.9006		–0.0417		0.4042	*	–1.6591		–0.0243		–2.0575		–104.9791		290	44	0.0421
	(3.6286)		(0.3297)		(0.2279)		(1.1229)		(0.0287)		(1.5194)		(93.4476)				
HS 850110	–0.4683		0.7665	***	0.0263		–1.2933	***	–0.0035		5.5535	***	6.4492		758	113	0.0160
	(0.3194)		(0.1128)		(0.0809)		(0.3894)		(0.0023)		(0.6893)		(8.5654)				
HS 853690	0.8876	*	1.0117	***	0.1165	*	–0.9430	***	0.0043		3.4956	***	–36.8362	***	834	123	0.0317
	(0.5187)		(0.1057)		(0.0655)		(0.3508)		(0.0029)		(0.6497)		(13.6228)				
HS 730429	6.4561	***	0.6671	***	0.0498		–0.5629		0.0060		3.5512	***	–176.5487	***	377	55	0.2114
	(1.1501)		(0.1497)		(0.1451)		(0.4241)		(0.0131)		(0.7131)		(29.5839)				

continued on next page

Table 6C.2 — cont'd

Variable	$LNRGDP_i$		$LNRGDP_j$		$LNRFEX_{ij}$		$LNDIST_{ij}$		$TARIFF_{ij}$		*CHINA*		*Constant*		Obs	Countries	R^2
HS 853710	0.8766		1.0823	***	0.1405	*	–1.1574	***	–0.0035		2.8178	***	–36.1360	**	810	120	0.0830
	(0.5843)		(0.1059)		(0.0762)		(0.3661)		(0.0033)		(0.6611)		(15.7862)				
HS 310530	2.1224		–0.2836		–0.1772		2.0251	**	–0.0098		8.2231	***	–61.3612		153	22	0.0218
	(3.9807)		(0.4780)		(0.2787)		(1.0114)		(0.0282)		(1.2198)		(102.6902)				
HS 280469	2.1306		–0.2845		–0.1750		2.0224	**	–0.0083		8.2235	***	–61.5513		153	22	0.0210
	(4.8265)		(0.4781)		(0.2783)		(1.0102)		(0.0326)		(1.2199)		(124.6736)				
HS 720719	–9.4787	**	0.5351	*	0.0422		–0.3361		–0.1891	*	4.4318	***	234.9078	**	167	24	0.0538
	(3.6782)		(0.2923)		(0.1093)		(0.3147)		(0.1003)		(0.7858)		(95.4845)				
HS 841430	–0.5635		0.8738	***	0.0281		–0.8006	**	–0.0034		4.2572	***	1.9723		789	118	0.0109
	(0.5036)		(0.1238)		(0.0535)		(0.3787)		(0.0036)		(0.7508)		(12.4351)				
HS 720838	–2.8187		0.3809		–0.1842		–0.3203		–0.0029		5.5898	***	67.6320		263	38	0.0133
	(2.1736)		(0.2673)		(0.2036)		(0.4200)		(0.0324)		(0.9918)		(56.4831)				
HS 850450	–0.1618		0.8883	***	0.0718		–1.4003	***	–0.0056		3.9337	***	–2.5809		683	100	0.0163
	(0.6689)		(0.1097)		(0.0876)		(0.3783)		(0.0038)		(0.6142)		(17.7060)				
HS 722990	2.2067	**	0.7397	***	–0.0863		–0.5495	*	0.0078		4.0944	***	–69.5783	***	2	1	0.7449
	(1.0095)		(0.1929)		(0.1156)		(0.3294)		(0.0067)		(0.7052)		(25.5099)				
HS 850440	0.1654		0.9425	***	0.1158	*	–0.5857	*	–0.0038		3.8609	***	–19.6572		758	113	0.0324
	(0.5638)		(0.1036)		(0.0608)		(0.3003)		(0.0025)		(0.5777)		(14.8683)				
HS 852580	–5.2955		0.9360	***	0.0139		–0.7048		–0.8064	*	4.6402	***	124.3492		143	73	0.0112
	(5.3667)		(0.1943)		(0.1075)		(0.5445)		(0.4475)		(0.8474)		(138.2226)				
HS 721049	–2.5250		0.7484	***	–0.4203	**	–0.2615		–0.0616	***	2.7771	***	51.1096		313	47	0.0551
	(1.5941)		(0.1675)		(0.2089)		(0.6200)		(0.0174)		(0.8057)		(41.2805)				

HS 847180	−0.5005		1.0075	***	0.0791		−0.4405		0.0020		3.8152	***	−5.5042		614	91	0.0135
	(0.5625)		(0.0989)		(0.0753)		(0.3835)		(0.0033)		(0.6026)		(14.4890)				
HS 854442	0.4741		1.0858	***	−0.1261		−0.4931		−0.1593		3.8912	***	−30.5451		134	68	0.0352
	(7.2404)		(0.1389)		(0.0931)		(0.6532)		(0.1475)		(0.8463)		(186.6225)				
HS 852190	−0.6430		0.6361	***	−0.0268		−0.9064	**	−0.0020		6.1387	***	10.2954		535	79	0.0008
	(0.5188)		(0.1120)		(0.0929)		(0.3613)		(0.0022)		(0.6494)		(13.4974)				
HS 310540	−1.2569		0.2313		−0.2166		0.7478		−0.0143		6.8027	***	21.8811		160	23	0.0047
	(2.8358)		(0.3063)		(0.2850)		(0.5940)		(0.0180)		(0.9896)		(72.0482)				
HS 760120	−0.4957		0.8051	***	0.0502		−1.1015	***	0.0224		2.7415	***	5.1633		473	69	0.0001
	(1.9382)		(0.1371)		(0.1281)		(0.3782)		(0.0591)		(0.6835)		(50.6259)				
HS 852290	−2.6628	***	0.6441	***	−0.1452		−1.5162	**	−0.0024		6.5226	***	67.4506	***	433	63	0.0477
	(0.8027)		(0.1599)		(0.1431)		(0.5926)		(0.0025)		(0.8612)		(20.3858)				
HS 848180	0.7211	*	0.9256	***	0.1557	**	−0.4184		0.0014		3.5410	***	−34.9408		878	129	0.0421
	(0.4024)		(0.0848)		(0.0692)		(0.2565)		(0.0027)		(0.5331)		(10.7462)				
HS 280920	0.2267		1.1921	***	0.0411		−1.4693	*	−0.0099	*	5.6288	***	−23.0674		160	23	0.0351
	(0.9307)		(0.2527)		(0.2194)		(0.8006)		(0.0059)		(0.7369)		(23.6517)				
HS 851770	9.5984		0.9121	***	0.2914	***	−0.4619		−3.9137	**	8.2383	***	−262.9234		152	77	0.0313
	(7.4671)		(0.1239)		(0.0862)		(0.4546)		(1.9745)		(2.5496)		(193.3162)				
HS 382490	−1.5221	***	1.0765	***	0.0929		−0.6768	**	−0.0082	**	3.0893	***	21.7491		829	122	0.0089
	(0.5259)		(0.0966)		(0.0728)		(0.2821)		(0.0034)		(0.5809)		(13.8097)				
HS 847160	−2.1296	***	0.8247	***	−0.0063		−1.1174	***	−0.0047	*	5.6980	***	46.3198		768	114	0.0154
	(0.5050)		(0.1182)		(0.0789)		(0.3600)		(0.0028)		(0.7066)		(12.9547)				
HS 850431	0.1425		0.8310	***	0.0492		−1.3041	***	−0.0006		4.6232	***	−10.6635		731	107	0.0162
	(0.4024)		(0.0972)		(0.0728)		(0.3166)		(0.0035)		(0.5685)		(9.4878)				
HS 310559	0.7769		0.3591	*	−0.2495		0.2128		0.0317		2.8357	***	−29.5779		196	29	0.0261
	(2.3905)		(0.2063)		(0.2746)		(0.5890)		(0.0226)		(0.9025)		(60.2091)				

continued on next page

Table 6C.2 — cont'd

Variable	$LNRGDP_i$		$LNRGDP_j$		$LNRFEX_{ij}$		$LNDIST_{ij}$		$TARIFF_{ij}$		*CHINA*		*Constant*		Obs	Countries	R^2
HS 854011	–4.5838	***	0.6500	***	–0.1390		–2.0454	**	–0.0173	**	6.5470	***	121.2311	***	411	60	0.0857
	(1.0721)		(0.2071)		(0.1808)		(0.8449)		(0.0077)		(1.0183)		(27.1104)				
HS 080810	–0.1648		0.4037	**	0.0268		0.5384		0.0052		7.6794	***	–8.9745		255	37	0.0117
	(1.3608)		(0.1903)		(0.0973)		(0.3469)		(0.0043)		(0.7518)		(34.1722)				
HS 853120	–2.2176	**	1.2040	***	–0.0008		–1.6228	***	–0.0093		3.6541	***	42.8039	*	366	53	0.0206
	(0.9417)		(0.2256)		(0.1533)		(0.4596)		(0.0061)		(0.8663)		(23.0898)				
HS 310210	–0.3251		0.3287	*	0.2760		–0.7469		–0.0085		3.3045	***	8.9548		251	38	0.0114
	(2.4709)		(0.1973)		(0.2841)		(0.7847)		(0.0119)		(0.9194)		(64.9508)				
HS 590210	1.9088	*	0.7626	***	–0.1306		–0.3383		–0.0038		6.9727	***	–64.5817	***	276	40	0.0653
	(1.0145)		(0.2444)		(0.1279)		(0.2815)		(0.0069)		(0.7043)		(24.5340)				
HS 844399	0.3299		1.0353	***	0.2714	**	–0.4747		–0.9934	***	3.6435	***	–23.9939		123	62	0.0018
	(6.9675)		(0.2278)		(0.1047)		(0.5280)		(0.2848)		(0.8911)		(181.0731)				
HS 283620	2.0124		0.0102		–0.1490		1.6419		–0.0022		7.6413	***	–62.9297		174	25	0.0395
	(1.7395)		(0.5296)		(0.2068)		(1.0593)		(0.0114)		(1.2929)		(42.1917)				
HS 847170	–0.6261		0.8864	***	0.0392		–0.9293	**	0.0017		5.3288	***	4.6087		641	94	0.0010
	(0.6757)		(0.1184)		(0.0933)		(0.4569)		(0.0035)		(0.7395)		(17.2786)				
HS 720839	–6.0207	***	0.5699	*	–0.1855		–0.1896		–0.0847	**	5.9662	***	144.4335	***	331	48	0.0589
	(2.2031)		(0.3017)		(0.1687)		(0.3542)		(0.0348)		(1.0544)		(56.4805)				
HS 520812	–0.7573		0.3288	***	–0.1186		–0.5082	***	–0.0012		8.1894	***	16.3962		447	65	0.0013
	(0.4748)		(0.0931)		(0.0727)		(0.1798)		(0.0016)		(0.4325)		(11.7812)				
HS 401699	–0.0159		0.8653	***	0.0843	*	–0.9370	***	–0.0014		3.4632	***	–10.0109		988	147	0.0241
	(0.3109)		(0.0833)		(0.0472)		(0.2731)		(0.0011)		(0.5509)		(8.1633)				

HS 551611	−2.5778	***	0.2765	***	−0.0629		−0.5705	*	−0.0033		8.5274	***	65.2552	***	339	49	0.0457
	(0.8232)		(0.0798)		(0.0954)		(0.3289)		(0.0024)		(0.4344)		(22.0945)				
HS 721499	−1.8480		0.8806	***	−0.2717		−0.2665		−0.0099		5.8528	***	29.1080		272	39	0.0025
	(1.3341)		(0.3018)		(0.2067)		(0.3590)		(0.0176)		(0.9246)		(33.1759)				
HS 761699	−0.4485		0.9056	***	0.0834		−1.0164	***	−0.0064	***	4.0499	***	0.4964		843	126	0.0124
	(0.2860)		(0.0979)		(0.0514)		(0.3254)		(0.0024)		(0.6310)		(7.6487)				
HS 722830	0.7180		1.0011	***	−0.2275		0.0684		−0.0396	*	3.7166	***	−41.5919		286	41	0.0414
	(1.4930)		(0.1982)		(0.1787)		(0.4640)		(0.0213)		(0.7761)		(38.1319)				
HS 850140	0.2452		0.5756	***	−0.0247		−0.7492	***	−0.0002		6.6970	***	−12.9948		545	82	0.0116
	(0.8477)		(0.1262)		(0.0672)		(0.2778)		(0.0034)		(0.6500)		(22.0324)				
HS 690790	1.0879	*	0.3229	***	−0.0603		−0.5900	*	−0.0025		6.0406	***	−30.4063	*	394	58	0.0532
	(0.6107)		(0.0829)		(0.1006)		(0.3565)		(0.0018)		(0.5066)		(15.6541)				
HS 731100	1.1690		0.6250	***	0.0705		−0.4492	*	−0.0132		4.1236	***	−39.6141		702	104	0.0453
	(0.7238)		(0.0778)		(0.0566)		(0.2472)		(0.0130)		(0.4775)		(18.6202)				
HS 720917	−1.0024		0.7119	***	−0.4578	*	−0.0295		−0.0466		5.3331	***	9.7966		256	37	0.0083
	(1.8379)		(0.2670)		(0.2503)		(0.4858)		(0.0299)		(0.9286)		(46.8950)				
HS 841940	1.8294		0.8342	***	0.0878		−0.4555		0.0007		2.8590	***	−62.3733	*	328	48	0.0195
	(1.1811)		(0.1856)		(0.1380)		(0.4777)		(0.0099)		(0.6962)		(29.9110)				
HS 720230	−2.2995		0.1611		0.0202		−0.5952		−0.1395		7.2630	***	62.0295		133	19	0.0150
	(3.2507)		(0.1467)		(0.1817)		(0.6241)		(0.1057)		(0.7774)		(82.1872)				
HS 720711	1.8294		0.8342	***	0.0878		−0.4555		0.0024		2.8590	***	−62.3733	**	328	48	0.0195
	(1.1811)		(0.1856)		(0.1380)		(0.4777)		(0.0347)		(0.6962)		(29.9110)				
HS 852340	17.7564		−0.1454		0.3418		−2.4426		0.9331		8.5432	***	−439.4175		38	19	0.0374
	(21.1425)		(0.2147)		(0.2657)		(1.8562)		(0.5815)		(1.0610)		(550.7122)				
HS 380891	22.2503	**	1.0347	***	0.0729		0.1579		−0.6099	***	3.2449	***	−598.5243	**	84	43	0.1177
	(10.5639)		(0.1862)		(0.1509)		(0.5970)		(0.2351)		(0.6739)		(273.0704)				

continued on ext page

Table 6C.2 — cont'd

Variable	$LNRGDP_i$		$LNRGDP_j$		$LNRFEX_{ij}$		$LNDIST_{ij}$		$TARIFF_{ij}$		$CHINA$		$Constant$		Obs	Countries	R^2
HS 847190	–1.0729	*	0.9171	***	0.0092		–0.6481	**	–0.0005		4.2709	***	12.9752		761	113	0.0160
	(0.5471)		(0.0999)		(0.0455)		(0.3234)		(0.0022)		(0.5971)						
HS 900190	3.1428		0.9695	***	0.0949		–1.1558	*	–0.1016		4.9744	***	–93.9430		86	44	0.0262
	(11.8370)		(0.2703)		(0.1366)		(0.6678)		(0.1377)		(0.9584)		(306.4374)				
HS 030343	2.4460		–0.1346		–0.2738		–1.7449	**	0.0042		5.0248	***	–40.5415		349	51	0.0293
	(1.5518)		(0.2133)		(0.2792)		(0.7178)		(0.0064)		(1.0511)		(41.7702)				
HS 741110	0.0420		0.5798	***	–0.0083		–0.9047	*	0.0052		5.1263	***	–6.6615		363	54	0.0043
	(0.5351)		(0.1370)		(0.1116)		(0.4670)		(0.0074)		(0.7611)		(15.0438)				
HS 380850	–29.4779	***	0.8246	***	0.1340		0.6339		–0.4644	***	4.1586	***	743.3471	***	134	69	0.1151
	(10.4198)		(0.1849)		(0.1204)		(0.5184)		(0.1610)		(0.7416)		(269.0955)				
HS 760719	–0.8835		1.2413	***	0.0656		–1.1203	**	0.0040		2.6328	***	3.2718		325	48	0.0066
	(0.9220)		(0.2097)		(0.1512)		(0.5201)		(0.0062)		(0.8318)		(23.2297)				
HS 853650	0.6480		1.0127	***	0.0080		–0.7331	**	0.0036		3.0480	***	–32.7650	***	779	117	0.0437
	(0.4596)		(0.0896)		(0.0518)		(0.3136)		(0.0033)		(0.5757)		(11.8541)				
HS 280300	0.4054		1.1800	***	0.0218		–0.5849		0.0046		2.9559	***	–34.0478		296	43	0.0302
	(1.0537)		(0.1960)		(0.1868)		(0.4699)		(0.0079)		(0.6959)		(27.3822)				
HS 950300	1.4811		0.4743	***	0.0746		–0.5227	*	–0.0607		6.8969	***	–43.1560		1	0	0.8832
	(2.9567)		(0.0723)		(0.0457)		(0.3023)		(0.0404)		(0.5443)		(76.3402)				
HS 720916	–1.0211		0.6479	**	–0.4769	**	–0.3505		–0.0271		3.5207	***	14.7177		196	28	0.0023
	(2.2551)		(0.3056)		(0.2213)		(0.5266)		(0.0293)		(0.9500)		(58.0727)				

HS 853669	1.3572	***	1.0766	***	0.0125		–1.0638	***	0.0037		2.6172	***	–49.8035	***	567	83	0.0844
	(0.5134)		(0.1130)		(0.0851)		(0.3817)		(0.0030)		(0.6395)		(13.3467)				
HS 481029	4.0869	**	0.9299	***	–0.1697		–0.4341		0.0106		1.1268	*	–122.7754	***	251	36	0.1183
	(1.8115)		(0.1883)		(0.1877)		(0.3586)		(0.0067)		(0.5975)		(47.0402)				
HS 854110	–0.6508		0.8158	***	–0.0216		–0.9479	*	0.0003		4.1267	***	7.3609		578	84	0.0002
	(0.6655)		(0.1271)		(0.1089)		(0.5022)		(0.0035)		(0.7074)		(16.6809)				
HS 871499	0.2722		0.5881	***	0.0466		–1.3728	***	–0.0006		5.0612	***	–8.5329		384	56	0.0145
	(0.6627)		(0.1392)		(0.1054)		(0.4083)		(0.0020)		(0.6588)		(16.5809)				
HS 840991	0.5719		0.8564	***	–0.0349		–0.7610	***	0.0020		3.6190	***	–27.2807	*	680	102	0.0182
	(0.6142)		(0.1142)		(0.0679)		(0.2687)		(0.0030)		(0.6301)		(15.4618)				
HS 847290	–2.4195	***	0.8661	***	0.1972	*	–1.3808	***	–0.0102		4.1018	***	54.4006	**	393	57	0.0308
	(0.8486)		(0.1831)		(0.1029)		(0.4145)		(0.0063)		(0.7086)		(21.1373)				
HS 848210	–1.4251	**	1.0196	***	0.0482		–0.9072	***	0.0002		3.5151	***	21.6395		638	94	0.0007
	(0.6187)		(0.1069)		(0.0764)		(0.2936)		(0.0054)		(0.5913)		(16.2255)				
HS 842810	–0.3578		0.6210	***	0.0407		–0.5437	*	–0.0021		5.0869	***	–0.4751		471	70	0.0058
	(0.7401)		(0.1423)		(0.0775)		(0.2973)		(0.0045)		(0.6667)		(17.8683)				
HS 640610	1.5517		0.3692	**	–0.3640	**	–0.0220		0.0032		6.0493	***	–48.0193		226	33	0.0325
	(1.5087)		(0.1544)		(0.1970)		(0.2580)		(0.0071)		(0.5118)		(39.2532)				
HS 710691	–0.9874		1.1203	***	–0.2126		–0.9029		–0.0012		4.0696	***	6.9264		228	33	0.0024
	(2.0424)		(0.3025)		(0.2163)		(0.6452)		(0.0133)		(0.9605)		(53.1710)				
HS 850511	–1.7317		0.8638	**	–0.0213		–1.6442	***	–0.0158	*	4.4020	***	38.9083		264	38	0.0209
	(1.1691)		(0.2406)		(0.1571)		(0.5013)		(0.0093)		(0.8369)		(30.0219)				
HS 441299	2.7421	***	0.3588	***	0.0336		–1.4456	***	0.0004		5.3180	***	–65.4489	*	355	52	0.0811
	(1.0339)		(0.1036)		(0.0891)		(0.4274)		(0.0038)		(0.4734)		(27.5203)				

Notes: *** denotes 1 per cent,**5 per cent ,* 10 per cent significance levels; robust standard errors are in parentheses; the list of products accounted for 40.91 per cent of the value of trade that occurred in 2008.

Appendix 6D

Calculation of FDI between Thailand and China on the employment of unskilled labour

Table 6D.1
Employment Effect from Thailand's FDI Inflows by Sector

Year	Employment Effect from Simulated Thailand's FDI Inflow by Sector										
	Financial Institutions	Trade	Construction	Mining and Quarrying	Agriculture	Industry	Services	Investment	Real estate	Others	Total
2000	0	1,851	493	0	0	1,295	167	0	0	2,796	6,601
2001	0	794	53	0	0	5,979	119	0	0	1,125	8,069
2002	0	559	37	0	0	4,211	84	0	0	1,990	6,880
2003	0	853	302	0	0	5,650	185	41	0	2,034	9,065
2004	0	5,342	0	0	0	2,769	393	0	0	3,424	11,928
2005	1,086	370	173	0	0	6,610	3,345	18	339	123	12,063
2006	11	156	1,377	3	12	7,248	1,685	0	2,555	57	13,104
2007	24	19	817	0	0	8,491	2,054	0	960	181	12,547
Total	1,120	9,944	3,252	3	12	42,252	8,032	59	3,854	11,729	80,257

Source: Authors' calculation.

Table 6D.2
Unskilled Labour Used from Thailand's FDI Inflows by Sector

Year	Unskilled Labour Used from Simulated Thailand's FDI Inflow by Sector (person)										
	Financial Institutions	Trade	Construction	Mining and Quarrying	Agriculture	Industry	Services	Investment	Real estate	Others	Total
2000[a]	0	319	136	0	0	519	62	0	0	1037	2073
2001	0	137	15	0	0	2,398	44	0	0	417	3,011
2002	0	94	12	0	0	1,617	30	0	0	793	2,546
2003	0	148	85	0	0	2,155	66	4	0	753	3,212
2004	0	981	0	0	0	1,142	140	0	0	1,261	3,522
2005	76	71	53	0	0	2,650	1,134	1	72	45	4,102
2006	1	28	438	2	12	2,976	576	0	485	22	4,539
2007	2	3	249	0	0	3,477	670	0	201	71	4,672
Total	78	1,781	988	2	12	16,935	2,722	5	758	4,398	27,678

Note: a. Because of lack of data on employment structure in this year, the ULI of 2001 is applied.
Source: Authors' calculation.

Table 6D.3
Employment Effect from Actual Thailand's FDI Outflows

Year	FDI (U$)	Exchange rate (B/U$)	FDI (Baht)	M/E Ratio (Baht/person)	Employment (Person)
	(1)	(2)	(3)=(1)*(2)	(4)	(5)=(3)/(4)
2000	809,775.68	40.11	32,481,562.74	41,636.73	780
2001	4,836,321.76	44.43	214,886,964.62	41,636.73	5,161
2002	2,367,466.42	42.96	101,706,554.84	41,636.73	2,443
2003	3,924,763.44	41.48	162,817,306.99	41,636.73	3,910
2004	13,987,790.60	40.22	562,622,717.33	41,636.73	13,513
2005	29,512,412.66	40.22	1,186,993,079.87	41,636.73	28,508
2006	56,066,366.60	37.88	2,123,905,159.01	41,636.73	51,010
2007	16,499,666.70	34.52	569,538,474.96	41,636.73	13,679
Total	128,004,563.9	—	4,954,951,820	—	119,004

Source: Actual FDI outflow from BOT.

Table 6D.4
Employment Effect from Actual Thailand's FDI Outflow by Sector

Year	Employment Effect from Simulated Thailand's FDI Outflow by Sector										
	Financial Institutions	Trade	Construction	Mining and Quarrying	Agriculture	Industry	Services	Investment	Real estate	Others	Total
2000	0	0	621	56	0	103	0	0	0	0	780
2001	0	0	3,158	1,138	0	0	0	0	0	865	5,161
2002	0	2,443	0	0	0	0	0	0	0	0	2,443
2003	0	0	0	0	0	3,910	0	0	0	0	3,910
2004	0	405	0	0	0	11,671	0	0	0	1,437	13,513
2005	37	1,671	633	8	353	23,365	291	58	2,062	30	28,508
2006	48	10,420	376	451	0	35,827	986	0	2,831	71	51,010
2007	839	2,021	2,750	0	0	7,434	32	0	602	0	13,679
Total	924	16,961	7,537	1,654	353	82,311	1,309	58	5,495	2,403	119,004

Source: Authors' calculation.

Table 6D.5
Estimated Unskilled Labour Used from Actual Thailand's FDI Outflow by Sector

Year	Unskilled Labour Used from Simulated Thailand's FDI Outflow by Sector (person)										
	Financial Institutions	Trade	Construction	Mining and Quarrying	Agriculture	Industry	Services	Investment	Real estate	Others	Total
2000[a]	0	0	171	26	0	41	0	0	0	0	239
2001	0	0	871	532	0	0	0	0	0	321	1,724
2002	0	411	0	0	0	0	0	0	0	0	411
2003	0	0	0	0	0	1,492	0	0	0	0	1,492
2004	0	74	0	0	0	4,812	0	0	0	529	5,416
2005	3	321	195	4	344	9,367	99	4	436	11	10,782
2006	3	1,869	120	274	0	14,711	337	0	538	27	17,879
2007	65	339	838	0	0	3,044	10	0	126	0	4,422
Total	71	3,015	2,194	837	344	33,467	446	4	1,099	888	42,365

Note: a. Because of lack of data on employment structure in this year, the ULI of 2001 is applied.
Source: Authors' calculation.

Notes

1. The authors note that while the gravity model has been widely used in studies of trade, its application to bilateral FDI flows is less common. However, a number of earlier studies have shown that the gravity model also has explanatory power when applied to foreign direct investment (Eichengreen and Tong 2005, p. 11).
2. The results of the calculation of simulated trade volumes are available from the authors on request.
3. The measurement is virtually an output per worker ratio, an index of labour productivity in the production of the commodity selected.
4. In 2008, the minimum daily wages were 203 baht in Bangkok and 150 baht in the provinces, giving the lowest monthly wages of 3,600 to 5,278 baht (US$109–160) (DLPW 2009).

References

Chayodom Sabhasri et al. "ASEAN and China Free Trade Area: Implications for Thailand" (in Thai). Ministry of Commerce, Bangkok, 2005.

Chia Siow Yue and Chalongphob Sussangkarn. "The Economic Rise of China: Challenges and Opportunities for ASEAN". *Asian Economic Policy Review* 1, no. 1 (2006): 102–28.

Department of Foreign Investment Cooperation (DFIC). "Summary Report of Foreign Investment in Thailand 2008" (in Thai). Bangkok, 2009.

Department of Labour Protection and Welfare (DLPW). *Yearbook of Labour Protection and Welfare Statistics 2008*. Bangkok: Ministry of Labour, 2009.

Dollar, D. and Lant Pritchett. "Assessing Aid: What Works, What Doesn't and Why?". World Bank Policy Research Report, Washington, D.C., 1998.

Eichengreen, B., Rhee Y. and Tong H. *The Impact of China on the Exports of other Asian Countries*. Working Paper No. 10768. Bangkok: National Bureau of Economic Research, 2004.

Eichengreen, B. and Tong H. *Is China's FDI Coming at the Expense of Other Countries?* Working Paper No. 11335. Bangkok: National Bureau of Economic Research, 2005.

Felt, E. and Wisarn Pupphavesa. "The Rise of China and Its Implications for Thailand in the Future: An Economic Analysis". *TDRI Quarterly Review* 10, no. 2 (1995): 3–12.

Jenkins, Rhys and Chris Edwards. *How Does China's Growth Affect Poverty Reduction in Asia, Africa and Latin America?* Latin America/Caribbean and Asia/Pacific Economics and Business Association, Working Paper Series No. 34. Presented at the 2004 LAEBA Annual Conference, Beijing, China, 3–4 December 2004.

Okamoto, Yumiko. "China and India: Challenges and Opportunities for ASEAN from Japanese Perspectives". Federation of ASEAN Economic Associations (FAEA), 2005.

Rose, Andrew. "Which International Institutions Promote International Trade?". *Review of International Economics* 13 (2005): 682–98.

Somkiat Tangkitvanich. "Reaping Benefits from Free Trade Agreements: Phase II" (in Thai). Ministry of Industry, Bangkok, 2008.

Sussawasd, Sasatra and Santi Chaisrisawatsuk. "Tigers and Dragons against Elephants: Does the Rising Chinese and Indian Share in Trade and Foreign Direct Investment Crowd out Thailand and other ASEAN Countries?". *Asia-Pacific Trade and Investment Review* 2, (2006): 93–114.

Wisarn Pupphavesa. "Economic and Social Effects of Agricultural Liberalisation under China-ASEAN FTA with Special Focus on EHP: A Case Study from Thailand". In *Economic and Social Impact of Liberalisation: A Study on Early Harvest Programme under China-ASEAN FTA*, edited by Yunling and Zhang. Beijing: Social Sciences Academic Press, 2008.

Websites:

Department of Export Promotion. <www.ryt9.com/s/expd/791634>. Accessed 1 August 2010.

National Economic and Social Development Board (NESDB). <www.nesdb.go.th>. Accessed 29 July 2010.

THAI BIZChina.com. <www.thaibizchina.com/thaibizchina/th/thai-china/>. Accessed 30 July 2010.

7

IMPACTS OF CHINA ON POVERTY REDUCTION IN CAMBODIA

Ouch Chandarany, Saing Chanhang and Phann Dalia

1. INTRODUCTION

Over the last three decades, China has witnessed dramatic economic transformation, rapid development and greater involvement in regional and global economic and political affairs. Such significant achievements have become the subject of intense debate, seeing China as both economic threat and opportunity.

Countries in the GMS are geographically close to China and constitute a highly dynamic region with great potential for development that could become a strategic market space and provide institutional arrangement prospects for strengthening China's regional integration. Likewise, China could become the gateway and main market destination for GMS countries, reducing their export dependency on the international market. Through connecting with countries in the GMS, China has built considerable trade and investment relations and provided support in the form of official development assistance (ODA), particularly infrastructure development.

Cambodia views China as a promising development partner that can expedite the country's development and reduce the gap with other Asian countries.[1] Clearly, the weight of China's presence is being increasingly felt in the country, drawing attention to its contributions and impacts. In discussing these issues, therefore, China's increasing role and its impacts within Cambodia should be studied.

1.1 Research Objectives

This study is one of a series of country studies conducted by GMS-DAN with support from the Rockefeller Foundation that seek to assess the potential impacts of China on the poor in the GMS countries, namely Cambodia, Vietnam, Laos and Thailand. This chapter focuses on Cambodia and analyses the poverty effects of China's rise through three critical components: (i) trade, (ii) investment, and (iii) official development assistance. It examines the trade relation between Cambodia and China and its poverty implication by mainly looking at the role of China's trade in labour-intensive products. The contribution that China's investment makes to the poor is reviewed through a case study on the garment sector. In recognition of China's support in developing Cambodia's infrastructure, two case studies on Chinese ODA funded projects in the transport sector explore the contributions of China's assistance to livelihood and social development of local people.

The chapter aims to raise awareness of the impacts of China's investment, trade and ODA in order to consider ways to mitigate the negative and promote the positive impacts for poverty reduction and the country's development. Section 2 reviews existing literature and the poverty situation in Cambodia, and presents a brief overview of policy on Cambodia-China trade and investment relations and Cambodia-China development assistance relations. Section 3 describes and analyses the trends in trade between Cambodia and China, explains the analytical framework on trade impact, and investigates the impact of China's trade and its contribution to poverty reduction in Cambodia. Section 4 looks at the trends of China's investment in Cambodia over the past decade, describes the methodologies and analytical framework of a case study on the garment sector and discusses the findings and poverty implications in terms of employment generation, remittance and skill development.

Section 5 illustrates the findings and analyses from two case studies on China's ODA-funded transport projects in Cambodia and their potential impacts on the local people. Finally, section 6 discusses the main issues and policy implications from the study's findings.

1.2 Methodological Approaches

The study adopts Jenkins and Edwards's (2004) framework to analyse the likely impact of China on poverty reduction in Cambodia by applying trade data at 3-digit SITC level. The study has three analytical levels. Level 1 includes export to China, import from China and export to the third market. Level 2 covers the scale of labour-intensive exports to China, the scale of competing import from China and pro-poor consumer goods and the scale of labour-intensive export to the third market. The third level focuses on likely poverty effects of increased or decreased employment in labour-intensive export to China, rising import competition from China, and the level of competition in labour-intensive products in the third markets.

By combining a disaggregated approach to examine the impacts of China on trade of the third countries at 3-digit SITC level with Winters' (2004) framework for the analysis of trade-poverty linkages using data from 1990 to 2002, Jenkins and Edwards (2004) find that in terms of export to China, Cambodia (among a few other Asian countries such as Bangladesh and Pakistan) predominantly exported labour-intensive manufactured products and some labour-intensive agricultural products[2] that have notable implications for poverty. Using an export similarity index — the closer the index is to 1, the greater the likelihood that China and Cambodia will be competitors — the study also found that Cambodia and China have strong export similarity for both overall export and manufactures export.

As the major proportion of manufactured exports is made up of labour-intensive textiles and garments, the study posits that rising competition from China in the third market could have negative effect on the poor. Although the import of manufactured products from China is substantial, it does not displace domestic industries, which employ unskilled workers, as those imports are mainly yarns and fabrics for garment export-oriented production. And thus, imports from China pose no significant threat to domestic manufacturing industries and therefore have minimal negative effects on the poor.

2. LOCAL LITERATURE REVIEW

2.1 China's Impacts on the Cambodian Economy

China's rapid growth during the last couple of decades has clearly stimulated curiosity among academics, researchers and policy-makers in both developed and developing countries about the magnitude of the effects, either complementary or competitive, that China could have on least developed countries. As the fourth largest world economy in terms of GDP at official exchange rate (Jenkins, Peters and Moreira 2007, p. 235), China has found its way into extracting productive resources in least developed countries in order to enhance its production capacity and to keep pace with accelerating world and domestic demand. This begs the question whether China contributes to the host least developed countries' development or hinders it.[3]

Hing and Nou (2006), using in-depth consultation with various stakeholders to explore the poverty implications of the Early Harvest Programme (EHP) under the framework of the ASEAN-China Free Trade Agreement, conclude that EHP provides Cambodia an opportunity to develop its agriculture as a source of growth and poverty alleviation through expanding export of products such as fresh fruit, livestock, fish, shrimps and prawns to China. Applying the industrial pollution projection approach developed by Hettige et al. (1995) in their investigation of China's impact on the environment in the region, Hing and Jalilian (2008) report that in the case of Cambodia, rising imports in the most polluting sectors from China between 2001 and 2007 led to a substantial gain from trade for the Cambodian environment, which comes at the cost of environmental degradation in China.

Chinese investors have been significantly involved in several sectors of Cambodia's economy, namely garment manufacturing, extractive industry, agro-industry and infrastructure development. Contribution from Chinese investors through their direct investment in the garment industry has been especially noteworthy. Data from the Garment Manufacturers Association in Cambodia indicates that of the total number of factories, approximately 20.7 per cent are owned by Hong Kong investors, followed by Taiwanese with 24.5 per cent and Chinese with 13.1 per cent, while only 8.6 per cent are owned by Cambodian investors (GMAC 2006 cited in USAID 2007, p. 8). Yamagata (2006), using firm-level data from 164 companies employing 147,000 females and 21,000 males in 2003, confirms that Cambodia's garment industry has substantially contributed to poverty reduction in the country through the employment of the poor as entry-level workers at wages far above the poverty line. Using overall food poverty lines of US$0.63 per capita per day for Phnom Penh and US$0.46 per capita per day for rural areas and data from Cambodia's Social Economic Survey 1999, the author estimated that the overall poverty line per capita per month for Phnom Penh in 1999 was US$18.9, which is far below garment workers' average monthly earnings of US$45.

The role of Chinese state-owned and private firms in the mining and extractive industry sector is also emerging. Although impact from these activities on Cambodia has yet to be quantified, several studies have shed light on the direction Chinese firms are taking. A map compiled by Oxfam America in 2007 indicates that two Chinese companies are engaged in Cambodia's offshore oil and gas sector (Ngo 2007, p. 10): China National Offshore Oil Corporation (CNOOC) in block F, and China Petro-tech in block D. Rutherford, Lazarus and Kelley (2008) state that six Chinese mining companies — one of which is China Petrotech — are known to be operating in Cambodia's mining sector, particularly metallic minerals, gold deposits, oil and gas (for a detailed list of firms see Rutherford, Lazarus and Kelley 2008, p. 52).

With respect to Chinese engagement in the agricultural sector, Tong and Hem (2009) report that as of March 2009, eleven Chinese companies had acquired investment licences in the form of economic land concessions (ELC) in the north and northeastern parts of the country, three of which had started crop cultivation (for details of other companies see Rutherford, Lazarus and Kelley 2008, p. 48). Hem, Tong and Ker (2009), through consultation with various stakeholders, namely commune and village chiefs, villagers and NGOs at various ELC sites, identified several problems caused by the arrival of Chinese investors: excessive felling of forest, no right of way on company-built roads for villagers, and denied access to forest products.

Tong and Hem (2009) confirm that several hydropower development projects have been awarded to Chinese firms — both private and state-owned. Those projects, both pre-feasibility and feasibility studies, include Lower Se San 2, Lower Srepok 2 and 4. Four major projects have been finalized for construction, including Kamchay, Stung Atai, Stung Tatay and Stung Russey Chrum (for detailed list of priority hydropower projects in Cambodia, see Hem, Tong and Ker 2009, p. 24). From their consultation with villagers, Hem, Tong and Ker (ibid.) note that roads constructed by Chinese companies in some project areas are closed to villagers as the companies fear that they might destroy construction facilities (specific location).

Coughlan (2007) notes China's involvement in the construction of roads and bridges in the central, north and northeastern parts of the country. Although his study reports both complaints from a number of villagers who had to relocate because they were displaced by the projects and as well as approval and consent from others who had benefited, no hard evidence on the impact of those projects on the communities in the surrounding areas was brought to light.

Overall, the above studies provide some insights into the effects of China's growth on Cambodia's economy. China has played a vital role in reducing poverty in Cambodia through its substantial direct investment in the garment industry. The export expansion of labour-intensive products to the Chinese market also has implications for poverty reduction in Cambodia. Meanwhile, concerns over Chinese involvement in agri-business development and infrastructure development, namely hydropower, onshore mining and offshore oil and gas sectors, persist.

2.2 Poverty Situation in Cambodia

Fighting poverty in developing countries is a resource-consuming challenge, and the outcome of such effort is characteristically slowed by various factors such as civil war and conflict, natural disaster, resource constraints and weak public institution among others. And these are the factors that have impeded poverty eradication in Cambodia. This section looks at the changing poverty trends over the last fifteen years and the likely factors influencing the poverty situation in Cambodia. It briefly reviews policy framework aimed at eliminating poverty and gives a general and practical definition of poverty and poverty measurement in Cambodia.

Poverty eradication has ranked high on the government's development agenda since the completion of the first Socio-Economic Development Plan I (SEDP I 1996–2000), which focused on macroeconomic stability and growth, social development and poverty alleviation, and the second government mandate 1998–2003, during which the Triangle Strategy — aiming at building peace, stability, security, integrating Cambodia into the region and the world, and promoting economic and social development through various programmes — was launched. The outcome of SEDP I laid the foundations for the National Poverty Reduction Strategy (NPRS) in late

2002, which was in line with SEDP II 2001–05 and Cambodia Millennium Development Goals (CMDG)[4] adopted in September 2000.

Since then, the government has pursued its commitment to reducing the number of Cambodians living in poverty by gearing considerable resources and efforts towards poverty alleviation through policy formulation and keeping poverty alleviation at the top of the agenda for government priority actions asset out in the National Strategic Development Plan 2006–10 and the Government Rectangular Strategy, both of which were formulated in the third government mandate 2003–07.

In order to grasp the nature of poverty, it is important to understand the concept and measurement of poverty. Poverty is commonly defined as "pronounced deprivation in well-being". In this sense, well-being is measured as the command of an individual or household over resources, and therefore, people are better off if they possess greater command over resources (World Bank 2008, p. 11). Monetary measurements of well-being use two key indicators whereby poverty is measured by comparing individuals' income or consumption against some threshold (poverty line) below which they are considered to be poor. Non-monetary measurements focus on literacy and nutrition. Education compares individuals' literacy against illiteracy as the threshold of poverty, and the number of years of education relative to the expected number of years that should be completed. Nutrition focuses on children's nutritional status,the incidence of specific diseases (diarrhoea, malaria, respiratory diseases) or the life expectancy of different groups within the population (Coudouel, Hentschel and Wodon 2002, pp. 30–33).

Before investigating poverty trends and to get a clear picture of poverty status in Cambodia, it is useful to outline how the poverty line is set. The food poverty line is based on the estimated cost of a basket of goods that would provide a subsistence-level dietary intake of 2,100 calories per day, and non-food allowances — minimum consumption of non-food goods and services — are derived from the non-food consumption of Cambodians whose total per capita household consumption is just equal to the food poverty line (World Bank 2006, p. 20). Table 7.1 summarizes food, non-food and total poverty lines over time in three geographical zones. The figures indicate that the cost of living (to maintain a decent standard of life) across the regions rose markedly between 1994 and 2007.

The poverty rate in Cambodia has declined markedly over the last fifteen years at an annual average rate of around 1.15 per cent, from 47 per cent in 1994 to 32 per cent in 2007, indicating a moderate outcome

TABLE 7.1
Updated Food Poverty Line, Non-food Allowances, and Total Poverty Line

Region	1993/94	2004	2007
Food poverty lines (current riels per capita per day)			
Phnom Penh	1,185	1,782	2,445
Other Urban	996	1,568	2,274
Rural	882	1,389	1,965
Non-food allowances (current riels per capita per day)			
Phnom Penh	393	569	647
Other Urban	269	384	430
Rural	236	364	302
Total poverty lines (current riels per capita per day)			
Phnom Penh	1,578	2,351	3,092
Other Urban	1,265	1,952	2,704
Rural	1,118	1,753	2,367

Note: 1993/94, 2004 data (World Bank 2006, p. 21); 2007 data (World Bank 2009*b*, p. 12). Exchange rates (NBC): 2,445.2 riels/US$ (1994), 4,019 riels/US$ (2004), 4,062.7 riels/US$ (2007).

Source: SESC 1993/94, CSES 2004, CSES 2007, World Bank staff projections.

from the government's poverty eradication efforts. Although poverty fell across geographical zones, (i.e. Phnom Penh, other urban and rural areas) improvement in poverty status was uneven. Poverty incidence remained high in rural areas, followed by other urban areas, while Phnom Penh marked the lowest rate of poverty (Figure 7.1). As approximately 40 per cent of the nation's total poor live in the Plains region and 50 per cent live in the Tonle Sap and Mountain/Plateau regions, it can be concluded that poverty in Cambodia is a rural phenomena (World Bank 2006, p. 35).

The slow reduction in poverty between 1994 and 2004 was due to one critical factor, the protracted civil war between the government and rebel Khmer Rouge fighters, who were finally demobilized and integrated into government troops in 1998. The conflict limited the outreach of public service delivery, namely health and education, to areas under rebel control and areas frequently plagued by the Khmer Rouge fighters' looting and destruction of community infrastructure between 1979, which marked the fall of the Khmer Rouge's absolute control of the country, and 1998.

FIGURE 7.1
Percentage of Population Living Below the Poverty Line by Region[a]

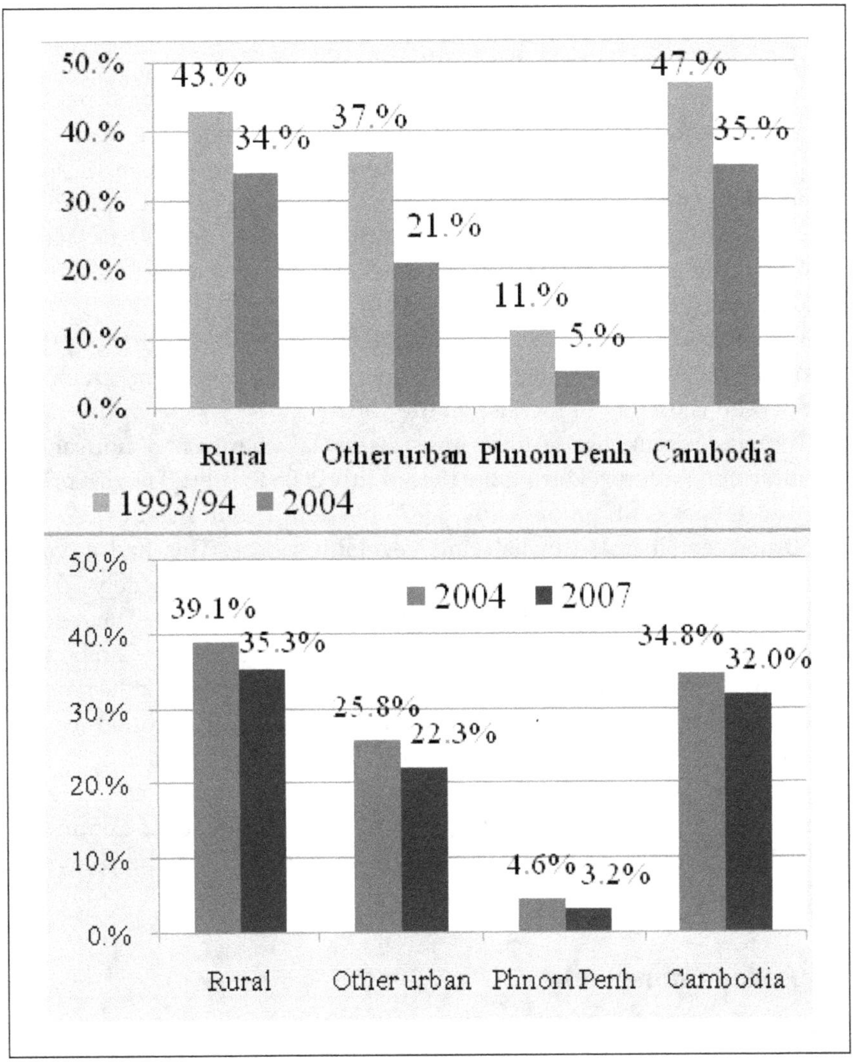

Notes: a. Figures are shown in two separate graphs because different sample frames, i.e. 1994–2004 and 2004–2007, were used for the estimations.
Source: SESC 1993/94, CSES 2004, CSES 2007, World Bank staff projections, 2006–2009.

Several other factors that could possibly be behind the sluggish decline in poverty include uncertain weather conditions and stagnant investment in rural infrastructure, particularly irrigation systems. The downward trend of poverty continued across all three regions from 2004 to 2007, but poverty incidence remained pronounced in the rural areas.

As of 2007, it appeared that government policy had been on track as it had brought about significant change in poverty outcome. However, inequality worsened as the Gini coefficient (a commonly used measure of inequality, ranging from a value of zero, signifying perfect equality, to one, signifying perfect inequality), rose from 0.35 in 1993/94 to 0.40 in 2004 and then to 0.43 in 2007 (World Bank 2007, p. iii; World Bank 2009*b*, p. 26). Poverty eradication outcomes of the fifteen years prior to the last quarter of 2007 were eroded by the sudden hike in food and energy prices from mid-2007 to mid-2008 and the global financial crisis that struck the Cambodian economy in the last quarter of 2008.

The first shock brought about substantial changes in household consumption patterns. During the period July 2008 to July 2009, rice prices rose by 100 per cent, followed by 50–70 per cent rise in meat prices and 20–30 per cent increase in fish and vegetable prices. This had adverse impacts on the poorest 40 per cent as they spend approximately 70 per cent of their income on food consumption (CDRI 2008, p. 9). The second shock, the global economic downturn, had a severe effect on the Cambodian economy. Garment manufacturing, a pro-poor industry,[5] was hit the hardest as approximately 70 per cent of total garment export is destined for the United States and 22 per cent to the EU. Between September 2008 and May 2009, 62,000 workers, the majority women, were laid off, bringing the sector's total workforce to 290,000 in May 2009 (Ministry of Commerce 2009). Low-income and vulnerable groups were particularly hard-hit and pushed deeper into poverty.

2.3 Policy Framework

Many policy and legal reforms to promote trade and investment have been put in place to boost economic growth and enhance poverty reduction. The Rectangular Strategy emphasizes the need to attract foreign investment and mainstream the development of trade in the country's poverty reduction efforts. Initiatives such as the Trade Integration Strategy known as the Diagnostic Trade Integration Study (DTIS) and the Sector-Wide

Approach (Trade SWAp) have been pinpointed as key instruments for the implementation of Cambodia's trade sector development strategy. In addition, because of Cambodia's participation in ASEAN and the WTO, as well as several bilateral deals, the government has overhauled the legal framework, procedures and institutional structures to be in line with international standards, including the implementation of harmonized customs nomenclature, computerized customs system, and a Single Window for customs.

Cambodia-China Trade and Investment Relations

Economic and trade relations between Cambodia and China have expanded in recent years. In 1996 Cambodia and China signed the agreement on trade, investment promotion and protection, and in 2000 they set up an economic and trade cooperation committee.[6] On 27–29 June 2008, the Embassy of China in Cambodia, the Ministry of Commerce (MoC) of Cambodia and the Council for the Development of Cambodia (CDC) jointly celebrated the fiftieth anniversary of Sino-Cambodian trade and economic cooperation achievement. They organized a large-scale exhibition, involving China's state-owned and private enterprises, local businesses and Chinese community groups in Cambodia, to build a high-level communication opportunity and expand investment, trade and encourage joint ventures.

The establishment of the ASEAN-China Free Trade Area (ACFTA) marks an important milestone in the development of ASEAN-China economic and trade relations. ASEAN and China signed a framework agreement in Phnom Penh in November 2002 that committed to establish the ACFTA within ten years, and for it to be fully operational by 2010 for the six original ASEAN members (Singapore, Thailand, Malaysia, Indonesia, Brunei and Philippines) and by 2015 for the four newer ASEAN members (Laos, Cambodia, Myanmar and Vietnam). This framework enhances trade and investment cooperation and reduces trade barriers between ASEAN and China as it covers trade in goods and services, investment and expansion of cooperation in various areas such as trade facilitation, technology transfer, human resources development and subregional development projects (including the ASEAN Mekong River Basin Development Cooperation).[7]

One of the most important arrangements in the framework agreement is the Early Harvest Programme (EHP), which took effect between 2004 and 2006 for the ASEAN-5, and is to come into effect in 2010 for the new members and the Philippines. Cambodia is expected to gain economic benefits and opportunities as well as challenges from ACFTA along with the EHP. Although a number of studies have examined the prospects for ACFTA as a whole, little information or research is available for the case of Cambodia. Hing and Nou (2006) explored the potential impacts of EHP on Cambodia's agricultural sector and conclude that it could provide opportunity to develop the country's agriculture sector as a source of growth and poverty reduction through expanding the export of products such as fresh fruits, livestock, fish, shrimps and prawns to China. However, they caution that Cambodia faces strong challenges, including unsound business climate, inadequate legal framework, insufficient infrastructure and weak public institutions, which could hinder agriculture and enterprises from taking advantage of the opportunities associated with the EHP.

The Greater Mekong Subregion (GMS) cooperation programme is another important economic and trade relation between Cambodia and China. The GMS agenda has concentrated on "hardware" in the form of physical infrastructure, especially cross-border infrastructure, to improve connections and communication across the region. In addition, the GMS programme has addressed "software" issues, including the facilitation of cross-border trade and investment, to support economic integration in the GMS and complement many of the liberalization measures pursued as part of ASEAN Free Trade Area (AFTA) membership.

Menon (2005) found that

> the GMS program is assisting its members to integrate more closely with the ASEAN region and, through this, with the rest of the world. As a program based on market rather than institutional integration, the GMS is promoting both regionalism and multilateralism. The sub-regional public goods provided through the program are spilling over to become not only regional but also global.

China is both a beneficiary and a contributor to the GMS programme. It provides financial and human resource development support to the GMS programme and its members because it aims to create more economic opportunities and growth in the southern parts of China (Yunnan and Guangxi provinces) and encourage increasing Chinese investment in GMS countries.

Cambodia-China Foreign Aid Relations

China has been providing foreign aid to Cambodia since the mid-1950s. Over recent years the two countries have seen continuous expansion of cooperation in culture, tourism and agriculture. There have also been exchange visits between the parliaments, armies, press, and health officials of the two countries.[8] China's foreign aid to Cambodia is now considered an essential channel for the promotion of trade and investment between the two countries.

China has gained popularity in Cambodia for development assistance due to its lesser burden of political pressure and economic conditions compared with other countries (Phoun n.d.). Because of its own experience with foreign assistance and not wanting to replicate what it perceives to be the ill behaviour of international donors, the Chinese government instituted a formal foreign aid or development assistance policy, including Cambodia, and set eight guiding principles for allocating disbursements that seem to take the pressure off recipient countries. The principles are (Chin and Frolic 2007):

- Ensure equality and mutual benefits for both donor and recipient countries
- Respect sovereignty and never impose conditions
- Give interest-free or low-interest loans in the name of the poor helping the poor
- Encourage recipient countries to develop independently and be less-reliant on foreign countries
- Support and endorse projects that require little investment and can be accomplished in the short term
- Allocate quality equipment and materials corresponding to market prices
- Deliver effective technical assistance
- Pay experts affordable fees according to local market prices.

In turn, Cambodia's government is also highly committed to ensuring that all the international aid provided is used effectively, with transparency and accountability, strengthening the role of key persons and relevance in programme planning and implementation, and undertaking assessment of the impact of NSDP (Chan et al. 2008).

3. CHINA'S IMPACT ON CAMBODIA'S TRADE

3.1 Magnitude and Changes

Significant progress in Cambodian-Chinese economic relations was evident in the mid-1990s when a number of Chinese investors flocked to the Cambodian garment industry to tap the benefits from Cambodia's special preferential treatment, namely Most Favoured Nation (MFN) status provided by the EU and the Generalized System of Preference (GSP) granted by the U.S. government. This could to a certain extent be a result of the Cambodia-China agreement on investment promotion and protection in July 1996 and the bilateral trade agreement in July 1997 coming into effect (Hing and Nou 2006, p. 17). Relations deepened further through the Framework Agreement of ASEAN-China FTA (ACFTA), particularly the Early Harvest Programme (EHP), which aims at accelerating agricultural trade liberalisation. Official Development Assistance (ODA) and capital inflow from China also played a vital role in boosting Cambodia's development during the last decade. Before examining Cambodia-China bilateral trade in greater detail, it would be useful to overview Cambodia's relations with its key trading partners in the region and the world during the last decade.

Cambodia's Trade with the World

In terms of import, the rate of import growth from the world, ASEAN and GMS-5 was considerably high between 2000 and 2008. By nominal trade values, Cambodia tends to import mostly from its traditional trading partners, namely its neighbours Thailand and Vietnam, followed by China, Singapore, Korea, Japan and Malaysia, and imports the least from India (see Table 7.2). What is noticeable is that the trends of import from these countries are all upwards, which begs the question whether said imports compete or complement the domestic market.

The pace of export growth lagged behind that of import during 2000–08, reflecting Cambodia's persistent negative trade balance during the period. Cambodia's negative trade balance with the world was almost US$2 billion in 2008, while its massive negative trade balance with ASEAN from 2000 to 2008 is striking, indicating the country's high dependence on commodity imports from the world and the region. By trading partner, severe negative balances with Thailand, Vietnam, China, Singapore and South Korea are

TABLE 7.2
Cambodia Bilateral Trade with World, 2000–08 (US$ million at nominal value)

Countries	2000	2001	2002	2003	2004	2005	2006	2007	2008
Import									
World	1,762.71	1,862.3	2,045.59	2,347.71	2,840.69	3,420.35	4,558.02	5,324.97	6,934.63
ASEAN-9	1,038.63	1,119.39	1,177.93	1,418.6	1,616.11	1,984.58	2,712.49	3,101.09	4,412.61
EU-15	106.57	93.6	111.39	103.57	125.76	145.82	155.19	199.14	211.99
GMS-5	651.58	819.1	945.66	1,254.54	1,558.35	2,006.66	2,730.07	3,281.52	4,641.17
CHN	164.06	205.65	251.56	294.65	451.77	536.03	697.76	883.59	1,095.54
IND	7.89	10.54	16.97	20.27	16.75	21.35	48.09	44.83	53.85
JPN	51.98	50.43	69.95	54.55	79.87	78.11	81.82	111.04	184.04
KOR	95.91	101.54	115.23	105.56	126.32	144.28	205.09	281.43	294.38
MYS	71.33	60.26	55.01	64.74	83.54	109.28	108.33	134.12	165.13
SGP	425.75	370.02	352.25	307.61	348.76	303.04	459.63	438.66	520.45
THA	345.9	467.44	515.69	692.61	722.6	914.99	1,251.69	1,356.85	2,014.03
USA	23.06	28.05	28.47	56.3	57.24	67.19	70.87	137.53	150.27
VNM	141.62	146	178.41	267.29	383.97	555.64	780.61	1,041.07	1531.6
Export									
World	1,529.75	1,778.26	2,013.67	2,384.22	2,950.36	3,150.85	4,019.03	4,605.79	4,955.64
ASEAN-9	138.35	112.24	182.84	192.95	218.07	302.47	338.88	362.24	438.86
EU-15	342.43	479.41	522.1	621.39	824.17	724.89	928.18	1,045.7	1,249.58
GMS-5	104.65	69.91	101.15	132.98	188.15	219.08	239.2	305.33	343.24
CHN	59.49	34.8	24.55	26	29.93	27.3	35.09	51.07	38.83
IND	1.27	1.11	0.68	0.31	0.23	0.42	1.48	1.24	4.27
JPN	52.18	66.01	74.92	89.43	99.76	105.46	120.23	138.99	121.01
KOR	2.31	7.1	3.03	4.2	6.95	5.96	5.46	8.87	14.38
MYS	16.84	19.01	19.36	8.32	9.03	8	20.27	21.31	14.38
SGP	74.84	54.64	84.03	74.48	48.35	100.42	112.35	84.87	116.58
THA	7.86	12.27	11.22	12.26	27.64	31.56	34.65	48.77	90.12
USA	879.95	1,016.77	1,145.81	1,335.84	1,591.48	1,766.6	2,328.27	2,599.41	2,545.83
VNM	37.3	22.83	65.39	94.71	130.58	160.22	169.45	205.5	214.28

Source: UN ComTrade (2009).

evident. It is imperative that potential effects from such trade balances, i.e., crowding-out effect on domestic producers, are investigated so that the domestic industrial or economic base is safeguarded by either horizontal or vertical interventions.

Cambodia-China Bilateral Trade

The deepening trade relation between Cambodia and China, i.e., ACFTA-EHP, has brought about significant changes in bilateral trade patterns between the two countries during the last decade. In general, total trade (import plus export) between the two countries expanded considerably at an average annual growth rate of 23.1 per cent between 2001 and 2008.

With low export value and highly fluctuating year-on-year export growth to China (averaging 0.3 per cent between 2001 and 2008) and substantial rise in year-on-year import growth from China (averaging 27.2 per cent between 2001 and 2008), Cambodia's trade balance (export minus import) with China worsened (Figure 7.2): year-on-year export growth dropped considerably and turned negative by 58.7 per cent in 2002 and by 24.5 per cent in 2008. Given the two slumps and the continued rise in China's imports, Cambodia's trade balance has widened substantially since the early 2000s, jumping from — US$146 million in 2001 to — US$1,057 million in 2008. Therefore it is useful to examine the pattern and nature of trade between the two countries to evaluate the potential benefits or losses from the ASEAN-China FTA, and the EHP in particular. This study does not intend to evaluate the impact of the agreement; rather, it looks at the likely effects of China's growth on poverty reduction in Cambodia through trade channels, which could shed light on potential gains or losses that might result from the framework agreement.

Prior to examining trade patterns in detail, it is important to look at Cambodia's top ten exports to China during the last decade. In 2008, the three major products — crude and synthetic rubber, cork and wood[9] (SITC 24), and textiles and clothing accessories — exported to China, contributed almost 89 per cent of total exports to China (Table 7.3). Other exports included agricultural products such as fish fresh/frozen, crustaceans/molluscs, and furniture/furnishings. Backtracking over the last ten years, we can see a tremendous decline in export (59.2 per cent) between 2000 and 2002, which marks a significant transition in the pattern of bilateral trade between China and Cambodia.

FIGURE 7.2
Cambodia's Bilateral Trade (y-on-y growth) with China and Its Trade Balance

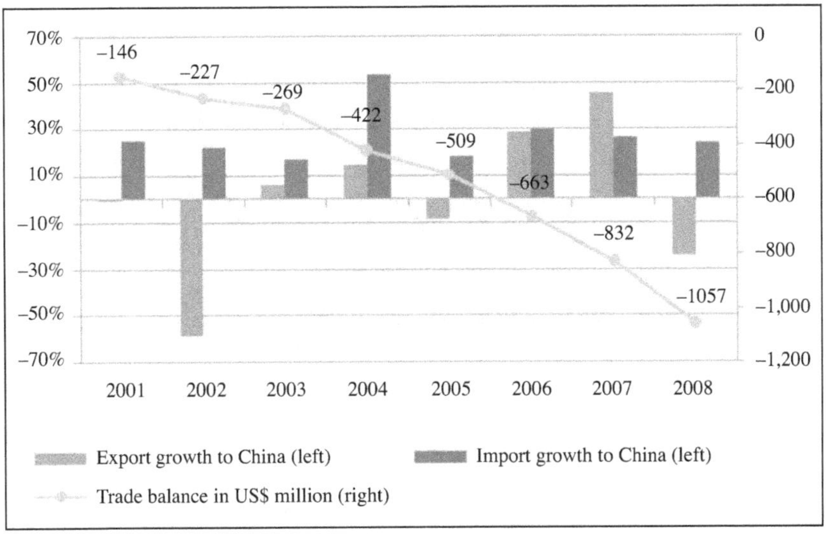

Source: UN ComTrade (2009).

The massive drop in total export in the early 2000s resulted primarily from a 71 per cent fall in cork and wood manufactures[10] (SITC 63) export from US$48.64 million in 2000 to US$14.05 million in 2002. This stemmed mainly from the government's cancellation of 40 per cent of all forest concessions, almost half the original area under concession, as well as the government's moratorium on logging in concession areas and log transports in January 2002. That said, despite the fall of cork and wood manufactures (SITC 63), natural cork and wood (SITC 24) increased markedly during the same period.

Despite the nosedive of total exports to China in the early 2000s a reverse trend became evident as export started to gradually rebound in 2008, though at a lower level than in the year 2000. Additionally, several other traditional exports, namely crude and synthetic rubber, apparel and clothing accessories, fish products, footwear and furniture grew moderately during the same period. It appears that more opportunities have been opened up for Cambodian products to enter the Chinese market, while the decline in wood export reflects the changing pattern of trade and the

TABLE 7.3
Cambodia's Top Ten Products Exported to China, 2000–08

SITC Rev.3	Production description	Value in US$ million					Share (%)				
		2000	2002	2004	2006	2008	2000	2002	2004	2006	2008
23	Crude/synthetic rubber	5.4	7.5	2.5	8.7	11.5	9.1	30.9	8.5	25.8	31.6
24	Cork and wood	1.6	1.1	10.1	12.1	10.6	2.7	4.4	33.6	35.8	29.2
84	Apparel/clothing/accessories	2.5	0.1	0.8	3	10.3	4.2	0.2	2.5	9	28.4
00	Textile fibres	—	—	0.1	0.7	1.2	—	—	0.3	2.2	3.3
26	Textile yarn/fabric/art.	0	0.2	9.1	7	0.6	0	0.6	30.6	20.9	1.7
03	Fish, live/fresh/chilled/frozen	0.5	1.1	0.5	0.6	0.5	0.8	4.4	1.7	1.8	1.3
65	Crustaceans molluscs	0.6	0.2	0.8	0.4	0.4	1	0.9	2.6	1.1	1
85	Footwear	—	0.1	0	0.1	0.4	—	0.2	0.1	0.4	1
82	Furniture/furnishings	—	0	0	0	0.3	—	0.1	0.1	0	0.9
89	Misc manufactures	0	0	0	0.2	0.2	0	0	0.1	0.5	0.4
	Others	48.7	14.1	5.9	0.9	0.4	82.1	58.3	19.9	2.7	1.2
	Total	59.3	24.2	29.9	33.7	36.4	100	100	100	100	100

Note: Author's ranking based on commodity export values in 2008.
Source: UN ComTrade (2009).

government's stance on environmental conservation and natural resource preservation.

The rate of growth of import from China has been far more rapid than the growth of export. The average year-on-year growth of import between 2001 and 2008 was around 27.2 per cent. Among the top ten products, textile yarn/fabric/articles ranked top and contributed about 50.3 per cent to total import from China in 2008 (Table 7.4). The first ranked product was imported mainly for domestic production and re-export to the third markets such as Japan, Canada, the EU and the United States as around 20.7 per cent of the total number of factories in the industry are from Hong Kong and 13.1 per cent from mainland China that source inputs mainly from parental factories in their hometown (GMAC 2006 cited in USAID 2007, p. 8).

Competition from China in the domestic market appears unlikely as import of the top ranked product is mainly for export-oriented production and backward linkages in the domestic economy are absent. In addition, six of the top nine imported products are not manufactured in Cambodia, and the activities and scale of the other three — apparel and clothing accessories and metal and non-metal manufactures — are insignificant.

On the whole, stronger trade relations between Cambodia and China, particularly through ACFTA-EHP, have provided wider opportunities for increasing bilateral trade in traditional commodities such as wood, fish, telecommunications equipment, textile yarns and fabrics, electrical machinery, iron and steel, metal and non-metal manufactures and several other new varieties of agricultural and manufactured products. However, Cambodia's yawning negative trade balance accrued over the last decade raises the question of whether Cambodia gains from trade with China, and if so, to what extent.

3.2 Methodologies and Analytical Framework

Figure 7.3 illustrates the analytical framework applied for analysing the impact of China's trade on poverty in Cambodia, following Jenkins and Edwards (2004).

3.3 Exports to China[11]

Table 7.5 indicates significant changes in the structure of Cambodian export to China during the last two decades. Between the early 1990s and 2000, all

TABLE 7.4
Cambodia's Top Ten Products Imported from China, 2008

SITC Rev.3	Production description	Value in US$ million					Share (%)				
		2000	2002	2004	2006	2008	2000	2002	2004	2006	2008
65	Textile yarn/fabric/art.	76	146.4	286	434.1	550.1	46.3	58.2	63.3	62.2	50.2
76	Telecomm equipment	11.4	5.9	11	23.1	59.7	6.9	2.3	2.4	3.3	5.4
66	Non-metal mineral manuf.	4.3	9.2	16.1	28.4	50.2	2.6	3.7	3.6	4.1	4.6
84	Apparel/clothing/accessories	8.2	8.2	11.9	30	48.4	5	3.2	2.6	4.3	4.4
71	Power generating equipment	4.3	8.1	11.6	17	47.4	2.6	3.2	2.6	2.4	4.3
77	Electrical equipment	1.3	2.5	2.7	11.2	37	0.8	1	0.6	1.6	3.4
67	Iron and steel	12.9	6.8	15.2	13.7	36.8	7.9	2.7	3.4	2	3.4
69	Metal manufactures	4.9	14.8	10.7	9.5	29.6	3	5.9	2.4	1.4	2.7
72	Industry special machine	6.5	11.4	7.7	21.6	29.1	3.9	4.6	1.7	3.1	2.7
74	Industrial equipment	1.5	2.5	4.7	17.1	28	0.9	1	1	2.5	2.6
	Others	32.8	35.3	73.9	91.8	176.4	20	14	16.4	13.2	16.1
	Total	164.1	251.1	451.7	697.5	1093	100	100	100	100	100

Source: UN ComTrade (2009).

FIGURE 7.3
Analytical Framework of Impact of China's Trade on Poverty Reduction in Cambodia

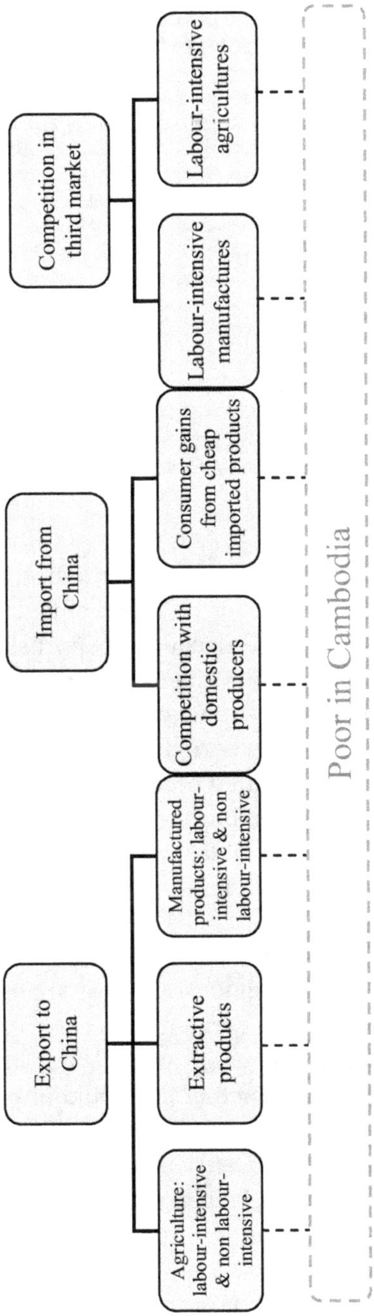

Source: Adapted from Jenkins and Edwards (2004).

TABLE 7.5
Share of Export to Total Export to China, 1992–2008, at 3-digit Level

P. Groups	RECODE of products	1992 (%)	2000 (%)	2007 (%)	2008 (%)
1	Labour-intensive agriculture	51.38	9.11	21.8	29.63
2	Other agriculture products	14.46	2.16	4.43	8.43
3	Forestry		2.73	47.06	27.42
4	Minerals & petroleum			0.02	0.32
5	Labour-intensive textiles & garments	3.26	4.21	19.34	28.19
6	Other labour-intensive manufactures		81.77	3.69	5.57
7	Other manufactured products	30.9	0.02	3.67	0.43
	Total	100	100	100	100

Note: Classification of products is indicated in Appendix A.
Source: UN ComTrade (2009).

product groups, except for other labour-intensive manufactures and forestry (data for which is not available for 1992) and other labour-intensive textiles and garments, show a marked decline in export shares. The tremendous drop in export share of labour-intensive agriculture in the early 2000s implies significant losses in export earnings and possibly employment in the sector. During the same period, export shares of other agricultural products and other manufactured products shrank substantially, marking the slump in export earnings, but any employment effects appear to be unlikely as those sectors are not labour-intensive. Interestingly, the share of export of labour-intensive textiles and garments shows a meagre rise during the period.

From 2000 to 2008, the trends of these product groups started to show a plausible turnaround (Table 7.5). Export shares of labour-intensive agriculture and textiles and garments increased considerably, but the immense drop in export shares of other labour-intensive manufactures gives a mixed picture as to whether this could imply reduction in export earnings and employment in the sectors. Additionally, the increase in export shares of non-labour-intensive agriculture, forestry, minerals and other manufactured products helped offset the decline in export of other labour-intensive manufactures.

Investigation of the detailed 3-digit level breakdown of products in each of the above product groups reveals more interesting findings

(Table 7.6). The tremendous drop in labour-intensive agriculture export stemmed primarily from declining export shares of fresh and dried fruits and nuts (SITC 057) from 16.8 per cent in 1992 to nil in 2000 and of natural rubber/latex (SITC 231) from 34.5 per cent in 1992 to 9.1 per cent in 2000. It should be noted that there was no rice export of any type at the time, and among fresh/dried fruits and nuts, only dried fruits (SITC 05799) were exported to China in 1992 and cashew nuts (SITC 05773) in 1995. The significant drop in natural rubber export resulted mainly from substantial reduction in the cultivated tapping area from 50,891 ha in 1992 to 29,119 ha in 2002 as large numbers of old (25–30 years of age) unproductive rubber trees were felled resulting in the reduction of total natural rubber/latex production, and thereby export.[12]

Between 2000 and 2008, the increase in the export share of natural rubber was the sole factor behind the surge in the export share of labour-intensive agriculture. It is also worth noting that two rice categories — glazed/polished (SITC 0422) and milled unbroken (SITC 04231)

TABLE 7.6
Detailed Breakdown of Share of Export to Total Export to China, 1992–2008

SITC 3	Product categories	1992 (%)	2000 (%)	2007 (%)	2008 (%)
001	Live animals except fish		0.352	2.012	6.223
034	Fish live/fresh/chilled/frozen		0.78	1.623	1.25
036	Crustaceans molluscs etc.		1.025	0.672	0.945
231	Natural rubber/latex/etc.	34.551	9.099	21.569	29.606
247	Wood in rough/squared		0.568	31.605	13.027
248	Wood simply worked		2.167	15.452	13.669
292	Crude vegetable materials	14.455		0.08	0.016
634	Veneer/plywood/etc.		79.439	0.051	
635	Wood manufactures nes		2.329	0.043	0.226
657	Special yarns/fabrics		0	0.02	0.046
661	Leather manufactures		0	0.001	0.005
841	Men/boys wear, woven		4.185	1.154	5.074
845	Articles of apparel nes		0	4.623	17.022
846	Clothing accessories		0.021	0.003	0.004
848	Headgear/non-textile clothing		0	0.001	0.001
893	Articles nes of plastics		0.001	0.036	0.058
899	Misc manufacture articles nes		0.001	0.135	0.33

Note: A detailed table is presented in Appendix Table 7B.1.
Source: UN ComTrade (2009).

— were exported in 2005 and 2008, but on a negligible scale. Export of natural rubber has picked up markedly during the last decade due to the government's rubber tree replanting programme started in 1993 (rubber trees are ready for tapping five years after planting) and the harvesting expansion of private and smallholder rubber plantations. As a result, the total area of rubber plantation — state, private and smallholder — in 2008 had reached 108,656 ha, around 31.58 per cent of which was ready for tapping (GDRP 2009).

The effect of natural rubber export on employment and poverty reduction in particular could be significant. A joint study by SOFRACO and CEDAC in 2005 estimated that the total workforce in the sector numbered around 26,300 in 2002, and a later UNDP (2007) estimate put the sector's workforce at 40,000 in 2007. In his study on the export competitiveness of the Cambodian rubber sector, Saing (2009*a*) indicates that the nominal daily wage of rubber labourers in 2008 was KHR15,000 equivalent to KHR9,814.8 at 2006 prices, which is far above the 2007 national rural poverty line — daily food and non-food consumption estimated by the World Bank — of KHR2,367 equivalent to KHR2,203.9 at 2006 prices.[13]

It is worth noting that the employment effect in the sector could be even more significant as a large proportion of Cambodian natural rubber is either formally or informally exported to Vietnam where it is processed and a certain proportion re-exported to China. Despite the low rubber price compared to Singapore's and Malaysia's markets, Cambodian rubber producers prefer Vietnam's market because its acceptance of low-grade natural rubber and low transport costs to the Vietnamese border (Saing 2009*a*, p. 13).

Other agricultural products showed a similar trend to labour-intensive agriculture between 1992 and 2000: the drop in the late 1990s to early 2000s resulted from a large decline in export of crude vegetable materials (SITC 292), and the rebound in the mid-2000s was due mainly to the increase in export of live animals (SITC 001) and fish live/fresh/chilled (SITC 034). Over the period 2000–08 there was a remarkable jump in the export of forestry products owing to the rise in export of wood rough/squared and wood simply worked. Export of mineral products, namely, ferrous waste/scrap (SITC 282) and base metal ore (SITC 287), emerged in 2007–08 but on an insignificant scale.

Export shares of labour-intensive textiles and garments show a constant upward trend between 1992 and 2008 due to the rise in exports of textile yarn, cotton fabrics/woven, man-made woven fabrics, woven textile fabrics, knit/crochet fabric, tulle/lace/embroidery, special yarn/fabrics (SITC 651–657) and men/boy wears, women/girl clothing woven, men/boy wear knit/crochet, women/girl wear knit/crochet, article of apparel, clothing accessories and headgear/non-textile clothing (SITC 841–848).

Unavailability of data and research on the number of garment factories that produce to export to the Chinese market makes it difficult to capture the employment and poverty effects of the increased export of garments and textiles. However, it could have implications for poverty reduction as the current monthly minimum wage in the sector is US$50 (approximately US$2.27 per working day at 2008 prices), which is higher than the 2007 Phnom Penh national poverty line of US$0.76 per day.[14]

In contrast, there was a significant fall in the export of other labour-intensive manufactures between 2000 and 2008. Substantial decreases in veneer/plywood (SITC 634) and other wood manufactures were the underlying reason behind the export slump. This was due to the government's moratorium on logging in concessions and log transports in January 2002. The significant slash in plywood production implies reduction in employment in the industry. Lack of data on job cuts and workers' daily earnings in the sector during this period prevents us from drawing any concrete conclusion on the poverty effect. However, it marked a significant change in the government's stance to a more environmental conservation-oriented trading position.

3.4 Domestic and 3rd Country Markets

Import from China (Producer Side)

Table 7.7 shows that agricultural products contributed only a small proportion of total import from China between 1992 and 2008. Thus, it appears that agriculture import from China posed no significant threat to and created no fierce competition against domestic agricultural producers. Overall, most of the various agricultural products from China are imported on an irregular basis, meaning that a product appears in one year but not in another. These products include several kinds of fish, fresh/chilled/preserved (SITC 034, 035), rice in husk and milled unbroken (SITC 0421, 04231), tapioca/sago (SITC 05645), dried vegetables (SITC 05619), melons/papaws (SITC 05791), pineapples prepared (SITC 05893) and apricots/cherries (SITC 05895).

TABLE 7.7
Share of Import to Total Import from China, 1992–2008, at 3-digit Level

P. Groups	RECODE of product	1992 (%)	2000 (%)	2007 (%)	2008 (%)
1	Labour-intensive agriculture	1.95	0.3	0.29	0.25
2	Other agriculture products	0.08	4.8	1.03	0.82
3	Forestry		0	0.01	0.01
4	Minerals & petroleum		0.44	0.73	1.66
5	Labour-intensive textiles & garments	0.06	51.33	60.22	54.63
6	Other labour-intensive manufactures	6.42	7.6	3.19	3.66
7	Other manufactured products	91.48	35.54	34.49	38.74
	Total	100	100	100	100

Note: Detailed table is presented in Appendix Table 7B.2.
Source: UN ComTrade (2009).

It should be noted that other products are regularly imported, but are not of Cambodian specialization, including frozen vegetables (SITC 05459), fresh apples (SITC 0574), dried grapes (SITC 05752), fresh pears/quinces (SITC 05792) and cooked pasta (SITC 09891). These imports are complementary to domestic production.

Although small in magnitude, given their constant rise in import value to Cambodian market and China's leading role among low-cost producers in the region, some products could compete with domestic producers. Such products include pork prepared/preserved (SITC 0175), onions/shallots (SITC 05451), garlic/leeks (SITC 05452), mushrooms/truffles dried or preserved (SITC 05613 & 05674), tomato puree (SITC 05673), other vegetables preserved (SITC 05679), fruit jams (SITC 0581), nuts/seeds (SITC 0581), fruit/nuts preserved (SITC 05896), natural honey (SITC 0616), sugar confectionery (SITC 06229), green tea (SITC 07411), black tea (SITC 07413), animal feed (SITC 08199), soy sauce (SITC 09841) and sauces/mixed seasonings (SITC 09849).

Before the mid-1990s, labour-intensive textiles and garments accounted for a minimal share of total imports while other manufactured products took the substantial share. Since then, textiles and garments import has grown rapidly — approximately half of the total import from China — because of the sector's dramatic expansion in the domestic economy between the mid-1990s and 2008. Of the total number of factories in the industry, around 20.7 per cent of investors are from Hong Kong and

13.1 per cent from China (GMAC 2006 cited in USAID 2007, p. 8). These Chinese factories, almost all of which are export-oriented, tend to source inputs for production in Cambodia from their parent firms in China and Hong Kong.[15] Therefore, the rising import share of such products poses no threat to domestic producers, but it does limit the development of domestic backward linkages.

The import share of other labour-intensive manufactures to total import from China was insignificant and declined from 7.6 in 2000 to 3.6 per cent in 2008. It seems that no severe effects are likely to emanate from this import as several products, such as animal hides, i.e. pig, sheep, goat, bovine (SITC 6112–6118), veneer sheets, plywood and fireboard (SITC 6341–6345), wooden tools/boxes (SITC 6351–6359), mattress support and bedding items (SITC 8212), metal and plastic furniture (SITC 82139 & 82171), handbags, leather trunks, plastic cases (SITC 8311–8312), and toy products (SITC 89421–89429) and vacuum flasks (SITC 89997), do not compete in the domestic market given the absence or meagre scale of such production activities in Cambodia.

However, other imported labour-intensive manufactures could pose potential competition for domestic producers given their regular and constant rise in share of import. Those products include glass bottles/jars, drinking glasses and kitchen/table glasses and other glassware and glass ornaments/beads (SITC 66511, 66522, 66523, 66529, 66593), kitchen/table porcelain (SITC 66611), wooden office, kitchen and bedroom furniture (SITC 82151–82159), bamboo furniture (SITC 82179), label paper and paperboards (SITC 89281), plastic bags/packaging and containers, plastic office equipment and other plastic articles (SITC 89311, 89319, 89394, 89399), pens of all kinds (SITC 89521), and brushes/brooms/mops (SITC 89972).

The import shares of other manufactured products constituted around one-third of total imports from China between 1992 and 2008. Although the magnitude of this import may not have any serious employment effect in the domestic economy given that the product group is not labour-intensive, it could hinder growth or expansion of similar domestic industries.

Some products could compete with local producers, such as beverages — alcoholic & non-alcoholic (SITC 111–112), pharmaceutical products (SITC 541–542), manufactured fertilizers (SITC 56211), paper/paperboard/cut paper products (SITC 641–642) and cement (SITC 66122). Other products, such as organic and inorganic chemicals (SITC 511–516, 522–524), plastics of non-primary form and chemical materials/products (SITC 581–583,

591–598), iron and steel and metal manufactures (SITC 673–679, 682–686, 691–699), and several other types of industrial and agricultural machinery (SITC 75–79, 81–83, 87–89) pose no threat to domestic producers due to the absence of the industries in the country.

Import from China (Consumer Side)

Besides examining the possible employment effect and competition arising from China's imports, it is also worth investigating whether Cambodian consumers could gain benefits from cheap products from China. Table 7.8 shows a mild rise in the import share of pro-poor consumer goods between 1992 and 2000, which dropped slightly to around 5.5 per cent in 2008. It appears that consumer gain is insignificant.

TABLE 7.8
Share of Poor Consumers' Goods Imported from China, 1992–2008 (%)

RECODE of product	1992	2000	2007	2008
Pro-poor consumer goods	2.27	9.55	4.82	5.49
Other product group	97.73	90.45	95.18	94.51

Note: Classification of products is indicated in Appendix 7A.
Source: UN ComTrade (2009).

Table 7.9 lists these pro-poor consumption goods in terms of their share of total import from China: agriculture contributed a minor share, live animals and fish/shellfish had tiny shares, while rice was imported occasionally and the import share of vegetables declined between 2000 and 2008. These are essential products commonly consumed by Cambodian middle- and low-income households, the poor in particular.

In contrast, shares of animal feed, edible products and non-alcoholic beverages increased slightly, and worn clothing emerged as a new import in 2007 and 2008. Import shares of clothing categories such as men/boys wear, women/girls wear, articles of apparel and clothing accessories, which were the main products in the group, marked a mild rise between 2000 and 2008. Consumer gain appears to be insignificant given that the major imports from China are inputs for the garments and textile sector

TABLE 7.9
Pro-poor Products Share of Total Imports from China, 1992–2008 (%)

SITC 3	Product categories	1992	2002	2007	2008
001	Live animals except fish				0.0095
037	Fish/shellfish, prep/pres		0.002	0.021	0.049
042	Rice		0.008		
048	Cereal etc. flour/starch		0.013	0.094	0.337
054	Vegetables, fresh/chilled/frozen		0.001	0.013	0.001
056	Vegetable root/tuber prep/pres	0.013	0.144	0.095	0.032
057	Fruit/nuts, fresh/dried		0.077	0.016	0.054
061	Sugar/molasses/honey	1.84	0.005	0.012	0
062	Sugar confectionery	0.095	0.023	0.102	0.096
081	Animal feed		0.026	0.001	0.006
098	Edible products n.e.s.		0.318	0.091	0.042
111	Beverage non-alcohol n.e.s.	0.663	0.107	0.037	0.067
269	Worn clothing etc.			0.004	0.009
841	Men/boys wear, woven		0.009	0.008	0.05
842	Women/girls clothing woven		0.097	0.001	0
843	Men/boy wear knit/crochet		0.27	0.07	0.652
844	Women/girl wear knit/crochet		0.129	0.165	0.733
845	Articles of apparel n.e.s.		3.188	2.448	2.034
846	Clothing accessories		0.78	0.959	0.845
848	Headgear/non-text clothing	0.065	0.506	0.19	0.116
851	Footwear	0.171	3.902	0.488	

Source: UN ComTrade (2009).

for domestic export-oriented production and in other chemicals and agriculture and industrial machinery.

Export to the 3rd Market

It is important to investigate similarities in the export structures of the two countries before examining the competition between Cambodia and China in the third market. To do so, the method used in the studies by Jenkins and Edwards (2004) and Okamoto (2005) was adopted and Spearman ranking was applied to check the correlation between the share of Cambodia's and China's SITC 3-digit export to their total export to the world. The closer the value is to 1, which would indicate identical export structures, the greater the likelihood that China and Cambodia will be competitors in the third market.

TABLE 7.10
Export Similarity between China and Cambodia, 1992 and 2008

Year	Agriculture[a]	*p*-value	Manufactures[a]	*p*-value	All Exports[a]	*p*-value
1992	–0.1125	0.66	0.1293	0.24	–0.0618	0.54
1995	–0.0455	0.84	0.2287	0.02**	0.0756	0.4
1998	0.0614	0.8	0.326	0.00***	0.1079	0.24
2001	–0.0818	0.69	0.3593	0.00***	0.2642	0.00***
2004	–0.0557	0.77	0.4731	0.00***	0.2388	0.00***
2007	–0.1921	0.32	0.4646	0.00***	0.2501	0.00***
2008	–0.1504	0.48	0.4685	0.00***	0.1771	0.03**

Note: Level of significance: * 10 per cent; ** 5 per cent; *** 1 per cent;
a: Spearman correlation ranking between export shares of Cambodia and China.
Source: Author's calculation based on data from UNComTrade (2009).

Table 7.10 indicates that Cambodia had low export similarity with China for all exports between 2001 and 2008, which is statistically significant at 1 per cent for 2001–07 and at 5 per cent for 2008. By product group classification, the structure of Cambodia's agriculture export had no similarity with that of China, but there was a rising level of similarity in the structure of its manufactures export, which is statistically significant at 5 per cent in 1995 and at 1 per cent for 1998–2008. This indicates rising competition from China in manufactured products in the third market.

As Cambodia's manufactures export is concentrated mainly in textiles and garments (particularly SITC Rev.3 84), the two countries are likely competitors in those products in the third markets. It should be noted that the marked correlation coefficients of the export structure of the two countries in manufactured products could be attributed to their strong similarities in the export structure of garments and textiles as Cambodia still has a narrow manufacturing base. Since the industry's establishment in the mid-1990s, Cambodia's garment products have traditionally been destined for three major markets, namely the United States (around 70 per cent), the EU (23 per cent) and Canada (5 per cent) (MoC 2009 cited in Saing 2009*b*, p. 2). Therefore, it is worthwhile examining the competition status between the two countries in both the U.S. and EU markets.

3.5 Competition in the U.S. Market

Figure 7.4 indicates substantial growth in China's market share of the U.S. garment market during the last decade, which was considerably

FIGURE 7.4
Market Shares of Asian Garments in the U.S. Market (SITC 841–848)

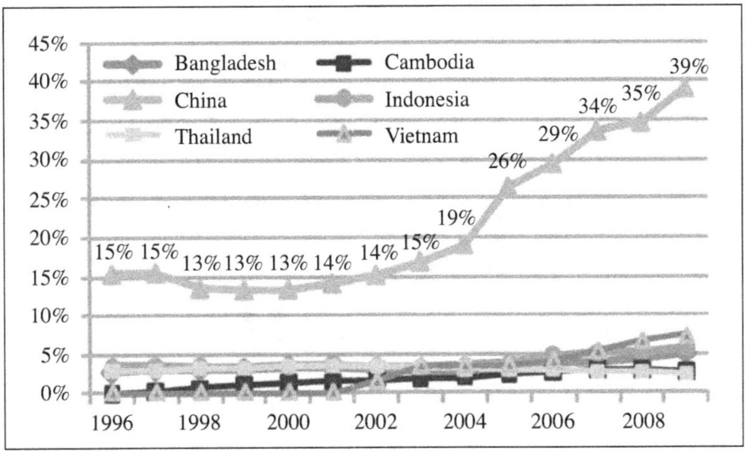

Source: USITC (2010).

high between the early 2000s and 2008, posing potential threat to countries specializing in these products, i.e. Bangladesh, Cambodia, Indonesia, Thailand and Vietnam. Despite the two shocks — hike in energy prices and the global economic recession — between late 2007 and 2009, the Chinese market share expanded markedly, while Cambodia's share slowed. During the same period, the rising shares of Vietnam and Bangladesh to a certain extent put further downward pressure on Cambodia's garment producers.

Table 7.11 lists Cambodia's top twelve garment exports to the U.S. market since the establishment of the industry in the early 1990s and highlights the products that Cambodia specializes in, i.e., jerseys/pullovers, men/women trousers, men/women outwear/underwear/nightwear, T-shirts, women/girl blouses and baby garments. Over the period 1990–2008, most products showed increasing export at current market value, while some marked a significant rise, for instance, jerseys and pullovers, women/girls trousers, men/boys trousers and women girls outerwear.

Given the increasing export value of Cambodia's top twelve products, it appears that the rising share of Chinese overall garment export to the United States does not seem to pose any serious concern to Cambodian products. However, a closer look at the relationship between market shares of the

TABLE 7.11
Cambodia's Top Twelve Garment Exports to the U.S. Market, 1990–2008 (US$ million)

No.	SITC	Product name	1990	1994	1997	2000	2003	2006	2008
1	8453	Jerseys/pullovers/etc.	–	0.001	25.92	200.65	182.64	456.08	591.75
2	8426	Women/girl trousers woven	–	–	11.4	139.66	273.21	350.95	373.5
3	8414	Men/boy trousers/etc. woven	–	–	34.73	163.42	140.79	195.9	236.69
4	8442	Women/girl outrwear knit/crochet	–	0.001	4.06	18.64	29.56	142.7	230.57
5	8448	Women/girl under/night wear k/c	–	–	1.32	27.23	123.86	185.63	160.00
6	8454	T-shirts/singlet knitted/crochet	–	–	0.70	12.74	13.33	107.62	136.82
7	8437	Men/boy knitted/crochet shirt	0.073	–	2.64	20.97	31.23	90.98	93.69
8	8447	Women/girl blouses knit/crochet	–	0.012	4.99	16.67	34.75	117.56	91.46
9	8438	Men/boy underwear etc. knit/crochet	–	–	2.39	11.45	74.54	76.13	73.18
10	8459	Apparel nes knit/crochet	–	–	0.42	3.26	6.23	60.98	72.62
11	8451	Babies garments etc.	–	–	0.08	21.03	16.91	35.24	66.47
12	8432	Men/boy suits knitted/crochet	–	–	1.21	3.59	4.78	35.75	50.32

Source: UN ComTrade (2009).

two countries at 4-digit product level gives a clearer picture of the likely competition between the two countries. Figure 7.5 shows that Cambodia could face potential threat from Chinese producers in some garment products, such as baby garments, jerseys/pullovers, men/boy underwear knit/crochet, men/boy trousers, women/girl outerwear, women/girl under/nightwear, women/girl blouses knit/crochet and women/girl trousers, but due to the declining share of other Chinese products, specifically apparel knit/crochet, could also grasp new opportunities.

3.6 Competition in the EU Market

The substantial growth in China's EU garment market share during the last decade gathered pace between 2000 and 2008, indicating potential threat to countries specializing in the same products, i.e. Bangladesh, Cambodia, Indonesia, Thailand and Vietnam. Again, China's market share continued to gain momentum despite the steep rise in energy prices and the global economic recession between late 2007 and 2009, while Cambodia's share slumped. However, given Cambodian products' minimal EU market share of 0.01 to 1.0 per cent between 1990 and 2008, China's and Bangladesh's surging market shares appear unlikely to have any effect on Cambodia (Figure 7.6).

Table 7.12 lists Cambodia's top twelve garment exports to the EU market between 1990 and 2008, the structure of which is similar to that to the U.S. market. Main exports are men/boy trousers, women/girl trousers, men/boy shirts, jerseys/pullover, men/boy knit/crochet shirts and men/boy suits, while others include women/girl outerwear and coats, apparel knit/crochet, T-shirts and women/girl blouses. The top six marked significant rise in export value, except for jerseys/pullovers and men/boy shirts; similar trends were also evident in the remaining top product groups.

Given the increasing export value of Cambodia's top twelve garment products, it appears that the rising share of Chinese overall garment export to the EU poses no threat to Cambodian products. Classified at 4-digit level, the picture of China's rising market shares is even more revealing. The Chinese market share of each of the top twelve grew rapidly, which could pose potential harm to Cambodian products. Nevertheless, as the Cambodian market share of each of the twelve products is minimal, negative effect appears unlikely.

FIGURE 7.5
Market Shares of Cambodia's Top Twelve Garment Products in the United States, 1990–2008[a]

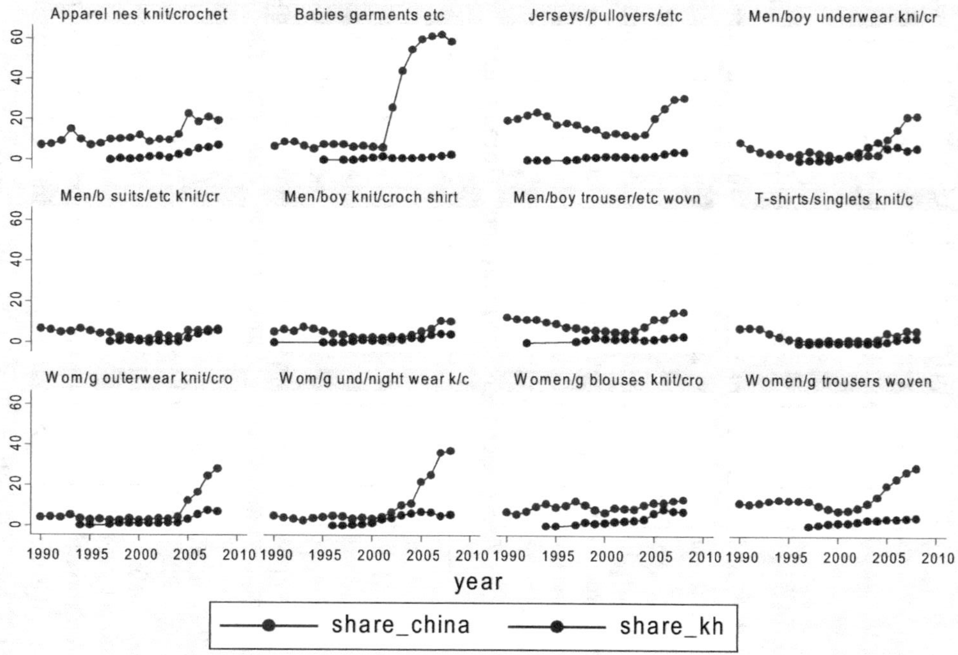

Note: a. All products are Cambodia's top twelve ranking among all garment exports to the United States (SITC 84) based on export value in 2008.
Source: UN ComTrade (2009).

FIGURE 7.6
Market Shares of Asian Garments in the EU Market[a] (SITC 841–848)

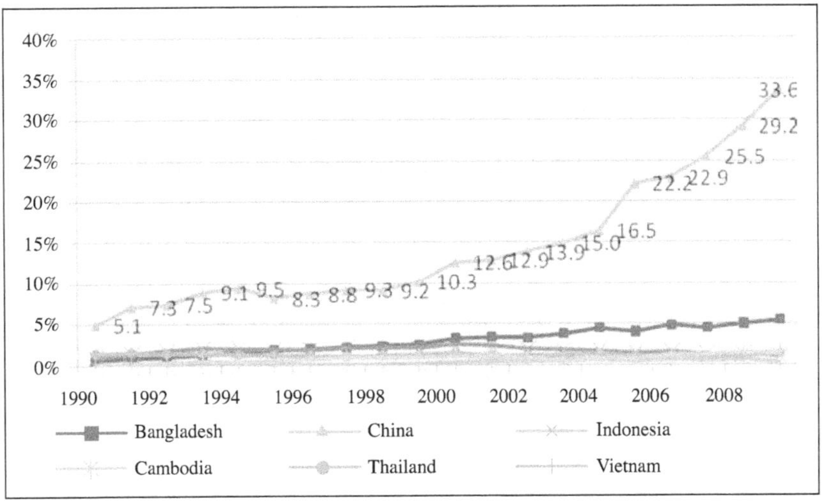

Note: a. EU12 includes Austria, Belgium, Denmark, Spain, Finland, France, Germany, Ireland, Italy, Luxembourg, Netherlands and Portugal.
Source: UN ComTrade (2010).

Overall, it appears that China could become a competitor in a number of Cambodian garment products, but not in the EU given Cambodia's negligible EU market share. However, the question whether Cambodia could compete against China in the U.S. and EU markets should be given serious consideration as a substantial 13.1 per cent of the industry belongs to China and 20.7 per cent to Hong Kong, while only a minor share of 8.6 per cent belongs to Cambodia (GMAC 2006 cited in USAID 2007, p. 8).

4. CHINA'S IMPACT ON CAPITAL INFLOWS TO CAMBODIA

4.1 FDI Inflow from China

Given its low domestic savings, FDI is a significant element in Cambodia's economy. From 1998 to 2008 the level of FDI in terms of fixed assets

TABLE 7.12
Cambodia's Top Twelve Garment Export to the EU Market, 1990–2008 (US$ million)

No.	SITC	Product name	1990	1994	1997	2000	2003	2006	2008
1	8414	Men/boy trousers/etc. woven	0.01	3.36	53.37	139.69	282.83	433.89	548.86
2	8426	Women/girl trousers woven	0.00	3.58	14.6	25.65	37.42	86.05	92.11
3	8415	Men/boys shirts, woven	0.00	0.16	3.36	5.04	11.01	15.53	54.23
4	8453	Jerseys/pullovers/etc.	0.21	0.87	13.8	31.12	54.67	49.52	43.31
5	8437	Men/boy knit/crochet shirt	–	0.51	2.88	19.43	57.49	43.27	42.28
6	8432	Men/boy suits/etc. knit/crochet	–	0.13	0.51	5.33	9.11	18.97	30.85
7	8442	Women/girl outerwear knit/crochet	–	0.57	6.06	5.84	21.85	31.9	24.89
8	8441	Women/girl coats etc. knit/crochet	–	1.78	3.41	2.57	6.51	8.25	17.52
9	8459	Apparel nes knit/crochet	–	5.64	4.19	0.91	8.79	11.5	16.66
10	8454	T-shirts/singlet knit/crochet	–	0.71	4.56	2.86	0.65	3.31	15.72
11	8447	Women/girl blouses knit/crochet	–	0.35	4.95	5.11	6.76	11.1	13.15
12	8458	Garments nes not knit/crochet	–	0.21	1.39	0.37	3.13	3.65	9.69

Source: UN ComTrade (2009).

FIGURE 7.7
Market Shares of Cambodia's Top Twelve Garment Products in the EU, 1990–2009

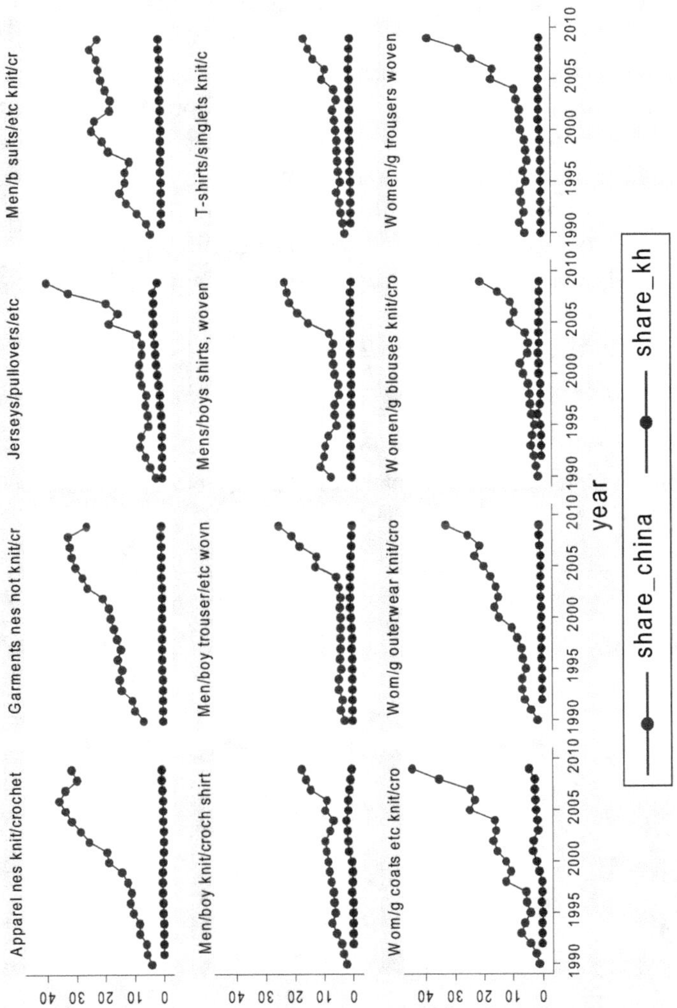

Source: UN ComTrade (2009).

approval contributed on average about 15 per cent of GDP and 56 per cent of total investment approvals (Figure 7.8). FDI was mainly concentrated in the tourism, construction and garment sectors. However, data from the National Institute of Statistics (NIS) Statistical Yearbook 2008 indicates that on average 60 per cent of total fixed asset approvals were implemented during 1994–2007.

Table 7.13 shows the top twelve investors in Cambodia from 1998 to 2009. China is the top investor, accounting for about 45.6 per cent of total foreign investments, followed by South Korea (17.6 per cent) and the United States (9.5 per cent). The average scale of China's investment is about US$25 million, lower than Russia's US$62 million, the United States' US$37.2 million and South Korea's US$30.9 million.

Table 7.14 illustrates the development of Chinese direct investment in Cambodia since 1998, and the substantial investment in Cambodia by Chinese enterprises from 2004 to 2009.

FIGURE 7.8
Foreign Direct Investment (Total Fixed Asset Approvals) in Cambodia (US$ million and GDP %)

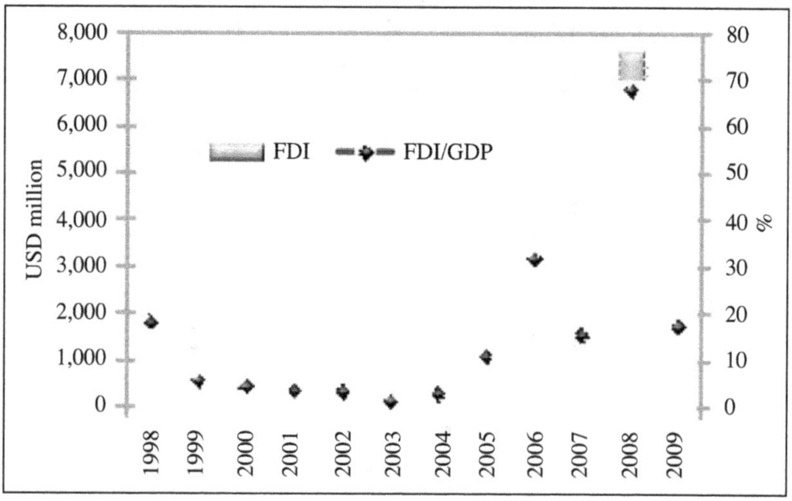

Source: CDC (2007, 2008, 2009); IMF (2010).

TABLE 7.13
Top Twelve Investors in Cambodia, 1998–2009

Country	No. of Project	Fixed Assets Approval (US$ million)	Average Investment Value (US$ million)	% of Total FDI
China	278	6,940.9	25.0	45.6
S. Korea	87	2,686.1	30.9	17.6
United States	39	1,452.5	37.2	9.5
Thailand	43	596.1	13.9	3.9
Malaysia	51	534.6	10.5	3.5
Vietnam	33	447.0	13.5	2.9
Taiwan	117	436.2	3.7	2.9
Russia	7	434.0	62.0	2.8
Singapore	46	403.8	8.8	2.7
Hong Kong	47	171.6	3.7	1.1
Japan	15	135.4	9.0	0.9
France	15	114.8	7.7	0.8

Source: CDC (2007, 2008, 2009).

TABLE 7.14
China's Investment in Cambodia, 1998–2009

Year	Number of projects			Fixed Assets Approval (US$ million)		
	Total	China	% China	Total	China	% China
1998	212	40	18.9	555.5	104.7	18.9
1999	135	27	20.0	196.2	46.0	23.5
2000	83	7	8.4	160.2	28.4	17.7
2001	47	5	10.6	139.5	5.0	3.6
2002	44	8	18.2	143.6	24.1	16.8
2003	58	10	17.2	64.7	32.9	50.9
2004	75	21	28.0	154.7	83.1	53.7
2005	123	41	33.3	682.4	452.0	66.2
2006	119	31	26.1	2,300.6	717.1	31.2
2007	166	32	19.3	1,344.6	180.3	13.4
2008	125	28	22.4	7,620.8	4,374.6	57.4
2009	122	28	23.0	1,871.3	892.7	47.7
1998–2009	1,309	278	21.2	15,234.0	6,940.9	45.6

Source: CDC (2007, 2008, 2009).

4.2 FDI Drivers

Sectoral distribution of China's investment in Cambodia shows that China is mostly attracted to natural resource development, such as petroleum, mining and energy (including hydropower plants), and tourism and garment sectors. From 1998 to 2009, 99.8 per cent of the total FDI in the petroleum sector, 91.7 per cent of that in mining and 83.5 per cent of that in the energy sector was China's investment (Figure 7.10). China's investment in tourism (60.7 per cent), garments (40.1 per cent), other industries (38.1 per cent) and agriculture (25.6 per cent) was also significant compared to the total FDI flows to each sector.

The scale of China's investment in Cambodia has gradually expanded from small-scale manufacturing companies, particularly in the garment sector, to medium- and large-sized resource development companies that have invested critically in natural resources, agriculture, construction, and hydropower plants. Notably, China invested heavily in Cambodia's tourism sector in 2008, in particular the development of Koh Kong coastal resort,

FIGURE 7.9
Fixed Asset Approvals in Selected Sectors, 1998–2008
(% of total FDI fixed asset approvals)

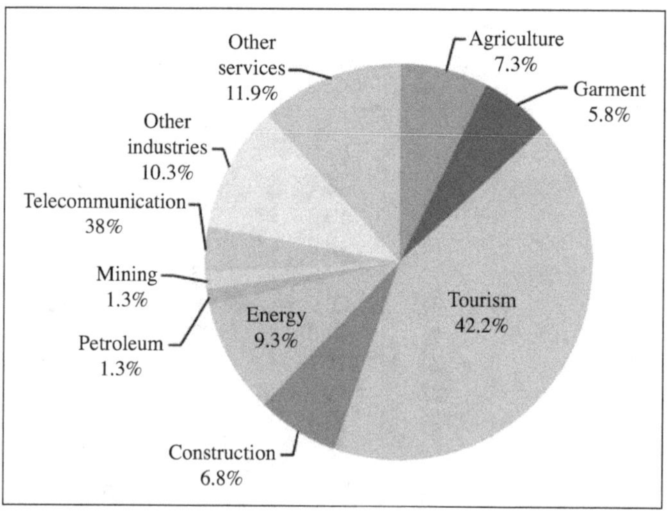

Source: CDC (2007, 2008, 2009).

FIGURE 7.10
China's Fixed Asset Approvals in Selected Sectors, 1998–2008
(% of total FDI fixed asset approvals in each sector)

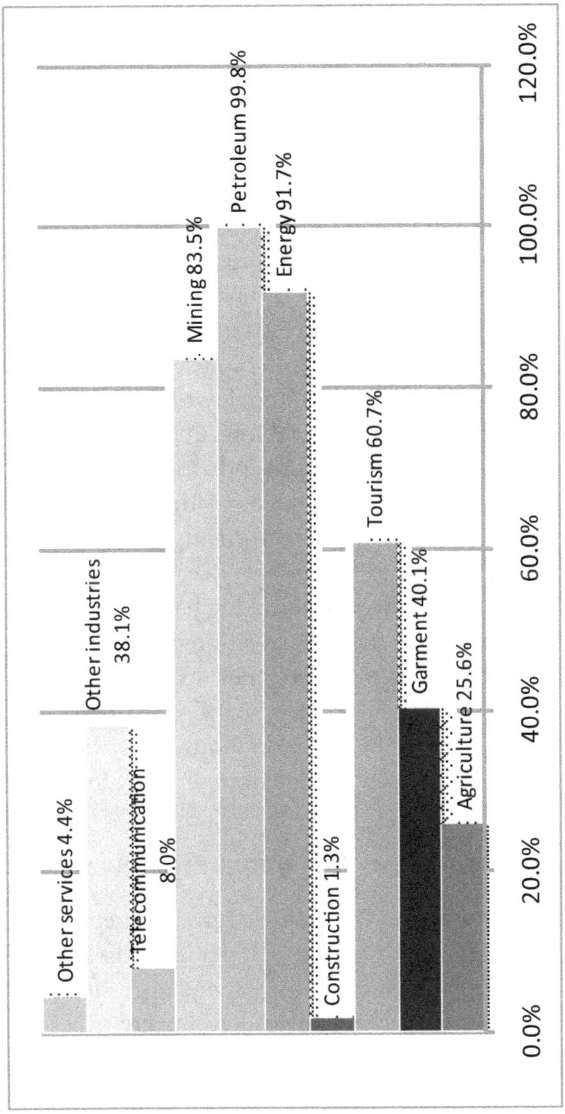

Source: CDC (2007, 2008, 2009).

amounting to US$3,805 million and accounting for about 98 per cent of China's total investment in this sector from 1998 to 2009.

Wu and Chen (2001) point out that the emergence of China's overseas investment is prompted by political motivation, market seeking, desire to take advantage of lower labour costs, and the availability and price of natural resources. The physical and human infrastructure, together with the macroeconomic situation and institutional structure of the host country, also play decisive roles in China's investment, as is evident in Cambodia.

The extensive Chinese investment in the export-oriented garment sector in the 1990s was largely attributed to Cambodia's Most Favoured Nation (MFN) status as well as the benefits that Cambodian exports were eligible for under the Generalized System of Preference (GSP) of the United States, the EU and other developed countries. China's investors took both advantages of market accession and lower labour costs. More recently, China has been investing in natural resource development such as energy (hydro-power plants), mining, agro-industry and construction.

Wu and Chen (2001) add that poor labour quality and low technical standards in developing nations have greatly encouraged the development of the contract market, and China has been able to move into this market on the basis of its experience, undertaking basic infrastructure construction through the provision of foreign aid. Moreover, it has helped to promote export sales of China's products. For example, China's construction companies have helped boost exports of China's construction equipment, facilities, materials, technology and labour. This will be discussed in the next section on China's official development aid to Cambodia.

4.3 Methodologies and Analytical Framework

In assessing the effects of FDI on poverty reduction, it is important to distinguish between its direct and indirect impacts. FDI can provide direct contribution mainly through employment and income generation. The indirect benefits of FDI can be transmitted through backward and forward linkages, spillover and demonstration effects; however, many of these effects are difficult to measure. On the other hand, the poverty effects of different types of FDI, i.e. labour-intensive or capital-intensive, can be identified. This is crucial for the country to design policies and strategies to attract FDI in those sectors that contribute to poverty reduction. Labour-intensive FDI, as a major generator of employment in a country like Cambodia, is important for poverty reduction. See Figure 7.11.

FIGURE 7.11
Analytical Framework of China's Investment in Cambodia

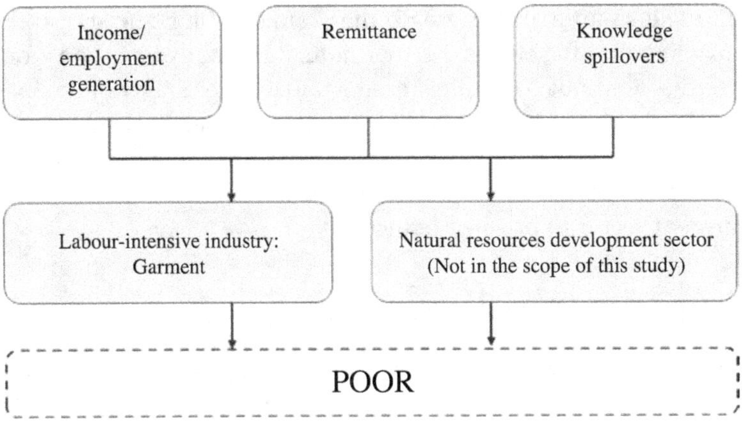

The labour-intensive investment of China is perceived as creating vast employment for unskilled workers, which positively affects the rural poor. Therefore, the research team undertook a case study on the garment sector, which is a labour-intensive industry and greatly attractive to investment from China, to assess the potential effects of China's FDI inflow on poverty reduction through exploring: (i) opportunities for the rural poor to increase earnings through employment creation and higher wages; (ii) remittance; and (iii) spillover effect on the rural poor's skill development and technology transfer to local enterprises. The effect of China's investment in the garment sector on the economy is also briefly discussed.

China has also invested heavily in natural resources (agriculture, agro-industry, mining, oil and gas, and hydropower), especially through economic land concessions. Such investment has significant positive and negative impacts on poverty reduction, local livelihoods and the environment. However, this aspect is not within the scope of this study.

4.4 Case Study on Cambodia's Garment Sector

Method and Limitations

A survey of 300 garment workers selected from both Chinese and non-Chinese owned companies (150 workers from each) to understand whether and how the poverty effects of China's FDI differ from other sources of

FDI was conducted in Phnom Penh. The sample was purposely selected at the location while factory size (i.e. the total number of workers employed) was not taken into account.

Since the sample size is small, the results of this survey cannot be used to generalize the effects. Furthermore, it is mainly based on workers' perspectives without balancing these against other stakeholders' views. This is due to difficulty accessing China's investors and other relevant agencies. Most importantly, the survey was not intended to be an in-depth analysis on the extent of the net benefit of China's investment in the garment sector to poverty reduction.

Overview of the Garment Sector

The garment sector accounts for around 10.5 per cent of GDP and has contributed tremendously to economic growth in the past decade. Data recorded by the Economic Institute of Cambodia indicates that the garment sector has added an estimated 2 per cent annually to GDP since 1995, though this trend seems to have been declining recently. The garment sector emerged in response to U.S. trade preferences. The USA-Cambodian Trade Agreement on Textiles and Apparel (1999–2004), which linked market access (increasing quota) to labour standards, was signed in 1998–99. A three-and-a-half year EU-Cambodian textile agreement, which provided duty and quota-free access for Cambodian garment products subject to rules of origin requirements being met, was set up in 1999. In addition, the EU introduced its "Everything but Arms" (EBA) scheme in 2001, which allows quota and duty-free access on all Cambodian exports to the EU market.

To date, Cambodia's share of its garment sector's value chain and value-added is relatively limited. Cambodia is only involved at the "cut, make and trim" phase of the value chain (World Bank 2009*a*). Cambodia does not have a textiles industry and most of the inputs for the sector are imported. Otherwise, the producing firm is supplied with materials by its customers and is paid a processing fee. More than 90 per cent of garment factories are foreign-owned, resulting in a significant repatriation of the profits. Direct contributions to the government budget have been limited since the sector enjoys import tax exemptions as well as tax holidays.

Even so, the benefits of the garment sector to Cambodia have been substantial in terms of boosting overall GDP, income generation and poverty reduction. Garments account for up to 80 per cent of recorded total exports. The garment industry not only contributes in terms of employment creation, but also through remittance to workers' families in rural areas. Many workers are young women who migrated from poor rural areas to Phnom Penh, where most garment factories are located. Thus, the majority of people who benefit from the industry are unskilled and poorly educated young women from rural areas, who typically would be among the most vulnerable within the labour market. The challenge is to what extent Cambodians are employed as technical workers and managers. It is estimated that China's recruitment agencies have sent approximately 5,000 Chinese garment technicians and supervisors to work in garment factories in Cambodia. Building domestic human resources capacity is crucial, and the circumstances in which local entrepreneurs gain experience from foreign firms should be established. Meanwhile, indirect job creation such as in transport, trade, restaurants, and other small businesses and services is also evident.

Findings

The case study presents basic information on garment workers' perceptions of the industry's contribution to poverty reduction through employment and income generation, remittance and opportunity for capacity and skill building.

(i) Employment Creation and Changes in Livelihood: Of the interviewed garment workers, 88 per cent are women and 82 per cent had been working in their current factories for three years or less. Sewing machinists represent 58 per cent of the total sample while office staff make up only 1.6 per cent. Table 7.15 details the sample workers by gender, job category and work experience.

Based on sample garment workers' recall of the last job they had when they were employed for at least three consecutive months, it was found that 63 per cent from the Chinese factories and 77 per cent from non-Chinese factories were previously self-employed as: (i) farmer, (ii) student, (iii) housewife or helping with housework, (iv) unemployed, and (v) other self-employment at home.

Not taking the size of factory (in terms of the number of workers employed) in the sample selection into account to some extent confirms

TABLE 7.15
Total Number of Sample Workers by Sex, Job Category and Work Experience

Job Category \ Experience	< 1 year		1–3 years		> 3–5 years		> 5–15 years		Total
	Male	Female	Male	Female	Male	Female	Male	Female	
Sample worker	0	2						1	3
Cutting operator	1	5	2	3	0	2		2	15
Sewing operator	8	42	4	68	0	27		25	175
Quality control worker	0	13	0	13				1	27
Worker (washing, ironing, packing…)	11	8	2	19	0	4		3	47
Warehouse worker	0	3	0	5	0	2			10
Cleaner/Guard/Cooker/Driver	0	1	2	5	1	0		1	10
Quality control inspector	0	1			0	2			3
Final inspector								2	2
Mechanic	1	0	1	0					2
Quality assurance assistant	0	1							1
Office staff			0	2	1	1		1	5
Total	22	76	11	115	2	38		36	300

Source: Survey conducted by CDRI in April 2010.

that Chinese investment in Cambodia's garment sector has generated employment for rural people. It must be noted, however, that the net benefits between previous (self-employment) and current employment were not considered.

The sample garment workers generally work eight to ten hours per day for six days per week. However, about 76 per cent of the workers from non-Chinese factories work ten hours per day compared to only 36.7 per cent in Chinese factories. At the time of survey in April 2010, the legal minimum wage for garment workers had been US$50 per month since 2006. Most of the workers interviewed were earning around US$80 per month, about US$2.67 per day on average.

To recap, the total poverty line in Phnom Penh in 2007 estimated by the World Bank was US$0.76 per day. That garment workers earned an average of US$2.03 per day (at 2006 prices), i.e., higher than the income needed to live above the overall poverty line in Phnom Penh of US$0.71 implies that to some extent employment in the garment industry reduces poverty.

Around half of the respondents from both Chinese and non-Chinese factories believed that their household's economic status had improved (Figure 7.12). The main reasons given for the changes include: (i) investment (purchase of land, motor boat, livestock), (ii) regular income (factory wages), (iii) more sources of household income, (iv) better rice yield, and (v) better living conditions in the village.

(ii) Remittance: When asked if they had ever sent money home, 47 per cent of workers from non-Chinese factories and 53 per cent from Chinese factories said they had. The sample workers' households mainly use remittance for: (i) daily food consumption, (ii) investing in agriculture, (iii) supporting education of family members, (iv) paying debt, (v) saving for children, and (vi) buying farm land (Figure 7.13).

(iii) Skill Development: Systematic skill or technical training had not been offered to employees at either Chinese or non-Chinese factories. Of the total sample of 300, only four respondents (two from Chinese factories) had received training — in new design and labour law. Similarly, most of the workers interviewed responded "don't know" and "no" when asked whether their factory would support opportunities to attend externally organized vocational training. Yet 41 per cent of Chinese factory workers

FIGURE 7.12
Sample Workers' Perception of Changes in Household Economic Status

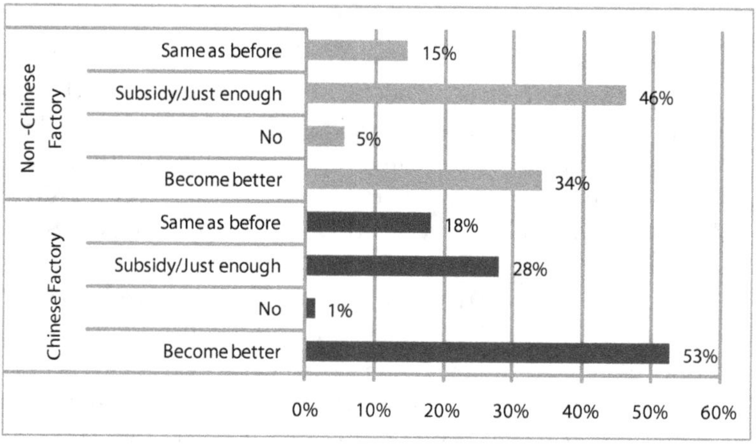

Source: Survey conducted by CDRI in April 2010.

FIGURE 7.13
Household Use of Workers' Remittance (Most important items)

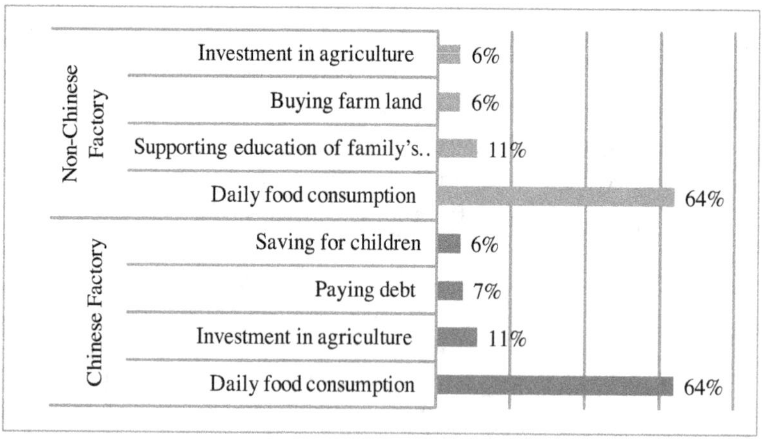

Source: Survey conducted by CDRI in April 2010.

and 63 per cent of non-Chinese workers felt they had gained specific skills or knowledge from their current job, though most of them had only attained basic skills through their daily work. They anticipated being able to use these skills and knowledge to: (i) find a job in a similar factory in the country, (ii) find a job in a similar factory abroad (Korea, Malaysia, Thailand), and (iii) run their own business, for example, a tailor shop. Only about 10 per cent of the workers interviewed had sought and paid for personal skill development such as sewing and designing and wedding design (Figure 7.15).

5. ODA FROM CHINA

5.1 Magnitude and Changes

Official development assistance (ODA) plays significant roles in financing Cambodia's development as an additional public resource through supporting public service delivery, and as a form of attracting private sector investment through infrastructure improvement and economic services.[16]

FIGURE 7.14
Garment Factory Training Programme

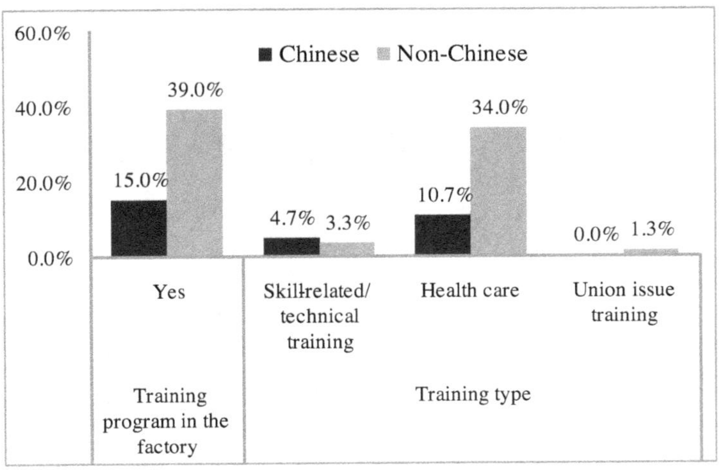

Source: Survey conducted by CDRI in April 2010.

FIGURE 7.15
Garment Factory Support to Attend External Vocational Training

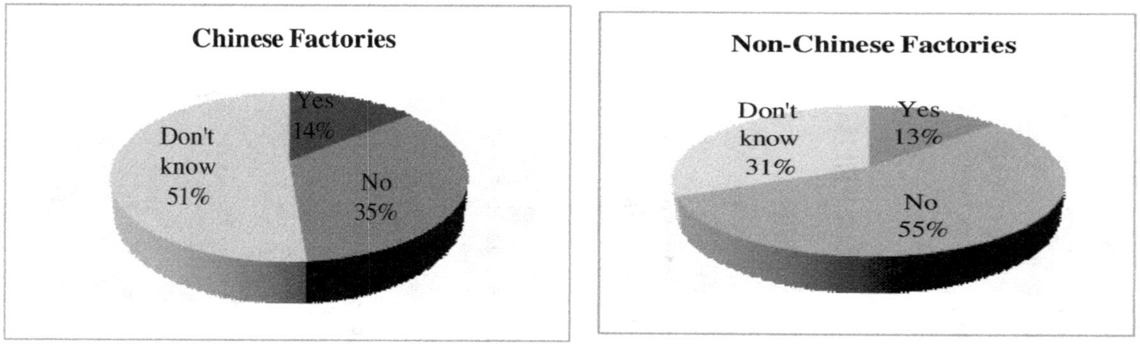

Source: Survey conducted by CDRI in April 2010.

The ODA database of the Cambodian Rehabilitation and Development Board of the Council for the Development of Cambodia (CRDB-CDC), the national aid coordination focal point, has recorded increasing financial disbursements since 2000. The average disbursement fund allocated by official bilateral and multilateral development partners and NGOs in the form of grant and loan between 2000 and 2009 totals US$662.3 million. In 2000, ODA per capita was US$37, rising to US$70.7 per capita in 2009. The main sectors targeted include health, education, agriculture, rural development, culture and arts, energy and electricity, governance and administration, transport, and community and social welfare, which is consistent with Cambodia's development priorities in the context of the Rectangular Strategy and the National Strategic Development Plan (NSDP). Each year during the period 2000–09, around 35 per cent of the total disbursement fund was allocated to technical cooperation, around 60 per cent to investment projects and programmes, and just 2.5 per cent went to food aid and emergency.

Given the fund disbursement, mutual trust and accountability are prerequisite for an effective development partnership. This perspective appeared following the recommendations of the Aid Effectiveness Reports in 2006 and 2007. The reports emphasize that acceleration of trust and understanding between Cambodia and its development partners is essential in order to ensure the improvement of development effectiveness.

Historically, several sources of assistance from different partners have financed Cambodia's development needs. Of these, China is emerging as a major donor for the country's improvement. Since the 1990s, once Cambodia was able to ensure security and political stability, the two countries have maintained frequent contact and exchanged visits, building on the strong diplomatic relations already forged over the previous fifty years. The two governments nominated the year 2008 as Sino-Cambodia Friendship celebration year to strengthen their relationship and enhance bilateral cooperation.

China has been a key source of foreign aid to Cambodia. During the period 2000–09, China's ODA to Cambodia totalled US$465 million, which represents 7 per cent of the overall endorsement from all Cambodia's partners. China's disbursement kept on increasing each year as is clearly illustrated in the rise from a mere US$2.6 million in 2000 to US$32.5 million in 2004 and then to US$114.7 million in 2009 (Table 7.16). As of 2009, its significant 11.6 per cent share of Cambodia's total disbursement,

TABLE 7.16
China's Disbursements in Terms of Assistance, 2000–09 (US$ million)

	Term	2000	2001	2002	2003	2004	2005	2006	2007	2008	2009 est.
Total disbursement by all the	Grant	—	347	347.7	373.4	367.2	438.8	458.6	567.3	681.7	699.1
	Loan	—	124.9	183.2	166.1	188.2	171.2	136.1	223.1	273.9	290.3
development partners	Total	466.8	471.9	530.9	539.5	555.4	610	594.7	790.4	955.6	989.4
	Grant	—	—	—	—	—	13.1	6.7	0.4	0.2	3
China	Loan	—	—	—	—	—	33.5	46.5	92	95.2	111.7
	Total	2.6	16.3	5.7	5.6	32.5	46.6	53.2	92.4	95.4	114.7
					Percentage of total						
	Grant	—	—	—	—	—	3	1.5	0.1	0	0.4
China	Loan	—	—	—	—	—	19.6	34.2	41.2	34.8	38.5
	Total	0.6	3.5	1.1	1	5.8	7.6	9	11.7	10	11.6

Source: The Cambodia Aid Effectiveness Report (CDC 2007, 2008, 2009).

an increase of 20 per cent on 2008, saw China ranked in second place after Japan.

The disbursement from China consists of three types of bilateral aid in the forms of grants, interest-free loans and concessional loans. Grants and interest-free loans are mostly channelled in kind through various projects, especially those directed to social welfare, material and technical assistance and personal training, according to the request of the country. Concessional loans are primarily captured in the profitability of the projects, namely infrastructure development, through contracting supplies of materials, technologies and services from China's state-owned companies (Davies 2008).

In terms of sectoral disbursement, China's disbursement was primarily allocated to the transport sector from 2005 to 2009 a robust trend that increased annually from 2006 to 2009 (Table 7.17), Compared to other major development partners, China was the largest contributor to this sector during 2007–09, followed by Japan and South Korea.

China has never hesitated to support Cambodia in areas that other lenders and donors have given up on due to related issues such as human rights, the lack of the Cambodian government's response on administrative procedures, the level of corruption, military and administrative reform, and the risky nature of the projects. Moreover, China actively encourages

TABLE 7.17
China's Disbursement by Sector, 2005–09 (US$ million)

Sector	2005	2006	2007	2008	2009	Total
Health		0.13				0.13
Education		0.38			0.08	0.46
Agriculture	1.71	0.07				1.78
Manufacturing, Mining and Trade	0.05					0.05
Information & Communication			8.85			8.85
Post & Telecommunications		8.46				8.46
Transportation	25.83	12.68	42.31	87.12	114.62	282.56
Community & Social Welfare Services	18.53	19.04	26.22			63.79
Culture & Arts		0.28	0.3			0.58
Environment & Conservation		0.02	0.02			0.04
Governance & Administration	0.52	12.18	14.75	8.29		35.75
Total	46.64	53.24	92.45	95.41	114.7	402.43

Source: The Cambodia Aid Effectiveness Report (CDC 2007, 2008, 2009).

FIGURE 7.16
Disbursement on Transportation by Major Partners (US$ million)

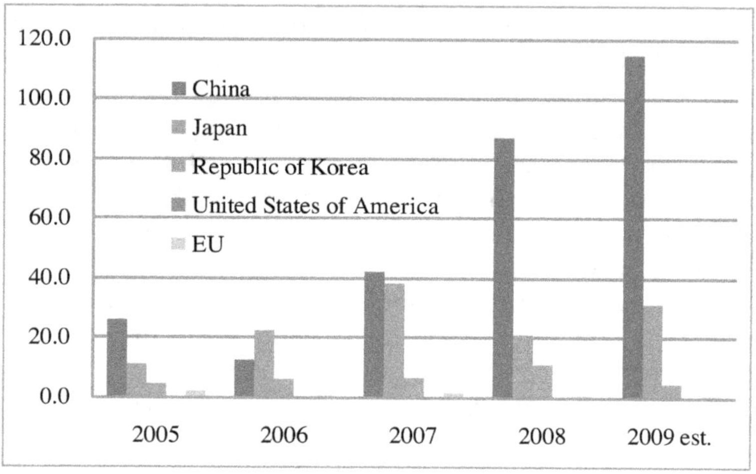

Source: The Cambodia Aid Effectiveness Report (CDC 2007, 2008, 2009).

business between its home investors and associates in Cambodia. This is indicated by approximately 90 per cent cooperation between Cambodian and Chinese private and semi-private firms (Phoun n.d.). Additionally, the aid from China is primarily based on the actual needs of Cambodia, and it is not linked to any condition or any repayment, i.e., "no strings attached". See Box 7.1. Therefore, Chinese development assistance has become increasingly attractive and demanded by the country.

Both Cambodia and China continue to strengthen their relationship through frequent mutual exchange visits. China is willing to expand commercial ties and allocate more disbursements to Cambodia for physical infrastructure and agriculture sector improvements (*Deum Ampil Newspaper* 2010). During the visit of Chinese Vice Premier Hui Liangy in March 2010, China signed three Memorandums of Understanding (MOU) with Cambodia, declaring its intention to boost crop production and upgrade the telecommunication systems in the country (Ek Madra 2010).

BOX 7.1

China's ODA to Improve Cambodia's Basic Physical Infrastructure, 2004–09

The notable rise of China's ODA can be chiefly chronicled through improvements in Cambodia's basic physical infrastructure, as evidenced in several main aid programmes:

- In 2004 China endorsed US$200 million as buyer's credit to build the Mekong and Tonle Sap bridges and two highways — Road Nos. 76 and 78. The company responsible for these constructions was Shanghai Construction Group of China.
- In 2006, RMB300 million was provided as non-refundable aid to build Cambodia's government office. Yunnan Construction Engineering Group undertook construction. Soon afterwards, under the GMS programme, China disbursed further concessional loans to build the Information Super Expressway. Another endorsement was the pledge of RMB100 million of interest-free loans for Cambodia's development activities.
- In 2007 China provided US$207 million under preferential buyer's credit loan for the construction of National Road No. 8 and a section of road No. 76, and Prek Tameak and Prek Kdam bridges. China further donated 200 small-sized diesel-powered water pumps for agricultural use to Cambodia and joined with multilateral donors in providing funds for the improvement of education and healthcare, improving infrastructure, rural development and agriculture. China's disbursement accounted for 13 per cent of the total US$690 million, which was a remarkable amount to Cambodia for its developopment process. As a bilateral donor, China kept allocating funds to Cambodia which was evident in the US$62,500 provided to Parliament and Inspection ministries for organizing their offices and transport equipment; the scholarships awarded to sixty Cambodian soldiers to undertake army training in China; and the nine naval patrol boats granted to safeguard oil installations in the Gulf of Thailand (*Rasmei Kampuchea 2007*).
- In 2008 China promised to endorse low-interest loans of US$55 million, at the same time allowing Cambodia to export extra volume of goods to China tax-free. China later pledged US$280 million in loans for infrastructure projects, the construction of irrigation systems in Battambang province, power transmission lines to Phnom Penh, the repair of a road linking Kapong Thom and Preah Vihear provinces, and the road from Stung Treng province to Ban-lung (*Rasmei Kampuchea 2008*).
- In May 2009, about US$73 million was provided as a concessional loan to build part of the main road in northeastern Cambodia to support the development of that area into a new economic zone. The road will be used for border trade, transport, and tourism with neighbouring countries in the GMS Triangle Development Framework. In July, approximately US$66.8 million was endorsed for road restoration in Kampong Thom, Kampong Cham, and Mondolkiri provinces (*Rasmei Kampuchea 2009*).

5.2 Methodologies and Analytical Framework

It appears that ODA plays an essential complementary role to other sources of development financing, especially in low-income countries like Cambodia. Also, ODA is a major vehicle for transferring both capital and technical knowledge from developed to developing countries. The challenge however is how to utilize ODA more efficiently and effectively in assisting the development and poverty reduction efforts of the recipient country.

Evaluating the impact of ODA in general or in a specific sector is a complex task as developmental outcomes and poverty dynamics are influenced by many factors outside the sphere of ODA operation. Importantly, the effects are even more difficult to quantify.

As stressed in the previous section on the magnitude of China's ODA, the marked increase in funding from China has mainly been directed to improving Cambodia's transport infrastructure. Hence, the impacts of China's ODA on poverty reduction are assessed through selected case studies on Chinese-funded transport infrastructure projects.

Transport infrastructure has long been assumed to contribute indirectly to poverty reduction. A number of studies, using different methodologies and with differing temporal and spatial coverage, provide considerable empirical evidence to validate the poverty impact of transport development. Setboonsarng (2006) reviews existing empirical findings and summarizes the 2005 ADBI Workshop on transport infrastructure and poverty reduction,[17] and presents the macro- and micro-level impacts of transport infrastructure. At macro-level, the transport infrastructure and poverty reduction linkage channels through economic growth. At micro-level, transport infrastructure contributes to poverty reduction in terms of the impact on income and non-income dimensions of poverty. In terms of income poverty, transport infrastructure opens up opportunities for the poor to raise the productivity of their limited resources (e.g. lowering the costs of inputs and facilitating access to credit, extension services, markets with better prices and agricultural diversification). Likewise, with non-income poverty, transport infrastructure can generate impacts by lowering the cost of services needed by the poor, and by complementing interventions that seek to improve access to health, education and other social services.

On this basis, two case studies were conducted using the analytical framework illustrated in Figure 7.17 to investigate the micro-level impacts

FIGURE 7.17
Analytical Framework of China's ODA in Cambodia

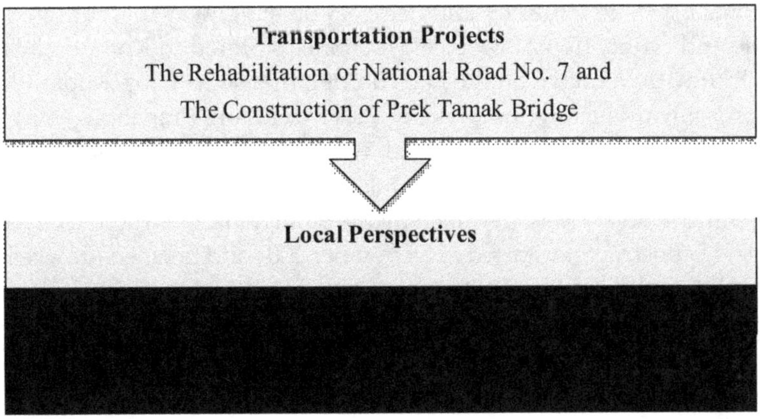

of Chinese-funded projects in Cambodia's transport sector in an attempt to assess the poverty effects of China's ODA.

5.3 Case Studies on China ODA Funded Projects in the Transport Sector

The two projects selected for case study are the rehabilitation of National Road No. 7 from Kratie to Trapeang Kriel (a border to Laos) which had been completed, and the construction of the Prek Tamak Bridge in Kandal province which was in progress at the time of study.

Focus group discussions (FGDs) with direct and indirect beneficiaries and target group representatives, and researchers' observations were used to gather mainly qualitative information primarily based on local people's perspectives. The main limitations of this assessment are the lack of quantitative data (conducting a survey would have been too costly given the budget) and the unevenness of time-series data on village social indicators (for example, school drop-out rate, mortality rate) to compare the situations before and after the road and bridge were built. Also, because the findings are largely dependent on subjective information, they cannot be used to generalize the impact of China's ODA on the whole of Cambodia.

Case Study: Rehabilitation of National Road No. 7 from Kratie to Trapeang Kriel (A Border to Laos)

National Road No. 7 is a 509-kilometre national highway that runs through Kratie and Stung Treng provinces. It connects Skuon in Kompong Cham province with Veun Sai on the Laos border, then joins Laos' Route 13 and runs northwards along the Mekong River to Luang Prabang.

The reconstruction of the road was funded by concessional loan of US$60.98 million and grant of US$2.43 million from the Chinese government, and was undertaken by the Shanghai Construction Group of China. Reconstruction started in November 2004 and finished in December 2007. National Road No. 7 is part of the road linkage for ASEAN countries and also completes Asian Highway No. 11: local people in Kratie and Stung Treng provinces generally refer to it as the ASEAN highway.

Findings

In each province, three villages located along the road and near the border were selected for focus group discussions to discover how the road construction had affected villagers' livelihoods. The villages of Ou Svay, O' Reussey Kandal and Reachea Nokol in Stung Treng province and O' Tanueng, Korsang and Sre Ror Neam in Kratie province were chosen.

The six to eleven participants in each FGD were selected with the help of the village chief, with a view to equal gender representation, diverse sources of income and a broad age range of 20–60 years old. The key points raised included the village situation before and after the road was repaired, likely impact on the villagers, and the relationship between villagers and outsiders throughout project implementation. The main sub-items covered travel time and costs, changes in livelihood patterns, access to market and social services, land values and investment development, safety, resettlement and rehabilitation, and possible impacts on other activities.

(a) Positive Impacts

The road has helped villagers by reducing the duration and cost of travelling to the provincial towns and markets. Villagers have better and easier access to education, healthcare services and credit, and the value of farm products and land has increased. The road has brought the villages within the reach of development organizations and new ideas on cultivation techniques and agricultural business. However, for villagers in Reachea Mongol, the road has only brought the opportunity of working for other people either outside or within the village as their land holdings are too small to grow much.

Travel time and costs: Villagers in Ou Svay village previously depended on boat transport to get to the capital of Stung Treng province, which would cost them up to KHR100,000 and they would have to spend a night in Stung Treng province. Now, they drive their own motorbike or travel by taxi and the journey takes just one to two hours. The cost of the 55-kilometre journey from O' Taneng village to Kratie province fell from KHR7,000 to KHR4,000 and now takes one hour by mini-bus or taxi compared to the three hours it used to take.

> Before, there was no point in buying a motorbike because there was no road. When we wanted to go somewhere, we had to wait until the taxi came to us or hitch a ride from a military truck. Now that there is a good road, we have been able to buy a motorbike with the money we have saved from selling our land and farm products, making it easier and faster for us to travel… Some grocers go to the provincial market almost every day.

Access to education and healthcare: Before the road was improved, the local school only taught grades 1 to 6 and children's education would stop at that point or some would even have dropped out earlier. This was due to the shortage of teachers, lack of school facilities and poor security when travelling to and from school. The school now teaches up to grade 9, and more children attend school because there are more teachers and better school facilities, i.e., tables, chairs and text books. Children can continue their education at secondary schools in nearby districts or provinces (8 to 55 kilometres away): a return fare costs KHR3,000 by motor-taxi or others who can afford the expense, rent a house close to the school. Prior to the road rehabilitation, access to health services was difficult and villagers used traditional medicines and treatment when ill. For childbirth, women just used herbs and relied on a traditional midwife which put them in imminent danger. The seriously ill would simply die at home or on the way to the healthcare centre, especially where health centres are located far from the village. With the better road, private healthcare providers have shown interest around the villages, and villagers have ready access to the public health centre. Also, the traditional midwife has been trained in safer delivery methods at the health centre. However, healthcare services in the villages are very slow to improve and can only deal with minor health problems. As a result, villagers still have to travel for better services available in nearby districts or to the province or Phnom Penh city, but they have better access to faster more readily available transport regardless of the circumstances.

Land value: Land prices have been escalating since the initial phase of the road construction which coincided with the land market boom in Cambodia. In O' Reussey Kandal village the land price along the road increased dramatically from virtually nil to US$100 for a 3 metres by 400 metres plot, and farm land was valued at US$2,000–3,000 per ha, whereas in Reachea Nokol village the price of 1 metre by 300 metres plot was US$600 and farm land was US$1,000 per ha. The buyers are from other provinces, namely Kampong Cham, Takeo, Prey Veng and Kampong Thom, and also Phnom Penh, and have bought land for farming and investment.

Access to markets: The prices of farm products rose because the road brings more buyers from further afield to the villages and villagers can now transport fresh produce to the market themselves, thereby increasing their bargaining power in setting prices. Crop prices rose from KHR200 per kilogram to KHR800–1,000 per kilogram, encouraging farmers to expand their farm production. The FGDs also reported that villagers used to let their produce rot because no one came to buy it or because transporting it to market was too difficult and costly.

> Brokers come to our house almost every day unlike before when they came only once a month... Even if they don't come to us, we can take our products to the provincial market ourselves.

Others: The villagers are enjoying a better quality of life with new motorcycles and house renovations paid for by selling their land and crops. Their children can now go to find work and learn new vocational skills such as crafts or motorcycle maintenance outside the villages. The road links the villages with development agencies, micro-finance institutes and tourists. This was reflected in the activities of Oxfam and Danida, such as digging wells, providing animal loans for livelihood earning, and helping to build paths in the villages. Micro-finance institutes such as Acleda, AMK and Thaneakea Phum provide opportunities for people to invest in their farming. CIVO has taught villagers handicraft skills. The road is attracting more tourists to visit potential eco-tourism sites near the villages (O' Reussey Kandal village).

(b) Negative Impacts

Some major concerns about the road construction were expressed:

Employment opportunities during construction: The construction project came complete in terms of labour, techniques and materials. Only a few local villagers were employed in the construction work and just for a few weeks.

Resettlement and rehabilitation: Some houses were damaged or demolished to make way for the road. Although compensation of US$1,000–2,500 for a house in good condition and US$300–600 for a poor one was paid, it was not much given the villagers had to move and resettle deeper into the forest.

Road safety and community security: The number of traffic accidents had increased due to the shortage of proper road warning signs, and poor quality road surface which is easily damaged. Incidence of theft had increased now that the villages are more accessible.

Conflict and the environment: The road has attracted several investment companies, mostly Chinese plantation and mining businesses, which have been granted government land affecting villagers' farmland and leading to conflict between villagers and the companies. Valuable wood has been lost where those companies have cleared forest to grow agro-industrial crops.

To sum up, the new road built under the Chinese disbursement project has provided villagers with more positive than negative benefits. The opportunity of growing more crops and learning from the experience of newcomers as well as passers-by has improved villagers quality of life. The road has been a complementary input, increasing the opportunity of getting more education as well as better healthcare services. The villagers can learn about the outside world from going to the provinces or Phnom Penh city. They can travel further and more easily to find work. The villages can be reached by development agencies which allocate social services to the villagers as well as help in taking care of forest resources. In short, the roads have brought more livelihood choices.

Case Study: Construction of Prek Tamak Bridge in Kandal Province

The Prek Tamak Bridge is located in Kandal province about 40 kilometres north of Phnom Penh city. The project was started in June 2007 and scheduled for completion in September 2010. By providing a crossing over the Mekong River, the project creates another east-west link for the country. Construction is supported by a concessional loan of US$43.5 million from the government of China under contract with China's Shanghai Construction Group.

Two FGDs were conducted, one in Kampong Domrey village, and the other in Svay Ath Leu village, Prek Tamaik commune, Kasach Kandal district. Kampong Domrey comprises 274 households. Eight participants (one male, seven females) were selected for the FGD by the village chief based on their standard of living which was defined as poor. One of the participants was a member of the commune council and a village chief. Svay Ath Leu has a total of 207 households. Seven people were purposely selected for the FGD according to their occupation as vendors around the ferry site. However, more people than expected joined the discussion which finally involved seventeen participants whose occupations or family members' occupations were vendors (cane juice, shell-fish, food, fruit and beverages) at the ferry dock. The FGDs were held in December 2009 while construction of the bridge was in progress and villagers were still using the ferry to cross the river. The FGD participants were asked what benefits they expected the new bridge to bring.

(a) Positive Impacts

Travel time and costs: Once the bridge is built they will be able to cross the river whenever they wish, whereas now they have to wait for the ferry, the crossing takes around one to one and a half hours, and the service only operates between 5 a.m. and 5 p.m. They will also spend less money on travelling. For example, the return trip from their village to Phnom Penh now costs KHR40,000. When they use the ferry, they have to pay KHR500 for a motor bike and KHR300 per person. If they travel by taxi, the return trip costs around KHR20,000. Because there is no night-time ferry service, in an emergency they would have to spend even more money on the ferry. When the bridge is open, they will not have those extra costs.

Changes in livelihood: People expected to have easier access to market because they will be able to travel at any time. In addition, the prices of goods produced in the village are going to increase because they will be able to sell direct to retailers rather than to middlemen. For instance, at the time of study the price of bricks in their village was KHR150 per piece, and without having to pay for the ferry crossing they would be able to get KHR200 per piece. In addition, villagers could get work in Phnom Penh because they will be able commute easily without having to spend money on accommodation in the city. Besides, they expected that new restaurants would open in their village, so there should be more local jobs available. Also, they were expecting their village to be connected to the national grid. At the time of study about 70 per cent of villagers were connected to a private electricity supply costing KHR2,800 per kilowatt. However, the participants reported hardship from the loss of family income, especially those whose sole income source is from selling around the ferry terminal. Still, they would prefer to have the bridge than not. This is because the income made from selling around the ferry site is minor or is intermittent at times; it is only supplementary income.

Access to social services: Students who study in Phnom Penh might be able to commute daily rather than renting accommodation and more students will be able to access school. When seriously ill, villagers will be able to get to hospital in good time.

Land value and investment: Land prices are expected to rise once the bridge is operational because of the easier accessibility. Land value around the site shot up during the initial stages of construction. Despite increasing land prices, villagers said they would not sell their residential land as they had nowhere to move to afterwards. The FGDs further revealed that the villagers expected to see future investment, though not immediately.

Resettlement and rehabilitation: The bridge had affected nearly 100 households. It was being constructed on people's land or houses and the government had paid compensation of US$18 per square metre for land or houses near the bridge, US$15 per square metre for other residential land, US$8 per square metre for farm land, US$5.30 per square metre for other land. Most of the people affected by the construction and who had to move resettled in the same village.

(b) Negative Impacts

Some local people who have small businesses near the ferry terminal may lose their supplementary income once the bridge is built, but they were optimistic about the new prospects the bridge might bring. On balance they felt they stood to gain, for instance the time and money that will be saved on travelling, the opportunity of finding jobs further a field, better access to more markets and getting higher prices for their products.

Mostly Chinese workers were employed in the bridge construction: no local workers were employed.

6. CONCLUSIONS AND POLICY IMPLICATIONS

This section outlines the evidence from each component of our impact analysis — trade, investment and ODA — linking them to poverty implications. It should be kept in mind that the findings are mainly drawn from the case studies.

6.1 Trade

The last decade and a half has seen a significant expansion of bilateral trade between Cambodia and China; however, Cambodia's negative trade balance continues to widen at an average annual growth rate of 34 per cent. Using framework developed by Jenkins and Edwards (2004), the study examined Cambodia's poverty effect from China through three specific dimensions, namely export to China, import from China and export to the third market. The results are summarized below.

There were noticeable changes in the pattern of export shares to China between 1992 and 2008. The share of labour-intensive agriculture dropped substantially from 51.4 per cent in 1992 to 9.1 per cent in 2000 and then rebounded to 29.6 per cent in 2008. The decline was mainly due to the reduction in natural rubber export when many old unproductive rubber trees were felled, while the rebound stemmed primarily from the rising export of natural rubber as several thousand recently replanted rubber trees matured for tapping and the increased export of live animals and fish between 2000 and 2008. Export of labour-intensive textiles and garments to China also showed a marked upward trend, rising from 3.2 per cent in 1992 to 28.2 per cent in 2008. The rising shares of these two product groups would have contributed to poverty reduction in Cambodia provided that they also generated significant employment. However, there was considerable drop in the export of other labour-intensive manufactures between 2000 and 2008, which was offset by the significant rise in the export of forestry products during the same period.

Data on Cambodia's imports from China show a small and declining share of labour-intensive agricultural products between 1992 and 2008. It appears that competition between the two countries in domestic agriculture markets is unlikely. Additionally, some of the products that are not of Cambodian specialization, such as fresh apples, dried grapes, fresh pears and quinces, are complementary. Despite labour-intensive agriculture's tiny import share, the regular and constant rise in the import share of certain products in this category, albeit small, could pose competitive threat in the future. More importantly, the substantial jump in labour-intensive textiles and garments' import share between 1992 and 2008 creates no competition in the domestic market provided that the products are assembled for re-export to the third market. The rising import share of said products appears to create employment in Cambodia, thereby having a positive poverty effect, but hinders opportunity for the development of domestic backward linkage industries in the domestic economy.

In terms of consumer gain, data show that the import share of pro-poor consumer goods increased between 1992 and 2000, but then declined from 2000 to 2008.This indicates that poor consumers' gain from the import of cheap Chinese consumer products abated slightly during the second half of the period, making China's contributing role to poverty reduction in Cambodia less likely. Pro-poor products that have been imported regularly include fish, cereal, vegetables, fruit, beverages, articles of apparel and worn clothing.

Analysis of export to the third market reveals that Cambodia and China could compete in the third market in manufactured goods, but not agricultural products. Further examination of the top twelve garment exports to the United States and the EU reveals potential competition with China in the U.S. market, but not in the EU given Cambodia's tiny EU garment market share of 0.01 to 1.0 per cent. Among the twelve products in the U.S. market, China's declining share and Cambodia's rising share of knit/crochet apparel (SITC 8459) creates opportunity for Cambodian producers, while the steep rise in China's market share of the remaining top twelve products could pose potential threat. This could have negative implications for poverty alleviation in Cambodia.

6.2 Investment

A major investor in Cambodia, China's investment in the country has grown substantially since 2004 and is concentrated in natural resource development (petroleum, mining, energy and hydropower plants), tourism and garment sectors. China's investors in Cambodia have explored low labour costs, political stability, investment incentives and newly emerging markets for Cambodia's MFN status.

The contribution of China's investment in Cambodia's garment sector is examined through the case study in terms of employment and income generation, remittance, and opportunity for skills transfer and capacity building. China's investment in this sector has shown a positive contribution to employment creation (63 per cent of the interviewed workers were self-employed before joining the Chinese factories). Their average earning is more than double the overall poverty line in Phnom Penh at 2006 prices. However, the net benefits between previous (self-employment) and current employment are not captured in the objectives of this study.

The case study also reveals that garment workers' remittance is chiefly used for household daily food consumption, followed by supporting the education of family members, paying debt and buying farm land, all of which would help their households move out of deficiency in the short and long run. This reflects workers' perceptions on the improvements in their household's economic status since they have been working in the garment factories, i.e., they are able to invest in buying land, motor boat and livestock in order to have regular income or more sources of income. On the other hand, most workers stated their dissatisfaction with the factory working environment including healthcare, work space, sanitation, and annual and sick leave entitlements. Opportunity and support for capacity and skill development were rated low, while the only skills and knowledge they have gained from their current job are basic skills learned from doing their daily work. Importantly, knowledge and skills transfer is a major gap in China's investment in Cambodia, especially in the garment sector. Although this sector does not require much skill, opportunity and support for skill development should be a complying component for foreign investment in Cambodia.

6.3 ODA

China has been a great development partner for either funds channelling or investment gathering for Cambodia. China's ODA also plays significant roles in financing Cambodia's development agenda as an additional public resource through supporting public service delivery. Cambodia has been granted aid with little quibbling over transparency and modality (Chan et al. 2008). China's assistance to Cambodia ranges from diplomatic ties to economic and investment interventions. But mostly China provides concessional loans to develop physical infrastructure, especially road construction and restoration. This study explored the contribution of two China ODA-funded transport projects to local people's livelihoods and local communities' social development.

Transport is crucial for the development of local communities as well as the nation as a whole. Without physical access to resources and markets, health, education and other social services, the quality of life suffers, growth stagnates and poverty reduction cannot be sustained. Also, poor roads limit the facilitating role of transport in both production and consumption activities.

The contribution of the China-funded projects to improve National Road No. 7 and construct Prek Tamak Bridge to livelihood changes and social development in the project areas are viewed from the perspectives of local people in terms of travel time and costs, access to market and social services, investment and business development, safety and other possible impacts. The findings of the two case studies suggest that villagers perceive they have gained more positive than negative benefits. In short, the better road and new bridge seem to be complementary inputs for developing or attracting both income earning and non-income opportunities that contribute to their livelihoods and social progress and to scaling down the poverty trap.

Case study respondents stressed that the road and bridge have significantly reduced travelling time and transport costs. This leads to the greater availability of inputs and consumption goods. Local farm produce can be sold at higher prices due to easier access to more markets and because more middlemen come to the villages. Crop diversification is another notable factor as newcomers and extension services bring in new information and techniques. The case studies also show villagers' increased use of education and health services resulting from road improvements as well as other interventions such as the greater willingness of professional staff to work in areas with guaranteed access and more reliable delivery of supplies. In addition, a new road encourages commercially operated services. Other positive impacts significantly raised by local people are the links to development agencies, micro-finance institutes, and tourists, which create business and employment opportunities for local people.

On the other hand, the idea that transport infrastructure can reduce poverty by creating employment is not confirmed by the local people in the two case studies. The construction and maintenance of a road is labour-intensive and could provide job opportunities to local people, though these activities are only occasional and therefore cannot represent a long-term strategy for reducing poverty. Construction activities were contracted with China's state-owned companies in the form of materials, technologies as well as labour — even unskilled workers. Only a few local people were employed during the construction period and just for a few weeks. Another concern raised by participants and local authorities is that since the road improvements, some Chinese plantation and mining investment companies have been granted concession land in the areas, leading to conflicts between villagers and companies, deforestation, and villagers' loss of access to land and forest resources. Issues of poor road safety due to inadequate traffic signs and increased theft in the villages were also raised.

Vendors who had a small business near the ferry terminal at the time of our survey stood to lose their supplementary income once the bridge is open, though they still felt optimistic about having the bridge.

6.4 Policy Implications

The discussion in the previous section highlights the main findings from each dimension of our analysis on China's trade, investment and ODA along with the poverty implications. In order to have more desired effect, some further steps should be taken into account.

Trade

From the empirical findings it is clear that deepening trade and investment relations with China could potentially contribute to poverty reduction in Cambodia through employment creation in labour-intensive sectors and the import of pro-poor consumer goods from China, which are complementary products for the domestic market. In order to better contribute to poverty reduction, it is imperative that the following steps be taken:

- Exploit opportunities to export labour-intensive agricultural products of Cambodian specialization, such as fish, live animals, rice, rubber and other light-manufactured products with preferential treatment from China under ACFTA framework, which would to a certain extent ease the burden of negative trade balance and enhance poverty reduction.

- Promote access to and increase availability of trade finance for small and medium enterprises as they indirectly engage in export activities.
- Promote Cambodian agricultural products through trade fairs or trade mission in China.
- Lobby Chinese garment producers to source their inputs from local producers and establish backward linkage industries in Cambodia.
- Encourage and support local producers to engage in backward linkage sectors in the garment industry.
- Adopt a computerized customs system to reduce the number of documents and signatures and informal fees, i.e. ASYCUDA World system at Sihanoukville Port, which will reduce unpredictability and improve investors' confidence.

Investment

The country's rich endowment of natural resources, extensive timber, mineral and hydropower potential, and petroleum reserves as well as its intensive low-cost labour force makes Cambodia attractive to China's investment and development assistance and assures the country of a positive attitude from China. As seen in the case study on the garment sector, China's investment impacted positively on employment and income generation, but not on skill development. The key issue is the extent to which benefits from China's investment spill over into the domestic sector in a synergistic relationship. Hence, policy interventions are needed to create necessary conditions for positive spillover and attract Chinese or other foreign investment to those sectors that have the potential to transfer skills and technologies, thus leading to innovation and increased productivity, improved domestic production and quality, and domestic backward and forward linkages.

ODA

Besides the positive impacts from the better road and new bridge, some courses of action at both local and national level should be considered:

- Diversification or expansion of livelihood opportunities for vendors and businesses that stand to lose income from trading at the ferry site and those who have lost access to land and forest resources.
- Dissemination of traffic information and road safety awareness guidelines to villagers through the commune councils.
- Negotiation with the Chinese government to employ Cambodian labour in China's ODA projects to promote the transfer of technologies and skills to Cambodia.
- Promotion of capacity building programmes at local level should be a complying condition for China's ODA.

6.5 Future Research

Based on the limitations of this study, more in-depth empirical analyses of the linkage between foreign investment and poverty reduction and the notion of infrastructure development and poverty reduction for Cambodia, at both macro and micro levels, should be undertaken.

APPENDICES

Appendix 7A

Classification of SITC 3-digit Products According to Production and Consumption Categories* (Jenkins & Edwards 2004, p. 38)

Production Categories

1. Labour-intensive agricultural products — 037; 042; 05; 06; 07; 231; 232
2. Other agricultural products — 00; 01; 02; 034; 035; 036; 04 (-042); 08; 09; 12; 21; 22; 26 (-266 and 269); 29; 411; 42; 43
3. Forestry — 24; 25
4. Minerals and petroleum — 233; 266; 27; 28; 32; 33; 34; 35; 68
5. Labour-intensive textiles and garment products — 65; 84
6. Other labour-intensive manufactures — 269; 61; 63; 665; 666; 821; 831; 851; 89 (-896 and 897)
7. Other manufactured products — 11; 51; 52; 53; 54; 55; 56; 58; 59; 62; 64; 66 (-665 and 666); 67; 69; 71; 72; 73; 74; 75; 76; 77; 78; 79; 812; 87; 88; 896; 897; 9

Consumption Categories

The following SITC products were identified as products likely to be consumed by low-income consumers. These consist of food, beverages, tobacco, garments and footwear.

00; 01; 02; 03; 04; 05; 06; 07; 09; 11; 12; 269; 84; 851

*Where a 2-digit SITC classification is indicated, this means that all 3-digit classes within it are included in the product group.

Appendix 7B

Table 7B.1
Share of All Products Exported to China, 1992–2008 at 3-digit Level (%)

SITC 3	Product names	1992	2000	2007	2008
001	Live animals except fish		0.3522	2.0122	6.2231
012	Meat neces. fresh/chilled/frozen		0.001		
034	Fish, live/fresh/chilled/frozen		0.7799	1.6226	1.2503
036	Crustaceans molluscs etc		1.0249	0.672	0.9446
037	Fish/shell-fish, prepared/preserved			0.1935	
042	Rice				0.0005
054	Vegetables, fresh/chilled/frozen		0.0047		
057	Fruit/nuts, fresh/dried	16.833			
058	Fruit preserved/fruit preps		0.0057		
059	Fruit/vegetable juices			0.0358	0.0248
112	Alcoholic beverages				0.0101
222	Oil seeds etc — soft oil			0.0381	
231	Natural rubber/latex/etc	34.551	9.0992	21.569	29.606
246	Wood chips/waste				0.7213
247	Wood in rough/squared		0.5677	31.605	13.027
248	Wood simply worked		2.1666	15.452	13.669
269	Worn clothing etc			2.6466	3.1204
273	Stone/sand/gravel			0.0141	0.066
282	Ferrous waste/scrap				0.2571
287	Base metal ore			0.0074	
292	Crude veg materials nes	14.455		0.0803	0.0159
335	Residual petrol. prods			0.0001	
524	Other inorganic chemical				0.0001
541	Pharmaceutical & medicament			0.0001	
542	Medicaments include vet			0.0125	
551	Essential oil/perfume/flavouring			3.6379	0.3337
581	Plastic tube/pipe/hose				0.001
598	Misc chemical prods nes		0.0010		
611	Leather			0.0042	0.0336
634	Veneer/plywood/etc		79.439	0.0506	
635	Wood manufactures nes		2.3286	0.043	0.2263
641	Paper/paperboard		0.0001		

SITC 3	Product names	1992	2000	2007	2008
642	Cut paper/board/articles			0.0003	
651	Textile yarn			8.5324	1.2187
652	Cotton fabrics, woven			0.843	0.0374
653	Man-made woven fabrics		0.003	0.2308	0.0458
654	Woven textile fabric nes		0.0001	0.1738	
655	Knit/crochet fabrics			0.7581	0.2251
656	Tulle/lace/embroidery/trim			0.0332	0.0076
657	Special yarns/fabrics		0.0001	0.0196	0.0462
658	Ready-made textile articles	3.2624		0.0016	
661	Leather manufactures		0.0002	0.0014	0.0045
664	Glass				0.0003
665	Glassware				0.0005
666	Pottery			0.0053	0.0277
667	Pearls/precious stones			0.0016	
679	Iron/steel pipe/tube/etc				0.0004
694	Nails/screws/nuts/bolts		0.0007		0.0008
697	Hold equipment				0.0003
699	Base metal manufacture		0.0003		0.006
716	Rotating electric plant			0.001	
718	Power generating equipment	6.3992			
723	Civil engineering plant				0.0144
724	Textile/leather machinery		0.0036		
728	Special industrial machinery				0.0009
742	Pumps for liquids				0.0022
744	Mechanical handling equipment	6.009			
747	Taps/cocks/valves				0.0007
752	Computer equipment				0.0045
763	Sound/television recorders etc				0.0002
764	Telecomm equipment nes			0.0102	0.0059
771	Elect power transmission equip				0.0017
772	Electric circuit equipment			0.0004	0.0405
776	Valves/transistors/etc			0.0024	0.001
778	Electrical equipment nes	18.491			0.0015
784	Motor vehicle parts/access			0.0001	
785	Motorcycles/cycles/etc			0.0016	

continued on next page

Table 7B.1 — *cont'd*

SITC 3	Product names	1992	2000	2007	2008
813	Lighting fixtures etc				0.0002
821	Furniture/stuff furnishing			0.1683	0.8679
831	Trunks and cases			0.001	
841	Men/boys wear, woven		4.1851	1.1544	5.0744
842	Women/girl clothing women			0.3848	0.6723
843	Men/boy wear knit/crochet			1.4856	1.793
844	Women/girl wear knit/crochet			1.0931	2.0472
845	Articles of apparel nes		0.0000	4.6233	17.022
846	Clothing accessories		0.0206	0.0031	0.004
848	Headgear/non-text clothing		0.0003	0.0009	0.0007
851	Footwear			0.5635	0.9043
874	Measure/control app nes			0.0014	0.0016
885	Watches and clocks		0.0126		
892	Printed matter		0.0013	0.0328	
893	Articles nes of plastics		0.001	0.0363	0.0575
894	Baby carriage/toy/game/sport				0.0007
897	Jewellery			0.0011	
898	Musical instrument/records			0.0026	
899	Misc manufacture articles nes		0.0007	0.135	0.3296

Note: Share of export to China to total export to China.
Source: UN ComTrade (2009).

Table 7B.2
Share of All Products Imported from China, 1992–2008 at 3-digit Level (%)

SITC 3	Product names	1992	2000	2007	2008
001	Live animals except fish				0.00952
016	Meat/offal preserved		0.00055		
017	Meat/offal preserved nes	0.08425		0.00095	
022	Milk prep. excluding butter/cheese		0.04319	0.00007	
025	Eggs, albumin		0.00018		
034	Fish, live/fresh/chilled/frozen		0.00007		
036	Crustaceans molluscs etc		0.00005		
037	Fish/shellfish, prep/pres		0.00236	0.02132	0.04885
042	Rice		0.00827		
048	Cereal etc flour/starch		0.0134	0.09388	0.337
054	Vegetables, fresh/chilled/frozen		0.00068	0.01321	0.00087
056	Vegetable root/tuber prep/pres	0.01262	0.14422	0.09495	0.03198
057	Fruit/nuts, fresh/dried		0.07736	0.0162	0.0539
058	Fruit preserved/fruit preps		0.02109	0.03298	
061	Sugar/molasses/honey	1.84029	0.00543	0.01187	0.00014
062	Sugar confectionery	0.09468	0.023	0.10214	0.09587
071	Coffee/coffee substitute		0.00829		
074	Tea and mate				0.00323
075	Spices		0.00299		
081	Animal feed		0.02587	0.00085	0.00591
091	Margarine/shortening			0.00718	0.00416
098	Edible products n.e.s.		0.31752	0.09061	0.04174
111	Beverage non-alcohol n.e.s.	0.66259	0.10683	0.03698	0.06718
112	Alcoholic beverages	0.30194	0.09179	0.89364	1.03233
121	Tobacco, raw and wastes		0.55311	0.34514	0.133
122	Tobacco, manufactured		3.83837	0.46196	0.28224
222	Oil seeds etc - soft oil			0.0023	
223	Oil seeds-not soft oil			0.001	
231	Natural rubber/latex/etc		0.00197		
232	Rubber synthetic/waste/etc		0.0003	0.00013	0.01169
248	Wood simply worked		0.00011	0.00664	0.00406

continued on next page

Table 7B.2 — *cont'd*

SITC 3	Product names	1992	2000	2007	2008
251	Pulp and waste paper			0.00281	0.00947
266	Synthetic spinning fibre			0.00168	0.00855
269	Worn clothing etc			0.00372	0.009
272	Fertilizers crude			0.0013	0.00021
273	Stone/sand/gravel		0.02655	0.07052	0.0179
277	Natural abrasives n.e.s.		0.00367	0.00094	0.00311
278	Other crude minerals		0.13092	0.00236	0.02637
281	Iron ore/concentrates				0.00015
283	Copper ores/concentrates		0.00152		
285	Aluminium ores/concentrates/etc			0.00016	
291	Crude animal material n.e.s.				0.00373
292	Crude vegetable materials n.e.s.		0.01051	0.02274	0.00099
322	Briquettes/lignite/peat			0.00068	
334	Heavy petrol/bitum oils		0.26001	0.36809	0.91359
335	Residual petrol. prods			0.00002	0.00314
342	Liquid propane/butane				0.51737
511	Hydrocarbons/derivatives		0.00392	0.0159	0.03792
512	Alcohols/phenols/derivatives		0.0073	0.00753	0.00075
513	Carboxylic acid compound		0.02104	0.01336	0.02302
514	Nitrogen function compound		1.05954	0.16193	0.06416
515	Organic-inorganic compounds		0.05858	0.03344	0.02539
516	Other organic compounds		0.04296	0.01211	0.0137
522	Elements/oxides/hal salt		0.11811	0.0385	0.01659
523	Metal salts of inorganic acid		0.10523	0.09365	0.09607
524	Other inorganic chemical		0.03267	0.00003	0.00077
531	Synthetic org colour agents		0.02146	0.00237	0.0014
532	Dyeing/tanning extracts		0.00005		
533	Pigments/paints/varnish		0.09016	0.06972	0.06407
541	Pharmaceuticals excluding medicaments		0.28184	0.21826	0.17008
542	Medicaments including vetinary supplies	0.03652	0.47826	0.86327	0.80181
551	Essential oil/perfume/flavouring		0.04672	0.10437	0.13017
553	Perfume/toiletries/cosmetics		0.00241	0.17828	0.10624

SITC 3	Product names	1992	2000	2007	2008
554	Soaps/cleansers/polishes	0.16069	0.20416	0.08388	0.04197
562	Manufactured fertilisers		0.0068	0.02985	0.03688
571	Primary ethylene polymer		0.00922	0.04005	0.02612
572	Styrene primary polymers			0.01741	0.00086
573	Vinyl chloride etc polymers			0.00145	0.01862
574	Polyacetals/polyesters		0.00107	0.00014	0.02518
575	Plastic nes-primary form		0.01034	0.01913	0.02286
581	Plastic tube/pipe/hose		0.00844	0.19971	0.14751
582	Plastic sheets/film/etc		0.07706	0.15332	0.17389
583	Monofilament rods/sticks		0.00455	0.00587	0.00562
591	Household/garden chemicals		0.04153	0.03352	0.03713
592	Starches/glues/etc.		0.02345	0.05477	0.07511
593	Explosives/pyrotechnics			0.03766	0.05766
597	Oil etc additives/fluids		0.00008	0.00168	0.00084
598	Misc chemical prods nes		0.01998	0.07384	0.16101
611	Leather		0.10046	0.22987	0.06989
612	Leather manufactures		0.00216	0.00165	0.00283
613	Fur skins tanned/dressed				0.01637
621	Rubber materials		0.04022	0.07521	0.05973
625	Rubber tyres/treads		0.76485	0.33168	0.30054
629	Articles of rubber nes		0.10853	0.06459	0.14593
633	Cork manufactures			0.00005	
634	Veneer/plywood/etc		0.00356	0.02489	0.07754
635	Wood manufactures n.e.s.		0.00328	0.04424	0.0194
641	Paper/paperboard		0.60196	0.31687	0.25305
642	Cut paper/board/articles		0.62733	0.43079	0.42958
651	Textile yarn		1.42078	2.48547	2.58503
652	Cotton fabrics, woven		21.2794	15.6682	13.4696
653	Man-made woven fabrics		6.55946	7.0439	5.38476
654	Woven textile fabric nes		2.94135	0.51125	0.69596
655	Knit/crochet fabrics		13.2108	28.5606	26.3276
656	Tulle/lace/embroidery/trimetc		0.28478	1.19186	0.94483
657	Special yarns/fabrics		0.60757	0.68895	0.69375
658	Made-up textile articles		0.02915	0.21196	0.20152
659	Floor coverings etc.		0.01237	0.03993	0.03245

continued on next page

Table 7B.2 — *cont'd*

SITC 3	Product names	1992	2000	2007	2008
661	Lime/cement/construction materials/	40.3933	0.10128	0.2819	0.37723
662	Clay/refractory material	1.786	0.49292	2.69139	3.08905
663	Mineral manufactures nes		0.06801	0.12127	0.07552
664	Glass	1.23345	0.47847	0.32501	0.48312
665	Glassware	3.08465	0.03021	0.14412	0.21236
666	Pottery	0.63646	1.45092	0.537	0.35556
673	Flat rolled iron/st prod	0.25065	0.09859	0.13819	0.01279
674	Rolled plated m-steel		0.00542	0.62191	0.54692
675	Flat rolled alloy steel		0.00064	0.00462	0.0722
676	Iron/steel bars/rods/etc	25.5067	6.9837	0.87978	2.25324
677	Iron/steel railway material			0.00452	
678	Iron/steel wire	0.07518	0.2353	0.04464	0.11492
679	Iron/steel pipe/tube/etc		0.54115	0.49922	0.36789
682	Copper		0.00333	0.05492	0.02731
684	Aluminium		0.01236	0.22761	0.14167
685	Lead		0.00003		
686	Zinc		0.00004	0.00004	
691	Iron/steel/aluminium structures		1.72209	0.80198	1.14679
692	Metal store/transport container		0.00918	0.37736	0.08989
693	Wire products excluding ins electricity		0.04572	0.10745	0.6551
694	Nails/screws/nuts/bolts		0.02194	0.10694	0.09939
695	Hand/machine tools	1.9072	0.34065	0.24378	0.23708
696	Cutlery		0.20313	0.0196	0.01493
697	Base metal household equipment		0.10399	0.04736	0.03666
699	Base metal manufacture nes	0.17153	0.51193	0.48182	0.43256
711	Steam generating boilers		0.08127	0.06753	0.87924
712	Steam/vapour turbines				0.17038
713	Internal combust engines	1.09634	1.89992	1.76467	2.16358
714	Engines non-electric nes			0.00001	
716	Rotating electrical plant	0.44833	0.65085	0.65028	1.07005
718	Power generating equipment nes	0.08661		0.00042	0.05799

SITC 3	Product names	1992	2000	2007	2008
721	Agriculture machine excluding tractor	0.47872	0.00939	0.02756	0.11745
722	Tractors	0.55781	0.06027	0.04352	0.10807
723	Civil engineering plant	0.08035	0.02686	0.64169	0.54447
724	Textile/leather machinery		2.43813	1.58974	0.93542
725	Paper industry machinery		0.20473	0.06741	0.05693
726	Printing industry machinery		0.02999	0.01022	0.02077
727	Food processing machines	0.49281	0.13988	0.08192	0.35903
728	Special industrial machines nes	7.8745	1.04036	0.58708	0.52136
731	Mach-tools remove material		0.01896	0.01326	0.02226
733	Mtl m-tools w/o mtl-rmvl		0.0161	0.00276	0.03128
735	Metal machine tool parts		0.00087		0.00042
737	Metalworking machine nes		0.00273	0.02966	0.05484
741	Industrial heat/cool equipment	1.31248	0.31729	0.70361	0.57535
742	Pumps for liquids	0.13706	0.15695	0.377	0.4076
743	Fans/filters/gas pumps	0.45103	0.13327	0.40265	0.29792
744	Mechanical handling equipment	1.34276	0.07906	0.61571	0.78082
745	Non-electrical machines nes	1.21536	0.09557	0.13078	0.22769
746	Ball/roller bearings		0.01415	0.02877	0.03141
747	Taps/cocks/valves	0.00641	0.03689	0.07573	0.06458
748	Mechanical transmission equipment		0.06318	0.03619	0.14016
749	Non-electrical parts/acc machine		0.0149	0.03835	0.03679
751	Office machines		0.01061	0.10893	0.06364
752	Computer equipment		0.0192	0.08929	0.06227
759	Office equipment parts/accessories		0.00326	0.04715	0.03563
761	Television receivers		5.0272	0.13524	0.08937
762	Radio broadcast receiver		0.03094	0.00146	0.0023
763	Sound/television recorders etc		0.00028	0.00067	0.05767
764	Telecomm equipment nes	0.21517	1.87375	5.71636	5.31392
771	Electric power transmission equipment	0.02912	0.03766	0.18374	0.75807
772	Electric circuit equipment	0.40462	0.12704	0.22214	0.62065
773	Electrical distribution equipment	0.28229	0.01354	0.82665	1.2714

continued on next page

Table 7B.2 — *cont'd*

SITC 3	Product names	1992	2000	2007	2008
774	Medical etc electro diagnose equipment		0.01581	0.02645	0.04526
775	Domestic equipment	0.05246	0.02691	0.0283	0.04356
776	Valves/transistors/etc	0.02527	0.00137	0.07706	0.0641
778	Electrical equipment nes	0.91781	0.57849	0.35895	0.58521
781	Passenger cars etc		0.01048	0.04338	0.02239
782	Goods/service vehicles	0.7972		0.65014	0.65833
783	Road motor vehicles nes			0.05197	0.00321
784	Motor vehicle parts/accessories	0.03052	0.02185	0.1907	0.25128
785	Motorcycles/cycles/etc	0.37667	2.10005	1.44051	1.48437
786	Trailers/caravans/etc	0.00424	0.00517	0.03102	0.01017
791	Railway vehicles/equipment			0.0045	
793	Ships/boats/etc		0.01069	3.10741	2.01862
811	Prefabricated buildings		0.00436	0.08251	0.11951
812	Sanitary/plumb/heat fixture		0.04137	0.06964	0.09925
813	Lighting fixtures etc	0.11955	0.20663	0.25854	0.33261
821	Furniture/stuff furnishing		0.07494	0.18578	0.30184
831	Trunks and cases		0.1649	0.04484	0.49168
841	Men/boys wear, woven		0.00949	0.00789	0.04977
842	Women/girl clothing woven		0.09733	0.0005	0.00046
843	Men/boy wear knit/crochet		0.26984	0.06986	0.65166
844	Women/girls wear knit/crochet		0.12894	0.16501	0.73263
845	Articles of apparel nes		3.1879	2.44795	2.03402
846	Clothing accessories		0.7803	0.95889	0.84454
848	Headgear/non-text clothing	0.06452	0.50618	0.19031	0.11617
851	Footwear	0.1705	3.90183	0.48847	0.42219
871	Optical instruments nes		0.0001	0.00234	0.00175
872	Medical/etc instruments	0.00507	0.04669	0.1053	0.19009
873	Meters and counters nes	0.11508	0.02697	0.01176	0.01818
874	Measure/control app nes	0.02464	0.04451	0.05894	0.06315
881	Photographic equipment		0.00001	0.00081	0.00298
882	Photographic supplies		0.02741	0.03857	0.02604
884	Optical fibres		0.04329	0.01215	0.03329
885	Watches and clocks	0.0141	0.57079	0.00259	0.00186

SITC 3	Product names	1992	2000	2007	2008
891	Arms and ammunition	0.28472	0.00031	0.01246	0.02617
892	Printed matter		0.0725	0.22723	0.18773
893	Articles nes of plastics	2.2192	0.78243	0.47005	0.43092
894	Baby carriage/toy/game/sport	0.0183	0.08321	0.0448	0.07383
895	Office/stationery supply		0.23431	0.06915	0.06686
896	Art/collections/antiques		0.00078	0.00013	
897	Jewellery		0.00035	0.02157	0.03019
898	Musical instruments/records		0.00759	0.10048	0.35234
899	Miscellaneous manufacture articles nes	0.00966	0.68267	0.56453	0.54788

Note: Share of import from China to total import to China.
Source: UN ComTrade (2009).

Table 7B.3
Garment Factories Registered as Members of GMAC, January 2010

Country	No. of Factory	Total No. of Worker*	Country	No. of Factory	Total No. of Worker*
Taiwan	61	77,245	Taiwan + USA	3	3,657
China	41	40,394	China + Hong Kong	4	3,632
Hong Kong	37	45,838	China + Taiwan	2	2,635
Korea	31	26,014	China + Cambodia	3	2,529
Malaysia	13	26,733	Korea + Cambodia	1	1,213
Cambodia	12	6,701	Malaysia + Taiwan	1	1,093
Singapore	10	20,575	Hong Kong + Canada	1	565
USA	8	4,916	Hong Kong + Macau	1	478
Macau	3	7,747	China + British	1	399
Bangladesh	1	2,126	Taiwan + Cambodia	1	356
British	1	1,400			
Canada	1	1,113			
Australia	1	713			
Indonesia	1	546			
Philippines	1	425			
Spain	1	350			
Thailand	1	306			
Total	224	263,142		18	16,557

Source: GMAC (2010).

Table 7B.4
Factories Selected and Number of Workers Interviewed

No.	Name of Factories	Owner of the factory	No. of garment workers interviewed
1	(Cambodia) Hongmei Imp & Exp Co., Ltd	Chinese (mainland China)	15
2	GDM Enterprise Co., Ltd	Chinese (mainland China)	15
3	GHG (Cambodia) Ltd	Chinese (mainland China)	15
4	Kimsheng Garment Co., Ltd	Chinese (mainland China)	15
5	Legend Garment (Cambodia) Co., Ltd	Chinese (mainland China)	15
6	New Orient (Cambodia) Garment Co., Ltd	Chinese (mainland China)	15
7	Pine Great (Cambodia) Garment Co., Ltd	Chinese (mainland China)	15
8	Shen Zhou (Cambodia) Co., Ltd	Chinese (mainland China)	15
9	Star Knitting & Garment Factory Ltd	Chinese (mainland China)	15
10	Su Tong Fang Group Ying Kan (Cam) Garment	Chinese (mainland China)	15
11	Gennon (Cambodia) Garment Manufacturing Ltd	Hong Kong	15
12	Supertex, Ltd	Hong Kong	15
13	Evergreen Garment Co., Ltd	Korea	15
14	Gawon Apparel Co., Ltd	Korea	15
15	June Textile Co., Ltd	Malaysia	15
16	PCCS Garment Limited	Malaysia	15
17	8 Star Sportswear Ltd	Singapore	15
18	Chean Ping Garment Co., Ltd	Taiwan	15
19	Phong Wan Enterprise Co., Ltd	Taiwan	10
20	Kin Tai Garment Co., Ltd	Taiwan	5
21	Sky High (Cambodia) Co., Ltd	USA	15
	Total		300

Source: Survey conducted by CDRI in April 2010.

Notes

1. H.E. Keat Chhon, Cambodia's deputy prime minister and minister of Economy and Finance, in an exclusive interview with *China Daily* on 18 September 2010 <http://www.cdeclips.com/en/business/fullstory.html?id=51941> (accessed 25 September 2010).
2. Based on Jenkins and Edwards's (2004) framework, the SITC-Rev2 product codes are: 037, 042, 05, 06, 07, 232 for labour-intensive agricultural products; 269, 61, 63, 665, 666, 821, 831, 851, 89 for labour-intensive manufactures; 65 and 84 for labour-intensive textile and garment products.
3. For the analysis and findings on impacts of China's growth on least developed countries, see papers by Jenkins and Edwards (2004); Jenkins, Peters and Moreira (2007); Kaplinsky and Messner (2007); Humphrey and Schmitz (2007).
4. Cambodia's MDGs cover nine broad indicators/goals, in which eradicating extreme poverty and hunger was set as MDG1. The overall target of MDG1 is to halve, between 1993 and 2015, the proportion of people whose income is less than the national poverty line.
5. The sector is considered pro-poor as the majority of the workers are from the provinces and their relatives depend on their remittance.
6. <http://www.mfa.gov.cn/eng/wjb/zzjg/yzs/gjlb/2696/> (accessed 26 May 2010).
7. The Development of the Singapore-Kunming Rail Link and the Bangkok-Kunming Highway.
8. <http://www.mfa.gov.cn/eng/wjb/zzjg/yzs/gjlb/2696/> (accessed 26 May 2010).
9. Using SITC Rev. 3, cork and wood includes cork natural/raw/waste, fuel wood/wood charcoal, wood chips/particles, wood rough/squared and wood simply worked, i.e., wood railway sleepers, soft wood shaped/grooved and hardwood sawn.
10. Using SITC Rev. 3, cork and wood manufactures (SITC 63) include corks and stoppers, veneer sheets, particle board (wood), plywood, fireboard and wood simply shaped.
11. This section is adapted from Jenkins and Edwards (2004) where products for export to China are classified into groups in terms of their labour-intensiveness and products imported from China are classed in pro-poor consumption categories to capture likely effect of bilateral trade on poverty reduction in Cambodia.
12. Link to MAFF statistics webpage <http://www.maff.gov.kh/eng/statistics/rubber.html#a2>.
13. Author's calculation using consumer price index (CPI 2006 = 100) data compiled by the National Institute of Statistics of Cambodia.
14. Adjusting for inflation using CPI constructed by the National Institute of Statistics: real daily wage = 2.27/1.51 = US$1.50 at 2006 prices ($CPI_{2008}$ = 151);

daily per capita consumption = 0.76/1.07 = US$0.71 at 2006 prices ($CPI_{2007}$ = 107).

15. A survey of 70 factories of the total 238 export-oriented members of the Garment Manufacturers Association in Cambodia (GMAC) by the Economic Institute of Cambodia (EIC) in February 2005 indicates that 79 per cent of the total number of factories in the sample import fabric from China and 14 per cent from Hong Kong, while 71 per cent import textile accessories from China and 24 per cent from Hong Kong (USAID 2005, p. 13).
16. The Cambodia Aid Effectiveness Report of the Council for the Development of Cambodia (CDC 2008, pp. 1 and 3).
17. This workshop was held in Manila on 18–22 July 2005. For more details, see <http://www.adbi.org/event/851.transport.infrastructure.poverty.reduction/>.

References

CDC (Council for the Development of Cambodia). *The Cambodia Aid Effectiveness Report*. Phnom Penh: CDC, 2007, 2008 and 2009.

CDRI (Cambodia Development Resource Institute). *Impact of High Food Prices in Cambodia: Survey Report*. Phnom Penh: CDRI, 2008.

Chan Sophal, Joel Mangahas, Pham Thi, Thanh An and Bernard Wood. *Cambodia Evaluation of Aid Effectiveness Final Report*. Phnom Penh: CDRI, 2008.

Chin, T. Gregory and B. Michael Frolic. *Emerging Donors in International Development Assistance: The China Case*. Singapore: IDRC, 2007. <http://www.globalcitizen.net/Data/Pages/1509/papers/2010051983431871.pdf>.

Coudouel, Aline, Jesko Hentschel and Quentin Wodon. *Poverty Measurement and Analysis*. Washington, D.C.: World Bank, 2002.

Coughlan, Mathew. *China's Poverty Footprint in Cambodia*. Phnom Penh: Oxfam, 2007.

Davies, Martyn. "How China Delivers Development Assistance to Africa". Centre for Chinese Studies, University of Stellenbosch, 2008.

Ek Madra. "China Signs Agreements with Cambodia to Boost Investment". 2010. <http://www.dap-news.com/en/news/582-china-signs-agreements-with-cambodia-to-boost-investment.html>. Accessed 18 March 2010.

GDRP (General Directorate of Rubber Plantations). "Cambodia Natural Rubber Areas, Yields and Production in 2008". Unpublished manuscript, 2009.

GMAC (Garment Manufacturers Association of Cambodia). "List of the Members of the Garment Manufacturers Association in Cambodia". Unpublished manuscript, 2010.

Hem Socheth, Tong Kimsun and Ker Bopha. *Maximising Opportunities of Chinese Investment in Natural Resources in Cambodia*. Phnom Penh: CDRI, 2009.

Hettige, Hemamala, Paul Martin, Manjula Singh and Davis Wheeler. "The Industrial

Pollution Projection System". World Bank Policy Research Working Paper No. 1431. World Bank, Washington, D.C., 1995.

Hing Vutha and Hossein Jalilian. *Environmental Impacts of the ASEAN-China Free Trade Agreement on the Greater Mekong Sub-Region*. Canada: International Institute for Sustainable Development, 2008.

Hing Vutha and Nou Keosothea. *The Early Harvest Programme: Implications for Cambodian Agriculture*. Special Report No. 4. Phnom Penh: CDRI, 2006.

Humphrey, John and Hubert Schmitz. "China: Its Impact on the Developing Asian Economies". Working Paper 295. Institute of Development Studies, University of Sussex, Brighton, 2007.

International Monetary Fund. "World Economic Outlook database". 2010. <http://www.imf.org/external/pubs/ft/weo/2010/01/weodata/index.aspx>. Accessed April 2010.

Jenkins, Rhys and Chris Edwards. "How Does China's Growth Affect Poverty Reduction in Asia, Africa and Latin America?". Expanded Report to DFID. Overseas Development Group, University of East Anglia, Norwich, 2004.

Jenkins, Rhys, Enrique Dussel Peters and Mauricio Mesquita Moreira. "The Impact of China on Latin America and the Caribbean". *World Development* 36, no. 2 (2007): 235–53.

Kaplinsky, Raphael and Dirk Messner. "The Impact of Asian Drivers on the Developing World". *World Development* 36, no. 2 (2007): 197–209.

Menon, Jayant. "Building Blocks or Stumbling Blocks? Regional Cooperation Arrangements in Southeast Asia". ADB Institute Discussion Paper No. 41. ADBI, Tokyo, 2005.

MOC (Ministry of Commerce). "Estimated Cambodian Export under GSP/MFN Scheme". Unpublished manuscript, 2009.

National Institute of Statistics (NIS). *Socioeconomic Survey of Cambodia 1993/94*. Phnom Penh: NIS, 1994.

———. *Cambodia Socioeconomic Survey 2004*. Phnom Penh: NIS, 2004.

———. *Cambodia Socioeconomic Survey 2007*. Phnom Penh: NIS, 2007.

———. *Statistical Year Book 2008*. Phnom Penh: Ministry of Planning, 2008.

Ngo, Ngoun Theary. "Extractive Industry Transparency Initiative in Cambodia". *Cambodia Development Watch* 3, no. 2 (2007): 7–10.

OECD. "China's Outward Direct Investment". *OECD Investment Policy Reviews*. Beijing: OECD, 2008.

Okamoto, Yumiko. "China and India: Challenges and Opportunities for ASEAN from Japanese Perspectives". Doshisha University, Kyoto, 2005.

Phou Sambath. "Cambodia-China Relation: Past, Present and Future". Ph.D. thesis. Indian Institute of Management, Bangalore, n.d.

Rutherford, Jeff, Kate Lazarus and Shawn Kelley. "Rethinking Investment in Natural Resources: China's Emerging Role in the Mekong Region". Heinrich Boll Stiftung Institute, 2008.

Saing Chan Hang. "Export Competitiveness of the Cambodian Rubber Sector Relative to Other Greater Mekong Sub-region Suppliers: A Simple Descriptive Analysis". ARTNeT-GMS Discussion Paper No. 1, 2009*a*.

———. "Impacts of the Global Financial Crisis on Garment Workers and Remittances: Lesson from Cambodia". ARTNeT-GMS Notes No. 3, 2009*b*.

Setboonsarng, Sununtar. "Transport Infrastructure and Poverty Reduction". ADBI Research Policy Brief No. 21. ADBI, Tokyo, 2006.

SOFRECO/CEDAC. "Study on the Evolution of the Cambodian Rubber Sector, Draft Report". Phnom Penh: MAFF, 2005.

Tong Kimsun and Hem Socheth. *China's Investment in Cambodia*. Phnom Penh: CDRI, 2009.

UN ComTrade. "United Nations Commodity Trade Statistics Database". 2009. <http://comtrade.un.org/db/>. Accessed April 2010.

UNDP and MOC. "Cambodia's 2007 Trade Integration Strategy: Executive Summary and Action Matrix". UNDP, Phnom Penh, 2007.

USAID. "Measuring Competitiveness and Labour Productivity in Cambodia's Garment Industry". Phnom Penh, 2005.

———. "Cambodia Garment Industry Workforce Assessment: Identifying Skill Needs and Sources of Supply". Phnom Penh, 2006.

———. "Factory-Level Value Chain Analysis of Cambodia's Apparel Industry". Phnom Penh, 2007.

Winters, L. Alan, Neil McCulloch & Andrew McKay. "Trade Liberalization and Poverty: The Evidence So Far". *Journal of Economic Literature* 42, no. 1 (2004): 72–115.

World Bank. "Cambodia at the Crossroads: Strengthening Accountability to Reduce Poverty". Phnom Penh, 2004.

———. "Cambodia: Halving Poverty by 2015?". World Bank, Phnom Penh, 2006.

———. "Cambodia: Sharing Growth, Equity and Development Report 2007". World Bank, Phnom Penh, 2007.

———. *Handbook of Poverty Analysis*. Washington, D.C.: World Bank, 2008.

———. "Sustaining Rapid Growth in a Challenging Environment". Cambodia Country Economic Memorandum. World Bank, Phnom Penh, 2009*a*.

———. "Poverty Profile and Trend in Cambodia: Findings from the 2007 Cambodia Socio-Economic Survey". World Bank, Washington, D.C., 2009*b*.

Wu, Hsiu-Ling and Chien-Hsun Chen. "An Assessment of Outward Foreign Direct Investment from China's Transitional Economy". *Europe-Asia Studies* 53, no. 8 (2001): 1235–54.

Yamagata, Tatsufumi. "The Garment Industry in Cambodia: Its Role in Poverty Reduction Through Export-Oriented Development". IDE Discussion Paper No. 62. JETRO, Chiba, 2006.

Yu, Ching Wong and Charles Adams. "Trends in Global and Regional Foreign

Direct Investment Flows". Regional Office for Asia and the Pacific International Monetary Fund, 2002. <http://www.imf.org/external/pubs/ft/seminar/2002/fdi/eng/pdf/wong.pdf>. Accessed April 2010.

Zhu, Zhenming. "China's Economic Aid to CLMV and Its Economic Cooperation with Them", no date. <http://www.ide.go.jp/English/Publish/Download/Brc/pdf/01_chinaseconomic.pdf>. Accessed April 2010.

8

IMPACTS OF CHINA ON POVERTY REDUCTION IN LAOS

Leeber Leebuapao and Saykham Voladet

1. INTRODUCTION

China's rapid economic growth has increasingly attracted the attention of scholars and policy-makers around the globe. There has been much discussion as to the potential impacts of China's rise on the world economy and on the economies of developing countries in particular. In this vein there have been a number of publications and research works related to China's trade, investment and overseas development assistance (ODA) flow in the Greater Mekong Subregion (GMS) (for example, Jenkins and Edwards 2004). However, so far most studies have only provided general overviews and data on China's trade, investment and ODA and lack in-depth analysis on how trade with China, and China's foreign direct investment (FDI) and ODA flows contribute to poverty reduction at local level, especially the flows that contribute to creating employment and income generation activities for local people as well as skill development, expertise and technological transformation. The aim of this chapter is to contribute to existing literature by providing a detailed empirical analysis of China's impact on poverty reduction in Laos through three mechanisms: trade, FDI and ODA.

1.1 Poverty in Laos

Classed as a low income country, Laos is not only one of the poorest in the world, but also one of the poorest in the GMS. Poverty is a major concern, and poverty reduction a priority focus of government policy. For policy-makers, poverty in Laos is defined in relation to the national poverty line based on the international standard developed by the World Health Organization (WHO). Using their calorie intake poverty line as a reference, Laos developed two corresponding national poverty lines by converting calories into rice consumption, setting 16 kilogram rice consumption per person per month as the food poverty line, and that plus 20 per cent of its value at local rice prices as the general poverty line. In order to make the poverty measure more practicable, rice consumption has been converted into monetary value. Due to the differing rice prices throughout the country, different poverty lines based on location, which vary from US$15 to US$20 per person per month, have been set by the Lao government.

The Lao Expenditure and Consumption Survey (LECS), which has been conducted regularly every five years since 1993 (1993, 1998, 2003, 2008), provides data that can be used for estimating the extent of poverty in the country. Using figures from the LECS, it is estimated that the incidence of poverty has been gradually reduced from 32.8 per cent in 2004 to 30.4 per cent in 2006 and 28 per cent in 2008. On average, poverty incidence is declining by around 1 per cent a year (Figure 8.1). This rate of reduction is relatively high in comparison with that of neighbouring countries, Cambodia (about 0.5 per cent a year) and Thailand (on average around 1.6 per cent during the last thirty years). However, as shown in Figure 8.2, just over 1.6 million Lao were still living below the poverty line in 2008.

Figure 8.3 illustrates the concentration of poverty in the remote northern and eastern parts of the country where the terrain is largely mountainous, road infrastructure not yet developed and access to market still difficult. In contrast, poverty concentration is relatively low in the pasture areas along the Mekong River, in the western part of the country where road infrastructure, telecommunication networks and access to market are relatively developed.

The National Growth and Poverty Eradication Strategy (NGPES) has identified two main dimensions of poverty in Laos: external and internal. External cost refers to the external environment; majority of the poor live in remote areas where road, information and telecommunication

FIGURE 8.1
Poverty Incidence in Laos, 2004–08

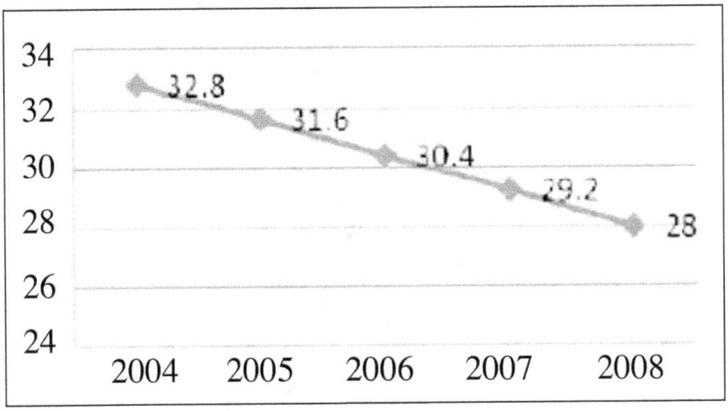

Source: MPI (2010).

FIGURE 8.2
Number of People (million) Living below the Poverty Line in Laos, 2004–08

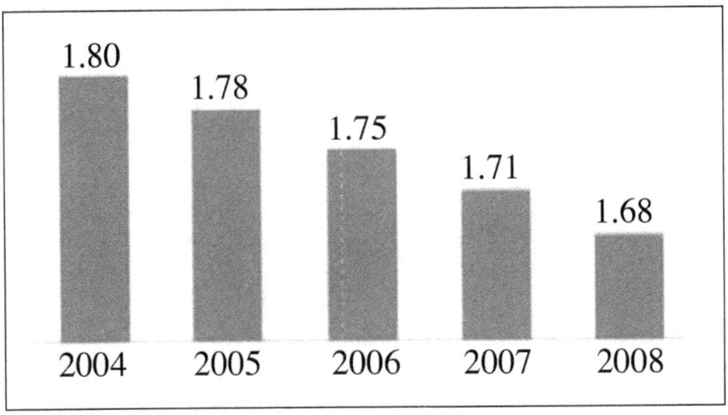

Source: MPI (2010).

infrastructure is underdeveloped and therefore have limited access to market and information. Internal cost refers to the abilities of the poor. Many poverty studies, including that on the poverty impacts of regional economic integration conducted by the National Economic Research

FIGURE 8.3
Poverty Distribution in Laos

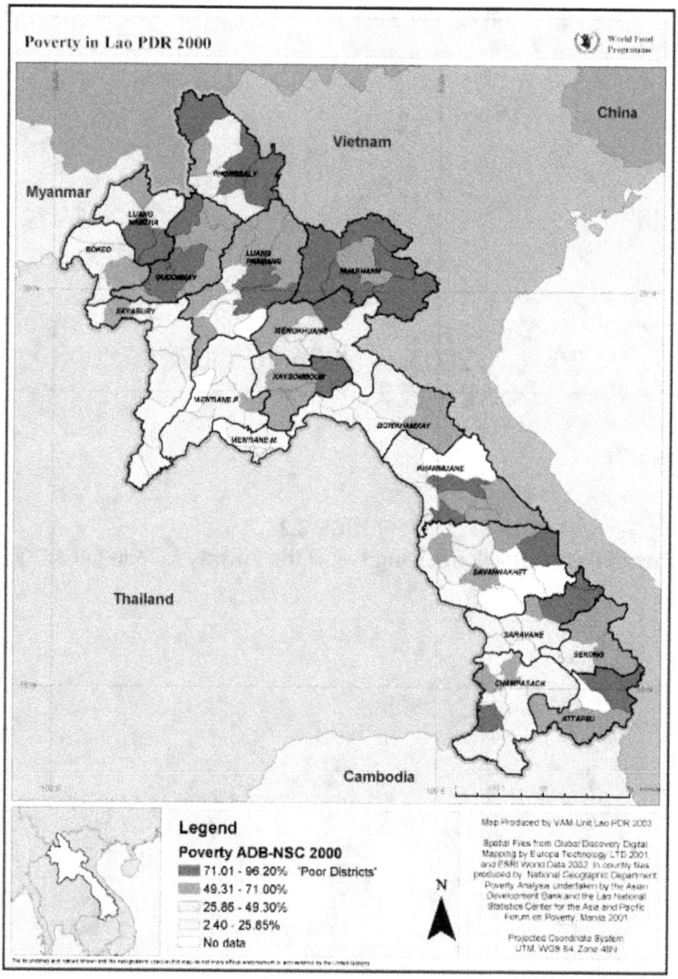

Source: World Food Programme (2000).

Institute (NERI) in 2007, confirm that the majority of the poor have low education and vocational training, and therefore, have low working skills. These combined factors make it difficult for them to get jobs and access income generating activities, especially the more highly paid occupations. Consequently, the poor are largely employed in subsistence agriculture.

2. RESEARCH OBJECTIVES AND METHODS

The objective of this country chapter is to evaluate the impacts of China's trade, investment and ODA on poverty in Laos. Employing the Jenkins and Edwards (2004) conceptual framework, we are concerned with establishing how poverty in Laos has responded to China's growing economy, through providing a pro-poor focused, disaggregated country analysis. To meet the needs of the study objectives, the assessment teams conducted the following research activities.

- *Literature review* to collect secondary data and information. The research team collected and analysed available publications, research reports, documents, data sheets and newspapers, which contain information and statistical data on China's trade with Laos and its FDI and ODA flow into the country.
- *Key informant interviews* to gain more in-depth information related to Laos-China trade, China's investment and ODA. Four officers with responsibility related to Laos-China trade, China's investment and ODA were interviewed, including representatives from the Laos-China Cooperation Committee, the Laos-China Cooperation Office, as well as the Investment Promotion Department and the Cooperation Department of the Ministry of Planning and Investment.
- *In-depth case studies* to examine in more detail how (1) trade with China, (2) Chinese investment, and (3) China's ODA affect poverty reduction at the local level, focusing on employment and income generation activities for local people. Key informants, including representatives from the Provincial Department for Planning and Investment, and the District Office for Planning and Investment, were interviewed for each case study. A community level focus group discussion was held for each case study.

The rest of the chapter is structured as follows. The next section considers the impact of trade with China and provides detailed information and statistical data on Laos-China trade flow over time by export and import products and by location. The findings of an in-depth study on sugar export to China in Sing district, Luang Numatha province, conducted to examine more closely how the trade flows contribute to poverty reduction at local level, especially in relation to job creation and income generation activities for local people, are discussed. Section 4 analyses how China's FDI outflow to Laos has impacted on poverty reduction, and reviews China's

FDI flow over time by sector and location. Observations and findings from an in-depth study looking at the poverty impacts of Sepone Mining in Vilabuti district, Savannakhet province, are presented and discussed. This case study was done to gain deeper insights into how China's investment affects poverty reduction at the local level, especially to examine in more detail how Chinese investment contributes to creating employment and income generation activities for the local populace as well the transfer of skills and technologies to local level. The poverty impacts of China's ODA are analysed in section 5, and statistical data on China's ODA over time by sector and location are reviewed. Discussion of an in-depth study on the poverty impacts of Road 3 (part of the North-South Corridor) examines in more detail how this Chinese ODA project is contributing to poverty reduction in the project area, i.e. in Luang Numtha province. Section 6 concludes and suggests some ways forward.

3. IMPACT OF LAOS-CHINA TRADE ON POVERTY REDUCTION

3.1 Macroscopic Analysis of Trade with China and Poverty

Characteristics of China-Laos Trade

Since the opening up of Laos in 1989, the government has implemented a number of policies and measures to facilitate increased trade, with a view to promoting growth and reducing poverty. These have included, for example, Decree No. 300/PM on One-Stop-Service Policy, Decree No. 169/PMO on abolishing export and import licences for regular goods with the exception of gold and copper, and Decree No. 0948/MoC on border trade facilitation.

Consequent of such measures, the volume of trade in general, and Laos-China trade in particular, has been increasing constantly and rapidly from US$30 million in 2004 to US$125 million in 2006 and US$137 million in 2008, which corresponds to a strong average growth rate of 71 per cent a year (Table 8.1). From 2004 to 2008, the accumulative Laos-China trade volume accounted for US$477 million, representing about 6.7 per cent of Laos' total external trade volume. China has become the country's third important trade partner after Thailand and Vietnam. As indicated in Table 8.1, total import from China between 2004 and 2008 accounted for about US$346 million, representing about 72 per cent of the Laos-China trade volume during the same period. Laos has a huge trade deficit to China

TABLE 8.1
External Trade in Laos, 2004–08 (US$ million)

External trade volume	2004	2005	2006	2007	2008	2004–08
Total trade volume	940	1,120	1,730	1,860	1,440	7,100
China	30	61	125	124	137	477
Non-China	910	1,059	1,605	1,736	1,303	6,623
Export	380	440	860	920	1,320	3,920
China	7	9	40	34	41	131
Non-China	373	431	820	886	1,279	3,789
Import	560	680	870	940	120	3,180
China	23	52	85	90	96	346
Non-China	537	628	785	850	24	2,834
Trade balance	–180	–240	–10	–20	1,200	740
China	–16	–43	–45	-56	–55	–215
Non-China	–164	–197	35	36	1,255	955
Terms of trade	0.7	0.6	1.0	1.0	11.0	1.2
China	0.3	0.2	0.5	0.4	0.4	0.4
Non-China	0.7	0.7	1.0	1.0	53.3	1.3

Source: Ministry of Industry and Commerce (2009).

which increased sharply from US$16 million in 2004 to US$45 million in 2006 and then rose more gradually to US$55 million in 2008, corresponding to a high average rate of increase of 48.8 per cent a year. From 2004 to 2008, the cumulative Lao trade deficit to China totalled US$215 million. Also, the terms of trade, i.e. the ratio of export to import, did not significantly improve during this period, showing a slight increase from 0.3 in 2004 to 0.4 in 2008.

Laos' main export products to China are wood and wood products, minerals, agricultural products — including sugar cane, vegetables, bananas, and non-timber forestry products (NTFP). The main imports from China are equipment and materials for investment projects, including machinery, vehicles, office equipment and construction materials, which account for about 40 per cent of total import from China between 2004 and 2008. These are followed by imports of other industrial products used both for consumption and production. Electronic equipment such as mobile-phones and televisions account for 25 per cent of total imports from China, raw materials for garment manufacturing for 18 per cent, agricultural production equipment for 10 per cent, and clothing and other daily consumption goods, 7 per cent (Figures 8.4 and 8.5).

FIGURE 8.4
Structure of Import from China, 2004–08

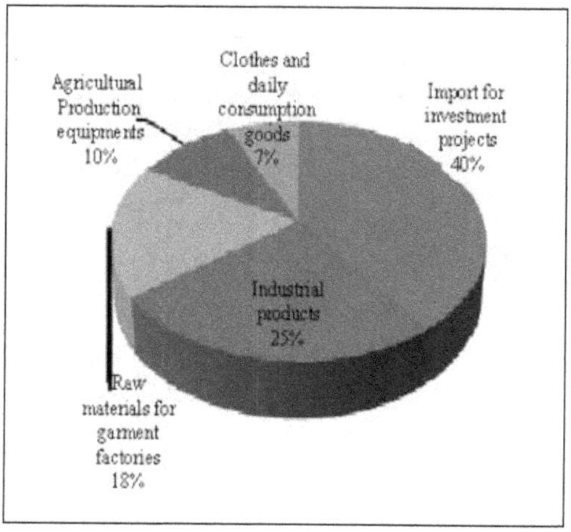

Source: Ministry of Industry and Commerce (2009).

FIGURE 8.5
Structure of Export to China, 2004–08

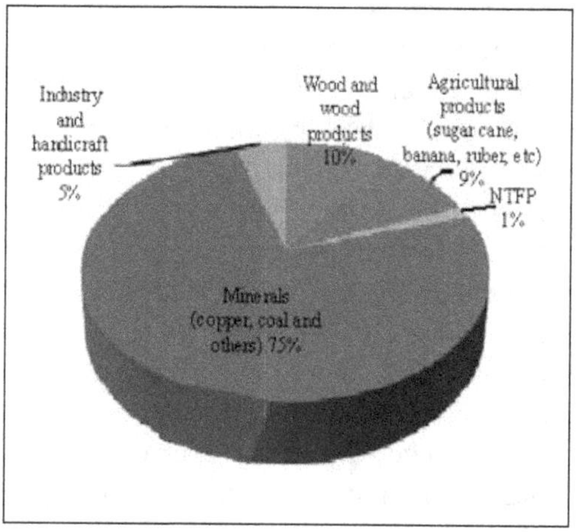

Source: Ministry of Industry and Commerce (2009).

Impact of China-Laos Trade on the Lao Poor

Looking at the structure of Laos' imports from China, it can be seen that the biggest share comprises capital goods and raw materials for production, which represented just over 60 per cent of total import from China between 2004 and 2008. The import of non-productive goods such as clothes and daily consumption goods shared 7 per cent of total import from China during the same period. This import structure has contributed positively to reducing poverty. The Ministry of Industry and Commerce (MIC) commented that imports from China could have positive long-term effects on economic growth and poverty reduction in Laos.

Consumer products imported from China are relatively low quality and low price. Therefore, poor local people have better access to said goods. In this sense, import from China has significant poverty reduction effects. The marketing of imported products from China is relatively simple. Chinese traders usually hire locations along streets within the town to establish their businesses and shops that are simply furbished and offer a basic service. The simple decor and service contribute to the low price of Chinese products, and thus help improve access of the poor to consumer goods.

Import of capital goods and other products used in production has the potential to promote industrial development in Laos. Capital goods used in capital-intensive processes have the power to reduce poverty indirectly through enhancing GDP growth. In addition, lower price products imported from China that are used in agricultural production, communication and information dissemination can have a direct positive impact on the lives of the poor, enhancing their consumption indicators. For example, equipment such as hand tractors enhances agricultural productivity, while mobile phones can improve access to market information, thus reducing transaction costs.

Although imports may benefit the poor, the nature of exports to China has few pro-poor attributes. The structure of exports to China has worried the MIC: 90 per cent of Laos' export to China comprises natural resources such as minerals, wood products and NTFP. The sectoral characteristics of Laos-China export industries have several negative attributes with regards to potential poverty reduction. First, Laos' exports to China are not labour intensive, but rather capital intensive involving large-scale natural resource extraction. These provide limited employment opportunities to poor Lao unskilled workers. Second, the current import-export structure with China has resulted in a large and growing trade deficit: raw materials, which are relatively low in value, account for Laos' biggest export share to China, and industrial products, which are relatively high in value, comprise the country's main imports from China. Third, raw mineral extraction can hinder industrial development by diverting resources away from other industrial development, increase vulnerability by leading to primary commodity dependency, and result in industrial stagnation by fomenting Dutch disease.

Laos' export structure not only has the potential to manifest economic problems, but may also lead to social and environmental dilemmas. For instance, the large-scale export of natural resources to China has high environmental impacts and is not sustainable. The import and export to China seems to contribute actively to declining forest cover, water quantity, NTFP stocks, and soil quality in Laos' northern provinces. China's trade in Laos is also associated with immigration. A number of Chinese came to Laos for trade or other income generation activities. Many of them have settled relatively permanently in the country. They have set up shops and import commodities from China such that China's markets are well established in many cities, for example, Vientiane, Luang Prabang, Outdoxay and Luang Numtha. Currently, there are no reliable statistical data on the number of Chinese traders settled in Laos. Many of them use a tourist visa to enter the country and then overstay and work without work permit. Chinese traders are particularly concentrated in many northern towns, which may lead to social problems in the future.

3.2 Case Study of Sugar Cane Plantation and Export to China in Sing District, Luang Numtha Province

Background

The research team conducted an in-depth case study on sugar cane plantation and export in Sing District to observe how Laos-China trade contributes to poverty reduction in the area. Among the many reasons for selecting the product and the area for case study, foremost are the area's close relationship to China, the significant activities of Chinese enterprises in the area as well as the high concentration of poverty. For these reasons, it was anticipated that the impact of Laos-China trade on poverty reduction in the area would be significant.

Sing District, with a population is 30,548,[1] is located in Luang Numtha province, about 60 kilometres north of the provincial capital. The district covers an area of 1,430 square kilometres (142,957 ha) and borders La district of China in the north, Long district in the south, Numtha district to the east and Myanmar to the west. However, the most important specific characteristics of the district are landscape, temperature and soil fertility. Over 60 per cent of the area is pastureland. The average temperature is estimated to be 25 degrees centigrade. The topographical and climatic conditions are excellent for agricultural production, including rubber and sugar cane plantation. In addition, the district has good road and information infrastructure links with China, especially with La district. A paved road crosses the district and connects it with China, and it has an international border gate which serves as the main gate for export and import from China. Chinese SIM cards are useable in the district. The road infrastructure and communication links provide good conditions for trading with China.

Socio-economically, Sing district has middle status in comparison with other cities in the country, but has a relatively high socio-economic status compared to other districts in northern Laos. In 2008, average per capita income was US$600 and poverty incidence was 11 per cent. During the last decade, the district has experienced relatively high economic growth and rapid poverty reduction. According to its Office for Planning and Investment, the district experienced an economic real growth rate of about 8 per cent and poverty reduction of 1.6 per cent a year during 2004 to 2006. Based on per capita income and poverty incidence, Sing district is identified as a relatively more developed district in Lunag Numtha province.

The main economic activity is agriculture which contributed about 70 per cent of the district's total production value and employed over 80 per cent of its labour force in 2008. The service sector, including tourism and other related industry, contributed about 20 per cent of total production value and employed about 15 per cent of the labour force. The industry sector is not yet developed, contributing only about 5 per cent of total production value in 2008. Sing district also has relatively good access to health and education services in comparison with the whole of Luang Numtha province. For example, it has fifty-six primary schools, the school attendance rate is about 85 per cent compared to 80.1 per cent for the whole province, while the maternity mortality rate is slightly lower at 300 per 100,000 births compared to 306 per 100,000 for the whole province.

Based on the area's favourable geographical and climatic conditions, sugar cane cultivation is a long tradition of people living in Sing district. However, before it started being exported to China, sugar cane plantation in the district was mainly subsistence level cultivation using traditional production techniques where just a small amount of produce was sold in the Laos-China border market.

In the mid-1990s, representatives of a Chinese sugar factory — located in Pong district bordering Sing district — approached local farmers to discuss the possibility of growing sugar cane commercially. The factory cooperated closely with the district authority. The district authority was obligated to encourage farmers to grow sugar cane while the factory itself provided technical assistance and financial support. The company also signed a purchase contract with villagers for when the sugar cane was harvested.

Initially, only a few villages and households joined the project. However, due to good experiences with the partner factory in China, the number of villages and households joining the sugar cane plantation projects in Sing district has been increasing continuously. Statistical data provided by the Office for Planning and Investment in Sing district indicates that by 2008, sixty-five villages or 3,200 households, corresponding to 67 per cent of villages or to about 52.3 per cent of total households in Sing district, Long province, had joined the project. In the same year, the project had a total production area of around 2,000 ha.

Sugar Cane Plantations' Contribution to Poverty Reduction in Sing District, Luang Numtha Province

Due to the import of techniques and technologies from China, including machinery, fertilizers and seed, as well as access to the Chinese market, sugar cane plantation in Sing district has been changing from subsistence agricultural production to commercial production, characterized by the use of higher level techniques and technologies, more intensive production as well as higher productivity. Discussion with the Office for Agriculture and Forestry in Sing district confirmed that the productivity of sugar cane plantation in the area is about 45 tonnes ha on average. In 2008, Sing district exported around 70,550 tonnes of sugar cane to China. With an average export price of US$18 per tonne, total sugar cane export value was estimated to be around US$1.6 million in 2008, corresponding to about 8.7 per cent of the district's total export value.

Resultant of this contribution of sugar production to export volume, Sing district has been experiencing significant economic growth rate and poverty reduction during the last decade. Statistical data provided by the District Office for Planning and Investment show that GDP per capita in Sing district has been increasing rapidly from US$379 per person per in 2004 to US$501 in 2006 and US$600 in 2008. During the same period, the district's average economic growth rate has been 15 per cent per year (nominal or equal to about 8 per cent real GDP growth). It is a significantly high growth rate in comparison with many districts in Laos, especially with other northern districts. Further details on the increase in GPD per capita between 2004 and 2008 are shown in Figure 8.6. In line with rapid economic growth, poverty incidence in the district has been also rapidly reducing from 28.2 per cent in 2004 to 25.4 per cent in 2006 and 20.1 per cent in 2008. This corresponds to an average rate of decline of 1.6 per cent a year, which is significantly high in comparison with many districts in Laos. Figure 8.7 presents more details on the reduction in poverty incidence over the five years from 2004 to 2008.

Accounting for nearly 9 per cent of Sing district's total export revenues, there is no doubt that sugar cane plantation exports to China contribute significantly to economic growth and poverty reduction in Sing district. However, discussion with many stakeholders including

FIGURE 8.6
GDP per capita (US$) in Sing District, 2004–08

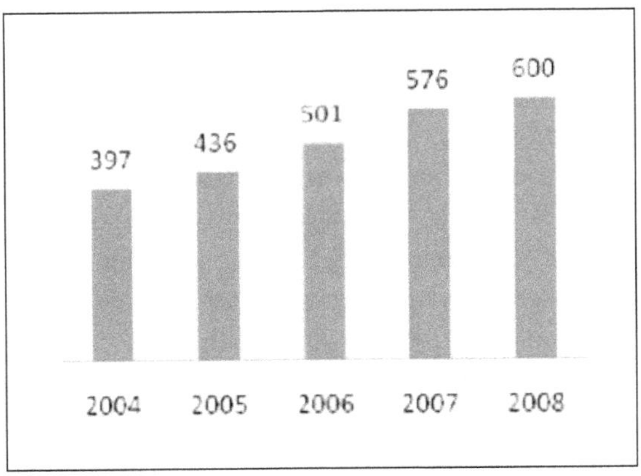

Source: Office for Planning and Investment of Sing District (2009).

FIGURE 8.7
Poverty Incidence (%) in Sing District, 2004–08

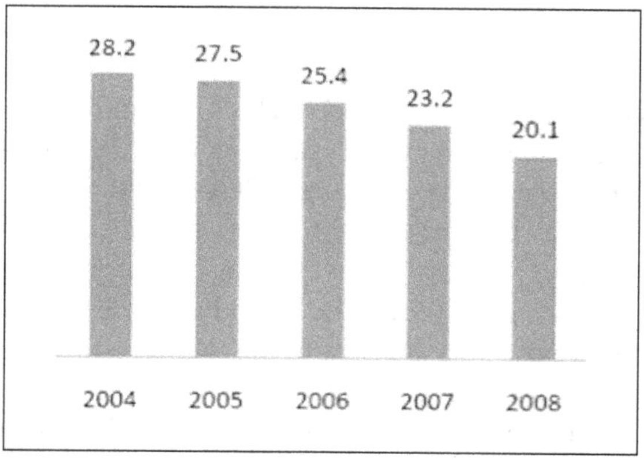

Source: Office for Planning and Investment of Sing District (2009).

sugar cane production households in the district, and the Water Resource and Environmental Office of Luang Numtha province, found that sugar cane plantation and export seems to have some negative effects on the environment. It was reported that the current sugar cane plantation areas used to be covered with productive forests where villagers grew land rice, collected NTFP and hunted wild animals, which were their main livelihood activities and income sources before commercial-scale sugar cane plantation and export to China. The loss of these self-sustaining habitats could leave many households vulnerable to shocks, for example, a major depreciation in the market value of sugar cane.

In addition, the once-forested areas used to serve as a protective watershed. The conversion of productive forest into sugar cane plantation, the more intensive land use, and the use of chemical fertilizers and insecticides to enhance productivity seem to have adversely affected the water shade area, and soil quality and fertility. According to the Water Resource and Environmental Agency in Luang Numtha and Oudomxay provinces, the water level in several rivers in northern Laos dropped significantly during the period 2004–08, further threatening vulnerable households' livelihood strategies. It is not suggested that sugar cane plantation and export alone are responsible for the reduced water level. There are many investments in other plantations, including rubber and banana, all of which impact on forest cover, so contributing to the reduction of water in several rivers in the northern provinces. However, it is observed that all of the plantations are related to China; some of them are Chinese FDI ventures, for example, rubber plantations, and some of these plantations produce goods for export to China.

It also emerged from discussions with farmers and sugar cane producers in Sing district, that sugar cane plantation in the area requires ever increasing amounts of chemical fertilizer to maintain productivity. They said that sugar cane cultivation needs the application of about 0.3 tonnes of chemical fertilizer per hectare. The amount of chemical fertilizer required increases by around 15 per cent a year which leads to increasing production costs of about 7 per cent a year. If such an increase in production costs is sustained over the long term, the profitability of sugar cane plantations would be greatly diminished. Consequently, poverty and food insecurity in the areas could return and at increased levels, exacerbated by the destruction of forestry resources and degraded soil fertility which would render the plantation of any crops impossible.

Analysis of the cane sugar industry shows that trade with China can have mixed results in reducing poverty. In the short term, the benefits to the poor are clear: increased employment and improvements in poor households' consumption indicators. In the longer term, cane sugar, like the majority of Laos' exports to China, is a relatively low value unprocessed product, as opposed to the high value-added manufactured or processed products that flow across the border from China. It is crucial that the balance of trade changes, and that Laos moves up the value chain, successfully transitioning from an exporter of primary commodities to an exporter of manufactured products. Further, there is evidence that the plantations have diminishing returns overtime as soil quality declines as a result of environmental degradation. This has the potential to damage future earnings of the local inhabitants, potentially increasing poverty.

4. CHINA'S FDI OUTFLOWS TO LAOS AND POVERTY REDUCTION

The main objectives of this section are to evaluate the poverty impacts of China's FDI. First, a general overview of China's FDI flow over time is presented, followed by the findings from the in-depth case study that was conducted to explore the poverty impact of Sepone Mining Project in Vilabury district, Savannakhet province. Many reasons led the research team to select this particular case study, especially the current activities of Chinese enterprises in Laos' mining sector and the location of the project in the eastern part of the country where poverty concentration is relatively high. By conducting the case study, the research team fully expected to be able to identify the poverty impacts of China's FDI to some extent.

4.1 Macroscopic Overview of FDI Inflows from China

General Overview of FDI Flow from China

The target of the Lao government is to eradicate poverty by 2015 and to advance Laos from the least developed country list by 2020. To achieve this target, the county needs economic growth of at least 8 per cent a year. With an incremental capital output ratio equal to 4, it needs an investment of at least 32 per cent of GDP and domestic saving rate equal to about 10 per cent of GDP. Thus, to realize the government's policy intentions the country needs to attract a large volume of capital inflows, including FDI and ODA. Regarding increasing FDI inflows, the government has implemented many policies and regulations, including on land management, taxation and trade facilitation. Due to cultural, political and economic similarities and interconnections, FDI from China is especially preferred and policy has been designed with this in mind.

As a consequence of the government's investment promotion policies and measures, a significant amount of FDI flows into Laos. Statistical data provided by the MPI indicates that FDI of over US$6,274.2 million flowed into Laos during 2004 to 2008, about 17.8 per cent of which came from China. Thus, China has become the country's third largest FDI source after Thailand and Vietnam. Table 8. 2 presents details on FDI flow into Laos from 2004 to 2008.

In general, as shown in Figure 8.8, FDI flow into Laos over the period 2004–08 is concentrated in natural resource-based capital-intensive and export-oriented sectors. The energy sector attracts 59.03 per cent of the investment followed by 10.83 per cent in industry and handicrafts, 9.42 per cent in agriculture and 6.99 per cent in the mining sector. FDI from China over the same period was similarly distributed as shown in Figure 8.9, with 43.33 per cent going to the energy sector followed by 22.3 per

TABLE 8.2
FDI in Laos, 2004–08 (US$ million)

Source	2004	2005	2006	2007	2008	2004–08
Total	533.1	1,245.3	2,699.7	1,136.9	659.2	6,274.2
Non-China	505	1,187.20	2,276.50	640.9	547.6	5,157.00
China	28.2	58.1	423.2	496.1	111.6	1,117.20
China's share (%)	5.3	4.7	15.7	43.6	16.9	17.8

Source: Ministry of Planning and Investment (2009*a*).

FIGURE 8.8
Share of Total FDI by Sector, 2004–08

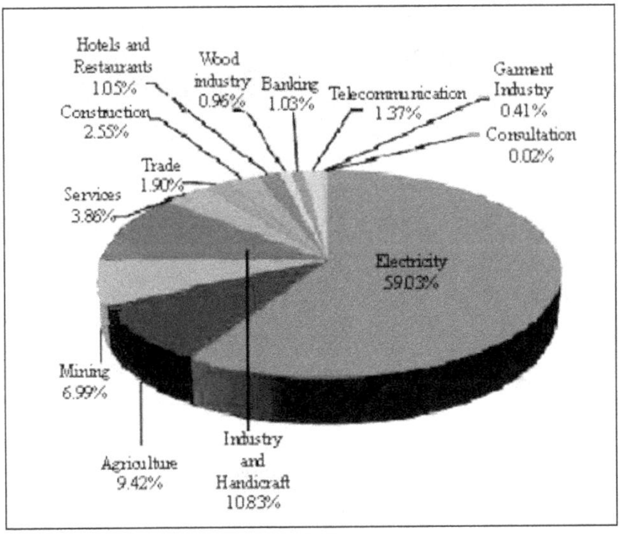

Source: Department of Investment MPI (2009*a*).

cent to industry and handicrafts, 11.58 per cent to mining, 8.81 per cent in services, and 7.53 per cent to the agriculture sector.

Despite similarities in overall composition of FDI, there are some differences between FDI from China and total FDI. FDI flow from China concentrates a little more in labour-intensive sectors, including industry and handicrafts, mining, services, agriculture and garment manufacturing, and thus has a greater potential impact on poverty through increasing

FIGURE 8.9
Share of Chinese FDI by Sector, 2004–08

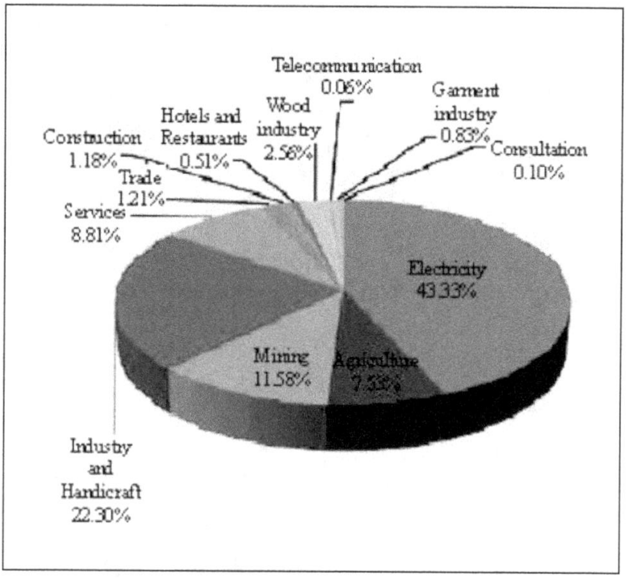

Source: Department of Investment MPI (2009*a*).

employment opportunities. As illustrated in Figure 8.9, just over 50 per cent of FDI flow from China in 2004–08 was concentrated in these sectors compared to less than 30 per cent of FDI from other countries. In addition, considering the location of FDI, it is clear that the biggest share of FDI flow from China is focused in Laos' northern provinces where the terrain is mountainous and poverty concentration is high. Table 8.3 presents more details on FDI structure in Laos by location. Based on structure and location, FDI flow from China seems to have higher impacts on poverty reduction in comparison with the same flow from other countries.

4.2 Poverty Impacts of FDI Flow from China: Case Study on Sepone Mining

The main objective of this subsection is to examine in detail how FDI flow from China effects poverty in Laos. To this end the research team conducted

TABLE 8.3
FDI Structure by Location, 2004–08

Location	Non-China (%)	China (%)
Northern provinces	15	65
Central provinces	50	25
Southern provinces	35	10
Total	100	100

Source: Estimated by NERI based on data provided by MPI (2009*c*).

an in-depth study on Sepone Mining which was selected for a number of reasons. First, it has been 100 per cent funded by Chinese investors since 2009, and thus is a good example of how Chinese FDI can impact on poverty reduction. Second, is has wide implications as mining is a major destination of Chinese FDI to Laos: over 11.5 per cent of China's FDI flow goes to the mining sector and about 15 per cent of mining exports from Laos go directly to China. Third, the geographical distribution of China's FDI is concentrated in the north of the country where Sepone Mining is located, so it is representative of Chinese FDI in this regard. Fourth, it is clear that poverty is concentrated in the north and eastern parts of Laos, and thus Sepone Mining has the potential to pay significant dividends in reducing poverty.

Background to the Area and Sepone Mining Project

Sepone Mining is located in Vilabury district, Savannakhet province, about 200 kilometres northeast of Savannakhet provincial centre. Vilabury district shares borders with Khammuane province in the north, Phine district in the south, Sepone district in the east and Atsaphone and Phalanxay districts in the west. The district covers an area of 1,141 square kilometres and has a population of 32,363. Just over 60 per cent of the population is of working age, i.e. fifteen to sixty years old; about 80 per cent of them are engaged in subsistence agriculture.

Agricultural production still plays a dominant role in the economy and livelihood activities of people in the area. In 2008, agricultural production contributed about 70 per cent of the total income of the population in the district, followed by around 20 per cent of total income from employment in the industrial sector (including Sepone Mining factory) and around 10 per cent from the services sector. The average per capita income in the district is estimated to be about US$717.60, which is about 20 per cent lower than the provincial average per capita income. Poverty incidence in the district is estimated to have been 28 per cent in 2009, which is relatively high in comparison with about 10 per cent in Savannakhet province. Thus, the district is identified as one of the least developed districts in Savannakhet province.

Due to the activities of Sepone Mining, the district has relatively good road and communication infrastructure linking it to the rest of Laos and beyond. It has a grade III paved road connecting to the East-West Corridor which links the area with Vietnam in the east and Thailand in the west. However, the road infrastructure is developed only in those areas around the project and in the district centre. In other parts of Vilaburi district, the road infrastructure is still underdeveloped in comparison with many other areas of Savannakhet province and other parts of the country. The mobile phone network covers about 40 per cent of its land area. Thus, in terms of infrastructure, Vilaburi is not only one of the least developed districts in Savannakhet province, but also one of the least developed districts in Laos.

The feasibility study for Sepone Mining project was conducted by Oxiana of Australia in 1989. In 1993, the investigation and production agreement was signed. Based on the agreement, Lane Xang Minerals Limited was established in the following year. At the beginning of the project, Oxiana held an 80 per cent share, the government of Laos had 10 per cent and a Chinese investor had 10 per cent. Thus, the project was initially an Australian investment. It established a relatively high standard of operational ethics, including social and environmental standards. Chinese investors took over the project in 2009. However, they have kept the management team and adopted the same social and environmental standards.

Sepone Mining Project and Poverty Reduction in Laos

Sepone Mining has played a significant role in enhancing Laos' macroeconomic indicators. It required an initial capital investment of around US$500 million, making it the largest mining project in Laos. It uses some of the most advanced techniques and technologies available, enabling it to produce 100,000 ounces of gold and 67,000 tonnes of copper per year. The mine has been operational since 2004 and since that time has produced a large volume of minerals: the accumulated gold production and export from Sepone Mining is about 1,000,000 ounces and copper about 290,000 tonnes (see Figures 8.10 and 8.11). This has had a significant impact on the Lao economy. During the period 2004–09, gold and copper export from Sepone Mining is estimated to have totalled around US$1,745.8 million, representing just over 34 per cent of total export from Laos during this period (see Figures 8.12 and 8.13).

According to statistical data provided by the factory, production and export from Sepone Mining contributes significantly to government budgetary revenues — Figures 8.14 and 8.15 provide details. From 2004 to 2009 Sepone Mining contributed about US$430 million to the government budget via the payment of profit tax, income tax, concession fees and dividends. This represents a staggering 12.6 per cent of the total government budget during the same period. As a good proportion of the government's budget will be spent on public infrastructure, health and education, Sepone Mining, by virtue of the sheer volume of its capital turnover and large tax bill, significantly contributes to poverty reduction

FIGURE 8.10
Accumulated Gold Production and Export of Sepone Mining (ozs), 2004–08

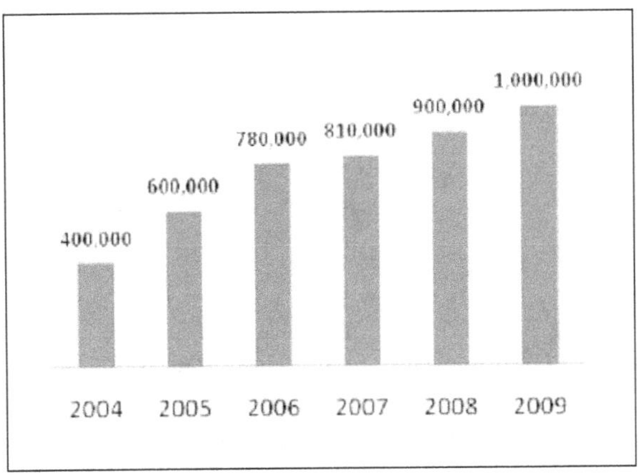

FIGURE 8.11
Accumulated Copper Production and Export of Sepone Mining (tonnes), 2004–08

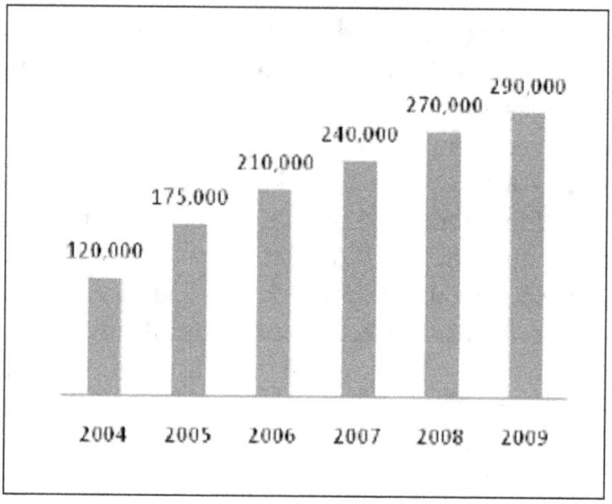

FIGURE 8.12
Accumulated Export Revenue of Sepone Mining (US$), 2004–09

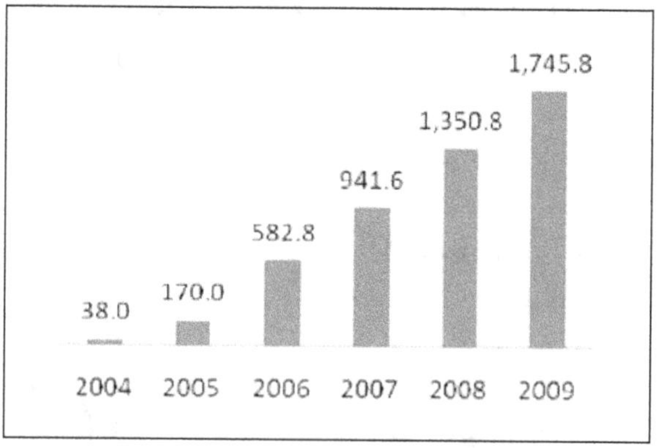

Source: Estimated by NERI based on data provided by Sepone Mining.

FIGURE 8.13
Export Share of Sepone Mining (%), 2004–09

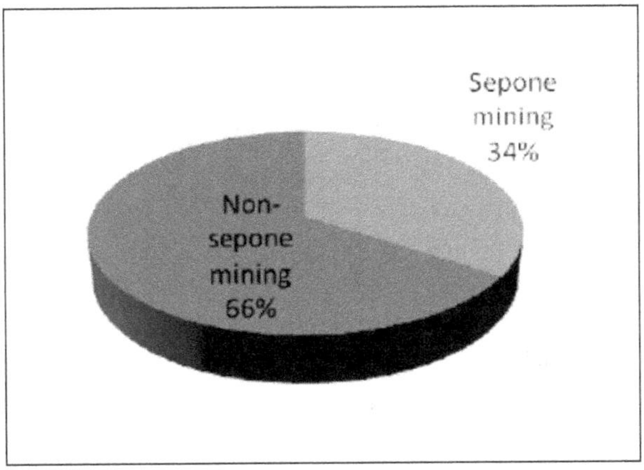

Source: Estimated by NERI based on data provided by Sepone Mining.

FIGURE 8.14
Accumulated Contribution to Government Budget by Sepone Mining, 2004–09

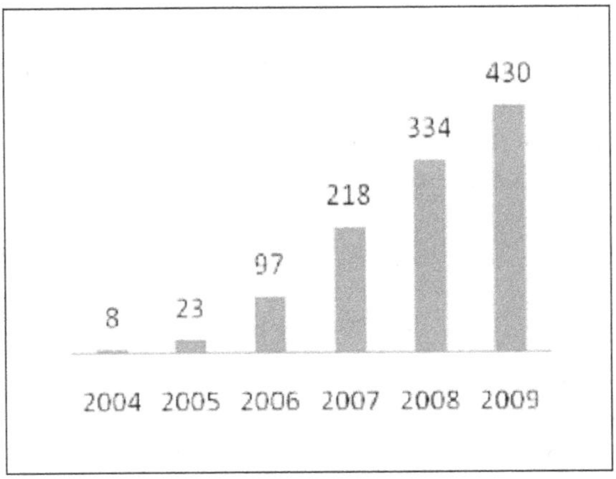

Source: Estimated by NERI based on data provided by Sepone Mining.

FIGURE 8.15
Share of Sepone Mining's Contribution of Total Government Budget, 2004–09

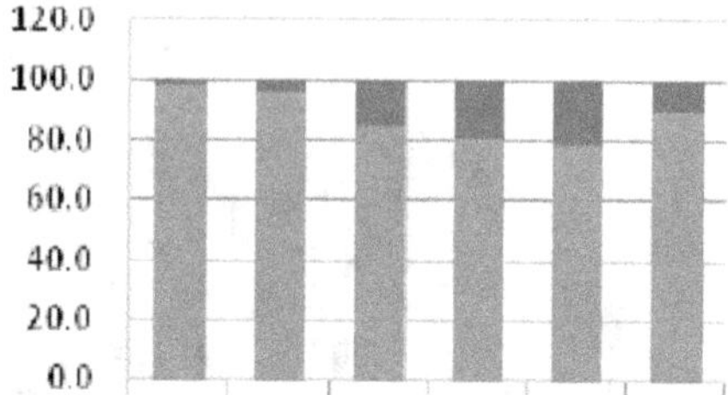

	2004	2005	2006	2007	2008	2009
Sepone mining	1.9	3.6	15.0	19.1	21.4	10.1
Non-sepone mining	98.1	96.4	85.0	80.9	78.6	89.9

Source: Estimated by NERI based on data provided by Sepone Mining.

in Laos as a whole through greatly contributing to the government's capital resources.

The mining factory also significantly contributes to local economic growth and poverty reduction in Vilaburi district. A key part of this has been its employment policy, which has focused on providing jobs and income generation activities for local people. Discussion with the personnel manager during the field trip found that Sepone Mining gives employment priority to local people. The employment policy of the factory states that people in Sepone Development Area (SPDA) get priority, Vilaburi people are second, and those from other areas of Savannakhet province are third, while workers from other provinces in Laos get the lowest priority. The personnel manager reported that of 2010 the factory employed a total of around 4,830 workers, of whom 3,360 are permanent staff and 1,470 are casual employees. As shown in Figures 8.16 and 8.17, the majority of employees are local people, especially those living in SPDA, Vilaburi district and Savannakhet province. In total, then, around 34.6 per cent of permanent staff and 72.4 per cent of casual labour in the Sepone mining factory live locally, meaning that about 46.1 per cent of total employees in Sepone Mining are local people (see Figure 8.18).

FIGURE 8.16
Structure of Permanent Employees in Sepone Mining, 2010

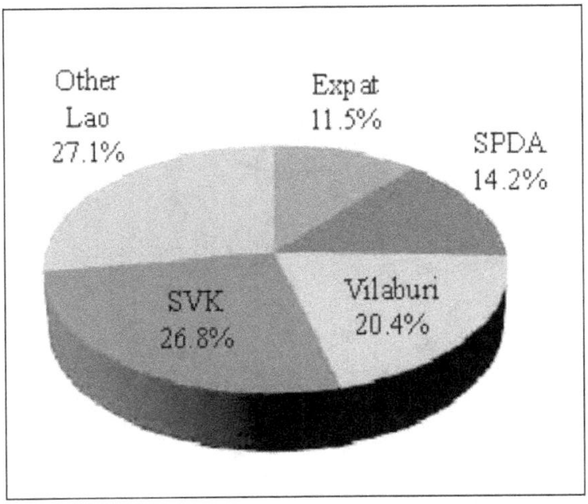

Source: Sepone Mining.

FIGURE 8.17
Structure of Casual Employees in Sepone Mining, 2010

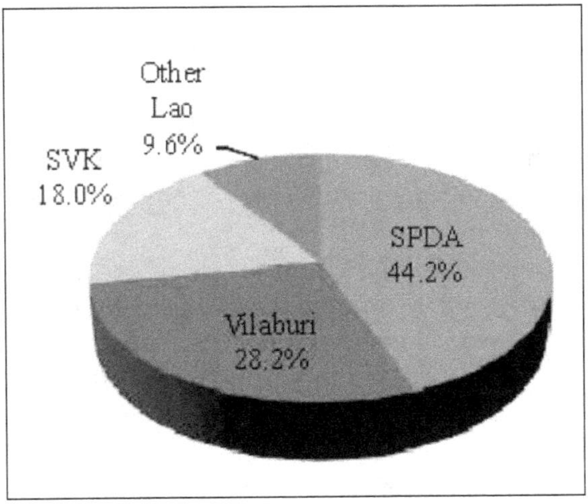

Source: Sepone Mining.

FIGURE 8.18
Structure of Employees in Sepone Mining, 2010

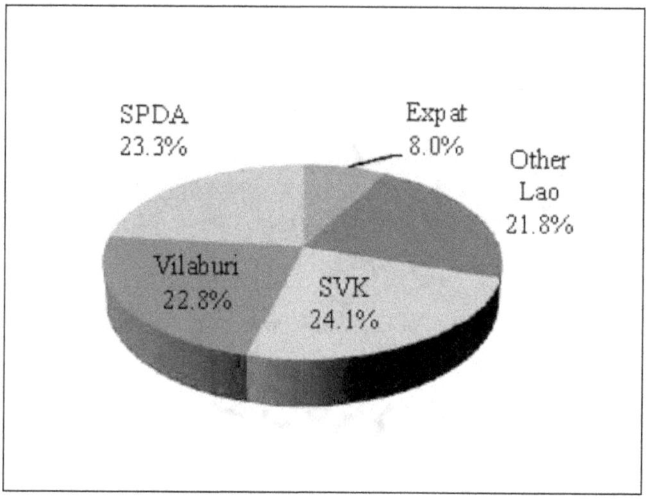

Source: Sepone Mining.

Although constituting a large proportion of the factory's workforce, the benefit that the local employees get is considerably small in comparison with the share of wages paid to foreign expatriates. Due to their relatively low education and limited skill base, most of the local people are employed in low-income jobs such as forest clearing. However, the personnel manager revealed that the lowest wage is about US$150 per person per month, which is far higher than the poverty line. As illustrated in Figure 8.19, local people (people in Vilaburi district) get only about 18.6 per cent of the factory's total factory payroll.

Despite the uneven distribution of wages among employees, Sepone Mining has contributed to local poverty alleviation both directly, in terms of providing work to the unskilled local populace, and indirectly by boosting the local economy. A study conducted by the Centre for International Economics (CIE 2010) found that 3 per cent of the Sepone mining factory's total revenue went on employee's wages. Based on this information, the total money flow from Sepone Mining into Vilaburi district through wage payment is estimated to have been US$9.7 million

FIGURE 8.19
Share of Payroll by Employee Groups, 2004–10

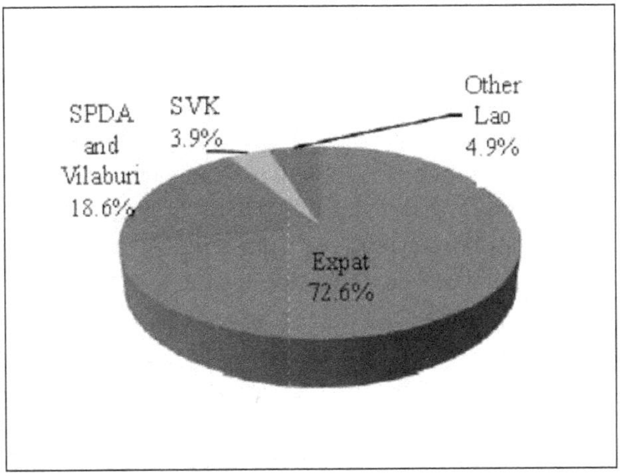

Source: Sepone Mining.

since 1989. This money contributes to economic growth and poverty reduction in the area.

The community development activities of the factory are another way for local people to benefit from the project. According to discussion with its manager, Sepone Mining has undertaken a number of social development activities since project establishment in 1989, including human resource development, the construction of roads, residential areas and schools, and setting up a primary healthcare facility. The project has established a rural development fund which aims to develop rural areas comprehensively and sustainably. Data provided by Lane Xang Minerals Limited indicates that the Sepone Mining Project has expended around US$2.9 million on community development.

Through the activities of Sepone Mining, the per capita income of people in the district has increased gradually from US$310.2 in 2004 to US$463.1 in 2006 and US$717.6 in 2009. This corresponds to an average rate of increase of about 15 per cent a year, which is a relatively high growth rate in comparison with that of Savannakhet province at 10.5 per cent and Laos at 6.7 per cent. At the same time, poverty incidence in the area has been gradually reducing from 45.6 per cent in 2004 to 36.8 per cent in 2006 and to 32.5 per cent in 2008 (Figures 8.20 and 8.21). Hence the poverty incidence in Vilaburi district has declined by around 2.9 per cent per year between 2004 and 2009, a significantly high reduction rate compared with 1.4 per cent for Savannakhet province and 1 per cent for Laos overall.

In line with economic growth and poverty reduction, other socio-economic indicators in Vilaburi district have been improving gradually. For example, the percentage of people with access to clean water has been increasing, from about 65 per cent in 2004 to 72 per cent in 2006 and 80 per cent in 2008. This corresponds to an average increase of 4.6 per cent a year which is also relatively high in comparison with the 3 per cent increase for the whole of Savannakhet province. The percentage of people with access to a toilet increased from 20 per cent in 2004 to 26 per cent in 2006 and 32 per cent in 2008, an average growth rate of 2.4 per cent a year. Mortality rate of children under five has been reducing gradually from 62 per 1,000 live births in 2004 to 58 per 1,000 live births in 2006 and 53 per 1,000 live births in 2008. However, despite these impressive figures, over 8,910 people, corresponding to 28 per cent of Vilaburi district's total population, were still living below the poverty line in 2009. Most of them

FIGURE 8.20
Per Capita Income (US$) in Vilaburi District, 2004–09

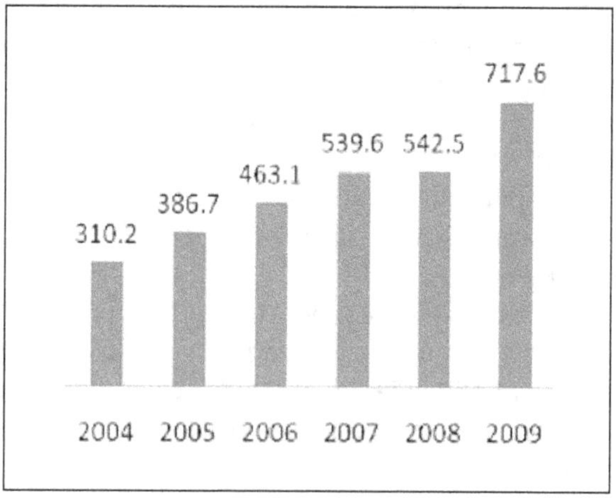

Source: Vilaburi District Office for Planning and Investment.

FIGURE 8.21
Poverty Incidence in Vilaburi District, 2004–09

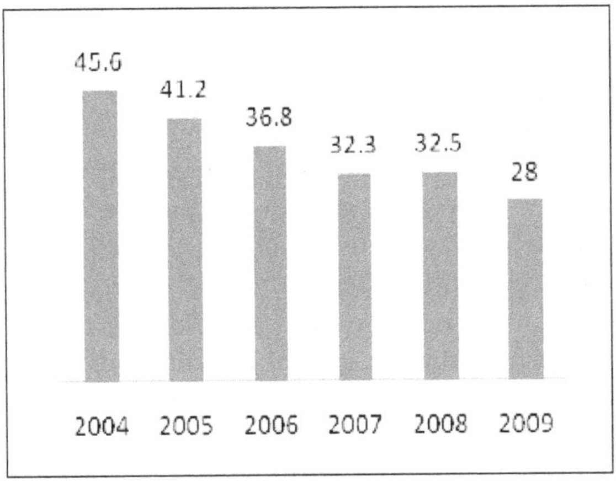

Source: Vilaburi District Office for Planning and Investment.

are living in remote areas where road access to Sapone Mining is difficult. Thus, Vilaburi district remains one of the poorest districts in Savannakhet province.

5. CHINA'S ODA TO LAOS AND POVERTY REDUCTION

The main objective of this section is to evaluate the impacts of China's ODA on poverty. To provide a comprehensive picture of China's ODA flow, including the respective policies of Laos', China's ODA flow over time and its specific characteristics have been included. After that, the findings from an in-depth case study on the poverty impacts of National Road 3, i.e. a section of the North-South Corridor, which was financed by China's ODA, is presented. The main reasons for selecting this particular case study are the scale and importance of the project itself and the prominence of Chinese actors in infrastructure development in general. Over 47.2 per cent of China's ODA in Laos is concentrated in the transport sector, including road infrastructure development. This section aims to highlight the salient issues in this important sector, which is a key destination of China's ODA.

5.1 Macroscopic Analysis of China's ODA to Laos

Along with external trade and FDI, ODA plays an important role in the socio-economic development of Laos, especially in the realms of public expenditure and investment. A study by NERI in 2009 found that almost half of public expenditure and over 80 per cent of public investment came from ODA in the period 1994 to 2001. Recognizing the role of ODA, the Lao government developed diplomatic relationships with over 120 countries and paved the way for assistance from all countries and organizations regardless of differences in political system and ideology. As a result of the "Open Door Policy" and the development of good diplomatic relations with other countries, a significant amount of ODA has been and is flowing into Laos. Statistics from the Ministry of Planning and Investment record ODA inflows of over US$1,060.2 million in the period 2004 to 2008; about 7.4 per cent of this ODA came from China. Thus, China is the fourth biggest ODA source for Laos, after Japan, France and Sweden. Table 8.4 presents more details on ODA flows to Laos, in 2004 to 2008.

Due to cultural, economic and political ties and similarities, ODA from China has been especially sought after by the Lao government. To secure solidarity and mutual cooperation, both countries signed an agreement on the establishment of the "Laos-China Cooperation Committee" in 1997. The Committee is a ministerial one and responsible for: (1) discussing and agreeing on possible cooperation in economic, trade and technical

TABLE 8.4
ODA Flow to Laos, 2004–08 (US$ million)

ODA	2004	2005	2006	2007	2008	2004–08
Total	184.2	205.5	223.8	233.3	213.4	1,060.20
Grant	113.4	146.9	150.2	131.3	155.7	697.5
Loan	70.8	58.6	73.6	102.0	57.7	362.7
Non-China	176.3	195.5	202.6	198.9	208.9	982.2
Grant	108.5	139.7	136.0	126.2	151.2	661.6
Loan	67.8	55.8	66.6	72.7	57.7	320.6
China	7.9	10	21.2	34.4	4.5	78
Grant	4.9	7.1	14.2	5.1	4.5	35.8
Loan	3.0	2.9	7.0	29.3	0	42.2
Chinese share	4.3	4.9	9.5	14.7	2.1	7.4

Source: MPI (2009*b*).

areas; (2) monitoring and controlling the implementation of bilateral contracts between the governments of both countries; and (3) monitoring and controlling the implementation of bilateral cooperation projects. The Committee organizes a regular meeting of politicians and high-ranking officials to discuss possible cooperation between both countries as well as to invite and arrange reciprocal exchange visits between politicians and high-ranking officials in both countries. Usually, ODA agreements are signed during these high-profile exchange visits. The Committee has worked actively and agreed upon many ODA projects, including the National Culture House, Laos-China Friendship Hospital in Luang Prabang, the Second Cement Factory in Vangvieng, Central Mobil Phone in Km 21 Vientiane Capital, Patu Xay (a renovation project), and the strengthening of the government's Printing and Mapping Department. Most of China's ODA projects have a politically symbolic character.

ODA from China to Laos comes either in the form of grants that don't have to be paid back, or in low or no interest loans. Regarding the former, China usually donates aid to finance social-oriented development projects such as the Laos-China Friendship Hospital in Luang Prabang, the National Culture House, Patu Xay Monument in Vientiane, as well as stipendiums to young people for studying in China. Low or no interest loans are generally provided to finance long-term profitable and strategically important projects such as the Second Cement Factory in Vanvieng, Vientiane province, Central Mobile Phone in Km 21, Vientiane Capital, the two ATR aircraft of Laos Air Line. In the period 2006–08, the Chinese government allocated grants to fund about ten projects in Laos and loans to finance another thirteen.

In general, Chinese ODA has been concentrated in a few areas including health, rural development, social development, education, human resource development and transport, especially the transport links from Laos to Yunnan province and some Chinese cities such as Nanning, as well as the development of transport infrastructure in urban and some rural northern provinces of Laos (see Figures 8.22 and 8.23). Over 47.2 per cent of China's total ODA to Laos is concentrated in the transport sector, especially in road infrastructure development. The most important road infrastructure financed by Chinese grant is the 70-kilometre section of the North-South road from the Laos-China border to Luang Numtha-Borkeo province border (Road 3) which cost about US$33 million. Following infrastructure development, just over 15.7 per cent of ODA has gone to rural development,

FIGURE 8.22
ODA in Laos by Sector, 2008–09

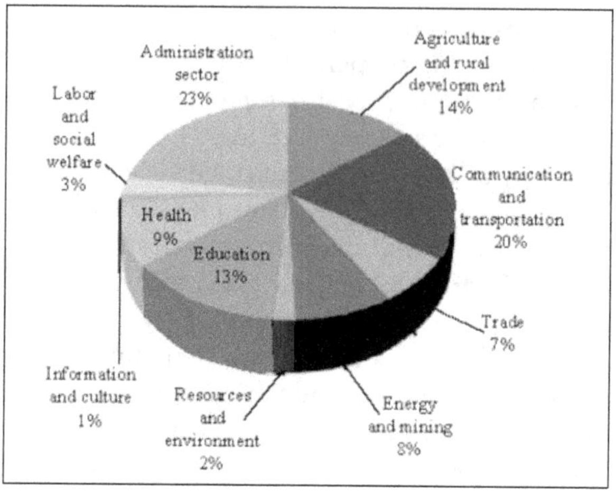

Source: Department for International Cooperation, MPI (2009*b*).

FIGURE 8.23
Chinese ODA by Sector, 2004–08

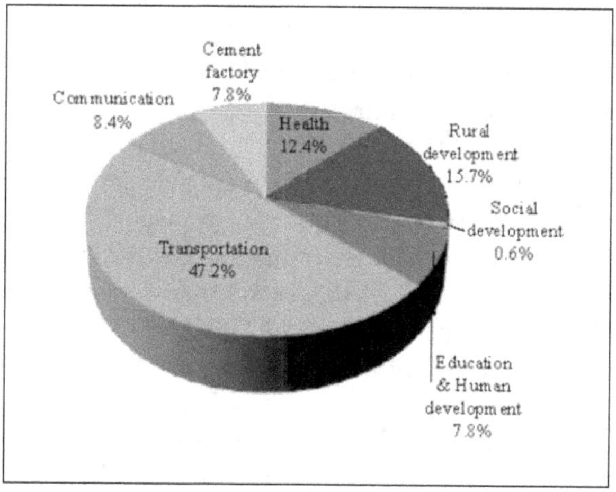

Source: Department for International Cooperation, MPI (2009*b*).

and 12.4 per cent to the health sector. The largest ODA health sector project is the Laos-China Friendship Hospital in Luang Prabang. About 7.8 per cent of ODA goes into education and human resource development; every year, the government of China provides over 200 Lao students with scholarships to study in China.

Comparing the structure of ODA from China to that from other countries, the difference is noticeable. ODA from China seems to concentrate a little more in the transport and communication sectors while the ODA of other countries appears to be slightly more diversified. Over half of China's ODA is in transport and communication while ODA from other countries concentrates in public administration, education, agricultural and rural development as well as in transport and communication.

The location of Chinese-funded projects is similar to that of its FDI. About 65 per cent of China's ODA project cost is located in northern Laos, about 30 per cent in the central area, and the remaining 5 per cent in the southern provinces (Table 8.5). Because of this geographical distribution of aid, ODA from China seems to have higher poverty effects in comparison with that from other countries: poverty concentration is significantly higher in the northern provinces where the terrain is mountainous and road infrastructure is less developed.

5.2 Case Study on Poverty Impacts of Road 3 (Part of North-South Corridor) in Luang Numtha Province

The construction of Road 3 (part of the North-South Corridor) is a good example of how China's ODA can affect poverty reduction in Laos. The Road 3 Project seems to be the biggest and most socio-economically important of all China's ODA projects in the country. In order to present

TABLE 8.5
Distribution of China's ODA by Location, 2004–08

Location	Non-China (%)	China (%)
Northern provinces	40	65
Central provinces	30	30
Southern provinces	30	5
Total	100	100

Source: Estimated by NERI based on data provided by MPI (2009*b*).

a comprehensive picture of how the road project has impacted on poverty, an overview of the socioeconomic status of the case study area, Luang Numtha province, is presented first. After that, the impacts of Road 3 on trade and investment flow in Luang Numtha province are examined, followed by an evaluation of how the road indirectly affects economic growth and poverty reduction in Luang Numtha province via increasing trade and investment flow.

Socio-economic Characteristics of Case Study Area, Luang Numtha Province

Luang Numtha province is located in the northern part of Laos, about 600 kilometres from Vientiane Capital. It has a total land area of 9,700 square kilometres and shares borders with China in the north, northeast and northwest, and with Oudomxay and Borkeo provinces in the south, southeast and southwest.

The province has a total population of about 150,000. About 62.4 per cent of the population is of working age, i.e., fifteen to sixty years old, 80 per cent of whom are engaged in the agriculture sector. Agricultural activities are the main economic activities in the province. In 2008, the sector contributed about 68.6 per cent of the province's total production value, the industry sector contributed about 15.2 per cent, while the service sector contributed about 16.2 per cent. Considering socio-economic status, Luang Numtha is a middle development province with per capita income of US$518.30 and poverty incidence of 23.9 per cent in 2008. Since 2004, the province has experienced rapid economic growth and poverty reduction.

In terms of infrastructure and communications, telecommunication and information infrastructure is relatively well developed in comparison with many northern provinces of Laos. The mobile phone network covers over 60 per cent of its total land area. Internet service is available in the provincial centre and in the main cities of the province such as Sing district, and Long district, where the number of tourist arrivals is significant. Television and radio are available and are the main information sources for people living in the province. Lao, Thai and Chinese television and radio broadcasting can be received in all residential areas. In addition, National Road 13 crosses the province and connects it with main cities in Laos such as Phonsaly in the north, Oudomxay, Luang Prabang and Vientiane in the south. Road 3 crosses the province from north to southeast and provides access to China and Thailand (via Borkeo), both of which are important export markets and import origins for Luang Numtha province.

Road 3 and Poverty Reduction

Road 3 is part of the North-South Corridor connecting Kunming in China with Bangkok, Thailand. The corridor is about 2,000 kilometres long; however, the section of the Corridor that crosses Laos from Boten Border International Gate (Laos-China border) to Houay Xay Border International Gate (Laos-Thailand border) is 228.3 kilometres long. The road was a dirt track before it was upgraded during 2005–08, but now it is classed as a grade III paved road, i.e., a two-lane paved road along which trucks can drive at a maximum speed of 80 kilometres per hour.

The total cost of the upgrading was US$63.5 million. Around 33 per cent of the total cost was funded by the Thai government, around 34 per cent was financed by soft loan from the Asian Development Bank (ADB) and the remaining 33 per cent was funded by grant from the Chinese government. The Thai-funded section of 73 kilometres runs from Houay Xay-Xienkhong International Border Gate, i.e., Laos-Thai border to Ban Sod, Borkeo province. The ADB-funded section from Ban Sod, Borkeo province to Nam Lung, Luang Numtha province is 73 kilometres long. Construction of the 72.8 kilometres section from Nam Lung, Luang Numtha province to Boten International Border Gate was funded by the government of China. The upgrading of the Chinese-funded section took only one year and was completed in 2006. This means Luang Numtha province has had an upgraded road connecting it to China since 2006. The other sections were completed in 2007 and 2008.

It is clear that the road is a driving force for economic growth and poverty reduction in Luang Numtha province. It crosses the economic centre of the province and connects it with other trade and economic centres in Laos and abroad, principally with China and Thailand, which are important trade partners of the province. The upgrading of Road 3 has significantly stimulated trade, investment and increased tourist inflows, which are main driving factors for economic growth and poverty reduction in the province. Table 8.6 shows that the trade flow (value of export + import) has increased from US$2.8 million in 2004 to US$5.8 million in 2006 and US$6.9 million in 2008. This corresponds to an average growth rate of 29.3 per cent a year, which is a significantly high growth rate in

TABLE 8.6
Trade, Investment and Tourism Flow in Luang Numtha Province, 2004–08

Items	2004	2005	2006	2007	2008
Trade flow (US$ million)	2.8	2.9	5.8	6.5	6.9
Investment flow (US$ million)	31.1	33.8	53.8	49.4	57.9
Tourism flow (1,000 people)	41.7	49.3	47.8	80.7	140.5

Source: Calculated by NERI based on data provided by provincial authority.

comparison with that of many provinces in Laos, especially the northern provinces where the average growth rate is 15–20 per cent a year. The capital investment inflow has also increased from US$31.1 million in 2004 to US$33.8 million in 2005 and US$57.9 in 2008, corresponding to an average growth rate of 17.2 per cent a year, which is a significantly high growth rate in comparison with the whole of Laos, i.e., about 9.8 per cent. Similarly, the number of tourist arrivals has increased from 41,700 in 2004 to 47,800 in 2006 and then to 140,500 in 2008. These figures correspond to an average growth rate of 47.4 per cent a year, a significantly high rate of increase compared to other parts of the country, especially provinces in northern Laos.

The significance of Road 3, and the Chinese-funded section in particular, in driving these changes is illustrated by the most noteworthy year, 2006, when the upgrading of the road connecting Luang Numtha with China was finally completed. From 2005 to 2006, the trade flow in Luang Numtha doubled and investment flow increased 59.2 per cent. The very high growth rate illustrates the very significant immediate effects of the road upgrading project on trade and investment in Luang Numtha province.

Through increasing trade, investment and tourism flow, Road 3 has contributed significantly to employment and income generation activities for local people. Sugar cane exports in Sing district alone provide jobs and income generation activities for around 1,200 local people. China's investment in rubber plantations in Luang Numtha province provides jobs and income generation activities for about 3,000. Indeed, as Figures 8.24 and 8.25 show, GDP per capita at market prices in Luang Numtha province has increased from US$304.80 per person in 2004 to US$376.80 in 2006 and US$518.30 in 2008, representing an average nominal growth rate of 14 per cent a year which corresponds to real GDP per capita growth of 6.5 per cent compared to a national average of 4.6 per cent during the

FIGURE 8.24
GDP per Capita (US$) in Luang Numtha Province, 2004–08

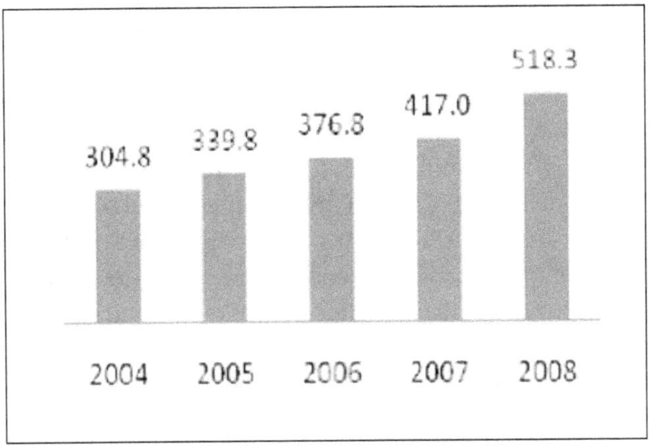

Source: Department of Planning and Investment, Luang Numtha province (2009).

FIGURE 8.25
Poverty Incidence (%) in Luang Numtha Province, 2004–08

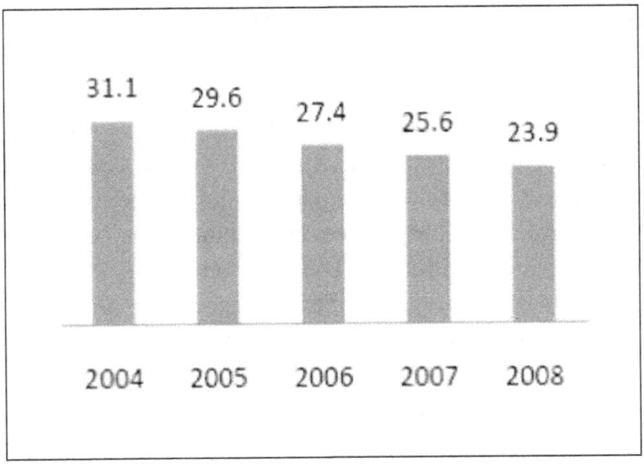

Source: Department of Planning and Investment, Luang Numtha province (2009).

same period. Simultaneously, poverty incidence in the province reduced from 31.1 per cent in 2004 to 27.4 per cent in 2006 and 23.9 per cent in 2008. The average rate of poverty reduction was 1.4 per cent a year while that of Laos over the same period was about 1 per cent a year. Consequently, it can be said that in increasing trade, investment and tourism flow, Chinese ODA in Road 3 has accelerated economic growth and poverty reduction in Luang Numtha province.

While no doubt contributing to economic growth and poverty reduction, the trade and investment growth stimulated by the construction of Road 3 also has negative attributes. The major share of investment and trade (especially export) which has stimulated rapid economic growth and poverty reduction in Luang Numtha province is natural resource-based investment and export, including investment in the plantation sector (sugar cane, rubber, watermelon), export of wood and wood products, mining products and NTFP. Therefore, as we have shown in our analysis of investment from and trade with China, there are a host of potential repercussions on the environment (for example, forest cover, watershed areas, soil fertility, water level, biodiversity). For example, statistical data provided by the Department for Planning and Investment of Luang Numtha province indicates that over 30,000 of hectares of forest have already been converted into plantation. From discussion with villagers in Sing district, the declining water level in several rivers in the province appears to be significant.

In addition, there are social and cultural problems associated with this growth in trade and investment inflow to the province, and the province's easier accessibility. There are problems associated with increased informal labour migration. Based on observations and discussions with people during the field trip, a significant number of Chinese migrants seem to flow into Luang Numtha province for income generation activities, especially for trading. They have established relatively permanent businesses, shops and residences. There is no reliable data on how many Chinese migrants are living and trading informally in Luang Numtha province. Moreover, increasing alcohol intake, human trafficking, commercial sex services, gambling, HIV/AIDS as well as criminal offences are particularly noticeable in Luang Numtha province. Before the corridor development, these phenomena were not outstanding or observable in the province.

6. CONCLUSION AND POLICY IMPLICATIONS

This chapter demonstrates the importance of China as a partner in the socio-economic development of Laos, but also highlights some challenges that have arisen through increasing socio-economic interactions with its rapidly growing neighbour. In general, China's economic activities in Laos can be said to have positive impacts on poverty. We have found that China's trade, FDI and ODA pay particularly high dividends because they are concentrated in the northern part of the country where the terrain is difficult, road infrastructure is less developed and poverty concentration is high.

Further analysis of the three main routes of impact also reveals the great and growing importance of China in poverty reduction in Laos. Regarding trade, China is the country's third most important trade partner after Thailand and Vietnam. From 2004 to 2008, trade with China accounted for about 9.5 per cent of Laos' external trade volume. The main products imported from China were found to be materials and equipment for use in investment projects and other manufactured products for use in consumption and production. Exports to China from Laos were found in the main to be primary products such as wood and wood products, agricultural products, NTFP and minerals. While it was found that imports and exports have contributed to economic growth and employment opportunities, the structure of exports is an area of concern. Cash crops and primary commodities constitute the majority of exports, resulting in environmental degradation, limited employment opportunities and present limited potential for the development of labour intensive manufacturing sector. Furthermore, cash crops like sugar cane have the potential to increase households' vulnerability to shocks through replacing subsistence agricultural processes and means.

China is also Laos' third most important source of FDI inflow, after Thailand and Vietnam. From 2004 to 2008, Laos received total investment flow of US$1,117.2 million from China, corresponding to about 17.8 per cent of total FDI inflow to the country during the same period. The main investment sectors for China's FDI are energy, industry, handicrafts, mining and agriculture. It was found that the distribution of China's FDI focuses more on labour-intensive pursuits than total FDI inflow. Moreover, Sepone Mining contributes significant capital revenues to the Lao government's budget (about 10 per cent) through tax payments and to GDP through substantial export revenues, as well as contributing to the local economy of Vilaburi district through utilizing the local labour force.

In terms of ODA, China is the fourth largest source for Laos after Japan, France and Sweden. From 2004 to 2008, Laos received ODA of over US$78 million from China, of which US$35.8 million was in the form of grant and US$42.2 million in soft loan. ODA from China accounts for about 7.4 per cent of total ODA in Laos. The biggest share (47.2 per cent) of China's ODA is concentrated in the transport sector. The upgrading of Road 3 was the biggest Chinese ODA project in Laos. After this project was completed in 2006, trade, tourism and investment in the area rapidly increased. While this has contributed to poverty reduction and economic growth on both macro and microscopic levels, there have also been environmental problems resulting from increased trade and investment. In addition, the new road has also facilitated growth in informal labour migration, human trafficking, commercial sex services and gambling.

Based on findings from in-depth studies, Laos-China trade, and China's FDI and ODA have significant effects on economic growth and poverty reduction in Laos. Due to the active contribution of China's trade, FDI and ODA, Laos has experienced rapid economic growth and poverty reduction during the last decade. However, the Lao government needs to design policy so it can better utilize the opportunities generated through economic interactions with China in order to maximize benefits and minimize costs. To this end we recommend the Lao government to take the following steps:

(1) Improve environmental protection and sustainable development mechanism, including institutions, regulations and laws. Principally, the country needs to strengthen natural resource protection, including forestry, watershed, soil and biodiversity. Rapid industrial growth in China will stimulate growing demand for raw materials for export to China and investment in natural resource-based sectors like agriculture and mining. The country needs to make sure that investment in this sector is environmentally friendly and sustainable.
(2) Improve security protection systems. Increasing trade, investment and tourism flow will stimulate migration from China as well as from other countries. Such migration will affect the security of

the local populace and migrants themselves. For example, crime, human trafficking, commercial sex services, HIV/AIDS infection would likely increase. Therefore, the country should make sure that its security system is able to provide sufficient precautions and safety measures.

(3) Provide training, technical assistance and financial support to local farmers producing food and raw materials for export to China so as to increase benefits, such as the development and transfer of technologies and skills, thus stimulating more economic growth and poverty reduction in Laos.

Note

1. Population census 2005.

References

Arshad, Imran. "Economic Theory, Transition & Alternatives: Application to Lao PDR". In *Annual Report 2007*, edited by National Economic Research Bank of the Lao PDR. Vientiane: GoL, 2003.

ASEAN Secretariat. "Framework Agreement on Comprehensive Economic Cooperation between ASEAN and the People's Republic of China". Jakarta, 2002.

Bank of Lao PDR. *Annual Report 2007*. Vientiane: GoL, 2007.

Centre for International Economics. *Economic Impact of Sepone Mining*. Canberra: CIE, 2010.

Chia, Siow Yue. "ASEAN-China Free Trade Area". Paper presented at the AEP Conference, Hong Kong, 12–13 April 2004.

Committee for Planning and Cooperation. *Foreign Aid Report 2000–2001*. Vientiane: GoL, 2002.

———. *All Foreign Direct Investment in the Lao PDR (1994–2002)*. Vientiane: GoL, 2002.

Department for Planning and Investment, Luang Numtha Province. "Summary on Implementing Socio-Economic Development Plan 2008 and Guidance for Socio-Economic Development for 2009". Unpublished manuscript, 2009.

Department of Statistics. *Statistic 2007*. Vientiane: DoS, MPI, 2007.

Government of Laos (GoL). *National Growth and Poverty Eradication Strategy*. Vientiane: GoL, 2004.

Haltmaier, Jane T., Ahmed Shaghil, Brahmina Couilbailey, Ross Knippenberg, Sylvain Leduc, Mario Marazzi and Beth Anne Wilson. "The Role of China in Asia: Engine, Conduit, or Steamroller?". International Finance Discussion Paper No. 904. Board of Governors of the Federal Reserve System, Washington, D.C., 2007.

Lazarus, Kate M. "In Search of Aluminium: China's Role in the Mekong Region". Heinrich Boll Stiftung, WWF and International Institute for Sustainable Development, Canada, 2009. <http://www.boell-cambodia.org/downloads/in_search_of_aluminum_RP.pdf>. Accessed 20 June 2010.

Leebouapao, Leeber, Darachanthra Souphit, Oraboune Syviengxay and Chaleunsinh Chansathith. "Regional Economic Integration of Lao PDR". NERI, Vientiane, 2002

Lim, Tin Seng. "China's Active Role in the Greater Mekong Sub-region: A 'Win-Win' Outcome?". East Asia Institute, National University of Singapore, 2008.

Limskul, Kitti. "ASEAN-Japan Comprehensive Economic Partnership", 2008. <http://www.jetro.go.jp/en/reports/survey/epa/sympo0311/s2-2s.pdf>. Accessed 12 May 2009.

Malaysian Institute Economic Research. "ASEAN Economic Integration". Sazakawa Peace Foundation, 2000.

Ministry of Industry and Commerce. *Statistics of Export and Import of Lao PDR*. Vientiane: GoL, 2009.

Ministry of Planning and Investment. *Statistics of FDI in Lao PDR*. Vientiane: MPI, 2009*a*.

———. *Statistics of ODA in Lao PDR*. Vientiane: Department. of International Cooperation, 2009*b*.

———. "FDI data sheet". Unpublished report, 2009*c*.

———. *Summary of Implementing Socio-Economic Development Plan 2009–2010 and Socio-Economic Development Plan for Fiscal Year 2010–2011*. Vientiane: MPI, 2010.

National Economic Research Institute. *Poverty Impact of Regional Economic Integration*. Vientiane: NERI, 2007.

———. "Evaluation of Socio-Economic Impacts of ODA". Unpublished draft report, 2009.

National Statistical Centre. *Lao Expenditure and Consumption Surveys (LECS III)*. Vientiane: NSC, CPI, 2004.

Natividad, Gabriel. "The ASEAN-China Free Trade Area, Inns and Prospects". University of California, Los Angeles, 2004.

Office for Planing and Investment of Sing District. *Summary on Implementing Socio-Economic Development Plan in 2008 and Guidance for Socio-Economic Development from 2009*. Sing District: OPI, 2009.

Oraboune Syviengxay. *One District One Product: Sample Survey — Rattan Works in Phone Village*. MAPS II Project. Vientiane: NERI/JICA, 2005.

Suzuki, Motoyoshi. "Cost and Benefit Analysis for Joining ASEAN". Suzuka International University, Japan, 2003.

UNDP. "National Human Development Report Lao PDR 2001: Advancing Rural Development". Vientiane, 2001.

———. "National Human Development Report Lao PDR 2006: International Trade and Human Development". Vientiane, 2006.

Vilaburi District Office for Planning and Investment. "Summary on Socio-Economic Development 2004–2009". Unpublished report, 2010.

World Food Program. "Poverty Map for Laos". 2000. <http://reliefweb.int/sites/reliefweb.int/files/resources/BD8AD3FF99493ACDC1256F2D00484B53-wfp_laoPov200104.pdf>. Accessed 14 April 2000.

Yin, Xingmin. "China's Trade and FDI to MRB Countries: An Advocacy Document". In *A China-Japan Comparison of Economic Relationships with the Mekong River Basin Countries*, edited by Mitsuhiro Kagami, pp. 17–69. Bangkok: IDE-JETRO, Bangkok Research Centre, 2009.

INDEX

www.ingramcontent.com/pod-product-compliance
Lightning Source LLC
LaVergne TN
LVHW011532200926
848484LV00001B/237